Chris Skidmore is the author of three previous books on medieval and Tudor history, and a Fellow of the Royal Historical Society and of the Society of Antiquaries. He was first elected in 2010 as the Member of Parliament for Kingswood. In December 2018 he was appointed Minister of State for Universities, Science, Research and Innovation.

www.chrisskidmore.com
🐦 @CSkidmoreUK

By the same author

Edward VI
Death and the Virgin
Bosworth

'Richard III, of all the English monarchs, deserves a fair hearing and Chris Skidmore's meticulous account does justice to this vilified king. With forensic detail, Skidmore looks at sources as well as rumours to build a picture of the last Plantagenet monarch. What shines out from this modern biography is the author's attempt to be fair to the last English king to ride in battle, who took murderous decisions in life; but died a hero'
Philippa Gregory, author of *The Kingmaker's Daughter*

'Skidmore's new biography of Richard is a full and measured account of his subject . . . [He] tells the story with style and the empathy of a well-trained historian . . . Skidmore has given us an eminently readable account of Richard's life and reign, firmly anchored in fifteenth-century politics and culture'
David Grummitt, *Times Literary Supplement*

'It is all but impossible to write either something fresh, or something fair, about Richard III, yet Chris Skidmore has pulled off both feats. Wide-ranging research brings out a Richard who is neither the crookbacked villain nor the victim, but a man for all political seasons, whose fall illumines his violent, complex age'
Sarah Gristwood, author of *Game of Queens*

'[Examines hostile indictments of Richard III] with sharp writing and a marvellously exhaustive command of contemporary documentary sources . . . In the author's hands, there's no lack of thrilling details in Richard's saga . . . His biography bids fair to become the definitive account for the twenty-first century'
Bob Duffy, *Washington Independent Review of Books*

'King Richard III is one of the most divisive figures in history, but this new biography aims to ignore the controversy and return to the facts: his personality, motivations and allegiances. How single-minded was his pursuit of power, and what role did he really play in the deaths of his young nephews?'
History Revealed

'This first-rate book . . . will be read with great profit and pleasure by fellow historians, and by all those who simply enjoy learning about dramatic episodes in the past from a fine writer'
Alistair Lexden, *The London Magazine*

RICHARD III

BROTHER
PROTECTOR
KING

CHRIS SKIDMORE

WEIDENFELD & NICOLSON

First published in Great Britain in 2017
This paperback edition published in 2019 by Weidenfeld & Nicolson
an imprint of The Orion Publishing Group Ltd
Carmelite House, 50 Victoria Embankment
London EC4Y 0DZ

An Hachette UK Company

1 3 5 7 9 10 8 6 4 2

A CIP catalogue record for this book is
available from the British Library.

ISBN (paperback) 978 1 78022 641 5
ISBN (audio) 978 1 4091 6593 4
ISBN (ebook) 978 0 297 87079 1

Typeset by Input Data Services Ltd, Somerset

Printed and bound by CPI Group (UK) Ltd, Croydon, CR0 4YY

www.orionbooks.co.uk

To Lydia

CONTENTS

ILLUSTRATIONS

1. Portrait of Richard III, English school, oil on panel, c.1510–40. © Society of Antiquaries of London / Bridgeman Images.
2. Page noting the birth of Richard III, from *The Book of Hours of Richard III*, English school, ink on vellum, 15th century. © Lambeth Palace Library / Bridgeman Images.
3. Church of St Mary and All Saints, Fotheringhay, Northamptonshire. Photo © NRT-Helena / Alamy.
4. Middleham Castle, Yorkshire. Photo © English Heritage / Heritage Images / Getty Images.
5. Letter from Richard, duke of Gloucester, to Sir John Say, 1469. British Library Cotton Vespasian MS F III fo. 19. © British Library Board / Bridgeman Images.
6. Portrait of Edward IV, English school, oil on panel, c.1510–40. © Society of Antiquaries of London / Bridgeman Images.
7. Portrait of George, duke of Clarence. © Paul Fearn / Alamy.
8. Edward IV on Fortune's wheel from *The Life of Edward IV*, English school, ink on vellum, 1460–c.1470. British Library Harley 7353. © British Library Board / Bridgeman Images.
9. Portrait of Elizabeth Woodville, Queen of Edward IV, English school, oil on panel, c.1500. © Ashmolean Museum, University of Oxford / Bridgeman Images.
10. Anthony Woodville and William Caxton presenting the first printed book in English to Edward IV. Lambeth Palace Library, London. © Bridgeman Images.
11. Battle of Barnet, English school, 15th century. Centrale Bibliotheek van de Universiteit, Ghent. © Bridgeman Images.
12. Battle of Tewkesbury in *Nouvelles du Recouvrement par Edouard IV de son Royaume d'Angleterre*, French school, 15th century. Bibliothèque municipale de Besançon MS 1168, fo. 4v. Courtesy of the Ville de Besançon Bibliothèque et archives municipales

28. Silver gilt boar badge discovered at the site of the battle of Bosworth. Image courtesy of Leicestershire County Council.
29. Cannon balls discovered at the battle site. Image courtesy of Leicestershire County Council.
30. Gold badge of an eagle with a snake. Image courtesy of Leicestershire County Council.
31. Tomb of Sir John Cheyne in Salisbury Cathedral. © Geoffrey Wheeler.
32. Tomb of Thomas, Lord Stanley, in the Church of St Peter and St Paul, Ormskirk, Lancashire. © Paula Martin.
33. The positions and movements of the forces at the battle of Bosworth. Map by John Gilkes, following an interpretation by Peter Foss.
34. The remains of Richard III in Leicester City Council Social Services car park. © University of Leicester / Rex Features.
35. The bones of Richard III. © University of Leicester.
36. The skull of Richard III. © University of Leicester.
37. Portrait of Richard III, English school, oil on panel, 1504–20. Royal Collection Trust © Her Majesty Queen Elizabeth II 2017.
38. Portrait of Richard III, English school, oil on panel, 16th century. © Society of Antiquaries of London / Bridgeman Images.

ENGLAND, FRANCE AND BRITTANY DURING THE WARS OF THE ROSES

The Itinerary of Richard III
Part 1: July 1483–January 1484

——— Post-coronation progress July–Oct 1483
- - - - - Movement against rebellion Oct–Nov 1483
·········· Kent progress Jan 1484

0   50
Miles

*North
Sea*

Tyne

Tees

Ure

Wharfe York

Pontefract

Gainsborough

Lincoln

Nottingham *Trent*

Grantham

Melton Mowbray

Leicester

Severn

Coventry

Worcester

Tewkesbury
Gloucester   Woodstock

Minster
Lovell   Oxford
        Thames

• Bristol   Reading Windsor   Greenwich

London

Farnham   Guildford   Canterbury   Sandwich

Bridgwater   Dover

Salisbury   Winchester

Exeter

Bridport Dorchester

English Channel

The Itinerary of Richard III
Part 2: February 1484–August 1485

——— Progress northwards 1484
- - - - Retreat southwards & Kent progress 1484
········· Progress northwards 1485

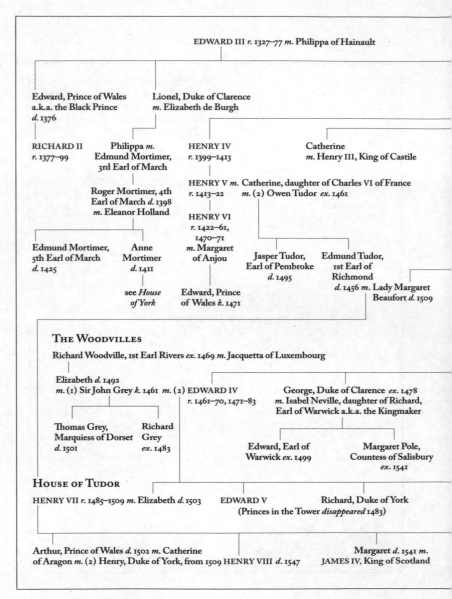

EDWARD III *r.* 1327–77 *m.* Philippa of Hainault

Edward, Prince of Wales
a.k.a. the Black Prince
d. 1376

Lionel, Duke of Clarence
m. Elizabeth de Burgh

RICHARD II
r. 1377–99

Philippa *m.*
Edmund Mortimer,
3rd Earl of March

HENRY IV
r. 1399–1413

Catherine
m. Henry III, King of Castile

Roger Mortimer, 4th
Earl of March *d.* 1398
m. Eleanor Holland

HENRY V *m.* Catherine, daughter of Charles VI of France
r. 1413–22   *m.* (2) Owen Tudor *ex.* 1461

HENRY VI
r. 1422–61,
1470–71
m. Margaret
of Anjou

Edmund Mortimer,
5th Earl of March
d. 1425

Anne
Mortimer
d. 1411

see *House
of York*

Jasper Tudor,
Earl of Pembroke
d. 1495

Edmund Tudor,
1st Earl of
Richmond
d. 1456 *m.* Lady Margaret
Beaufort *d.* 1509

Edward, Prince
of Wales *k.* 1471

The Woodvilles

Richard Woodville, 1st Earl Rivers *ex.* 1469 *m.* Jacquetta of Luxembourg

Elizabeth *d.* 1492
m. (1) Sir John Grey *k.* 1461 *m.* (2) EDWARD IV
r. 1461–70, 1471–83

George, Duke of Clarence *ex.* 1478
m. Isabel Neville, daughter of Richard,
Earl of Warwick a.k.a. the Kingmaker

Thomas Grey,
Marquiess of Dorset
d. 1501

Richard
Grey
ex. 1483

Edward, Earl of
Warwick *ex.* 1499

Margaret Pole,
Countess of Salisbury
ex. 1541

House of Tudor

HENRY VII *r.* 1485–1509 *m.* Elizabeth *d.* 1503

EDWARD V

Richard, Duke of York

(Princes in the Tower *disappeared* 1483)

Arthur, Prince of Wales *d.* 1502 *m.* Catherine
of Aragon *m.* (2) Henry, Duke of York, from 1509 HENRY VIII *d.* 1547

Margaret *d.* 1541 *m.*
JAMES IV, King of Scotland

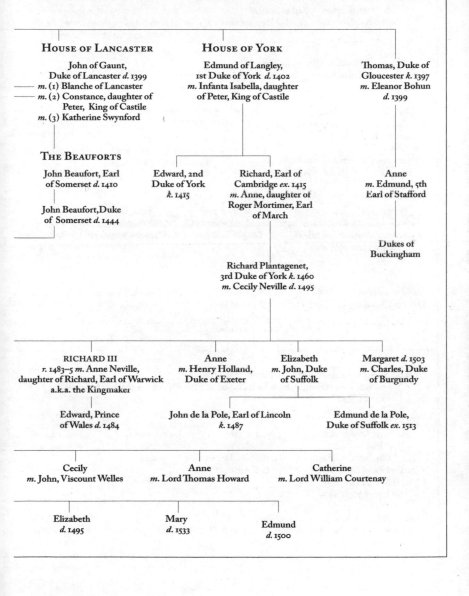

HOUSES OF LANCASTER AND YORK AND THE HOUSE OF TUDOR

HOUSE OF LANCASTER

John of Gaunt,
Duke of Lancaster *d.* 1399
—— *m.* (1) Blanche of Lancaster
—— *m.* (2) Constance, daughter of
Peter, King of Castile
m. (3) Katherine Swynford

THE BEAUFORTS

John Beaufort, Earl
of Somerset *d.* 1410

John Beaufort, Duke
of Somerset *d.* 1444

HOUSE OF YORK

Edmund of Langley,
1st Duke of York *d.* 1402
m. Infanta Isabella, daughter
of Peter, King of Castile

Edward, 2nd
Duke of York
k. 1415

Richard, Earl of
Cambridge *ex.* 1415
m. Anne, daughter of
Roger Mortimer, Earl
of March

Thomas, Duke of
Gloucester *k.* 1397
m. Eleanor Bohun
d. 1399

Anne
m. Edmund, 5th
Earl of Stafford

Dukes of
Buckingham

Richard Plantagenet,
3rd Duke of York *k.* 1460
m. Cecily Neville *d.* 1495

RICHARD III
r. 1483–5 *m.* Anne Neville,
daughter of Richard, Earl of Warwick
a.k.a. the Kingmaker

Anne
m. Henry Holland,
Duke of Exeter

Elizabeth
m. John, Duke
of Suffolk

Margaret *d.* 1503
m. Charles, Duke
of Burgundy

Edward, Prince
of Wales *d.* 1484

John de la Pole, Earl of Lincoln
k. 1487

Edmund de la Pole,
Duke of Suffolk *ex.* 1513

Cecily
m. John, Viscount Welles

Anne
m. Lord Thomas Howard

Catherine
m. Lord William Courtenay

Elizabeth
d. 1495

Mary
d. 1533

Edmund
d. 1500

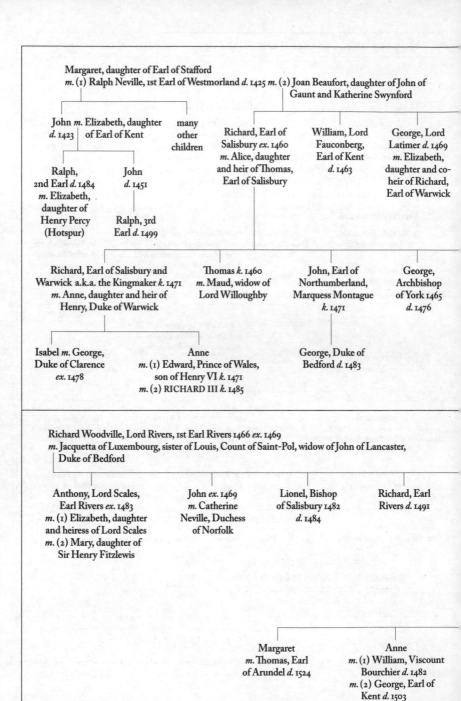

Margaret, daughter of Earl of Stafford
m. (1) Ralph Neville, 1st Earl of Westmorland *d.* 1425 *m.* (2) Joan Beaufort, daughter of John of
Gaunt and Katherine Swynford

John *m.* Elizabeth, daughter
d. 1423 of Earl of Kent

many
other
children

Richard, Earl of
Salisbury *ex.* 1460
m. Alice, daughter
and heir of Thomas,
Earl of Salisbury

William, Lord
Fauconberg,
Earl of Kent
d. 1463

George, Lord
Latimer *d.* 1469
m. Elizabeth,
daughter and co-
heir of Richard,
Earl of Warwick

Ralph,
2nd Earl *d.* 1484
m. Elizabeth,
daughter of
Henry Percy
(Hotspur)

John
d. 1451

Ralph, 3rd
Earl *d.* 1499

Richard, Earl of Salisbury and
Warwick a.k.a. the Kingmaker *k.* 1471
m. Anne, daughter and heir of
Henry, Duke of Warwick

Thomas *k.* 1460
m. Maud, widow of
Lord Willoughby

John, Earl of
Northumberland,
Marquess Montague
k. 1471

George,
Archbishop
of York 1465
d. 1476

Isabel *m.* George,
Duke of Clarence
ex. 1478

Anne
m. (1) Edward, Prince of Wales,
son of Henry VI *k.* 1471
m. (2) RICHARD III *k.* 1485

George, Duke of
Bedford *d.* 1483

Richard Woodville, Lord Rivers, 1st Earl Rivers 1466 *ex.* 1469
m. Jacquetta of Luxembourg, sister of Louis, Count of Saint-Pol, widow of John of Lancaster,
Duke of Bedford

Anthony, Lord Scales,
Earl Rivers *ex.* 1483
m. (1) Elizabeth, daughter
and heiress of Lord Scales
m. (2) Mary, daughter of
Sir Henry Fitzlewis

John *ex.* 1469
m. Catherine
Neville, Duchess
of Norfolk

Lionel, Bishop
of Salisbury 1482
d. 1484

Richard, Earl
Rivers *d.* 1491

Margaret
m. Thomas, Earl
of Arundel *d.* 1524

Anne
m. (1) William, Viscount
Bourchier *d.* 1482
m. (2) George, Earl of
Kent *d.* 1503

Robert,
Bishop of
Salisbury 1427
Durham 1438
d. 1457

Edward, Lord
Abergavenny d. 1476
m. (1) Elizabeth, daughter
and coheir of Richard,
Earl of Worcester
m. (2) Catherine, sister
of John, Lord Howard

Catherine m. (1) John,
2nd Duke of Norfolk d. 1432
m. (2) Thomas Strangeways
m. (3) Viscount Beaumont
m. (4) John Woodville
ex. 1469

Anne m. (1) Humphrey,
Duke of Buckingham
k. 1460
m. (2) Walter, Lord
Mountjoy d. 1474

Cecily
m. Richard,
Duke of
York k. 1460

EDWARD IV

Eleanor
m. (1) Richard, Lord
Despenser d. 1414
m. (2) Henry, Earl
of Northumberland
d. 1455

Joan
m. William, Earl
of Arundel 1465
d. 1487

Cecily
m. (1) Henry, Duke
of Warwick d. 1466
m. (2) John, Earl of
Worcester ex. 1470

Alice
m. Henry, Lord
Fitzhugh d. 1472

Eleanor m. Thomas,
Lord Stanley d. 1503

Catherine m. William,
Lord Hastings ex. 1483

Margaret m. John,
Earl of Oxford d. 1513

Edward
d. 1488

Elizabeth
m. (1) Sir John Grey, son of
Lord Ferrars of Groby k. 1461
m. (2) EDWARD IV

Eleanor
m. Anthony, Lord
Grey of Ruthin
d. 1480

Thomas, Marquess of Dorset d. 1501
m. (1) Anne, daughter of Duke of Exeter
m. (2) Cecily, daughter and heir of Lord
Bonville d. 1529

Thomas

Richard
ex. 1483

Jacquetta
m. John, Lord Strange
of Knockin d. 1479

Catherine
m. (1) Henry, Duke of Buckingham ex. 1483
m. (2) Jasper Tudor, Duke of Bedford d. 1495
m. (3) Sir Richard Wingfield

Mary
m. William, 2nd Earl
of Pembroke d. 1491

A NOTE ON MONEY AND DATES

English monetary values are recorded in pounds (*l*), shillings (*s*) and pence (*d*), with twenty shillings in the pound and twelve pence in the shilling. The mark was a unit of account, with one mark being worth 160 pence or thirteen shillings and four pence, therefore two-thirds of a pound. There are many pitfalls to estimating the value of currently across the centuries; however, a useful guide is the National Archives' Currency Converter (see www.nationalarchives.gov.uk/currency) that suggests one pound in 1480 would have been worth an equivalent of £504.59 at 2005 prices, with one shilling worth an equivalent of £25.23 and one penny equalling £2.10. The standard unit of French money was the *livre tournois*, divided into twenty *sols* (later *sous*), each worth twelve *denier*. One *ecu* was worth the equivalent of six *livres tournois*. The value of the *livre tournois* to the pound fluctuated, but it is generally estimated that there were ten *livres tournois* in the pound, with one shilling being worth two *livres tournois*.

Dates are given according to contemporary sources that followed the Julian calendar in use at the time. With the adoption of the Gregorian Calendar in 1752, account should be taken of the fact that these dates do not match with the exact dates of our current calendar. The difference between the two calendars in the fifteenth century is nine days, so the battle of Bosworth, while fought on 22 August in 1485, would have actually been 31 August in our contemporary calendar.

INTRODUCTION

Shortly after Palm Sunday, 1484, a Silesian knight, Niclas von Popplau, arrived in England. His first journey had been from the Kentish coast, where
he had landed, to pay his own pilgrimage to the internationally renowned
shrine of Thomas Becket at Canterbury, which Popplau later noted in
a journal he made of his visit 'was more beautiful than any I have seen
before, decorated beyond all measure with many gem stones'.[1] Journeying
to the capital, Popplau visited Westminster Abbey, where, among others,
he saw the tomb of Edward the Confessor. Eight days after Easter, Popplau
set off from London with the intention of visiting the king himself, currently residing in Yorkshire. As the Silesian travelled northwards, through
Ware, Cambridge, Stamford and Newark, he found himself something
of a novelty to the local population, at times being pursued by 'beautiful
women who followed me around' attempting to kiss him. 'If I refused to
kiss one', he later wrote, 'she would depart in embarrassment, but would
return half an hour later, and with much deference offered me food and
drink. And all this they did just so as to deprive me of my virginity.' Still,
Popplau found them to be the 'most beautiful women, the likes of which
I have not seen anywhere in the world. They love the Germans, they like
to be flirted with, they have more beautiful home-spun breasts, and by
nature from head to foot larger and sturdier limbs, than German women.'
As for the men, Popplau found them 'hot headed and choleric disposition,
and when they burst out in anger take no pity on anyone'.

Passing through Doncaster and on to York, Popplau noted how the city
'was the patrimony of the present king of England, before he was elected
or became king by his own power'.[2] Arriving in York, he found the minster

there 'an even more beautiful church than in London, and much more ostentatious, in all its buildings more extensively decorated'. On 1 May, Popplau arrived at a 'strong castle' not far from York, likely to have been Pontefract Castle.* 'Here are kept the king's treasure', Popplau noted, 'and great lords like the king's children and the sons of princes which are kept like prisoners.'[3]

The following day, Popplau was granted an audience with King Richard III, 'in the presence of all princes, earls, councillors and all his nobility'. Popplau addressed Richard in Latin, delivering letters from the Holy Roman Emperor as well as the king's sister, Margaret, the duchess of Burgundy. Richard was apparently 'astonished' at Popplau's eloquence; reading the letters, Popplau later wrote, Richard 'himself approached me, took me by the hand and drew me to him. He answered me in Latin through an interpreter that his majesty the king would gladly do everything I asked as far as lay within his power to do, for the sake of His Imperial Majesty the Prince of Burgundy and also for my own sake, on account of my eloquence, which he would not have expected of me, had he not heard it himself.'[4] Richard then addressed Popplau three times ('as is the custom in England', Popplau noted): 'I welcome you, and be freely welcome with me.'[5] After Popplau left the king's court, he was conducted to a nearby inn by one of Richard's gentlemen of the royal chamber, though they quickly found that they were not alone; 'many people followed us to the house, including women and maidens. They entered the inn secretly, but with the hostess's permission, so that they might look at me alone.'

The next day Richard sent for Popplau to attend mass at the nearby church, no doubt designed to impress the Silesian with the quality of musicianship that he had already collected from across the country. Popplau was suitably impressed. 'There I heard the most delightful music that I heard in all my life, which in the purity of the voices might well be compared to the angels.' After mass, Richard ordered a Flemish nobleman who was currently residing at court, John, lord of Bergen op Zoom, to take Popplau by the hand and lead him to his chamber, in a tent erected near to the church. Going inside, Popplau was struck by its lavish contents:

* Richard himself told Popplau in a later conversation that the castle was called 'Pons Fractus'.

'There I saw the King's bed, covered in red velvet and a cloth of gold . . . in the same way as His Imperial Majesty's bed is so adorned. And in the king's tent there was also a table covered all around with cloths of silk embroidered with gold, set up next to the bed.' Catching sight of Richard himself as the king prepared to sit down to dinner, Popplau was equally impressed at the splendour Richard had cloaked himself in. 'The king went to dinner and wore a collar of gold with many pearls the size of peas, and diamonds. The collar was as thick as a man's hand, and was worn over his left shoulder across his back and under his right arm.'

It was a display, Popplau believed, that had been 'deliberately placed by the wise men of his court in such a way that I should see him sit at table in his regal splendour'. At the king's table were 'his princes and Lords'; Popplau observed how when Richard 'had sat down there sat with him two princes, the king's blood-relatives, and the earl of Northumberland, who is the most powerful in all England. But they sat a long way from the King at the very end of the table.'

When Richard noticed Popplau had entered the tent, he ordered that he should sit at the table 'alongside his two kinsmen'. Popplau replied that rather than sit with the king's companions, his 'greatest pleasure and desire', especially since he was due to depart shortly, was to sit close to the king, 'to see his royal majesty's face and exceedingly famous virtues', an answer which, Popplau noted, 'greatly pleased the king'.

As the pair conversed at the table, Popplau observed how Richard 'grew animated' at his answers, 'so that he barely ate of any dish, but continually talked with me':

He asked me about his Imperial majesty, all kings and princes of the Empire who were known to me, about their customs, fortunes, dealings, and virtues. I answered with everything that was to their honour. Then the king was silent for a while. Afterwards he began again to question me, of many things and dealings, and finally also of the Turks. And I replied to him that before Martinmas 1483 his Majesty the King of Hungary with the aid of forces sent by His Imperial Majesty and his Imperial Majesty's lands, had slain more than 12,000 Turks of the Turkish emperor. When the king heard this, he was greatly pleased and answered 'I would that this kingdom and land of mine lay on the Turkish border instead of the kingdom of Hungary.

Then I would certainly just with my own people and without the aid of other kings, princes and lords drive away not only the Turks but all my enemies and opponents.¹⁶

'O Dear God, what a gracious lord I recognised in that king', Popplau wrote, full of praise for his royal host. The German also noted how the king was 'three fingers taller than I, but a little slimmer, and not as muscular⁷ and much thinner', adding that 'he has very delicate arms and legs, also a great heart'.

Several days later, Richard gave Popplau a gift of fifty nobles. Popplau stayed at the royal court for around eight days, when he 'was almost always present at court at his meals', before finally deciding to continue his journey. Informing the king of his departure, Richard replied that he would 'not impede my intended way. But should, my planned journey complete, I care to return to his majesty on the way back, I should be even more welcome to him than now.' Richard then gave Popplau a gold collar 'which he took from the neck of a gentleman'. Overwhelmed by the king's generosity, Popplau begged 'that he should not grant such a gift to me, being entirely undeserving, for I had not come to his Majesty to seek handouts or gifts, but his royal majesty's favour'. To this Richard, almost offended, retorted that 'if for the sake of my own honour I would refuse his gifts, which it was his honour to give, how did I expect to gain his favour? Therefore, if I desired his good grace, I should also accept this gracious mark of honour, and not reject it.' Popplau meekly thanked Richard and with hesitation accepted the gift, though he could not help but notice that the collar was of significant weight, weighing thirteen ounces in gold.

Popplau was given safe conduct to travel the country unharmed, though for the moment he was 'commanded' by the king to rent an inn, where he continued to be visited by members of Richard's chamber, together with 'the king's musicians, shawms, pipers and lutenists', whom Popplau rewarded with a gift of four crowns. Richard gave Popplau an additional fifty nobles, and when the German attempted to refuse yet another gift, the king became 'animated' and 'sent me a message asking whether I were of royal or princely blood that I should hold his gifts in contempt, to whom I replied that I had refused his majesty's gifts not out of contempt, but simply on account of honour. And he rebuked me with harsh words, and pressed me to such a degree that I had to accept it.'

When Popplau was ready to depart, he was given letters of safe conduct by the king, while one of Richard's men, a Spanish captain called Juan de Salazar, a soldier of fortune who would later fight on Richard's behalf, approached the German with 'letters and instructions for his good friends in his own country, that they should show me friendship and favour, and he did this of his own free will, even though I had not ever approached or asked him for it'.[8]

Popplau would soon depart England for Portugal, where he visited the court of King John II. Once again, Popplau gave ample descriptions of the generosity with which he was treated at a royal court. Throughout his work, his willingness to describe the courts and holy places across Europe suggests that the knight had been sent on a mission for political purposes, rather than for his own pleasure. The same year as his visit to Richard's court, Popplau had been promoted to the rank of palatinus at the court of Emperor Frederick III, becoming one of the monarch's close associates. His tours across Europe seem to have been to gather information for his master, which would include descriptions of the castles that he saw, in particular the military installations at the French naval base of Honfleur and detailed accounts of Portuguese expeditions to Africa.[9] Yet it is striking that Popplau had clearly been impressed with his English host, noting that, when he had finally departed, 'the king of England had given me a dead boar' (either a boar to eat during the farewell party that Richard had commanded be held at the local inn, or referring to the collar of gold, which would have been decorated with Richard's insignia of the white boar).

Popplau's description of Richard provides us with a rare, contemporary glimpse into the world of Richard III. Of course, we are viewing Richard as he would wish to be seen, knowing that Popplau was likely to pass on any report of his conduct to his royal master, Frederick III. Richard's personality and behaviour had become the talk of the courts of Europe. Barely over a year before, Richard had been the unswervingly loyal younger brother of Edward IV, the Yorkist king who had reigned, albeit with one deposition in 1470, for over twenty years. Edward's death, aged just forty-one, in April 1483 had transformed everything. Many had expected his eldest son, Prince Edward, aged thirteen, to inherit the throne as Edward V. A coronation was planned, but would never take place. Richard, having been entrusted as the new king's Protector, eventually chose to accept the crown for himself, being crowned Richard III on 6 July 1483. In the whirlwind of political events, Edward V and his younger brother, Richard, duke of York, disappeared into the Tower of London, never to be seen again. Within eighty-eight days, Richard had gone from brother to Protector to king. Immediately, his unforeseen reign had been beset by rebellion, including by his closest ally, Henry, duke of Buckingham.

Popplau's visit to Richard's court was against the backdrop of a king determined to demonstrate his military capabilities and defend his kingdom; for several weeks afterwards, Richard would continue to remain in the north, basing himself at Scarborough, where he prepared for naval warfare against the Scots. If Richard was able to express his generosity to Popplau in a confident manner, he hid well his own anxieties and concerns, as well as his own significant personal grief for the sudden loss of his son, Prince Edward, who had died at Middleham in April 1484. Without an heir, Richard's dynasty seemed even more uncertain than that of his elder brother at the time of his sudden death. Richard, aged only thirty-one, would have time to father future heirs; far harder was it to rid himself of the rumours that were swirling around the courts of Europe that he had actively initiated the deaths of his brother's heirs, Edward V and Prince Richard. Just months before, in January 1484, the French chancellor, Guillaume de Rochefort, had warned the Estates General at Tours, faced with the minority of the thirteen-year-old king, Charles VIII, that the French nobility must not follow the example set in England the previous year. 'Think, I beg you', de Rochefort had pleaded, 'what happened in that land after the death of King Edward, that his children already grown up and remarkable, were killed with impunity, and the royal crown was passed, with the people's blessing, to their killer.' Hearing the same rumours that surrounded Richard's ascent to the throne, Popplau noted that 'King Richard, who reigns at the moment, has also killed King Edward's sons, as is said, so that he and not they might be crowned.' Yet Popplau had also heard a different version of the tale, one which he was inclined to agree with, that 'some say they are still alive and are kept in a dark cellar'.[10]

Popplau's account of Richard's court presents itself in stark contrast to later accounts of Richard's reign, providing us with a sense of the 'real'

Richard, a king both generous, impassioned and learned. Yet if we are to place Richard in the context of his own time, and not that of later accounts such as William Shakespeare's fabled *Richard III*, it is to the contemporary sources that we must return if we are to divorce fact from fiction.

The Richard III we have ourselves inherited through historical tradition is one that has been shaped and moulded by that convenient fiction, of viewing Richard as the personification of evil, a child-killer, a man whom nothing, or no one, would stop him from obtaining his ambition of wearing the royal crown. This later re-invention of Richard III has already been decried by so-called 'Ricardians' as 'Tudor propaganda', but in many respects the nature of historical debate surrounding Richard III still remains depressingly predictable.

As far back as 1788, the antiquary William Hutton, in his book *The Battle of Bosworth Field*, recognised that Richard, 'of all the English monarchs, bears the greatest contrariety of character': 'Some few have conferred upon him almost angelic excellence, have clouded his errors, and blazoned every virtue that could adorn a man. Others, as if only extremes would prevail, present him in the blackest dye; his thoughts were evil, and that continually, and his actions diabolical; the most degraded mind inhabited the most deformed body.' Yet, Hutton admitted, 'Richard's character, like every man's, had two sides . . . though most writers display but one.'[11] Nearly 230 years on, historical scholarship has ensured that more information has been unearthed on Richard III than most medieval monarchs, yet the popular debate has stubbornly refused to move on. All too often, Richard III's life and reign remain defined by the question, 'Was he a good or bad king?', or, more predictably, 'Did he kill the princes in the Tower?'

It is difficult to break out of the dramatic cycle of events, moulded by the sources that we are reliant upon. Richard's fame often has more to do with the deeply ingrained portrait of the king that we have inherited from Shakespeare. Through the dramatist's pen, Richard was transformed from an historical figure into the archetypal villain. Throughout Shakespeare's first history cycle, Richard appears as a 'carnal cur', 'hell's black intelligencer', a 'bottled toad', 'an indigested and ill-formed lump' and a 'lump of foul deformity', whose penchant for evil deeds and appearance are formed into one hideous personality.

Shakespeare's Richard III was not entirely a dramatic invention. Over the past century since Richard's death, historical writing had sought to denigrate Richard's name. In the years immediately following the battle of Bosworth, the Warwickshire antiquary John Rous, who had in Richard's own lifetime praised the king as 'a mighty prince and especial good lord' who was 'full commendably punishing offenders of the laws, especially oppressors of the Commons, and cherishing those that were virtuous, by the which discreet guiding he got great thanks and love of all his subjects great and poor', now turned against the dead king, who he declared was 'excessively cruel in his days . . . in the way that Antichrist is to reign. And like the Antichrist to come, he was confounded at his moment of greatest pride.' He described the king as 'small of stature, with a short face and unequal shoulders, the right higher and the left lower', though even this had been later altered in the manuscript so that Richard's left shoulder was to be higher than his right, just as portraits of the king would be altered to depict Richard as a hunchback.[12]

Popplau's account of his stay at Richard's court is the most detailed contemporary description of Richard and his royal household, though further glimpses of Richard's personality can be gleaned from the king's own letters, together with surviving payments and warrants. Other contemporary chronicles and accounts also exist to provide flesh to the bones of our knowledge, though, compared to the sixteenth century, the fifteenth century and the narrative accounts of its politics fall into an unsteady period of historical writing, departing from the monastic chronicles of the medieval period, yet not fully ensconced in the humanist histories of the Tudor period. The consequences of this mean that, particularly for the reign of Edward IV, historians possess less strictly contemporary information than any other reign in English history since Henry III. If establishing the precise sequence of events proves problematic at times, still more elusive is the establishment of motive or the understanding of personality in politics. If it is difficult to discern the intentions behind Richard's actions at times, it is, as Geoffrey Elton observed, 'because no sound contemporary history exists for this age that its shape and meaning are so much in dispute now'.[13] Many authors now considered to be crucial sources of information were unaware that they were writing 'history' for a public audience; many simply considered that they were making notes in private commonplace books or letters, interspersing important national events occasionally among events of a more personal or local nature. Personal letters such as those from the Paston, Plumpton, Stonor or Cely collections provide an invaluable window into the private thoughts of individuals reacting to political circumstance, yet compared to the voluminous State Papers collected in the reign of Henry VIII, they are meagre. Other professional recorders of events did so with an agenda that suited their own needs, and not those of the twenty-first-century historian.

One of the most important sources for the years 1471–85 is the account generally known as the 'Second Continuation of the Croyland Chronicle', yet its authorship, and by inference its purpose and bias, remains contested among historians.[14] While we know that its author was a doctor of canon law and a councillor of Edward IV, elsewhere he claims that he wrote and completed the narrative within ten days, ending on the last day of April 1486. Even if the work's direct authorship cannot be concluded upon, it is clear that reference has been made to official documentation in its compilation. Certain elements even demonstrate a distinct personal knowledge of Richard's reign, such as the recording of an oath taken by the nobility to Richard's son, Edward, in 'a certain room near the corridor which leads to the queen's chambers'.[15] One gets the sense that the narrator of events, perhaps told to the scribe who composed the chronicle, was at the heart of power: the fact that John Russell, bishop of Lincoln and Chancellor during Richard's reign, is known to have resided at Crowland Abbey during April 1486 surely points to his guiding influence in the composition of the political sections.[16]

For Richard specifically, recent discoveries in the twentieth century have transformed our understanding of his reign. *The Great Chronicle of London*, first published from a manuscript in 1938, was the product of the industry of the draper Robert Fabyan, who was writing up to his death in February 1513. It provides us with important near-contemporary evidence of the reign from a London perspective; the equally important discovery of Dominic Mancini's manuscript account of the 'Usurpation of Richard the Third', in the archives at Lille, reveals another first-hand account of Richard's ascent to the throne, written no more than six months after the event. Yet even Mancini is the product of what rumours, information and disinformation were circulating throughout the capital during that heady summer of 1483; no source is beyond reproach as truly independent. It was the Italian historian Polydore Vergil, writing in the early sixteenth century, yet whose work, the *Anglia Historica*, was not published until 1534, who imposed a new pattern of historical development upon the events of the fifteenth century. Instead of writing history in an annalistic fashion, as previously employed by medieval chroniclers, Vergil chose to divide English history into royal reigns. As a result, the personality of a king would now play an ever greater role than before. For Vergil, Richard's own personality would be critical in understanding the failure of his reign. He was 'little of stature, deformed of body, the one shoulder being higher than the other', while he had 'a short and sour countenance, which seemed to savour of mischief, and utter evidently craft and deceit. The while he was thinking of any matter, he did continually bite his nether lip, as though that cruel nature of his did so rage against itself in that little carcass. Also he was wont to be ever with his right hand pulling out of the sheath to the midst, and putting in again, the dagger which he did always wear. Truly he had a sharp wit, provident and subtle, apt to both counterfeit and dissemble; his courage also high and fierce.'[17] It was a highly influential portrait of Richard that would remain for centuries, establishing a template that would be followed by Thomas More, and the later Tudor chroniclers Edward Hall and Ralph Hollinshed, before being cast into literary legend by Shakespeare.

Admittedly, much has been done to dispel the myth of the 'black legend' of Richard III. Since the publication of Horace Walpole's *Historic Doubts on the Life and Reign of Richard III*, published in 1768, Richard's memory has found loyal defenders, from Clements Markham to Josephine Tey. Richard's generosity, his piety and his pronouncements on the dispensing of justice have been held up as signs that he was a 'good king', whose virtues have been suppressed, yet these features of Richard's personality and reign should not be gathered together in an attempt to make a case for the defence of the king, for it ignores the wider context of medieval nobility and kingship that Richard was immersed in. His behaviour and words cannot be taken in isolation; kings before and after Richard acted in a similar manner, for that was what was expected of them. Yet to create a white legend of Richard's personality seems merely to perpetuate the sterile debate of a 'good' Richard versus an 'evil' Richard. The history of Richard III needs to be treated with balance and more accurate scholarship, something that can only be achieved by returning where possible to the original sources and contemporary accounts of Richard's life and reign, exploring his life as it was, not as it was later to be seen.

Nor can our understanding of Richard's personality, his motives and ambitions, be gleaned from the last few years of his life alone. For over a decade, Richard stood by Edward IV as his loyal brother, following him into exile and earning his spurs fighting successfully at the battles of Barnet and Tewkesbury. Richard's experiences in the wars against Scotland shaped his sense of leadership and longing for military glory, while an early taste of Richard's ruthlessness can be witnessed in his early land transactions and determination to build an affinity and power base of his own. The fact that Richard managed to establish himself as one of the greatest and most powerful noblemen of his age, in spite of his status as one of Edward IV's younger brothers, demonstrates Richard's early determination to succeed. Richard's early career as duke of Gloucester, built as it was on the shifting sands of the brutal world of fifteenth-century politics, is important for understanding why Richard later chose to take the decisions he did in becoming king.

This work has unapologetically been written as a narrative history of Richard's life and reign; in doing so, attention has been paid mainly to the high court politics of the age, and Richard's role within this world. I have attempted to focus also on how Richard constructed his own power base, for it was his northern affinity, constructed in his early years as duke, that would prove so crucial for him obtaining the throne. Richard's accession to the throne had only been made possible, not just through Richard's own personality, but through a coalition of support that placed the crown on Richard's head. Too much attention is traditionally paid to Richard's individual role in his accession, when, like any political coronation, this was only possible with the support of certain key members of the nobility, who backed regime change. Richard's success depended as much upon their own individual grievances and ambitions as his own.

This is surely the key point about the battle of Bosworth, where Richard fell defeated, not by Henry Tudor, but by the defection and loss of support of his own army and his 'northern men' on whom he had relied to build his career first as duke of Gloucester, then as Protector and finally as king. While individual personalities are crucial for understanding the nature of

power in the fifteenth century, it is important not to forget that kings and
noblemen were the corporate representation of a far wider range of ideals,
and, more realistically, ambitions, of the men who served them.

Richard III reigned for just 788 days, yet his reign is unique in late-
medieval history for the wealth of archival evidence we have inherited,
partly through the survival of his signet docket book, together with privy
seal and Exchequer warrants, many of which remain unpublished. It is
possible to fashion from these an almost day-by-day account of Richard's
reign, and it is through this detail, of returning to the original sources,
that I have attempted to bring a fresh perspective on Richard's reign.

Aged only thirty-two at his death, Richard III remains a strong candidate for being our most celebrated and controversial king. Hundreds of
books have been written about him, while he remains the only English
king with two organisations dedicated to his name, with the Richard III
Society, originally founded in 1924, 'in the belief that many features of the
traditional accounts of the character and career of Richard III are neither
supported by sufficient evidence nor reasonably tenable', currently with a
membership of several thousand. Recently, popular interest in Richard III
has surged with the discovery of the king's remains in Leicester, prompting even more books, articles and television programmes. This book is
not an attempt to compete with the popular mania surrounding Richard.
Instead, by exploring Richard's life in fresh detail, its aim is not only to see
the king's life and reign through the lens of the fifteenth century, but to
gain a sense of why Richard behaved and ruled in the fashion he did, for
'good' or for 'evil'.

PART ONE

BROTHER

1

SONS OF YORK

On 21 May 1471, Edward IV rode into the capital in triumph. He was escorted by thousands of horsemen, 'well accompanied and mightily with great lords, and in substance all the noblemen of the land', the author of one account recorded, 'well arrayed for war'.[1] It was not the only time during his reign that the king had marched into London 'in state', to declare his reign restored. Ten years ago, aged just nineteen, Edward had marched into the capital to claim the throne as rightfully his, displacing the hapless Lancastrian king, Henry VI. Now he returned once more the victor, having won back his kingdom for a second time. This time, however, he had made sure that the Lancastrian cause was all but destroyed. At the battles of Barnet and Tewkesbury, fought just weeks before, not only had Richard Neville, the earl of Warwick, been killed at Barnet, but the Lancastrian prince and heir, Edward, had been slain at Tewkesbury. Henry's queen, Margaret of Anjou, had been captured, and was now paraded through the streets of London in a heavily guarded carriage, the symbol of his victory of victories on a day of Roman triumph.

The mayor and aldermen of London went out to meet their restored king in the meadows between Islington and Shoreditch, where they were knighted, the number of knighthoods distributed without parallel. Edward then made his way through the streets of the capital, at the head of a huge force, numbered by several chroniclers as approaching 30,000 men, as banners and tattered standards of war were unfurled, with trumpets and clarions playing. Alongside, or following just behind, rode Edward's two brothers, George, duke of Clarence, and Richard, duke of Gloucester, together with the dukes of Norfolk, Suffolk and Buckingham, six earls and sixteen barons, 'together with other nobles, knights, esquires and a host of horsemen larger than had ever been seen before'.[2]

Edward's victory against his enemies was complete. 'Upon this occasion', the Crowland chronicler observed, 'many were struck with surprise and astonishment, seeing there was now no enemy left for him to encounter.'[3] The Lancastrian dynasty was effectively over. As the author of a tract known as the 'Arrivall of Edward IV' noted, 'it appeared to every man at eye the said party was extinct and repressed for ever, without any manner hope of again quickening; utterly despaired of any manner of hope or relief'.[4]

The three brothers, Edward IV, George, duke of Clarence, and Richard, duke of Gloucester, presented what seemed a united front: the Yorkist dynasty in all its pomp. But behind this display of unity lay the reality that the dynasty had nearly been torn apart by division and disloyalty. Clarence had himself been a prime mover in the rebellion that had led to Edward IV's forced exile to Burgundy, and an ally of Warwick, only coming back into his brother's fold and gaining his pardon at the eleventh hour. Victory had been achieved not without its costs, and indeed not without new loyalties that the king had come to depend upon in his years of greatest crisis. His brother Clarence may have failed him, but Richard, duke of Gloucester, still aged just eighteen, had proved an invaluable companion and campaigner. With his military record unsurpassed, the past year, which had seen exile alongside his brother and the experience of two hard-fought battles, now placed him arguably as the king's most important ally and support. For Richard, recovering from his wounds, his first taste of battle had proved not only his usefulness and loyalty to his brother, but had shown that he could withstand the brutality of combat. Leading the Yorkist vanguard, he had managed to hold his own in a 'sharp fight'. If the battle at Barnet was a rite of passage, Richard had come of age. For the first time, his own fortunes had begun to transform him from obscure younger brother to powerful lord in his own right, rewarded with land and office. From this moment, Richard, duke of Gloucester, would continue to hold the centre stage of fifteenth-century politics. Richard's reputation as a loyal brother had been forged in the tumultuous events of 1471: yet it was a reputation that already was not without controversy.

That same night, Henry VI was found dead in the Tower of London.

The coincidence would not go unremarked upon. The Yorkist version of the story attempted to suggest that the former king had died of grief, discovering that night the death of his son and the end of his cause, 'not having, afore that, knowledge of the said matters, he took it to so great dispite, ire, and indignation, that, of pure displeasure, and melancholy', he died two days later.[5] Other chroniclers told a different tale. 'I would pass over in silence the fact that at this period King Henry was found dead in the Tower of London', the Crowland chronicler remarked; adding only, 'may God spare and grant time for repentance to the person, whoever he was, who thus dared to lay sacrilegious hands upon the Lord's anointed!' Cryptically, the chronicler hinted that he knew who had committed the deed. 'He who perpetrated this has justly earned the title of tyrant, while he who thus suffered had gained that of a glorious Martyr.'[6]

Henry's body was exhibited at St Paul's Cathedral for several days, before being carried by barge 'solemnly prepared for the purpose, provided with lighted torches', to Chertsey Abbey, and there 'honourably interred'. Ceremony, no matter how honourable, could not mask the sinister rumours that now swirled around the capital. After Henry's body had been 'chested', one chronicler wrote, his coffin had been brought to St Paul's, where its lid was opened, placing the king's face on display, 'that every man might see him'. Yet it was noted that 'in his lying there he bled on the pavement there', while afterwards, the corpse having been brought to Blackfriars, 'there he bled new and fresh'.[7]

If Henry had been silenced in the Tower, the finger of blame pointed immediately at his successor, King Edward. 'King Edward caused King Henry to be secretly assassinated', the Milanese ambassador in France reported, 'he has, in short, chosen to crush the seed'.[8]

If Edward had been responsible for the king's death, giving the order for his execution, then, it was said, another had performed the deed, or followed through with the king's wishes. Richard, duke of Gloucester, had not yet turned nineteen, but already he had been appointed Constable of England in reward for his services to his brother the king, having loyally served him throughout his exile the previous year; as Constable, Richard was also in command of the Tower itself, and the welfare of its royal prisoner. One chronicler wrote how it had been on the night of 21 May, at between eleven and twelve o'clock at night, that Richard himself had been present at the Tower when Henry, 'being inward in prison . . . was put to death'.[9]

Whatever the truth of the stories, no one could deny that the long-suffering Henry VI was now dead, and the Lancastrian dynasty and its royal line were effectively extinct. In contrast, while in sanctuary at Westminster, where she had fled after discovering that the king had been forced into exile, Edward's queen, Elizabeth, had given birth to the couple's first son, Edward. The Yorkist dynasty, triumphant in battle, had now been blessed with a male heir, securing its future.

Just two months after Edward had gambled his reign in battle, on 3 July 1471, in the Parliament chamber at Westminster, the Yorkist court gathered to celebrate its new-found stability, in the form of the baby prince. Restating their loyalty to the dynasty, an oath of homage was taken by all members of the nobility, recognising Edward IV's newborn son, Edward, as Prince of Wales. The prince's uncle, Richard, had travelled south especially for the ceremony. He swore that the young baby, 'first begotten son of our sovereign lord', was 'to be very and undoubted heir to our said lord as to the crowns and realms of England and France and lordship of Ireland'. He promised and swore that 'in case hereafter it happen you by God's disposition to overlive our sovereign lord; I shall then take and accept you for the very true and rightwise King of England'. Pledging his 'faith and truth', he further swore that 'in all things truly and faithfully behave me towards you and your heirs as a true and faithful subject oweth to behave him to his sovereign lord', ending, 'So help me God and Holy Dom and this holy Evangelist.'[10]

As other members of the nobility followed Richard, lining up to declare their loyalty to the new prince as their future king, it must have seemed to Edward IV that the instability of the past, the bloodshed of the civil wars that had plagued England since the 1450s, had now finally drawn to a close. His rivals had been destroyed, and that uncertain chapter in England's history seemed to be at an end. The future, Edward must have considered, would now be one of stability and security, personified in the image of his loyal brother Richard, now a trusted stalwart of his regime, pledging his undying loyalty to his newborn son as his future sovereign lord. With a brother such as Richard by his son's side, his fidelity proven in exile and in battle, there could be no doubt that the future of the Yorkist dynasty was complete.

Richard's had been a difficult birth. Much later, rumours spread that the baby had been born breech, or feet first; wilder tales included stories that the pregnancy had lasted two years, that the child had to be cut from the mother's womb, that it had emerged 'with teeth and hair down to his shoulders'.[11] Even in birth, men sought means to blacken his name. For those who studied the skies and astrological charts, he had been born when 'Scorpio was in the ascendant . . . And as Scorpio was smooth in countenance but deadly in his tail, so Richard showed himself.'[12] The only facts one can truly discern about the birth of Richard, the youngest son of Richard, duke of York, are those later recorded by Richard himself, who wrote in his own hand in his Book of Hours the date of his birth. By the date 2 October, in Latin are the words: 'On this day was born Richard the Third, King of England, at Fotheringhay in the year of our Lord 1452.'[13]

Richard had been born into surroundings that reflected his family's illustrious heritage. The castle and keep of Fotheringhay had belonged to the house of York since Edmund Langley, the first duke of York, had taken possession of the castle in the fourteenth century. Situated close to the Great North Road, eighty miles away from London, the castle overlooked the banks of the River Nene, surrounded by the large hunting forest of Rockingham. Edmund had rebuilt the castle, and the family's heraldic symbol of the falcon and the fetterlock stood guard over the castle's grey keep. It was surrounded by a double moat, its main entrance through an impressive gatehouse on its north-west side; a range of buildings including the original keep, a manor house and two chapels stood out among the range of workshops, kitchens, brewhouses, bakeries, stables and barns. Later, it would be described as 'a castle fair, and meatly strong, with very good lodgings in it, defended by double ditches, with a very ancient and strong keep'.[14]

Richard's father, Richard, duke of York, was at the time of Richard's birth considered, in the line of succession, a strong contender as heir to the throne. Though he was descended in the male line from John of Gaunt's next brother and fourth surviving son of King Edward III, Edmund of

Langley, York's claim to the throne could be found not just on his father's side, but also through his mother, Anne Mortimer. Through her, York was also able to claim descent from Edward III through his second son, Lionel, duke of Clarence, through Clarence's daughter, Philippa, the grandmother of Anne Mortimer. Through a combination of circumstance and fortune, in particular the death of all three brothers of Henry V without issue, York could legitimately expect to be considered heir to the throne. There is little doubt that York was fully aware of his royal ancestry; as early as 1450, he began to adopt the surname 'Plantagenet' as if to emphasise the purity of his claim to the throne. But he was also, when Richard was born in 1452, financially in trouble and banished from the king's court, his long-term power struggle with the duke of Somerset and Henry's queen, Margaret of Anjou, having caused his humiliation and disgrace.

His wife, Richard's mother, Cecily, the duchess of York, was thirty-seven, and coming to the end of her childbearing years. She had already given birth to ten children, five of whom had survived. This time, she had struggled through pregnancy with 'disease and infirmity' she later wrote, forcing her to make a pilgrimage to the shrine of our Lady of Walsingham. As she recuperated from a difficult labour, in spite of all her physical pain, Cecily's 'immeasurable sorrow and heaviness' were not for herself but for her husband's own 'infinite sorrow' at his estrangement and exile from court.[15] This exile coincided with a period of recovery in the fortunes of the beleaguered King Henry VI. By 1453 Queen Margaret was pregnant, potentially pushing Richard of York further down the line of succession.

Then, in August, Henry VI suffered a complete nervous breakdown. As he lay unable to speak or move, for months the king's condition was kept a secret in the hope that he would make a sudden recovery. On 13 October 1453, Margaret gave birth to a son, Prince Edward. The baby was presented to the king by the queen herself, taking the prince in her arms, 'desiring that he should bless it'. Yet Henry remained motionless. Margaret departed 'without any answer or countenance, saving only that he looked on the Prince and cast his eyes down again without any more'.[16] Unaware of the world around him in his catatonic state, Henry VI finally had his heir to the Lancastrian dynasty; yet, for the rest of the king's council, it was a sign that something would need to be done to overcome an impending national crisis caused by the king's incapacity. The following month, in spite of repeated attempts by Queen Margaret to prevent it, York was appointed Protector and Defender of the Realm. Somerset was denounced and committed to the Tower, awaiting charges of treason.

York's sudden change of fortune instantly raised the status of his own children. As Protector, the duke was allowed the privilege not only of having his heir Edward titled as an earl, but his second son, Edmund, too, who was granted the earldom of Rutland by 1454. While the infant Richard would have simply been too young to have been placed in his own household with governors and tutors, and would most likely have been under the direct care of his mother at Fotheringhay, his elder brothers had been set up with their own household at Ludlow Castle in the heart of York's estates in the Welsh Marches, in preparation for their future roles.

York's tenure as Protector was not to last the year. On Christmas Day 1454, Henry VI awoke: presented with his baby son, 'he said he never knew him till that time, nor knew what was said to him, nor knew where he had been whilst he hath been sick till now'.[17] Henry's recovery transformed everything. York's protectorate was suddenly over, and his great enemy, Somerset, was released from prison, baying for revenge. York, together with the earl of Salisbury and the earl of Warwick, departed from the capital without taking formal leave of the king. They were summoned to attend a great council at Leicester on 21 May, in order 'to provide for the king's safety'.[18] The meeting was to be packed by Somerset's allies at court. York knew that the assembly was nothing more than a trap, possibly to seek his own trial and execution. He had no choice but to act first, and no other option than to take military action. When news that a large Yorkist force was advancing rapidly southwards, Somerset and the king were taken by surprise.

On 22 May the two armies met at St Albans. After negotiations had broken down, a short and violent fight broke out in the streets of the town. Cornered in a tavern, Somerset was killed. Henry, who had been injured in the 'battle', was seized and taken back to London. As soon as the fighting had ceased, York went to the king and knelt before him, begging his forgiveness. He had not meant for the king to be harmed; he only wished to defeat the king's enemies at court. Henry had little choice but to forgive. Led back to London surrounded by an armed procession of York's men, with the duke riding close by at his right hand, it was obvious to everyone watching that Henry was nothing more than a captive king.

The new government, with York at its head, sought to bring about reconciliation and heal old wounds. Three days later, York placed the crown on Henry's head at a staged ceremony at St Paul's. Parliament was summoned, issuing a general pardon to those who had taken up arms on York's side against the king.

Then during the summer of 1455, Henry fell ill again. Once more, York stepped in to assume the mantle of Protector. Three months later, in February 1456, the duke resigned after the king made a partial recovery. In York's place, Queen Margaret now exerted her influence over the king, effectively ruling in his name. In June 1459, Margaret summoned a royal council to meet at Coventry: York, Salisbury and Warwick were excluded, and in their absence indictments were laid against them.

The Yorkist lords had separate plans. They intended to hold their own meeting at Ludlow, where York, who had arrived in the town with his entire family, including Duchess Cecily and their youngest children, George, Richard and Margaret, would be joined by an army of northerners brought by the earl of Salisbury from the Neville estates in Middleham, together with a contingent from the Calais garrison, led by Warwick. On 23 September, Salisbury and his forces were confronted by a royalist detachment led by Lord Audley at Blore Heath. The fighting lasted for four hours. Audley was killed and the Lancastrians defeated, though the engagement resolved nothing, for the main Lancastrian army, led by Queen Margaret and with Henry VI in attendance, was closing in. By the time Salisbury joined with York's forces at Ludlow, the Yorkist leaders realised they were trapped. York chose to hold his ground; on 12 October, his forces 'fortified their chosen ground, their carts with guns set before their battles, made their skirmishes, laid their ambushes' on the opposite side of the River Teme, south of Ludlow, near Ludford Bridge.[19] In comparison to the size and scale of the Lancastrian forces, a royal army led in person by the king himself, York had managed to muster just six peers, two of whom were his own sons. During that night, the duke faced another blow: the Calais garrison, unwilling to bear arms against the king in person, had defected. Now there could be no hope of victory. Around midnight, York, together with his military leaders, his sons Edward and Edmund, Salisbury and

Warwick, left their army in the field, their standards and banners still flying, claiming that they needed to 'refresh' themselves in the town.

They did not return. Abandoning their men, York and Edmund fled to Ireland. Edward, earl of March, took a different route, to Calais. It was a shameful flight from the field, but for Cecily and her young children, as dawn broke the following morning, the nightmare had only just begun. As chaos erupted outside the castle walls, it would not be long until the Lancastrians would discover that York had left his own wife and children to their fates. One chronicler recorded that 'King Harry rode into Ludlow, and spoiled the Town and Castle, where at he found the Duchess of York with her two young sons [then] children.'[20] Another recalled that 'The town of Ludlow belonging then to the duke of York, was robbed to the bare walls, and the noble duchess of York unmanly and cruelly was entreated and spoiled.'[21] What exact treatment was meted out to the duchess remains vague: while 'entreated' might be interpreted as 'dealt with' or 'persuaded', spoiled could refer to any serious crime from robbery to rape. For Richard, having just turned seven, the terrifying experience must have taught him at this early age the catastrophic consequences that defeat could bring. Having witnessed at first hand the humiliation and horror of war, heard the sound of cannon fire and sensed the fear that accompanied his father's defection and defeat, Ludlow marked for Richard the end of his childhood years. If Richard had been allowed to live his early years in a sheltered existence, his age of innocence had been suddenly shattered.

Cecily and her three youngest children were taken to Coventry, where, during the 'Parliament of Devils', York and other leading Yorkists were 'for their traitorous rearing of war . . . at Ludford afore specified, in the fields of the same . . . reputed, taken, declared, adjudged, deemed and attainted of High Treason, as false traitors and enemies' to the king.[22] By now there could be no turning back. All of York's estates in England and Ireland were to be confiscated. Stripped of his title, his lands, his inheritance, York now became a man with nothing to lose. Still, Cecily was determined to protect her children from the impact that their father's attainder might have upon their family's fortunes. Once again, the duchess employed her familiar tone of reconciliation, this time appearing in front of King Henry in person, begging that her husband be allowed to 'come to his answer and to be received unto his grace'. This Henry 'humbly granted ... and to all hers that would come with her'. Cecily was granted a royal pardon together with an allowance of 1,000 marks out of York's former estates to support herself and her children. The duchess, her two sons and her daughter were to be transferred to the custody of Cecily's sister, Anne, duchess of Buckingham, where they were to be placed effectively under house arrest at Tonbridge Castle, Kent. 'She was kept full straight and many a great rebuke', one chronicler noted.

The outbreak of fighting at Blore Heath and Ludford Bridge marked the end of York's ambitions for a renewed protectorate and the acknowledgement and acceptance of his heirs as future kings of England. There could be no more reconciliation. The only way forward was to claim the throne for himself, and to do so by force. The duke understood that disillusion with the Lancastrian regime still prevailed: with a king incapable of ruling, surrounded by a self-serving clique of advisers, change was needed. From Ireland and Calais, York and his followers began a ruthless propaganda assault, sending letters and broadsheets into the realm, presenting themselves as champions of good government and reform.

In March 1460, York and Warwick met in Ireland to plan an invasion. This time they aimed to place the duke on the throne. Three months later, Warwick, together with Salisbury and Edward, earl of March, and a force of 2,000 men, landed in Kent. Men flocked to their standards 'like bees to a hive'; compared to the disaster at Ludlow, the Yorkists now found seventeen peers prepared to lend support to their cause. Entering London several days later, the Yorkist army's sudden advance threw Henry VI and the Lancastrians into panic.[23] By the time the Lancastrian forces had gathered at Northampton, the Yorkists had already marched out of the capital in pursuit. Brief the battle of Northampton may have been, but its outcome could hardly have been more dramatic or successful: the leading Lancastrian noblemen, the duke of Buckingham, the earl of Shrewsbury, Viscount Beaumont and Lord Egremont, were all killed defending the royal tent. With the battle over, Henry VI was seized and led back to London, a prisoner in all but name. In an incredible turnaround in their fortunes since their flight from Ludlow, the Yorkist lords controlled both the king and the capital, while Queen Margaret was forced to flee to Scotland.

York himself, though their figurehead, was yet to return from Ireland. When he finally landed at Chester on 9 September 1460, his first thoughts were to be reunited with his duchess. Meanwhile he delayed his entry into London, touring his estates, where he recruited men for his march upon the capital. As he made slow progress southwards, the duke's intentions could not have been clearer: with his banners emblazoned with the royal arms, a drawn sword was carried before him, its point facing upwards, a sign of majesty and a privilege only granted to kings. Warwick prepared the way for the duke's arrival, condemning Henry VI publicly as 'a dolt and a fool', stating that York 'would now be on the throne if there were any regard to justice'.[24] Three days after Parliament had assembled, York entered the capital and made his procession to Westminster. Arriving at the palace through an entrance reserved for the monarch, in the Parliament chamber in front of an assembled audience of lords, he strode up to the marble chair of the king's bench and laid his hand upon it, 'to take possession of his right'. York had miscalculated badly. There were no cheers, no acclamation in support of his attempt to claim the throne that the duke had expected. His peers stood in embarrassed silence. Several days later, York chose to address the lords once more. Convinced of his right to rule, the duke would not take no for an answer. This time, he did not hesitate to sit on the throne itself, declaring to the assembled lords that the crown was his by right of inheritance. Once again, he was met with stony silence.

York would not be deterred. Instead he would continue to press his case, to be recognised officially and in law as heir to the throne. With the stand-off continuing, a compromise was offered: an 'Accord' was formulated and eventually accepted, whereby Henry VI would remain king for life, but he would be succeeded by York and his heirs. Finally, York had achieved his dream of recognition: from this moment he formally titled himself Richard Plantagenet, openly signalling his belief that his was the true line of succession from Edward III. On All Saints' Day, 1 November, another solemn ceremony was staged at St Paul's: Henry wore his crown, but this time York walked in procession, while Warwick bore the sword before the king and Edward, earl of March, carried the king's train.

While Henry may have been content to accept the compromise offered by the Accord, his queen, Margaret, was hardly prepared to allow her

son, Edward, to be disinherited without a fight. She was soon planning
for an invasion and a rising of the Lancastrian nobility. The threat could
not be ignored, and on 9 December, York marched out of London with
Salisbury and Edmund, earl of Rutland, to confront Margaret and the
growing Lancastrian forces. By 21 December, the duke had reached his
castle at Sandal, where his men spent Christmas. It soon became clear
that the castle was vastly understocked with supplies, and the duke and
his men were forced to undertake foraging missions into the surrounding
countryside. Within days, York and his men were encircled by Lancastrian
forces. On 30 December, the duke chose to confront his enemies, with disastrous consequences. Treachery in his own ranks left York outnumbered
and outflanked. The duke was dragged from his horse and killed, while
his son, Edmund, was killed trying to escape. Salisbury, at first imprisoned, was later executed by 'the common people', who dragged him out
of the castle and 'smote off his head'. Rumours swirled of the humiliations
inflicted upon York's dead body, that it had been made to wear 'a vile garland' fashioned from reeds and propped up while the Lancastrian leaders
taunted and abused it, before decapitating it, and, having adorned the
duke's head with a paper crown, placed it upon a spike on the city gates at
York.[25]

Edward, earl of March, had been sent to Ludlow to raise men from the
duke's estates when he discovered news of his father's and brother's deaths.
There was little time to mourn their loss. Edward not only now inherited
his father's dukedom of York, but his claim to the crown also. He could
be in little doubt that Queen Margaret would seek his blood too; already
the Lancastrian army was travelling southwards towards the capital,
described by various commentators as a 'whirlwind of the north' and 'a
plague of locusts' that intended to wreak destruction upon the south. But
first Edward had to contend with a Lancastrian army led by Henry VI's
half-brother, Jasper Tudor, earl of Pembroke, that had landed in south-
west Wales and was marching on Hereford. On 2 February, the two armies
met in the freezing cold at Mortimer's Cross, not far from Edward's castle
at Wigmore. Just before the battle, three suns had appeared in the sky,
leaving Edward's followers distraught at the portent. To Edward, however,

it was auspicious: 'Be of good comfort, and fear not', he told his men, 'this is a good sign, for these three suns stand in token of the Father, the Son and the Holy Ghost, and therefore let us have a good heart.'[26] The reality behind the strange, miraculous vision was somewhat more prosaic: the phenomenon was caused by an optical illusion known as a parhelion, in which light refracted through ice crystals in the atmosphere causes the appearance of multiple suns to form in the frosted air.

The following day, Edward's forces routed the Lancastrians. The new duke was determined to have vengeance: 4,000 Lancastrians were killed, more soldiers than in all previous battles of the civil war combined.

In honour of his devastating victory, Edward adopted the 'sun in splendour' as one of his own devices. Yet his celebrations were premature. Faced with the advance of the queen's Lancastrian forces towards London, Warwick had hastily dissolved Parliament and marched his troops out of the city. On 17 February, engaging with the Lancastrian army at St Albans, the earl suffered a bloody defeat: he fled the battle, though many Yorkist leaders were taken prisoner. Worse still, Henry VI had been recaptured by the Lancastrians and was now back under his wife's control. The road to London was open for the Lancastrians to seize the capital. The advance of the 'northern men' seemed a terrifying prospect: 'the people in the north rob and steal and are planning to pillage all this country, and give away men's goods and livelihoods in all the south country', Clement Paston warned his brother John.[27] Fear of northern violence and 'countless acts of cruelty' stirred talk in London of armed resistance. Everything pointed towards the horrifying prospect of civil war being fought in open combat among the streets of the capital.

Since her return to London, Duchess Cecily and her younger children, Margaret, George and Richard, had been lodged in the duke's residence at Baynard's Castle. Located on the banks of the River Thames, the large house featured several courtyards and undercrofts, with an imposing great hall that gave it the appearance of a royal palace. It was also a convenient strong house, whose thick walls could be compared to the Tower down-stream, while the building was capable of accommodating over 400 armed men in York's retinue when necessary. But Cecily realised that, with her husband now in exile, it would also be a beacon for Lancastrian attacks. As she awaited her husband's return from Ireland, Cecily decided to move her children into Fastolf Place on the banks of the Thames in Southwark, belonging to an old acquaintance of the family, Sir John Fastolf. The house was guarded by a retired German soldier, Christopher Hausson, who took charge of his new guests. The family arrived on 15 September; two days later, however, Cecily heard news of York's landing at Chester. On 23 September, after receiving a request from her husband that she should join him in Hereford, Cecily left the three children in Hausson's care, though their elder brother, Edward, earl of March, 'cometh every day to see them'.[28] The violent deaths of her husband and her son Edmund at Wakefield brought home to Duchess Cecily the necessity to protect her younger children, especially her other sons, who provided a succession down York's male line. 'Fearing the fortune of that world', she placed the two boys, George and Richard, in the care of one Alice Martyn, a widow who was charged with keeping them 'from danger and peril in their troubles'.[29] From there they were sent into exile abroad, 'over the sea . . . unto a town in Flanders named Utrecht, where they rested a while'.[30]

Cecily entrusted the care of George and Richard to Duke Philip the Good of Burgundy, the head of a family with whom York had already sought out marriage alliances. Philip's magnificent court reflected the wealth of his independent duchy that stretched across most of modern-day Belgium, Luxembourg, most of the Netherlands and areas of northern France. The arrival of the two young boys from a noble family that had been engaged in violent civil war with the ruling house of Lancaster – the dynasty of Henry V, whom Philip had held in high regard as an ally – was an embarrassment. News of the disaster at Wakefield and the death of York had reached Burgundy, and while the exiled French dauphin, Louis, who was living in Burgundy at the time, was keen to support the Yorkist cause, Philip, with his own court centred on Flanders and Brabant, preferred to retain a neutral stance, especially while Charles VII of France, who was hostile to his son Louis's influence on Burgundian policy, remained supportive of the Lancastrian cause. The arrival of York's own sons George and Richard presented Philip with a dilemma. In the end, the duke chose what he considered the best course of action for now: to do nothing and keep the two boys at a distance from his own court. Instead, George and Richard were to remain in Utrecht.

Meanwhile the threat of the Lancastrian entry into London did not materialise. After a delegation led by Anne, duchess of Buckingham, and Jacquetta, Lady Rivers, pleaded with the queen not to allow her northern army entrance into the city, on 19 February Margaret decided to return to Dunstable. It was to prove a catastrophic mistake. The same day, Edward, earl of March, moved swiftly east with his army after hearing news of Warwick's defeat at St Albans. Three days later, Edward was reunited with his cousin in the Cotswolds, allowing their united force to march on London, which they entered on 26 February to popular acclaim. The eighteen-year-old earl of March was recognised as the city's saviour, who had rescued London from the ravages of the 'northern' men.[31] Unlike Warwick, whose defeat had placed the city under threat in the first place, damaging his reputation, Edward's unbroken record of victory marked him out as the true inheritor of the Yorkist claim to the throne.

Edward had learnt from his father's mistakes the previous autumn. While the celebrations marking his arrival continued, he kept himself out of sight, hidden away in Baynard's Castle. Rather than rush to claim the crown, he would wait for the crown to come to him, or at least create the pretence of having done so. Conveniently, with Parliament not sitting and many lords having fled the capital, Edward was free to plan his own accession, stage by stage, in carefully co-ordinated and stage-managed ceremonies.

On Sunday, 1 March, Edward's cousin, George Neville, the bishop of Exeter, preached a sermon in front of a specially chosen assembly of soldiers and citizens in St John's Field. Here he set out Edward's title to the throne, while reading a list of articles that showed how Henry VI had broken the Accord reached the previous October. Asking his audience whether they believed Henry was fit to continue as king, Neville stirred the crowd to make their own acclamation that they would accept Edward as king in Henry's place. Messengers were then sent to Edward to inform him of 'the people's' decision: for this, Edward 'thanked God and them'. Two days later, proclamations were sent out summoning people to assemble at St Paul's the following morning, Wednesday, 4 March. There, at the cross, Neville once again asked the people whether they would accept Edward as their king. While the same loud and enthusiastic cheers were made, Edward, who had arrived in a solemn procession accompanied by Yorkist lords, heard mass in the cathedral before riding to Westminster. There he took his seat on the marble chair of the king's bench, wearing royal robes and holding the sceptre in his hand, while a formal document setting out Edward's claim to the throne, the *Titulus Regius*, was read out. When this had been done, for a third time the assembled crowds were asked if they wished Edward to become their king, which was met with loud shouts of 'Ye, Ye,' proclaiming the duke as their new king, Edward IV.

News of Edward's accession travelled quickly, with reports making their way across the Channel within days. In Utrecht, news that the two young boys in the bishop's charge were now brothers of a king, and royal princes of England themselves, was marked by festivities. The town's accounts reveal that payment was made on 9 March, by order of the *oversten*, the eight aldermen who ran the town, for three *aem* (a jug of 170 litres), minus five *taec* (4.25 litres), meaning around 489 litres of wine, at a cost of £46 15s, were drunk in celebration of 'the two sons of the duke of York'.[32] Still Duke Philip remained cautious of welcoming Richard and George to his court. When further news reached Burgundy that Edward had led his forces into the north, where he had won a remarkable victory over the Lancastrians at Towton on 29 March – an assault of such magnitude that over 20,000 lost their lives, with Queen Margaret and Henry VI forced to flee into exile in Scotland – Philip suddenly reconsidered his opinion of the two boys, whose status as royal princes now seemed beyond doubt.

George and Richard were summoned to the Burgundian court at Bruges. They were welcomed personally by Duke Philip, and 'received, cherished and honoured' at court. The Milanese ambassador at the French court wrote from Bruges on 18 April how 'the two brothers of King Edward have arrived, one eleven and the other twelve years of age. The duke, who is most kind in everything, has been to visit them at their lodging, and showed them great reverence.'[33] The town accounts of Bruges reveal the entertainment that was organised for the boys' arrival, recording payment 'for a banquet given to our dread lord and the children of York in the aldermen's hall' to which were invited 'the ladies of the city ... and where also many other noble lords of our aforesaid dread lord's blood and council were present'[34] By 28 April, George and

Richard had arrived at Calais, where they were shortly to sail to England.

Meanwhile Edward remained in the north, hunting down Lancastrian lords and enforcing his authority on the region, including removing the impaled heads of his father and brother from their spikes on the city gates of York, interring their remains at Pontefract. The new king's coronation was planned for June. In preparation of their own role in the coronation, Richard and George began their final journey to the capital. Arriving in Canterbury on Saturday, 30 May 1461, the two brothers were presented with three capons, two oxen, twenty sheep and three gallons of wine. Since the day was also the Vigil of the Holy Trinity, Richard and George journeyed to the cathedral, where they were greeted by the prior of Christ Church and the rest of the convent, wearing green copes. They attended vespers, and the following day walked in the procession to high mass.[35]

Preparations were made by the city to receive the new royal princes with suitable honour. On 1 June 1461, it was agreed that the Common Council of the city of London, together with 'the most worthy citizens of the guilds', should assemble the following day at Billingsgate, the mayor and aldermen dressed in crimson, to meet 'the Lords George and Richard, brothers of the Lord King'.[36] Both brothers were then most likely taken to their mother at Baynard's Castle, before travelling to Sheen to be reunited with their brother, Edward, upon his arrival on 14 June. With the king's coronation planned for two weeks' time, Edward appointed his brother and heir George as steward for the coronation banquet, although since 'he was but young and tender of age' he was to be assisted by Lord Wenlock, who was to take over the tiresome duties of assessing the various claims of those desperate to perform the honorary offices at the ceremony.

There is no indication that Richard was given a specific role in the coronation itself, though as the king rode into London on 26 June, he was met by both his brothers at the Tower, along with thirty others who were formally dubbed knights of the Bath, the second-highest order of chivalry, that evening. The heralds were paid an additional twenty marks 'for the gift and largesse of our dearest beloved brethren at the same place made knights'.[37]

The following morning, Edward rode in procession to Westminster, preceded by his brothers and the other knights, all wearing blue gowns trimmed with white fur and white hoods, with tokens of white silk lace on their left shoulders. On Sunday, 28 June, Edward was crowned at Westminster. Richard and George watched as the archbishops of Canterbury and York placed St Edward's crown on their brother's head. In the banqueting and celebrations that followed over the next two days, both brothers were once again in attendance, while their elder brother, the king, wore his crown constantly as if to continually remind everyone that he really was their monarch. Barely six months before, the house of York had seemed doomed, destroyed by their father's death: now, with their lives transformed, it seemed as if fortune smiled upon them.

The accession of the nineteen-year-old Edward brought joy in the capital, which Yorkist balladeers would swiftly capitalise on, with one poet exhorting: 'let us walk in a new vineyard, and let us make a gay garden in the month of March with this fair white rose and herb, the Earl of March'.[38] 'I am unable to declare how well the commons love and adore him, as if he were their God', an Italian merchant in London wrote to a friend in Bruges that April. 'The entire kingdom keeps holiday for the event, which seems a boon from above.'[39] Over six foot three inches tall and with a strong warrior-like physique, Edward appeared the very opposite of the mentally frail and weak Henry VI, who had reigned, a king in name only, for more than thirty-eight years. After decades of decline, during which England had lost most of its territory in France, a new world seemed on the horizon.

Henry VI had managed to flee to Scotland with his wife, Queen Margaret of Anjou, arguably the power behind the Lancastrian throne, yet a succession of smaller battles eventually ground down any resistance, until, in July 1465, Henry VI was captured and taken to the Tower. Edward's victory against his enemies appeared complete: the long period of civil war and political upheaval was finally at an end, or so it seemed. The reversal in the brothers' fortunes had been remarkable, but also demonstrated how fragile political life could be, or might become. Fortune's wheel might turn at any time. For now, they were in the ascendant; whatever the future held for them, they remained confident that God was on their side. In an illustrated manuscript produced shortly after his coronation, there is an image that depicts Edward, wearing the crown and his royal regalia, at the top of Fortune's wheel, while Henry VI is being crushed beneath it. Clarence and Richard are on the left-hand side, ascending, being watched by the bishops and the nobility in their plate armour. A small cloaked figure depicting Reason has stopped the wheel by driving a spoke into it. With the wheel prevented from turning once more, the illustrator evidently hoped that Edward, sitting securely at the top, would long remain as king.

2

THE WHEEL TURNS

The day after the coronation, on Monday, 29 June, Edward created his brother and heir, George, the duke of Clarence. The choice of the title of Clarence was significant. First created for Lionel of Antwerp, son of Edward III, it was now a symbol that the Yorkist claim to the throne descended directly from Edward III, a claim that was far stronger than that of their Lancastrian predecessors. The speed at which Clarence was elevated to his dukedom highlighted that he was to be considered Edward's heir presumptive and honoured as such; as the youngest of the king's brothers, Richard would have to wait several months until he was finally elevated to the higher ranks of the peerage: on 1 November he was finally created duke of Gloucester, with an annuity of £40 attached to the title that would be paid by the county whose name Richard bore.[1]

Still only nine years old, Richard was to remain under his brother's watch at court. Richard and Clarence seem to have lodged at the royal palace at Greenwich, known as Placentia, 'the pleasant place', which had been built in 200 acres of grounds by Duke Humphrey in 1427. During the summer of 1461, the two boys may have been briefly housed together in a tower at Greenwich, whose rooms included a hall, parlour and six chambers, each furnished with hangings made of worsted.[2] The wardrobe accounts of Robert Cousin, the Keeper of the Great Wardrobe, indicate that he conveyed clothes and furniture to Richard at Greenwich: the account, dated 30 September 1462, lists 'diverse robes, mantels, gowns, tunics, caps, hose, and other diverse ornaments, things and material necessary for the duke's rank', along with several hundred marten furs, forty pelts of black lambskin, hats, over seventy pairs of shoes, boots, twelve bowstrings, 'one saddle of antique fashion with a harness, one saddle gilt, one sword with a belt and white scabbard, and one harness'.[3] Clarence had four henchmen, a herald and two footmen in his own small household, while Richard only had unspecified 'servants' with him; the large number of shoes (seventy-six pairs), bonnets (ninety-one) and over fifty-two yards of frise suggest that the supplies were not for Richard alone.

The wardrobe account is an unusual survival for the amount of information it reveals about the duke's existence at a time when only infrequent mention of Richard can be found. Within two weeks of his creation as duke of Gloucester, on 13 November 1461, Richard is listed among those given commissions of array to raise troops for the king's defence against his enemies in Scotland.[4] On 4 February 1462, Edward ordered that his 'right entirely beloved brother' Gloucester should receive a helmet, a crest and a sword, which should be set in the chapel of the college of St George at Windsor, 'according for him to the honour and order of the Garter'.[5]

While residing at court, young Richard continued training to become a knight, following the traditional form of education reserved for members of the nobility. Sir John Fortescue praised the royal household as a 'supreme academy for the nobles of the realm, and a school of vigour, probity and manners'. Education was focused on military training, vital for men who would be tasked with protecting the realm, but royal princes should also have a knowledge of law to be inspired with a love of justice, though learning should be only 'in general terms'. Scripture should be studied, but not 'profoundly'.[6] Richard's day-to-day routine probably followed that set down by royal household ordinances under Edward IV several years later. After being awakened, Richard would have attended matins before hearing mass in his chapel or closet. Breakfast would follow, before being 'occupied in such virtuous learning as his age shall now suffice to receive'. At dinner, which Richard would himself later suggest should be observed no later than eleven o'clock in the morning, he would take 'meat' while listening to noble stories that would be read to him, encouraging the practice of virtue and honour and 'acts of worship'. The afternoon was taken up with 'disports and exercises as behoveth his estate to have experience in' before attending evensong and supper.[7] Part of Richard's training in his later youth would have included jousting and horse-riding. In his *Chronicle*, John Hardyng noted that 'at fourteen year they shall to field I sure, at hunt the deer, and catch a hardiness . . . at sixteen year to array and to wage, to joust and ride, and castles to assail'.[8] The wardrobe accounts attest to the fact that riding gear was purchased for both Richard and his brother George, while in March 1465 the fletcher William Love was paid £20 6s 1d 'for divers sheaves of arrows and other chattels' that had been delivered to John Younge, yeoman of the king's bows, for 'the use of our brethren the duke of Clarence and Gloucester'.[9]

Richard and Clarence seem to have been looked after by other leading figures in the realm during their visits across the country. On 12 September 1462, Edward granted Thomas, Lord Stanley, an annuity in recognition of his services done to the king and his brothers Clarence and Gloucester[10] while Thomas Bourchier, the archbishop of Canterbury, would later be rewarded because he had 'at the king's request . . . supported the king's brothers . . . for a long time at great charges'.[11] In late August 1463, Richard attended mass at Canterbury Cathedral with his brother Clarence, who as heir presumptive, ordered that a sword be carried before him with its point raised upwards. As for Richard, his presence went unremarked. The chronicler John Stone noted the arrival of the dukes at Canterbury, 'the lord George Duke of Clarence with his brother'. Richard remained very much in the shadow of his elder brother.[12]

As heir presumptive, Clarence was also given the lion's share of royal grants; in contrast, Edward's grants to Richard were considerably less generous. In September 1461, there had been rumours that Richard was to receive lands in Norfolk, though this came to nothing.[13] On 12 August 1462, he was granted a sizeable number of lands; however, unlike Clarence's landed estate, none of these amounted to any specific territorial affinity: the grant included the lordships of Richmond in Yorkshire, Pembroke in West Wales and a scattering of lands from the forfeited de Vere estates in Cambridgeshire, Essex and Suffolk, confiscated from the earl of Oxford. Two months later, on 2 October, Richard was appointed Admiral of England, Ireland and Aquitaine, to complement his constableship of Corfe Castle in Dorset.[14]

Since Richard had yet to obtain his majority, any grants that were made by the king were provisional, with the king free to revise his arrangements as he chose. As soon as the lordship of Richmond had been granted to Richard, it was to be taken away, for it seems that Clarence, who already held the Honour of Richmond, wanted the lands for himself; after Clarence had protested, Edward duly complied.[15] Though Richard was eventually compensated for this, the process was characterised by hesitation and contradiction, with no guarantee that he would be given an estate that would not only secure his income as a royal duke, but more importantly would allow him the opportunity to build up a territory that he might call his own. In the absence of stability over his own future, Richard must have learnt from an early age that, in contrast to his elder brother Clarence, the heir to the throne, his life was set to be very different, a life in which he would need to seize every opportunity that presented itself to him.

Richard, earl of Warwick, was the greatest nobleman of his age. The earl was second in the realm only to Edward himself, though some would say Warwick regarded himself as more important than the king. One Italian visitor observed how Warwick 'seems to be everything in this kingdom', while others joked how 'there are at present two chiefs in England, of which Monsieur de Warwick is one, and they forget the name of the other'.[16]

As Richard approached his teenage years, it was time to be sent into the household of a nobleman to complete his military training and to learn what was expected from a royal member of the nobility. There could be no better place to discover this than in the magnificence of Warwick's household, one of the greatest of its day, which in 1465 Richard duly entered. He is likely to have first journeyed to the Midlands, to the earl's principal castle, at Warwick: later that year one account roll notes payment of £1,000, 'to Richard Earl of Warwick, for costs and expenses incurred by him for the Duke of Gloucester, the King's brother'.[17] That same year Richard was to be found at the Collegiate Church of St Mary in Warwick, making an offering at the high altar in the presence of the earl and countess of Warwick, Lord Fitzhugh and Lord Hastings. By now Richard's household also included minstrels, who were present at Stratford upon Avon with the earl of Warwick's minstrels in 1465.[18] The surviving wardrobe account for Richard, dated 20 March 1465, indicates that the king still paid for his brother's 'diverse robes, gowns, tunics, caps, hose, shoes and other diverse ornaments, things and material the same as necessary for the duke's rank',[19] with additional luxuries including two covers of tapestry work, two pairs of falconry gloves, four dozen bowstrings, twelve arrowheads, a bowcase, two standing basins and a significant amount of riding equipment.[20]

Warwick's landed wealth was unsurpassed, making him the most powerful nobleman since John of Gaunt. Through his Neville ancestors, the earl had inherited vast estates in the north of England, particularly in Yorkshire, where Warwick held the strongholds of Middleham and Sheriff Hutton castles, lying north of York. Warwick also held the wardenship of the West March, with his base at Carlisle. Through his mother, the dowager countess of Salisbury, Warwick had inherited the estates of the Montagu earldom of Salisbury, while his marriage to the heiress Anne Beauchamp, the daughter of Richard Beauchamp, the original earl of Warwick, had given the earl his title and the family's lands in the Midlands and the south, as well as the lordship of Glamorgan in south Wales. Following his accession, Edward IV granted the earl a number of lucrative offices north of the Trent confiscated from Lancastrian supporters. Warwick's Neville family members were equally well rewarded, with his youngest brother, John, being created earl of Northumberland and granted the estates of their rivals, the Percy family, in the county, while another brother, George, was appointed Chancellor of England.

With his wealth and power, Warwick was able to ensure that his household was one of the largest and most renowned outside of the royal court. The earl's northern household at Middleham and Sheriff Hutton would also have allowed Richard to become familiar with the large inter-connecting circle of northern noblemen and gentry who were associated with the Neville patrimony, including the Scropes, the Fitzhughs, the Greystokes and the Dacres. Another ward in Warwick's guardianship was Francis, Lord Lovell, who would remain a life-long friend and supporter of Richard's.

As a royal duke, Richard would have spent most of his time among Warwick's close family within the inner chambers of his castles at Warwick, Middleham and Sheriff Hutton. The earl's countess, Anne, was described as a 'full devout lady in God's service' who was 'free of her speech to every person familiarly according to her and their degree'.[21] The couple had two daughters, Isabel, born in 1452, and Anne, born in 1456, whom the earl had yet to marry off. For while the earl had his youngest sister, Margaret, married to John, earl of Oxford, in 1462, and his niece Alice, daughter of his sister Lady Fitzhugh, wed to Lord Lovell, Warwick clearly expected a much greater match for his two daughters.

The Neville family influence and wealth can be glimpsed at a feast held in September 1465, at the archbishop's palace at York, to celebrate the promotion of Warwick's brother, George Neville, as archbishop of York. Over 2,000 people were in attendance including bishops, eighteen heads of religious houses, two dukes, six earls, seven barons, eighteen knights, sixty-nine esquires, as well as thirty-three judges, sergeants and lawyers, the mayor of Calais, and the mayor and aldermen of York. The feast was nothing less than a northern coronation, the celebration itself a demonstration of the apogee of Neville power and their dominance in the region. Over 500 stags, bucks and deer were prepared by sixty-two cooks, along with 1,500 hot venison pasties, 500 partridge, 400 woodcocks, 1,000 egrets, 2,000 pikes and breams, and twelve porpoises and seals. Other cold dishes included 4,000 cold venison pasties, 4,000 'dishes of jelly' and 3,000 cold baked tarts and cold custards, together with 'spices, sugared delicates and wafers plenty'.[22] Like a royal coronation, roles were given to the nobility serving at the high table, with Warwick as head steward, his brother Northumberland treasurer, and William, Lord Hastings, the controller. Other members of the nobility played out their roles dutifully: Lord Willoughby acted as carver, the late duke of Buckingham's son, John Stafford, was cupbearer. Four of Warwick's sisters were also present with their husbands, the earl of Oxford, Lord Fitzhugh and Thomas, Lord Stanley; other members of the northern peerage were in attendance, represented by the earl of Westmorland and Lords Scrope, Dacre and Ogle. In all, thirteen tables were crammed into the main hall and second chamber with 412 men fed in the lower hall and 400 servants in the gallery.

For Richard, on the cusp of turning thirteen, sitting in the 'chief chamber' witnessing this spectacle must have made a significant impression. Yet, for the moment, the young duke would be excluded from the company of the male members of the household; still considered too young to be a part of the high tables occupied by Warwick and the northern nobles, Richard sat among the women of the Neville court that night. On his right-hand side sat his sister, Elizabeth, the duchess of Suffolk, while on his left hand sat the countesses of Westmorland and Northumberland, 'and two of the Lord of Warwick's daughters', Isabel and Anne Neville.[23]

The feast may have reflected the splendour of the Nevilles' regional power and their glittering northern connections, but it hid the fact that at the royal court Warwick's formidable authority and command over the king had begun to wane.

The cracks had first begun to appear only three years after his accession, when Edward, thought of as the most eligible bachelor in the whole of Christendom, suddenly declared that he was already married. His choice of bride stunned the world. Elizabeth Grey was the widow of a Lancastrian knight who had died fighting the Yorkists at the battle of St Albans in 1461, and by whom she already had two young sons. On Edwards announcement it must have seemed as if the world had been turned on its head. Edward had already developed a reputation as a playboy, linked to several women at court, yet his promiscuity was hardly considered an issue while the king remained a young and headstrong single man. Matrimony might wait, but still the king was expected to choose carefully the mother of the nation's royal heirs. Edward's marriage broke all the accepted rules. Elizabeth was not a virgin, while their marriage, having taken place in secret, with no banns and no public demonstration of the ceremony, ran the risk of accusations of illegitimacy. Politically, the marriage could not have been more disastrous. While it may have been clear that the king both loved and was physically enamoured of his new wife, in marriage neither love nor passion mattered; what did was land, money and power, of which Elizabeth had nothing to offer. The Burgundian chronicler Jean de Waurin described the king's council's reaction to the news of the king's secret marriage: 'they answered that she was not his match, however good and however fair she might be, and he must know well that she was no wife for a prince such as himself; for she was not the daughter of a duke or earl, but her mother, the Duchess of Bedford, had married a simple knight, so that though she was the child of a duchess . . . still she was no wife for him'.[24]

What Richard and his elder brother Clarence may have thought of their brother's marriage relies on a later account, which, if it is to be believed, stated how Richard and Clarence were 'both sorely displeased' at the marriage. Clarence supposedly 'vented his wrath more conspicuously, by his bitter and public denunciation of Elizabeth's obscure family; and by proclaiming that the king, who ought to have married a virgin wife, had married a widow in violation of the established custom'. Richard, however, 'being better at concealing his thoughts and besides younger and less influential, neither did nor said anything that could be brought against him'.[25] As he was only eleven years old, it seems likely that Richard's personal views of his brother's marriage would have been considered of little significance; as for Clarence, contemporary accounts suggest that he was prepared to ride alongside the new Queen Elizabeth during her official procession into the capital, as well as play a prominent role during her coronation several months later, acting as Steward for the occasion.

If Edward's marriage to the low-born Elizabeth Woodville was seen as a humiliation, no one could have felt this more strongly than Warwick. He himself was acutely aware of her family's humble origins. Just four years previously, the earl and Edward had together openly berated the bride's father, Lord Rivers, at Calais in 1460 after they had captured him. Then Warwick had told Rivers to his face that 'his father was but a squire . . . and that it was not his part to have language of lords'.[26] Now the earl had little choice but to accept the king's choice of wife, though ultimately he could not forget, nor forgive his cousin for ignoring his advice.

Warwick had been determined to ensure that Edward would be married to a suitably impressive foreign bride. In October 1461, a Burgundian marriage had been proposed; the following year, Warwick suggested that Edward should marry the Scottish regent, Mary of Guelders, while in 1464 the king of Castile offered up his sister and heiress, Isabella, to become Edward's queen. Yet, in his early twenties, Edward seemed in no mood to settle down. Still, Warwick persisted; hopeful of an Anglo-French agreement with Louis XI of France, who had begun to flatter the earl, sending him presents and entertaining him as if he were a monarch himself when he visited the French court, in March 1464 the earl negotiated a truce with France, together with a planned conference in the autumn, that might finally seal a perpetual peace between the two nations. As part of the deal, Warwick intended for Edward to marry the French king's daughter, Anne. Since the child was only three years old, Louis's sister-in-law, Bona, the daughter of the duke of Savoy, was proposed instead.[27] The conference was eventually set for 1 October, to take place at Saint-Omer, and Warwick was charged with leading the English delegation. Only two weeks beforehand, in front of a stunned audience, Edward had revealed that he was in fact already married.

Edward's marriage would later be recognised as the point at which relations between the king and Warwick began to sour. The chronicler Warkworth stated that 'after that rose great dissention ever more and more between the King and him, for that, and other', admitting that while the pair were 'accorded divers times: but they never loved together after' while the *Great Chronicle* reported how the marriage caused 'much unkindness' between the king and Warwick, and 'kindled the sparkle of envy, which by continuance grew to so great a blaze'.[28]

The queen's Woodville kin were rapidly married off to leading members of the nobility through the king's influence; in the two years between October 1464 and 1466, the queen's five sisters were married to the earls of Arundel, Essex, Kent and Pembroke and the young duke of Buckingham, who would come to bitterly regret his bride being forced upon him by the king. The entire Woodville clan 'were certainly detested by the nobles', the Italian writer Dominic Mancini had been informed, 'because they, who were ignoble and newly made men, were advanced beyond those who far excelled them in breeding and wisdom'.[29] Hardly a month seemed to pass without another member of the queen's family receiving yet another preferment or grant of patronage and office. The queen's rapacity was seen by observers as the driving force behind the alienation of Warwick and the nobility. 'Since her coronation she has always exerted herself to aggrandise her relations, to wit, her father, mother, brothers and sisters', one Italian correspondent wrote. 'She had five brothers and as many sisters, and had brought things to such a pass that they had the entire government of this realm.'[30]

Warwick was powerless as he watched the Woodville family sweep up every marriage prospect at court. Even the queen's younger brother, the twenty-year-old John Woodville, was found a bride – no less than Warwick's own rich and elderly aunt, Katherine Neville, the dowager duchess of Norfolk, who at sixty-five was, as one chronicler commented, a mere 'slip of a girl'.[31]

With no male heir himself, Warwick knew that the survival of his own dynasty depended on finding suitable husbands for his two daughters,

Isabel and Anne. Privately, Warwick had his heart set on a far grander scheme. One story recalled how the earl had taken both the king's younger brothers, George, duke of Clarence, and Richard, duke of Gloucester, off to Cambridge, where he had promised to marry them to Isabel and Anne.

When Edward discovered what had happened, he was furious, berating his brothers. But once the seed of the idea had been planted, it seemed that Clarence, proud and ambitious, and still technically the king's heir in the absence of any male children born to the king and queen, could not be dissuaded from the prospect of marriage to the eldest daughter of one of the largest landowners in the country. Secretly Warwick began to seek out a papal dispensation for Clarence's marriage to Isabel.

Meanwhile, rifts over foreign policy and England's relations with France and Burgundy saw the faction fighting between Edward and the Woodvilles and Warwick intensify. No one could have predicted the king's next move, however, when, on 8 June 1467, he rode in person to the residence of his Chancellor and Warwick's brother, George Neville, the archbishop of York, at Charing Cross, accompanied by his brother Clarence and several of his nobility. Ordering Neville to hand over the Great Seal, Edward took the seal from the archbishop with his 'own hands'. Neville's downfall could scarcely have been more of a public humiliation, especially for Warwick, who returned from France just over two weeks later; the news of his brother's dismissal, one chronicler reported, was 'to the great secret displeasure of the earl of Warwick'.[32] As if to add further insult to injury, on his return the earl brought with him a French embassy, whose members were lodged in unimpressive residences and made to wait for six weeks for an audience with the king. If Warwick still believed that he could maintain his former influence over the young king, the events of June 1467 proved a sudden awakening to the new reality of Edward's independence.

When Earl Rivers' house in Maidstone was pillaged in 1468, Warwick was considered to be behind the sacking. A standoff ensued between the king and the earl, who had refused to depart from his northern residence at Middleham to attend court, even when promised a safe conduct. 'Many murmurous tales ran in the city between the earl of Warwick and the Queen's blood', wrote one London chronicler.[33] While it would remain the view of many, particularly on the continent, that Edward's marriage would become the cause of 'mortal war betwixt him and the earl of Warwick', the Crowland chronicler noted that there was another reason for the widening split between the earl and the young king.³⁴ In July 1467, Edward agreed that his sister, Margaret of York, should be betrothed to Charles, the eldest son of Philip, duke of Burgundy. The agreement marked a wider alliance between England and Burgundy, something which Warwick, who favoured an alliance with France, opposed, since he 'bore a bitter hatred' for Charles himself. According to the chronicler, Warwick was 'deeply offended' by Margaret's marriage, adding, 'it is my belief that this was the real cause of dissention between the king and the earl'. Warwick had 'grumbled a bit' at Edward's Woodville marriage, yet had become reconciled to the match and had 'continued to show favour to all the queen's relatives until her kindred and affinity, in accordance with the king's will, arranged the marriage of Charles and Margaret and many other affairs likewise, against the earl's will'.³⁵

Still, Warwick was present at Margaret's official departure the following year, in June 1468, when she processed from London via Canterbury to Margate, accompanied by the king himself and his two brothers, Clarence and Richard. The final scene of England that Margaret would have witnessed before embarking on her voyage to Sluys was of the Yorkist court apparently united. Yet behind the pageantry, rumours swirled of dissent within the realm. It was at this time that Richard's stay in Warwick's household finally came to an end. Aged sixteen in 1468, he had reached his majority; immediately he was to be thrust into the responsibilities of adulthood, and the duties that came with his position as one of the most senior noblemen in the realm. On 25 October 1468, just weeks after his sixteenth birthday, Richard was granted lands formerly belonging to Lord Hungerford, who had been executed as a traitor four years earlier. The grant may have been linked to Richard's first official political duties, for in December he was appointed as the leading member of a commission of 'oyer et terminer', to deal with events such as rebellion. Before him, Hungerford's son, Thomas, and Henry Courtenay, the brother of the earl of Devon, were charged with treason, accused of conspiring with Margaret of Anjou on 21 May 1468 to bring about 'the final ... destruction' of Edward IV.³⁶ Both men were found guilty. In the presence of the king, Richard passed the sentence, stating that they were to be hanged, drawn and quartered. It was an early lesson for the duke in the brutal reality of high politics, in an age when disloyalty paid a heavy price. Hungerford's treason placed Richard in an enviable position to benefit from the remainder of the Hungerford lands, yet he chose to spare the ruin of Thomas's mother, Margaret; while she surrendered the 'prize' castle and manor of Farleigh Hungerford to Richard immediately, Richard still allowed her to retain a life interest in nineteen manors, and to receive profits on other lands held in trust. The income from six other manors was to be used to found a chantry in Salisbury Cathedral and an almshouse for twelve poor men in Haytesbury.[37]

Discontent with Edward's reign erupted finally into open opposition in the spring and summer of 1469, with a growing rebellion led by one 'Robin of Redesdale'. Soon after, Warwick and Clarence escaped to Calais, where Clarence was married to the earl's eldest daughter, Isabel, in defiance of Edward's wishes. Clarence had little reason on the surface to be discontented with his lot. Yet the corrosive effect of Edward's promotion of the Woodvilles had affected Clarence too. The duke was no longer heir presumptive, though the birth of only daughters to Edward and Elizabeth – Elizabeth of York in February 1466, followed by Mary in August 1467 and Cecily in March 1469 – ensured that the king's eldest brother retained a pre-eminence at court, and with it the possibility that, while the king remained without a male heir, he might become inheritor of the Yorkist dynasty himself. At the very least, Clarence expected that the king should not only provide for him materially, but with the best possible marriage he could find.

Edward had different ideas. In 1466, as part of the marriage negotiations for Margaret of York with Charles of Burgundy, a double marriage had been proposed: as well as the king's sister Margaret's marriage to Duke Charles, Clarence would wed the heir of the duke by his first marriage, Mary of Burgundy. Meanwhile, Warwick's secretive French negotiations with Louis XI intended for Clarence to be married off, his becoming lord of Holland if an Anglo-French attack on Burgundy was successful. In the end, neither proposal materialised. Clarence's ambitions, for so long fostered by his favourable treatment from the king, seem to have remained unfulfilled. His alliance with Warwick provided the duke with the possibility not only of a marriage that would secure his future by inheritance, but also that he would be able to become his own man, securing for himself an independence and freedom from his brother's patronage and influence that Clarence longed for.

It seems that Clarence had had Isabel in his sights for some time. In one of his household books, it had been noted that Isabel was 'one of the daughters and heirs of the said Richard earl of Warwick'.[38] Clarence's name had already been linked with Isabel back in April 1467, but by February 1468 the Milanese ambassador related news that 'in England the country is in arms. The Earl of Warwick has drawn a brother of the king against the king himself. They have not yet come to open hostilities, but are treating for an accommodation. The Earl has sent word here.'[39] Aside from the king's opposition to his brother marrying Warwick's heiress, the other significant obstacle to any marriage was of consanguinity: George and Isabel were first cousins once removed, and were also related in several other degrees, meaning that the couple would need to obtain a dispensation from Pope Paul II in order to marry. Edward was determined to use all his authority and influence to prevent any such application. He managed to stop Warwick's agent from securing an audience with the pope; however, the earl refused to give up and managed to secure the necessary dispensation on 14 March 1469.[40]

In contrast to his wayward elder brother, Richard remained loyal to the king. He himself must have faced a choice: between his former guardian, Warwick, and Edward, yet Richard was in no doubt as to where his duty lay. By Saturday, 24 June, Richard had arrived at Castle Rising, where he dictated the first letter that survives of the duke's correspondence. Written to Sir John Say, the chancellor of the duchy of Lancaster and a close associate of the king's, who had previously lent money to the crown, the letter read:

> Right trusty and wellbeloved We greet you well. And forasmuch as the King's good Grace hath appointed me to attend upon His Highness into the North parts of his land, which will be to me great cost and charge, whereunto I am so suddenly called that I am not so well purveyed of money therefore as behoves me to be, and therefore pray you as my special trust is in you,

to lend me an hundred pound of money unto Easter next coming, at which time I promise you ye shall be truly thereof content and paid again, as the bearer hereof shall inform you: to whom I pray you to give credence therin, and show me such friendliness in the same as I may do for you hereafter, wherein ye shall find me ready. Written at Rising the xxiiiith day of June.

R. GLOUCESTER

A postscript, written in Richard's own hand, reads: 'Sir J[ohn] say I pray you that ye fail me not at this time in my great need, as ye wule that I show you my good lordship in that matter that ye labour to me for.'[41] Despite Richard being just sixteen years old, his own words reveal that Sir John had already sought out the duke's 'good lordship' and influence, while perhaps more importantly Richard himself understood his own position in the bargain. In recognising the bonds of loyalty and service that tied a master to his faithful following, and the need for reciprocal support, in this case a financial loan in return for the duke's own influence and assistance in Sir John Say's personal 'matter' over which he had already been approached, Richard demonstrated that he recognised the nature of medieval aristocratic life and the importance of his own 'lordship' to those beneath him, if he was to succeed in establishing his own authority and client network. As the younger brother to the king, Richard knew that he was in a unique position to be able to bend the king's ear or gain preferment for men at court. It was a powerful bargaining tool, one which the duke was prepared to wield to his advantage. The letter also demonstrates that, in Richard's early years at least, he remained desperately short of money: although he might have been the king's brother, away from the royal court, for now he had scant resources of his own to draw upon, relying on temporary loans to bridge any shortfalls in his finances, which might be later paid off by his brother. Nevertheless, Richard remained a loyal stalwart to the king, and, as his actions reveal, was determined to do all he could in his own power to draw men into the king's service at a time of need.

Events rapidly spiralled back into civil war, as Warwick and Clarence returned, raising troops and demanding an end to Woodville dominance. During the battle of Edgecote and its aftermath, over 4,000 Welsh troops were killed, along with two of Edward's detested favourites, William

Herbert, earl of Pembroke, and Humphrey Stafford, earl of Devon. Soon the queen's own father, Earl Rivers, and her brother, Sir John Woodville, were arrested and executed. Edward himself was arrested as Warwick sought to govern alone. Unable to do so without royal authority, he had little choice but to release the king.

Warwick had clearly overstepped his position, yet Edward had no alternative but to reconcile himself to Warwick and Clarence. A general pardon was granted, forgiving all offences that they had committed, while a Great Council was held in the great chamber of Parliament, where Clarence, Warwick and their supporters swore peace, 'and it was agreed that all disagreements should be abandoned'.[42] Warwick had been fortunate to retain his lands and inheritance, in spite of his actions during the summer. Still, he must have known that, after he had ordered the execution of the queen's father, Earl Rivers, and her brother, along with the king's own close associates, one day revenge would be sought by the queen. As the Crowland chronicler remarked, 'there remained a sense of outraged majesty, deep in the heart, on the one side and on the other a guilty mind conscious of an over-daring deed'.[43]

For the moment, a fragile truce between both sides remained. 'The King himself hath good language of the Lords of Clarence, of Warwick', Sir John Paston wrote shortly after Edward's return to the capital, 'saying they be his best friends.' Yet even Paston recognised that behind Edward's façade of unity and forgiveness, 'his household men have other language, so that what shall hastily fall I cannot say'.[44]

If the crisis of 1469 had shaken Edward into realising that he could no longer rely on his cousin Warwick or his brother Clarence for support, the events of the summer had marked a turning point in the king's relationship with his other brother, Richard. The duke had stuck loyally by his side, raising men on his behalf in his hour of need: whereas previously Edward had struggled to find a role for Richard, the king now recognised that his brother had emerged as a mainstay of support for his regime. With few friends to count as his own, Edward also understood that Richard needed to be rewarded for his services. Following the execution of many of the king's closest advisers, and with both Warwick and Clarence barely able to be trusted, Richard would be given a series of important grants of titles, offices and lands to reflect his new position. On 17 October, he was appointed Constable of England, an office vacated by the execution of Richard Woodville, Earl Rivers, two months previously. Woodville had been granted the office on the understanding that it would pass to his son Anthony; however, any claim seems to have been ignored or set aside. It seems that the appointment had been made with the queen's tacit support, for two days later Elizabeth granted Richard the stewardship of her land with an accompanying fee of £100.[45] The same day, on 19 October, Richard was awarded a further £100, with the king ordering the Exchequer to 'make ready payment immediately after the sight of this our letter without any longer delay of the sum of £100 which we have assigned and granted unto him towards the provision of such certain things and stuff as we have commanded him to buy and ordain to his use and wear at this time'.[46]

No one could have been prepared for the events that were about to unfold. Late in February 1470, rebellion broke out once more, this time in Lincolnshire. Once again, it rapidly became apparent that the shadowy hand of Warwick was pulling the strings. Chastened by the dire consequences of his complacency the previous year, this time Edward moved swiftly to crush the rebellion, marching northwards with an army. Before the rebels could join forces with Warwick and Clarence as intended, Edward managed to catch and disperse the insurgents at 'Lose-Cote field' on 12 March. During the battle, the rebels had cried Clarence's name out loud as they advanced. Sir Robert Welles was captured wearing the duke's livery, while treasonable messages from both Clarence and Warwick were found inside an abandoned helmet.[47] Interrogating the captured rebels confirmed Edward's worst suspicions, for they 'knowledged and confessed the said duke and earl to be partners and chief provocateurs of all their treasons. And this plainly, their purpose was to destroy the king, and to have made the said duke king.'[48]

Edward journeyed to York, where he proclaimed both men 'his great rebels', demanding that they appear before him. If they disbanded their forces and promised loyalty, reconciliation was offered, though no promises of pardon were made. For Warwick and Clarence, there was no other choice but to take flight across the Channel, taking Clarence's heavily pregnant wife, Isabel, and Warwick's younger daughter, Anne Neville, with them. The earl had hoped to disembark at Calais; however, he had underestimated the resolve of the lieutenant, Lord Wenlock, who made it clear by firing warning shots to sea that the earl was not welcome to land. The trauma was too much for Isabel, who went into premature labour on the voyage: her child, a son, died soon after birth and was buried at sea. Unable to land, Warwick had little choice but to head for the Normandy coast, and into the arms of the French king, Louis XI.

For Louis, Warwick's unexpected arrival seemed at first more a hindrance than a help, and he spent weeks attempting to persuade the rebels to depart. Warwick's response was to make him an offer so remarkable that he could hardly refuse. In return for the French king's support for an invasion, Warwick agreed to place the Lancastrian king, Henry VI, currently languishing in the Tower, back upon the throne. Still, Margaret of Anjou, now residing in exile in France, where she had been since fleeing the realm after the arrest of Henry VI in 1465, would need to be persuaded of the merits of the scheme. This was no easy task. At a meeting with Louis in June, a 'very hard and difficult' Margaret told the French king directly that she 'might not, nor could not pardon the said Earl, which hath been the greatest causes of the fall of King Henry, of her, and of their son'. It would take a further month before the queen was finally persuaded to meet Warwick on 22 July at Angers, when the earl fell to his knees in front of Margaret, begging her 'pardon for the injuries and wrong done to her in the past'.[49] It was a full fifteen minutes before the queen allowed the earl to rise. The display was enough to convince the queen of the earl's conversion.

As a sign of this conversion, and in order to seal the agreement, the earl would marry his younger daughter, Anne, to Prince Edward, the son of Queen Margaret of Anjou and Henry VI. England would then renounce its friendship with France's rival, Burgundy, and instead ally itself with the French. Forged out of desperation on Warwick's part, the agreement was a masterstroke on the part of the French king, who on this occasion fully lived up to his nickname: 'the universal spider'. An agreement was reached, to be sealed by the marriage. Clarence was to be cut out of the deal altogether.

King Edward must have recognised that his victory over Warwick and Clarence in their flight to France was a pyrrhic one. Portents foretold of future division and strife: 'there appeared a blazing star in the west, and the flame thereof like a spear head, the which divers of the King's house saw it, whereof they were full sore adread'.[50] While the earl remained at large, he would remain free to return. Duke Charles of Burgundy, having now inherited the kingdom from his father, frantically tried to warn his brother-in-law in a stream of letters detailing Warwick's negotiations with the French king. Yet, for the moment, it seemed that Edward paid little notice, not recognising the seriousness of Warwick's preparations for a forthcoming invasion, or perhaps refusing to believe that the earl would really throw his lot in with his nemesis, Margaret of Anjou, in what must have seemed a fantastical proposal.

In spite of recent warnings and reports from his spies that Warwick's invasion was imminent, Edward found himself caught by surprise. For weeks, rumours of Warwick's impending invasion had filled the capital. Edward wrote on 7 September that he had received information that his 'rebels and traitors' with the help of 'our ancient enemies of France' intended to land in Kent; he proposed to travel to the region shortly.[51] Yet the king had underestimated the speed at which Warwick's preparations had progressed. On 9 September, Warwick and Clarence, together with their followers on board a fleet of sixty ships provided by King Louis, sailed from the Seine port of Honfleur. Six days later the Lancastrian army landed at Dartmouth and Plymouth, where Warwick issued his own proclamation in the name of Henry VI, the 'very true and undoubted King of England' in the 'hands of his rebels and great enemy Edward, late the Earl of March, usurper, oppressor'.[52]

Hearing news of the rebels' landing, Edward had quickly departed from York, aiming for London. The king had only reached Doncaster, however, when he was woken in the middle of the night by his minstrel, Alexander Carlisle, with the news that not only had Warwick's brother, John Neville, marquess of Montagu, chosen to defect to join his brother's side, but that Montagu's army was closing in around the king, and was only a few miles from Edward's camp, and 'coming for to take him'. Edward was stunned by the defection and 'greatly marvelled' at the news that had apparently been brought by defectors from Montagu's own camp.[53] Arming himself and

placing guards around his tent, Edward nervously awaited further news.
When confirmation came that Montagu's army was swiftly approaching,
Edward decided that his only safety lay in flight. Edward knew that he
had to reach the nearest available port with ships available to escape the
country as soon as he possibly could. He was accompanied by his brother-
in-law Earl Rivers, Lord Hastings and the earl of Worcester, together with
Lords Saye and Duras, and his brother Richard.

The port of Bishop's Lynn (now King's Lynn) was the nearest friendly
port; however, it was located on the south side of the Wash. The crossing was a dangerous one, and out of the several hundred men who chose
to make the journey, a few men drowned before the party drew into the
harbour of the port on the night of Sunday, 30 September. Earl Rivers
commanded significant regional influence in the area, and would have
ensured that Edward was received favourably: the town's accounts reveal
that the king 'tarried there until Tuesday and then took ship overseas'.[54]

It was at this point that the king's party decided to separate. Lying at
anchor several Dutch 'hulks' – flat-bottomed merchant ships – and a small
English vessel were now commandeered for the king's use. Edward and his
party set sail on Tuesday, 2 October, Richard's eighteenth birthday, with
members of the nobility placed in separate ships.

Richard was to travel separately from his brother, possibly accompanied
by Earl Rivers, and may have sailed several days later, while the earl of
Worcester set sail towards Huntingdon to seek further support. Richard
was certainly absent from the king's flight across the Wash, for he does not
appear in the records detailing the king's arrival at King's Lynn.[55] Edward
meanwhile began his journey across the North Sea with several hundred
followers, 'who possessed no other clothes than the ones they were fighting in; they did not have a penny between them and scarcely knew where
they were going'.[56] A strong westerly wind ensured that the crossing was a
rapid one, certainly no longer than thirty-six hours, though the ships were
pursued by several Hanse ships, which caused the fleet to scatter and the
king's ship to be driven ashore on 3 October.

With low tide approaching, the king and his men had little choice but
to anchor and run aground in the bay harbour of South Texel. Followed by
the Hanse ships, who waited in the mouth of the bay for high tide to board
and ransack the ships, they were rescued by local residents, who helped

them ashore, forcing the Hanse ships to sail away. Later, the chronicler Philippe de Commynes placed Edward's survival in the hands of Louis de Bruges, Seigneur de la Gruthuyse, the duke of Burgundy's governor of Holland. 'The king was completely penniless and gave the ship's master a robe lined with fine marten's fur, promising to reward him better in the future', Commynes later wrote, describing how 'There never was such a beggarly company. But my lord of Gruthuyse dealt honourably with them, because he gave them several robes and paid all their expenses for the journey to The Hague in Holland, where he took them, and then informed the Duke of Burgundy about this event.'[57]

As news of Edward and Richard's flight abroad spread, an astonished Warwick made his journey to the capital unopposed. Queen Elizabeth, by now heavily pregnant, fled to sanctuary at Westminster. Meanwhile, dazed and confused, Henry VI was taken from the Tower, where he was discovered 'not so worshipfully arrayed as a Prince, and not so cleanly kept as should seem such a Prince'. Cleaned up and given new clothes, Henry was brought to Westminster with 'great reverence', much to his bewilderment.[58] A sermon was preached by John Goddard, proving 'by certain bills' that Edward had no claim to the throne, and that Henry was the rightful king.[59] Several days later, Warwick, together with Clarence and Thomas, Lord Stanley, entered the city through Newgate. The earl's first actions were to journey to the Tower, where he knelt before King Henry, pleading forgiveness for his past actions. Henry was then led once more out into the streets, paraded in a new long blue velvet gown, to St Paul's, where he made an offering. This time, it was Warwick by his side, who would hold power in all but name. Once more, the earl had proved himself to be a kingmaker: this time, however, he was determined to wield real authority. He styled himself 'lieutenant to our sovereign lord, King Henry the Sixth', whose restoration was now officially described as 'our readeption of our royal power'.[60]

By 13 October, Edward had been reunited with Hastings and Rivers at The Hague. Strangely, almost a month after Edward's arrival in Holland, there is no record of Richard being present in his brother's company. It is only by the second week of November that Richard's arrival in Holland is finally

documented. The bailiff accounts of the city of Veere record: 'Item paid by order of my Lord of Boucham the bailiff of Veere which he had loaned when my lord of Gloucester travelled in Holland 3 pounds, 2 shillings, 3 pennies.'[61] Yet the accounts suggest that Richard's arrival was somewhat unexpected: there is no wine to greet him, and no lord present to receive him as a royal visitor. If Richard was not with his brother Edward at the time of his arrival in Holland, where exactly was he? And why did it take Richard almost a month to be reunited with his brother in exile?

One possible answer is found in the chronicle of Adrian de But, a Cistercian monk residing at Les Dunes Abbey, on the road between Bruges and Calais, who recorded how 'the younger brother of the now fugitive King Edward . . . Duke of Gloucester, put up as much resistance as he could'. While de But noted the help that had been given to Edward by Charles the Bold, he also described how Edward was now 'with his younger brother, the Duke of Gloucester, who had come to him from England with many men'.[62] It seems plausible that instead of taking flight from King's Lynn with Edward, Hastings and Rivers, Richard had remained behind in England, acting as a recruiting agent for men who wished to join the king in exile.

Eventually they were reunited at The Hague. The English party remained there until Christmas. De Gruthuyse's hospitality was lavish, providing the exiles with new clothes and covering their living expenses, while his library of illuminated manuscripts, filled with histories and chivalric romances, must have made a significant impression upon his guests. Yet despite the warm reception provided by de Gruthuyse, both Edward and Richard could not have failed to notice that Duke Charles remained distinctly lukewarm about the sudden and unexpected arrival of his brothers-in-law.

In fact, Charles's reaction to the news of Edward's surprise landing could hardly have been more hostile. 'The duke was extremely alarmed by this news and would rather the king had been dead, since he was very uneasy about the earl of Warwick who was his enemy and now had mastery in England', wrote the chronicler Commynes.[63] Yet it was not so much Warwick's influence at home that made Charles nervous, rather his friendship with the French king, Louis XI. Wanting peace with England to continue, Charles was unwilling to be drawn into a prolonged civil war abroad, the victor in which seemed far from certain. For the moment, the duke preferred to keep Edward and his company at arm's length, limiting his contact with them to messengers and official correspondence. Edward and his small band of exiles were to be left waiting, pondering their eventual fates. For the king himself, the sudden nature of his flight and the seemingly hopeless spectre of his exile must have come as a shocking blow. 'Less than a fortnight before, he would have been astounded if anyone had said to him "The earl of Warwick will drive you out of England and make himself her master in eleven days"', remarked Commynes, who had access to many of the courtiers who had accompanied Edward in his flight, adding, 'what excuse could he find after suffering this great loss through his own fault, except to say, "I didn't think that such a thing could possibly happen?"'[64]

For Richard, the sudden shift in fortune must have reminded him of his first exile as a child, ten years previously, when he had been sent with Clarence to the Low Countries, safe from harm. At that time he had learnt how fickle men's favour could be; it was here that he witnessed how his treatment in the care of his foreign hosts altered almost overnight with his transformation from an insignificant son of a dead nobleman to the brother of a king. Now it was a different story, with Clarence on the other side of the Channel, enjoying the favour of the newly restored Lancastrian court. Judging by Duke Charles's delayed reaction to his arrival, the signs were hardly promising. For the second time in his life, Richard was cast out into the cold.

Warwick understood that moderation in the treatment of his enemies would be essential if he was to stand a chance of bringing peace to the kingdom. No attainders were issued against the Yorkists, while those who had fled into sanctuary were given protection by a proclamation forbidding any disturbance of sanctuaries. This was to the benefit of Queen Elizabeth, who gave birth to her first son, Edward, on 2 November, helped in her confinement by Elizabeth, Lady Scrope, who had been sent by Henry VI, 'by the advice of our council'.[65] What would have once been a cause of celebration, the birth of a son and Edward IV's heir, a Yorkist Prince of Wales, was now just another inconvenience to Warwick and the newly re-established Lancastrian regime; in a sign of how devastating contemporaries viewed their triumph over Edward IV to have been, the birth of the child went largely unremarked.

Without the ability to reward his supporters with grants of land from the forfeited estates of his enemies, the earl's position would remain weak. A far greater problem for Warwick, however, was the agreement he had reached with Louis XI. In committing his new regime to an alliance with France, Warwick had set himself on a direct course against Burgundy. The earl himself seems to have been blinded to the risk that such a policy of aggression might place upon England's trade relationship with the Netherlands, having been seduced by the French king. Louis had already organised three days of thanksgiving for Henry VI's restoration in October. The following month he sent his ambassadors to England to agree the terms of a treaty between the two countries, where, according to the Milanese ambassador, they were received with 'a marvellous demonstration of love and affection'.[66] On 28 November, Louis XI signed a treaty with Prince Edward of Lancaster, on behalf of his father, Henry VI, which included a secret pact to make war with Burgundy until the duchy was completely subdued.[67] In the document, Louis was referred to tellingly as Louis, 'King of France', suggesting that Warwick, in his desperate search for support, was willing to recognise the Valois title to the French kingdom, something which every English king since the mid-fourteenth century had refused to do. On the same day, a dispensation for Prince Edward to marry Warwick's daughter Anne was finally granted, allowing the couple to marry two weeks later, at Amboise, on 13 December.

Meanwhile, Edward IV's fortunes appeared bleak. For the past two months, having been forced to depend on the hospitality of Louis de Gruthuyse, Edward had waited, at the mercy of Duke Charles of Burgundy. No response to his pleas had been forthcoming. But now Edward found the wheel of fortune turning suddenly in his favour. Bolstered by the promise of support from Warwick and the Lancastrians, in early December Louis XI publicly denounced the Treaty of Péronne, a previous alliance between France and Burgundy, effectively declaring war on the duchy, while he rapidly launched an invasion on Saint-Quentin, moving forces into Picardy. Having been embarrassed at the presence of the exiled Yorkists in Burgundy, Charles had little choice but to embrace Edward and his band of exiles as his only hope against a combined force of French and English aggression. On 26 December, Edward was finally summoned to a personal meeting with the duke, while five days later he had been granted £20,000 'for their departure from my lord the duke's lands to return to England'.[68] Edward began his preparations to recover the kingdom he had so suddenly lost. Gathering men and ships for an invasion, he also reached out to those disaffected by the new regime – including his wayward brother, George, duke of Clarence. As soon as Warwick had established Henry VI back on the throne, Clarence realised that he had been sold short of his dream to be recognised as joint ruler of the realm, and heir to the throne. According to one chronicler, Clarence found himself 'held in great suspicion, despite, distain, and hatred, with all the lords, noblemen, and other, that were adherents and full partakers with Henry . . . he saw also that they daily laboured amongst them, breaking their appointments made with him, and, of likelihood after that, should continually more and more fervently intend, conspire, and procure the destruction of him and all his blood'.[69] When Edward discovered news of Clarence's treatment, he decided that he might be won back to the Yorkist cause, and arranged for messages to be sent through his mother, the duchess of York, and his sisters, including 'most specially' Margaret, duchess of Burgundy, who 'at no season ceased to send her servants and messengers . . . so that a perfect accord was appointed, accorded, concluded and assured betwixt them'.[70]

On the afternoon of Thursday, 14 March, Edward's small fleet, scattered by storms, landed at Ravenspur, the port where, seventy-two years before, Henry Bolingbroke had landed in 1399 on his way to depose Richard II. Marching to York, where he managed to convince the citizens that he merely wished to recover his earldom, Edward and his troops continued unhindered southwards. By the time he reached the town of Warwick, he was greeted with the joyous news of Clarence's defection. As proof of his decision, Clarence had ordered his troops to wear on their breasts the rose of York on top of their Lancastrian collars, indicating that when Clarence had begun raising his men on 16 March, they must have originally believed that they would be fighting for Warwick and the Lancastrians. A meeting between Clarence, Edward, Richard, duke of Gloucester, and the king's closest friend, William, Lord Hastings, then took place between the two armies, at which there was 'right kind and loving language betwixt them two, with perfect accord knight together for ever hereafter, with as heartily loving cheer and countenance, as might be betwixt two brethren'. Richard and Clarence again spoke with each other, while all those watching 'were right glad and joyous', with trumpets sounding the news of the reunion.[71] 'Not war but peace was in every man's mouth', Vergil commented; with armour and weapons on both sides laid down, the brothers embraced each other 'gladly'.[72]

The three brothers then went 'with great gladness' to Warwickshire, where once again Edward challenged the earl of Warwick to depart from behind the city walls of Coventry and give fight. News of Clarence's defection must have been a serious blow to Warwick. Again the earl refused to leave the city. Despite Clarence being dispatched as a negotiator to offer 'a good accord', the earl still refused to countenance surrender. With Warwick dug in at Coventry, Edward faced the choice of having to lay siege to the city, with the prospect of a bloody and protracted conflict that would leave many casualties on both sides, or to march onwards to London, where Edward knew he could expect to find a favourable reception. Control of the capital would allow Edward to gain 'the assistance of his true lords, lovers and servants, which were there, in those parts, in great number', one chronicler noted. On Friday, 5 April, Edward decided to strike out on his march to the capital.

Meanwhile, in London, the city had been thrown into a state of panic. The Common Council had received letters from both Edward and Warwick urging their support. Warwick's brother, George Neville, the archbishop of York, was already present in the city, and attempted to rally support to the Lancastrian cause by parading Henry VI through the streets. Led 'by the hand', the king, a broken man and a shadow of his former self, was taken in procession from St Paul's through Cheapside, dressed in only 'a long blue gown of velvet as though he had no more to change with'.[73] Accompanied by a meagre following of 600 supporters – including the seventy-year-old Lord Sudeley, a veteran of the French wars who bore the king's sword in front of him – the display of the rapidly fading Lancastrian dynasty evinced more pity than pride, with the city chronicle noting that the procession was 'more like a play than the showing of a prince to win men's hearts', while the sight of Henry 'pleased the citizens as a fire painted on the wall warmed the old woman'.[74]

As the lamentable procession came to an end, news reached the city that Edward and his army were fast approaching the city walls. With the mayor having taken to his bed, other members of the Common Council decided to flee to France. Eventually, after anxious discussion, it was resolved that since Edward 'was hastening towards the city with a powerful army, and as the inhabitants were not sufficiently versed in the use of arms to withstand so large a force, no attempt should be made to resist him'.[75] By this time, Edward had marched through Dunstable and reached St Albans on 10 April. The next day he entered London in triumph, with his army led by a 'black and smoky sort of Flemish gunners'.[76] After Edward and his brothers made an offering at St Paul's, Edward then made his way to the bishop's palace to secure Henry VI's person. Edward gave Henry his hand, while the Lancastrian king, unaware of what exact events were unfurling around him, embraced his longstanding enemy, reportedly exclaiming, 'My cousin of York, you are very welcome. I know that my life will be in no danger in your hands', to which Edward replied that 'he should have no worries and should be of good cheer'.[77] Soon after, Henry was 'seized' and taken to the Tower, where he was placed along with the archbishop of York.

Several days later, on 14 April, Easter Sunday, the king met Warwick's forces just outside Barnet. As dawn broke around half past four in the morning, a thick mist enveloped the surrounding fields. Unfurling his banners and blowing trumpets, Edward's army descended upon Warwick's forces – estimated at a superior number of around 15,000 men, compared to Edward's 12,000 troops – attacking first with cannon fire and, as they drew closer, 'hand strokes'. The 'great mist' that had descended was now so thick that it 'would not suffer no man to see but a little from him'. Edward, 'about the middest of the battle', fought on and 'manly, vigorously and valiantly assailed' Warwick's forces, 'where he, with great violence, beat and bare down afore him all that stood in his way'.[78] In the mist, the fact that the two armies were not directly aligned against each other soon began to tell. According to the accepted version of events, Edward's right wing and

vanguard, led by his brother Richard, had been arranged to extend beyond
Warwick's opposing left wing, while Edward's left wing, led by William,
Lord Hastings, in turn overlapped Warwick's right wing, led by John, earl
of Oxford. The result of this was that Richard, advancing into the mist,
discovered that he was not only unopposed, but found that he was going
downhill, off the high ground. Realising what had happened, and hearing
the noise of the battle taking place at the centre, Richard ordered his men
to swing left, and, attacking up the slope, began to launch an attack into
Warwick's left flank, led by the earl of Exeter. Richard may have found
that his initial advance downwards led him onto marshy ground, and the
consequent fighting seems to have been fierce, with those in his household
and fighting close by him sorely injured and killed. Six years later, Richard
would remember in his prayers Thomas Parr, John Milewater, Christopher
Worsley, Thomas Huddleston and John Harper, 'slain in his service'.[79]

But it was at the other end of the line of Warwick's forces that the outcome
of the battle was to be eventually decided. On the Lancastrian right-hand
flank, towards the west of the battlefield, the earl of Oxford found that his
advance was also unopposed as a result of the two sides overlapping, and
quickly succeeded in putting to flight most of Lord Hastings's division of
3,000 men, routing them as they were chased towards Barnet.

Oxford's men, confident that the battle had been won, returned to pick
over the spoils of the dead. Regrouping in the heavy fog, they would have
advanced up along the road from London, where the earl would have
planned to attack the rear of the Yorkist forces once more. Yet the shifting
movements of the battle lines meant that, instead, Oxford's troops came
in direct confrontation with the flank of the Lancastrian forces, led by
the marquess of Montagu. In the confusion, and with the mist impairing
their own vision, Montagu's men turned to see what they thought were
soldiers wearing the Yorkist livery of the sun with streams on their coats,
and, fearing a Yorkist attack, began to fight back. In fact, the troops in
front of them wore Oxford's own livery of 'a star with streams', but, as the
chronicler Warkworth observed, 'the mist was so thick, that a man might
not profitly judge one thing from another'.

Chaos ensued. Warwick's troops turned on the earl of Oxford's forces,
believing them to be their Yorkist enemy. Crying, 'Treason', Oxford and
his men fled away from the field.[80] The cries of treason were perhaps not

unfounded. During the battle, according to one account, Montagu decided to switch his allegiance, putting on the king's livery after he 'agreed and appointed with King Edward'. When one of Warwick's men caught sight of the marquess's defection, he 'fell upon him, and killed him'.

The Lancastrian army rapidly disintegrated. For Warwick, there seemed little choice: seeing 'his brother dead, and the Earl of Oxford fled, he left on horseback, and fled to a wood'. Soon the earl realised that he was trapped, with no means of escape. When one of Edward's men 'espied him', he was set upon, killed and 'despoiled . . . naked'.[81]

It was not yet eight o'clock on the morning of Easter Sunday. After four hours of close fighting Edward's forces had 'won a marvellous, unexpected and glorious victory'.[82] Along with Warwick and Montagu, 3,000 men lay dead on the field. Other Lancastrian lords had taken flight, such as the earl of Oxford, who did not pause until he had reached the Scottish Borders. At least Henry VI had been discovered remarkably unharmed, having been placed 'in the forward during the battle'.[83] The same afternoon, Edward rode into the capital with the former king by his side, pathetically still dressed in the old blue gown he had worn days before. As soon as he reached the city, Henry was placed in his familiar home, the Tower, 'there to be kept'.[84] Arriving at the door of St Paul's, Edward was greeted by the archbishop of Canterbury. The king brought with him two banners, 'badly torn by missiles', which he offered up at the rood of the north door as the Easter hymn 'Salve festa dies' was sung. Edward then returned to Westminster, to the queen, who had not believed her husband's victory until a messenger carrying one of Edward's gauntlets had been sent to her.

The following day, on Easter Monday, 15 April, at around seven o'clock in the morning, those going about their early-morning business witnessed two chests being brought into St Paul's Cathedral. There, inside, on open display, were the naked bodies of Warwick and his brother the marquess of Montagu, 'except for a cloth tied around the private parts of either'. The chests were set upon stones within the church, where thousands would flock to see them over the next few days.[85] Edward's intent in making this humiliating display was clear, ensuring that 'the people should not be abused by feigned seditious tales . . . for, doubtless else the rumour should have been sown about, in all countries, that they both, or else, at the least the earl of Warwick, was yet alive, upon cursed intent thereby to have caused new murmurs, insurrections and rebellions against indisposed people'.[86] The kingmaker was dead. Nevertheless, Edward spared his cousin the indignity of having his body quartered and sent across the kingdom; instead both corpses were allowed to be interred in the family vault at Bisham Abbey.

The battle had been won, but the war was far from over. The Lancastrian Sir John Paston, who had fought alongside his patron, the earl of Oxford, wrote to his cousin, warning him not to rally to the Yorkist cause too soon. 'For the world, I assure you, is right queasy, as ye shall know within the month; the people here feareth it sore. God hath showed himself marvellously like him that made all, and can undo again when him list; and I can think that by all likelihood shall show himself as marvellous again, and that in short time.'[87] Events would prove Paston right. On the evening of Easter Sunday, as the cries of the wounded could still be heard on the battlefield at Barnet, as men despoiled the dead of their weapons and armour, Queen Margaret and her son, Prince Edward, and his new wife, Anne, together with 'other men of the King of France', came ashore at Weymouth. The countess of Warwick also landed at Portsmouth. When Anne arrived at Southampton, the news of her husband's and brother-in-law's deaths was broken to her. She fled instead into sanctuary at Beaulieu Abbey in the New Forest. When she discovered the outcome of the battle the queen was 'right heavy and sorry', though she was persuaded that if the Lancastrians were able to assemble a great army, Edward and his forces would not be able to withstand another battle so soon after Barnet. Now was the perfect time to strike.

Edward was informed of Margaret's arrival on 16 April. He lost no time in raising fresh troops to replace the men he had lost at Barnet, through either death, injury or exhaustion, 'which were right many in number'. Three days later, the Yorkist army departed out of London. After a cat-and-mouse game, which saw both armies nearly engage in battle on the outskirts of Bristol, only to track each other across the Cotswolds, past Gloucester and on to Tewkesbury, Edward prepared his army for battle. It was vital that he struck first, preventing the Lancastrians from escaping and marching towards the Severn and into Wales. Edward chose to deploy his forces in a similar formation to that which had proved so successful for him at Barnet: his brother Richard would once more be given command of the vanguard; the middle 'ward' or main 'battle' would be commanded by Edward himself, together with Clarence, kept close by under the king's watchful eye; the rearguard was placed under the control of William, Lord Hastings, and the marquess of Dorset.

Once the three 'battles' had been arranged into formation and banners were unfurled, Edward ordered the blaring of trumpets, upon which he 'committed his cause and quarrel to Almighty God, to our most blessed lady his mother, Virgin Mary, the glorious martyr Saint George, and all the saints; and advanced, directly upon his enemies'.[88] Edward's first move saw him bombard the Lancastrian camp with gunfire and the arrow fire of over 3,000 archers, fronting Richard's vanguard. 'The king's ordnance was so conveniently laid afore them, and his vanguard so sore oppressed them, with shot of arrows, that they gave them a right-a-sharp shower.' The Lancastrian forces returned their fire, 'both with shot of arrows and guns, whereof nonetheless they had not so great plenty as had the king'.[89] Once again, as commander of the king's vanguard, Richard was at the centre of Edward's strategy. 'The Duke of Gloucester, who lacked no policy, galled them grievously with the shot of arrows.' Meanwhile, the Lancastrian force 'rewarded their adversaries home again with like payment, both with shot of arrows and great artillery', though they stood little chance against the 'plenty of guns as the king had'.[90]

If it was Edward's tactic to provoke his enemies into a panicked and rash response, it worked. The Lancastrian earl of Somerset ordered his troops to move down the hill, passing by the side of the king's vanguard led by Richard, by means of a lane which led his troops into a close where Somerset now launched a direct attack 'right fiercely' on Edward's own men. If the Lancastrians had made a general advance, Somerset's man-oeuvre may have worked: instead, the other Lancastrian commanders, John, earl of Devon, and John, Lord Wenlock, remained in their place. With the Lancastrian army now split, and Somerset left isolated after his charge, Edward seized his opportunity. 'The King, full manly, set forth even upon them, entered and won the dyke, and hedge, upon them, into the close, and, with great violence, put them up towards the hill, and, so also, the King's vanguard, being in the rule of the Duke of Gloucester.'[91] In combining their forces, Edward and his brother Richard began to repulse Somerset's attack, pushing his troops backwards through the ditch and back up the hill.

It was at this point that fortune played straight into Edward's hands. Before the battle had begun, he had spotted to the right-hand side of the field a wooded park. Thinking that it might give the Lancastrians the opportunity to spring an ambush, Edward sent a detachment of 200 spears (men-at-arms carrying lances) on horseback into the woods, where he ordered them to hide in formation, a quarter of a mile from the field, 'giving them charge to have good eye upon that corner of the wood, in case that any need were, and to put them in devoir, and, if they saw none such as they thought most behoveful for time and space, to employ themselves in the best wise as they could'.[92] When the spears found no evidence of an ambush in the woods, they had hidden themselves, waiting for the best moment to appear. Now they rushed headlong into battle, charging at Somerset's vanguard from the side. Turning to see the spears charging at them, Somerset's men were astonished. Already struggling against the king's forces, they were, one chronicler observed, 'greatly dismayed and abashed, and so took them to flight into the park, and into the meadow that was near, and into lanes, and dykes, where they best hoped to escape the danger'.[93] The very means by which the Lancastrians had hoped to entrap their Yorkist opponents now proved to be their own prison. Unable to escape, pinned in by the narrow lanes and dykes, 'many were distressed, taken, and slain'.

Soon Somerset's forces realised they were becoming overwhelmed. When Somerset recognised that his troops were 'overlaid with the multitude of his enemies', he ordered his men to draw back to their standards, 'that being close together, they might more easily resist'. His soldiers' courage was 'somewhat refreshed' and they began to fight more fiercely than before. Yet without any fresh soldiers to replace the rising number of wounded and dead, it was a losing battle. They were 'overmatched of the multitude, and in the end vanquished'. Soon the Lancastrians were in full flight: as they fled towards the town, many were hacked down, including the earl of Devon, Somerset's brother, John Beaufort, and John, Lord Wenlock, earning the fields near the abbey the sobriquet of the 'bloody furlong' within thirty years of the battle.[94] For now, a fortunate few, including Somerset himself, managed to make it inside the doors of Tewkesbury Abbey, hoping to find sanctuary behind its holy walls. The great hope of the Lancastrian dynasty, the young Edward, Prince of Wales, was not so fortunate.

The official version of events, the *Arrivall of Edward IV*, states merely that 'in the winning of the field such as abode hand-strokes were slain incontinent; Edward, called Prince, was taken, fleeing to the town wards, and slain, in the field'.[95] Yet rumours of the young prince's cold-blooded and brutal dispatch in the aftermath of the battle would continue to circulate. Warkworth believed that Prince Edward had been slain in the field, only after he had 'cried for succour to his brother-in-law the Duke of Clarence'.[96] The Crowland chronicler stated that 'upon this occasion, there were slain on the Queen's side, either on the field or after the battle, by the avenging hands of certain persons, Prince Edward'.[97] Twenty-five years later, the *Great Chronicle* described how the Yorkist forces had captured both Queen Margaret and Prince Edward alive. The prince was brought into Edward's presence, where 'the king had questioned a few words of the cause of his so landing within his realm'. When the prince 'gave unto the king an answer contrary [to] his pleasure', the Chronicle reported that 'the King smote him on the face with the back of his gauntlet, after which stroke so by him received, the king's servants rid him out of life forthwith'.[98] The Tudor historian Polydore Vergil elaborated the story further, describing how when brought to the king, who demanded to know how 'he durst be so bold as to enter and make war in his realm', the prince insouciantly replied, 'that he came to recover his ancient inheritance'. Edward fell silent, 'only thrusting the young man from him with his hand, whom forthwith, those that were present were George duke of Clarence, Richard duke of Gloucester, and William lord Hastings, cruelly murdered'.[99]

The further the sources are removed from the event itself, the wilder the accusations of murder and foul play surrounding Prince Edward's death become. According to the Tudor chronicler Edward Hall, Prince Edward was himself hauled before Edward IV, having been captured by Sir Richard Croft, the king's tutor, who was knighted at Tewkesbury. When the prince replied discourteously to the king, Edward struck him across the face with his gauntlet before the young man was murdered in the king's presence by Clarence, Gloucester, Thomas Grey, marquess of Dorset, and William, Lord Hastings.[100] Much contained within these later tales can be dismissed as interpolation, especially as every contemporary source, including a letter from Clarence on 6 May, noted how the prince and other Lancastrians 'were slain in plain battle'.[101] One illuminated French manuscript, however, circulating shortly after the battle and certainly within a year of the event, suggests that there may be more than a grain of truth to the later accusations. The scene depicted shows that the battle has finished; King Edward with three other men in armour is standing at the head of a company of knights on horseback. The king's arm is raised, about to strike at a man standing before him. The man is held captive by two others. As to the identity of the prisoner, the illuminator had made this clear by the royal coat of arms hanging on the shield. There is no hint of the identity of the prince's captors, while his fate is held in the suspense of the frozen image of the illumination. But it is clear that, from the image alone, the prince's fate was already sealed.[102]

Prince Edward's death was not the only controversy that Edward and the Yorkists would later face. After the battle, Edward went to the abbey, where, according to the official Yorkist account, he planned to 'give unto Almighty God laud and thanks for the victory, that, of his mercy, he had that day granted and given him; where he was received with procession, and so conveyed through the church, and the choir, to the high altar, with great devotion praising God, and yielding unto him convenient laud'. The account continues by saying that Edward, as a merciful king, gave to his enemies on the field 'all his free pardon', adding somewhat cautiously that this had 'not at any time been granted, any franchise to that place for any offenders against their prince having recourse thither'; if Edward so wished, it would have 'been lawful to the King to have commanded them to have been drawn out of the church, and had done them to be executed as his traitors, if so had been his pleasure'.[103]

The reality suggested in other contemporary accounts of what happened in the aftermath of the battle is somewhat different. Edward and his men forcibly entered the abbey, determined to chase Somerset and his men out of their sanctuary. As Edward 'came with his sword into the church', the king was only stopped in his tracks by a priest carrying the sacrament 'in his hands', who 'required him by the virtue of the sacrament that he should pardon all those' who had sought sanctuary in the church, including the earl of Somserset and a dozen other knights. Edward eventually agreed, and 'upon trust of the King's pardon given' the men were left alone in the abbey.[104]

Further evidence of affray or violence breaking out in the abbey itself can be found in the *Chronicle of Tewkesbury Abbey*, which describes how Edward and his men entered the abbey wielding arms; before the fighting could be broken up, several Lancastrians were attacked and killed, forcing the abbey to be reconsecrated on 30 May by the bishop of Worcester; a nearby church at Didbrook was also reconsecrated by the bishop the following year, after it too had been 'notoriously polluted by violence and shedding of blood'.[105]

If Edward agreed to issue a royal pardon to all those who had fled into the church, he soon changed his mind. Two days later, on Monday, 6 May, the remaining Lancastrians in the abbey were dragged out as captives, where they were brought to trial before Richard as Constable of England and the duke of Norfolk as marshal. Accused of having 'provoked the great rebellion that so long had endured in the land against the King, and contrary to the weal of the realm', they were judged guilty: as diehard Lancastrians, the men had already shown themselves irreconcilable to the Yorkist dynasty, having been pardoned by the king before, only to rebel once more. The sentence of execution was carried out instantly, 'in the midst of the town, upon a scaffold therefore made', upon which Somerset and his companions were 'beheaded, each one, and without any other dismembering, or setting up, licensed to be buried'.[106] This time, Edward would not give his enemies any opportunity to avenge their defeat.

In the capital, there was still further resistance to overcome, in the form of an armed raid mounted upon London by the Bastard of Fauconberg, one of Warwick's cousins, who had arrived in Kent from Calais. Managing to persuade hundreds of Kentishmen to march with him, incited by the prospect of plundering wealthy Londoners, the rabble arrived outside the city armed with 'heavy and great clubs and long pitchforks and ashen staves'.[107] Fauconberg had also moored his Calais fleet at Southwark, where the ships' cannons opened fire on the Tower. The following day, he attacked London Bridge, yet the retinues of Earl Rivers were able to mount a counter-attack, driving the rebels to Stepney, where many of Fauconberg's followers were slaughtered. Still unwilling to surrender, Fauconberg withdrew to Blackheath, where he received news that the king was hastening back to London with a large army. As his own forces began to disperse in panic, Fauconberg had no other option but to withdraw, taking a ship to Sandwich, where he waited in the hope of being pardoned.

Edward and his forces arrived in the capital on 21 May in triumph. His victory was complete. The following morning, news began to leak out that Henry VI had died in the Tower the previous night. On 22 May, Henry's body was brought from the Tower to St Paul's Cathedral in a procession. As the procession made its way through the city, past Cheapside, one city chronicle noted how there were 'about the bier more glaives and staves than torches'; 'the corpse of King Henry VI was brought through Cornhill from the Tower with a great company of men of that place bearing weapons as if they would have led him to some place of execution'.[108]

Ten years after he had first won the throne, Edward had been forced to demonstrate the same determination and zeal to win back his kingdom. His victory was all the sweeter for the fact that the Lancastrian dynasty had finally been destroyed and lay in tatters, without an heir. Not only were Henry VI and his son, Edward, dead, and Margaret of Anjou a broken woman, but he had faced down the man who had made him king, and won. For the first time, Edward was his own man.

3

'NOT ALTOGETHER BROTHERLY EYES'

The events of 1468 to 1471 had seen a major realignment in the royal brothers' fortunes: while Clarence had plotted his elder brother's downfall, Richard had distinguished himself as a loyal servant to the crown. Clarence also had to face a new uncomfortable truth: that he was no longer the next in line to the throne. Returning to the capital, Edward had been reunited with Queen Elizabeth in Westminster Abbey's sanctuary. There he had held his newborn son, the prince and heir to his throne, in his arms. After three daughters, the sight of his first male child came 'to his heart's singular comfort and gladness, and to all them that him truly loved', and the child was quickly named Edward, after his father: 'the sight of his baby released part of his woe', Edward's sister Margaret later observed.[1]

Richard's guardian through childhood, the earl of Warwick, had been ruthless in destroying his political rivals, and had demonstrated the power of his vast northern estates that brought with them a northern affinity of men, nothing less than a private army, with which he had come close to overturning the Yorkist succession. Richard had learnt first hand how the threat of military power and violence could beat a path to success. He had witnessed, both in his time spent at Middleham or Sheriff Hutton in Warwick's household and during the enthronement banquet of Archbishop George Neville in September 1465, the allure of the Neville authority. Now, with the deaths of both Warwick and his brother the marquess of Montagu, the Neville ascendancy in the north had been irretrievably broken.

Richard's bravery on the field had been singled out for praise in a poem written to celebrate the return of the Yorkist army to London following the battle:

The duke of Gloucester, that noble prince
Young of age, and victorious in battle
To the honour of Hector that he might comens
Grace him followeth, fortune and good speed
I suppose he is the same that clerkis of red
Fortune hath him chosen, and forth with him will go
Her husband to be, the will of God is so.[2]

Edward, recognising Richard's service and devoted loyalty to his campaign to reclaim the throne, accepted that his younger brother would need to be fully rewarded. It seemed that Edward was willing to consider Richard's desire to step into Warwick's shoes. On 18 May, Richard was appointed Great Chamberlain, 'in the same manner as Richard, late Earl of Warwick, receiving such fees as the said Earl had at the receipt of the Exchequer, with all other profits', while on 29 June Richard was granted Warwick's former lordships of Middleham, Sheriff Hutton and Penrith.[3]

During the summer, Richard was tasked with mopping up any remaining vestiges of rebellion. The same day that Henry's body was carried from the Tower, Edward sent Richard to Kent, leading the vanguard of the king's army to apprehend Fauconberg at Sandwich. Negotiations seem to have already opened, and after some deliberation Edward chose to grant Fauconberg his pardon. It was left to his brother to travel to the Kentish coast in his role as Admiral, while Edward himself had by now reached Canterbury. Four days later, a warrant was issued under the king's privy seal for safe conduct to be granted to Fauconberg to travel to the north, where he was to journey in attendance upon Richard as warden of Carlisle and the West March.[4]

Suddenly, however, something went very wrong. The *Vitellius Chronicle* records how, by the end of the year, Fauconberg 'was taken at Southampton and beheaded; and his head sent to London, and set upon the bridge'.[5] Polydore Vergil, writing later, also described the events after Fauconberg's surrender: 'sometime afterwards, having incautiously gone to the port of Southampton, he was captured and forfeited his head'.[6] On 28 September, the news was confirmed, as Sir John Paston noted coolly in his memoranda: 'Item, Thomas Fauconberg his head was yesterday set upon London Bridge, looking into Kent ward.'[7]

What had occurred during a matter of weeks that could cause such a rapid change in fortune? Jean de Waurin, writing before 1474, wrote that Fauconberg had been sent with Richard 'for his good surety' to 'a place called Merlan' (probably Middleham Castle).[8] The purpose of Richard's journey northwards was to restore Edward's authority in the north: as a Neville restored to the king's favour, by his presence Fauconberg would have been a valuable means to achieve this. According to Waurin, Fauconberg 'came and went with Gloucester's other servants without being constrained or harmed', suggesting that he was not in custody, but rather the terms of the safe conduct were being observed. But by late summer Fauconberg had returned to the south coast, where he had taken to the sea. Here he was arrested 'for a new offence'; Waurin believed that he had taken to his ship 'to harm King Edward again'. Waurin maintained that his offence had been 'discovered' by Richard, who ordered his execution.[9] Sir John Paston was uncertain as to whether Fauconberg deserved his fate: 'some men say he would have deserved it, and some say nay'.

According to Warkworth's chronicle, it was 'by the Duke of Gloucester in Yorkshire, the said Bastard was beheaded'.[10] Fauconberg's death was not Richard's own private enterprise; in his role as Constable, overseeing cases of treason, he was obeying Edward's wishes. It was a role he took very seriously indeed. On 4 July 1471, Richard issued a letter to the bishop of Bath and Wells ordering that Thomas Dagsell, Thomas Bylsby and John Blamehall, having been found guilty of treason, were to be arraigned by the sheriff and brought to London, 'to the town of Southwark to be dragged and after hanged'.[11]

Regardless of Richard's role in the execution, Fauconberg's death must have been ordered by the king; it was Edward's own royal warrant which ordered that thirty shillings be paid to one Henry Cappe 'in payment for his expenses in carrying the head of Bastard Fauconberg'. The head was taken to London Bridge, where it was 'pitched upon a stake or pole where it stood long after'.[12]

Richard should have been pleased with his grants from the king. His new wealth and the ties of service and loyalty that stemmed from possession of Warwick's Neville lands in the north, together with the duchy of

Lancaster and wardenship of the West March appointments, ensured that the duke's future would be a promising one. Yet looking around, Richard still had cause to feel embittered. Not only did his new livelihood hang on the thread of a royal grant, with all the risks that it might one day be rescinded; it seemed that his loyalty and devotion had counted for little, especially when compared to Edward's generosity to his brother, George, duke of Clarence, whose past treachery had been the cause of so much strife. Since Clarence's reconciliation, as a reward for his defection, he had been immediately granted all the Warwick inheritance that his wife Isabel had been entitled to inherit, while Clarence was also restored to his former estates. It was, given Clarence's past behaviour, an act of remarkable generosity, ensuring that the duke enjoyed a landed income of around £7,000. Edward himself would later claim that he 'gave him so large portion of possessions, that no memory is of, or seldom hath been, that any King of England heretofore within his realm gave so largely to any of his brothers'.[13]

For Richard, Clarence's treatment merely underlined, in comparison, his somewhat lowly status. During the 1460s, as a young child, he had had to patiently wait his turn: while Clarence was made a duke on the eve of the coronation, Richard's own creation as duke of Gloucester was delayed several months; Clarence had been one of the first additions to the ranks of the Order of the Garter, yet Richard had to wait five years until he joined the order. Many of the lands that Edward had initially provided for Richard, much smaller in size than Clarence's, were later to be taken from him, as politics and patronage required a redistribution of the royal grants; even the title of Great Chamberlain, gifted to Richard, was removed from him when Clarence demanded that the office should be his. Clarence always seemed to get what he wanted; Richard, on the other hand, was treated as if his interests were dispensable.

Still Clarence wanted more. Since his wife Isabel's mother, Anne, the countess of Warwick, had lodged in sanctuary at Beaulieu, the duke had taken Isabel's younger sister, Anne, into his household for her protection. Anne was now the widow of the young Prince Edward, and had just turned fifteen in June 1471. Clarence's altruism was little more than skin deep. He had hoped to keep the entire inheritance of the earl of Warwick to himself. To achieve this, he needed to ensure that Anne's rights were denied. As her mother was in sanctuary, Anne had no one to represent her own interests. Faced with being left in a captive limbo, the only way that she would be able to secure her inheritance was through marriage. In order to do so, she would need a husband powerful enough to face up to Clarence. Only the king's brother Richard, her father's original choice for her marriage, would suffice. Whether Richard himself had become acquainted with Warwick's daughter already is unknown, though their proximity during the banquet held in honour of George Neville in 1465 suggests that they must have been familiar with one another.

Realising what his brother was attempting to achieve by confining Anne, probably at his London house, Coldharbour, near Dowgate, Richard knew he would have to act fast in order to prevent Clarence from subsuming the entire Warwick and Despenser inheritance to himself. He must have also known that it would only be through marriage that he might finally break his dependence upon royal favour, and found his own inheritance and personal stability. It was obvious that no potential wife offered a greater inheritance than Anne Neville.

Exactly when Richard decided that he would marry Anne Neville is uncertain; however, the duke departed the capital in August 1471, travelling to Norwich on 23 August, before journeying to the north for the rest of the autumn and winter, where grants confirmed by Richard are dated 4 and 6 October, 20 November and 11 December. Richard, the Crowland chronicler wrote, had sought Anne's hand in marriage shortly after the death of Prince Edward at Tewkesbury; 'this proposal, however, did not suit the views of his brother, the duke of Clarence . . . such being the case, he caused the damsel to be concealed, in order that it might not be known by his brother where he was; as he was afraid of a division of the earl's property, which he wished to come to himself alone in right of his wife, and not to be obliged to share it with any other person'. Yet Clarence had underestimated his younger brother, whose 'craftiness' enabled Richard to scout out where Anne had been hidden. Discovering her in the city of London, 'disguised in the habit of a cookmaid', Richard removed Anne to the sanctuary of St Martin's le Grand, located between the Guildhall and St Paul's.[14]

Clarence was furious. Richard was attempting to take from him and his wife a share of lands they had already entered possession of, challenging his right of inheritance that seems to have already been accepted by the king. The Milanese ambassador wrote how, 'because his brother King Edward had promised him Warwick's country', Clarence 'did not want the former [Richard] to have it, by reason of the marriage with the earl's second daughter'.[15] For Richard to marry Anne and claim her share of the Warwick inheritance went not just against common law, but against canon law too. As was often the case with interwoven family ties between the nobility, Richard and Anne were related: as first cousins once removed, the couple were related in the second degree, while Clarence's marriage to Anne's sister, Isabel, had added further complexity in the legality of Richard's relationship with Anne. As brother- and sister-in-law, Anne and Richard were now related in the first degree of consanguinity. Any relationship between them would have been considered shocking, while also unlikely if not impossible to have secured a dispensation: Warwick had struggled to obtain permission for his daughter Isabel to marry Clarence, related in the second degree of consanguinity. Yet Richard was undeterred in applying to the papacy for a dispensation. 'Richard, duke of Gloucester, layman of the diocese of Lincoln, and Anne Neville, woman of the diocese of York, wish to contract marriage between them', the request states, 'but as they are related in the third and fourth degrees of affinity, they request a dispensation from the same'. It succeeded: Richard's wishes were finally granted by the pope in April 1472.[16]

Edward attempted to mediate between the two brothers. Clarence told the king bluntly that Richard was welcome to Anne, if only he could keep her lands. A month later, Clarence finally conceded to his brother's demands, but only after a deal was struck, granting Clarence the titles of earl of Warwick and Salisbury, and the office of Great Chamberlain of England, previously held by Richard. In return, the entire Warwick inheritance was to be divided, leaving Clarence with only the Neville lands in the West Country and the west Midlands. The warrant itself was signed not by the authority of the council, but with the king's own signature, testament to his personal interest in resolving the fraternal dispute.[17]

The eventual division of lands between the two brothers, the Crowland chronicler observed, 'left little or nothing at the disposal' of their wives' mother, Anne, the countess of Warwick.[18] In late 1472, the countess petitioned Parliament, beseeching them to 'weigh in your consciences her right and true title of her inheritance' of the earldom of Warwick and the Despenser lands, 'to which she is rightfully born by lineal succession'.[19] No one listened to her pleas. Now the countess believed that she was effectively under house arrest, being confined to sanctuary by force.

In May 1473, Richard, growing frustrated at Clarence's delay in implementing the king's agreement, decided to take matters into his own hands. If he was unable to gain Clarence's permission to enjoy the lands of his wife's mother – those that belonged not only to the Neville family, but the countess of Warwick's Despenser inheritance also – he had no choice but to take them by force. With the king's apparent consent, Richard ordered that the countess be escorted from her sanctuary, to join Richard's household in the north. Rumours circulated that the countess, having been restored to her lands, had granted them entirely to the duke, her new son-in-law, tales at which, as one contemporary wrote, 'folks greatly marvel'.[20] It may be that the countess's removal was at her own accord; John Rous later wrote how she had 'fled' to Richard 'as her chief refuge', while Anne may have also had a part to play in her mother's removal, with Rous describing her mother's treatment as Anne's 'choice'.[21]

In the end, Parliament gave her lands to be split between George and Isabel, and Richard and Anne. The dowager countess of Warwick was to be treated, the Act continued, as if she 'were now naturally dead': she was to be 'barrable, barred and excluded' from any of her late husband's possessions and lands.[22]

The frailty of Richard's claim to the Neville inheritance, first acknowledged as a royal grant in 1471, is key to understanding the duke's own ambitions and insecurities. Richard had fought desperately to obtain the inheritance of the earl of Warwick, but the laws of inheritance had foiled him from making the lands entirely his own. Richard could not prevent the fact that the Neville lands had been settled down the male line of Richard Neville, the earl of Salisbury, which passed to his son Richard Neville, the earl of Warwick. Since Warwick only had two daughters, the line of succession passed to his brother, John, marquess of Montagu, and his male heirs, of which the young George Neville, the duke of Bedford, born in 1465, was Montagu's only son. The male line of succession then passed to Warwick's third brother, George, the celibate archbishop of

York, then to the male line of Salisbury's brother, George, Lord Latimer.

Of course, the natural line of male succession had been broken by Warwick's and Montagu's deaths as traitors at the battle of Barnet. Edward
had intended to attaint them both, confiscating their property, which
would then be given to Richard as a royal grant. This was essentially what
occurred with Edward's July 1471 grant of the Neville property to Richard,
despite the fact that Warwick and Montagu had not been attainted. Yet
it suited neither Richard nor Clarence for Warwick or Montagu to be
officially attainted, since they would lose their own rights of inheritance
through their wives to the lands; even if they were re-granted to them, it
would be by royal grant only, with all the uncertainty of tenure that this
involved – it would be in the king's gift to revoke the grant at his pleasure.

One thing both brothers could agree upon was their mutual desire to
have the security of inheriting their wives' shares of the earl and countess
of Warwick's lands. Yet if Warwick's and Montagu's lands were to remain
unattainted, then this meant the claims of the male line of succession of
the Neville family still stood, with Montagu's son, George Neville, able
to lay claim to the lands upon his majority. In order to prevent this from
happening, nothing less than an Act of Parliament would be needed to
settle a new line of inheritance upon the lands.

In early 1475, Richard secured an Act that gave the Neville lands to him
by right of inheritance of his wife, Anne. The Act barred the rights of Montagu's son, George Neville, and instead passed the lands direct to Richard
and Anne to enjoy, as long as George continued to survive and produce
a male heir. The real heirs of the Neville inheritance, the Act claimed,
were the heirs of Richard, earl of Salisbury, who could not be penalised as
they themselves had committed no offence to justify forfeiture. If George
Neville were to die without any living male child, then Richard was to
'have and enjoy' the Neville lands for the 'term of his life' only; he would
be unable to pass the lands to his heirs. Instead, they would pass down
the male line of succession of the Neville family, to Richard Neville, Lord
Latimer, then just a child of four.[23]

Why Richard agreed to these terms is unknown, except that it may
have been the only way he could secure a share of the tail male estates
by right of inheritance rather than royal grant. Possibly Richard calculated that George was young enough to live on to marry and continue the

male line of succession, allowing him to continue to hold the lands.

Richard was in fate's hands: if the young George Neville were to die without any male heirs, Richard and Anne's possession of the Neville lands would revert to a life interest, disinheriting Richard's own dynasty.

Family divisions between the brothers seem to have been contained by Edward's decision to invade France in 1475. His 'Great Enterprise' offered both Clarence and Richard the opportunity for military glory. Both raised thousands of men for what was the largest English invasion to set foot on the continent, with Richard alone bringing 3,000 of the 14,000 troops assembled. Yet the launch of this new crusade ended in bitter disappointment for those hopeful of armed combat. Weeks into the expedition, Edward instead preferred to sign a treaty at Picquigny with the French king, Louis XI, who effectively bought himself peace with England, lavishing pensions worth tens of thousands of pounds upon Edward and his noblemen. Richard refused to be present at the signing of the treaty at Picquigny, with the chronicler Philippe de Commynes stating that he was 'mal content' with the arrangement, though it seems that the duke may have been inspecting French troops at the time. Likewise Richard refused to be kept in the pocket of the French king, even if he would later accept a present of a large cannon from Louis, along with horses and costly plate.[24]

Having marched his country to war, raising taxes to pay for troops and equipment, Edward knew that he would face trouble at home. 'There is no doubt that there was deep anxiety in the king's heart over this state of affairs', the Crowland chronicler wrote, 'and that he was not unaware of the condition of his people and how easily they might be drawn into rebellions and strange schemes, if they were to find a leader.'[25] Picquigny led to popular discontent that Clarence may have hoped to use to his advantage. In late September, the Milanese ambassador to the Burgundian court reported that 'Edward did not want his brothers to proceed to England before him, as he feared some disturbance, especially as the Duke of Clarence, on a previous occasion, aspired to make himself king'.[26] Memories proved hard to forget, both for the king and for Clarence, who continued to believe that he was owed further advancement.

The sudden death of his wife, probably in childbirth, at the end of

December 1476 seems to have led to a heightened state of instability in Clarence's mind. When Charles, duke of Burgundy, was killed in battle in early 1477, Clarence sought the opportunity of marrying the duke's daughter, Mary, the heiress of the kingdom. Edward was determined to place every obstacle in the path of such a match. When the match fell through, and Mary was instead married to Archduke Maximilian, Clarence placed the blame at Edward's feet. 'Each one began to look upon the other with not altogether brotherly eyes', the Crowland chronicler wrote.[27] Sycophants of both the duke and the king spread disparaging remarks about each other: Clarence, who by now had absented himself from court and was holed up in Warwick Castle, was playing a dangerous game.

Clarence did not seem to care. Unstable and unbalanced, he acted next in a way that scandalised the political establishment. On 12 April 1477, two of his servants broke into the house of Ankarette Twynyho, a former servant of Clarence's wife, Duchess Isabel. Ankarette was dragged to Warwick, where she stood trial on charges of having poisoned her mistress. The hastily assembled and coerced jury convicted her in less than three hours. She was immediately executed. Clarence had committed nothing less than judicial murder, but for the moment Edward took no action, refusing to reveal his hand.

Behind the scenes, the king prepared to gather evidence that would lead to the final downfall of his wayward brother. An Oxford astronomer, Dr John Stacey, who had been arrested under suspicion of using magic arts for evil purposes, had recently confessed under torture that he had been involved with a member of Clarence's household, Thomas Burdett, and another astronomer, Thomas Blake, a chaplain of Merton College. According to the confession, several years earlier at Thomas Burdett's request, Stacey and Blake had calculated the horoscopes of both Edward IV and Prince Edward. In May 1475, they revealed their findings, claiming that the horoscope foretold an early death for both the king and his son.

This was evidence enough for Edward to seek his revenge. On 12 May 1477, Burdett, Stacey and Blake were tried at King's Bench on charges that they had 'imagined and compassed' the death of the king and the Prince of Wales, using magic arts to accomplish their designs. The indictment further claimed that Thomas Burdett 'did ... falsely and treacherously disperse and disseminate divers and seditious bills, rhymes and ballads, containing complaints, seditions and treasonable arguments, to the intent that the people should withdraw their cordial love from the King and abandon him, and rise and make war against the King, to the final destruction of the King and Prince'.[28]

On 19 May all three defendants were found guilty and were sentenced to death. Blake successfully sought pardon, though Burdett and Stacey were to be hanged at Tyburn. 'They were drawn to the gallows at Tyburn and permitted to say anything they wished, briefly, before they died', the Crowland chronicler wrote, 'they declared their innocence, Stacey, indeed, faintly, but Burdett with great spirit and many words, as though, like Susanna, in the end he was saying, "Behold I die, though I have done none of these things."'[29]

The trial and execution of a member of Clarence's household for treason had clear implications for the duke himself. The same day, writs were also issued to the Warwickshire justices, ordering that they send their records of the Twynyho court case to Westminster.[30] The net was closing in around Clarence. In a desperate attempt to clear his name, the duke decided to act first. The following day he burst into a meeting of the council at Westminster, forcing them to listen to his spokesman, Dr John Goddard, who 'upon the duke's instigation' read out the declarations of innocence which Burdett and Stacey had made at the gallows. Clarence's choice of Goddard as his spokesman was tactless in the extreme, since the preacher was best known for previously having defended Henry VI's right to the throne at St Paul's Cross in September 1470. Edward was at Windsor when he heard the news. According to the Crowland chronicler, the king was 'greatly displeased and recalled information laid against his brother which he had long kept in his breast'.[31] This time, in a whirlwind of defiance towards the king and his law, Clarence had gone too far.

The next day, Clarence was summoned to Westminster, where, in the presence of the mayor and aldermen of London, Edward 'from his own lips, began to treat the duke's action . . . as a most serious matter, as if it were in contempt of the law of the land and a great threat to the judges and jurors of the kingdom'. Clarence was immediately arrested and placed in the Tower some time in June 1477.

It would be a further six months before Clarence's eventual fate was decided. 'No one argued against the duke except the king; no one answered the king except the duke', the Crowland chronicler wrote of the proceedings in January 1478. 'Some persons, however, were introduced concerning whom many people wondered whether they performed the offices of accusers or witnesses. It is not really fitting that both offices should be held at the same time, by the same persons, in the same case. The duke swept aside all charges with a disclaimer offering, if it were acceptable, to uphold his case by personal combat.'[32] Pitted against each other, brother against brother, Clarence even offered to clear his name in a duel. The verdict was never in doubt. Clarence was formally condemned in January 1478, though his execution was delayed while Cecily, the dowager duchess of York, fought hopelessly to persuade Edward to pardon his brother.[33] Her efforts were in vain: Clarence was executed in private in the Tower, possibly at his own request in a bath of malmsey wine.

Two days after Clarence's death, Edward assigned 'certain lords' to travel with Clarence's body to Tewkesbury Abbey, to prepare for the duke's burial there. 'The King intends to do right worshipfully for his soul', the royal councillor, Thomas Langton, wrote on 20 February.[34] Edward took over responsibility for paying Clarence's debts to the abbey of 560 marks, to be paid in instalments, while he paid outstanding debts to Clarence's household totalling over £325. Edward soon regretted his brother's death. Thomas More later described how, although Edward had 'commanded' Clarence's death, 'when he wist it was done, he piteously bewailed and sorrowfully repented'.[35] Polydore Vergil believed that 'it is very likely that king Edward right soon repented that deed; for (as men say) when so ever any sued for saving a man's life, he was wont to cry out in a rage, "O unfortunate brother, for whose life no man in this world would once make request"'.[36] Whether Edward's sorrow was genuine, given that he had been the prime mover in his brother's execution, it may be that the king found cause to doubt his judgement, believing that he had been influenced to take such drastic measures. Polydore Vergil mused on Edward's regret, remarking how the king was 'affirming in that manifestly' that Clarence had been 'cast away by the envy of the nobility'.[37] Clarence's destruction had been ordered by the king, but it had very much been authored by the Woodvilles. Relatives and servants of the family had combined to remove their common enemy. Four bridegrooms of Woodville marriages arranged in the 1460s, including the duke of Buckingham, who pronounced sentence upon Clarence, were members of the jury on the trial, while just days before the trial began the royal family, including Richard, gathered to celebrate the marriage of Edward's youngest son, Richard, duke of York, to Anne Mowbray, the duchess of Norfolk. The scenes of a united royal family, surrounded by extended Woodville kin, sent out the clear message that Clarence was now permanently excluded from the fold.[38] For Thomas More, it was clear that Clarence's death had been brought about 'by the Queen and the Lords of her blood which highly maligned the king's kindred'.[39] Dominic Mancini had heard told a story that 'The queen then remembered the insults to her family and the calumnies with which she was reproached, namely that according to established usage she was not the legitimate wife of the king. Thus she concluded that her offspring by the king would never come to the throne, unless the duke of Clarence were removed; and of this she easily persuaded the king.'[40]

Clarence's death was viewed nationally as nothing less than a tragedy. 'These three brothers', the Crowland chronicler mused, 'possessed such outstanding talent that if they had been able to avoid dissension that triple cord could have been broken only with the utmost difficulty.'[41] Edward now ruled, according to the chronicler, 'so haughtily thereafter that he seemed to be feared by all his subjects while he himself feared no man'. 'After this deed many people deserted King Edward', he noted, 'who was persuaded that he could rule as he pleased throughout the whole kingdom now that all those idols had been destroyed to whom the eyes of the common folk, ever eager for change, used to turn in times gone by. They regarded the earl of Warwick, the duke of Clarence and any other great man in the land who withdrew from royal circles as idols of this kind.'[42] If this was the case, then one man seemed to fill the vacancy left behind by their deaths. Writing several years later, Dominic Mancini implied that Richard, after his brother's death, 'came very rarely to court', claiming that Richard himself 'was so overcome with grief for his brother that he could not dissimulate so well, but that he was overheard to say that he would one day avenge his brother's death':

He kept himself within his own lands and set out to acquire the loyalty of his people through favours and justice. The good reputation of his private life and public activities powerfully attracted the esteem of strangers. Such was his renown in warfare that, whenever a difficult and dangerous policy had to be undertaken, it would be entrusted to his discretion and his generalship. By these skills Richard acquired the favour of the people and avoided the jealousy of the queen, from whom he lived far separated.[43]

Whether this was entirely the case, or whether Mancini was simply portraying an image of Richard as somehow separate from the king and his court, no one could deny that, with the death of Clarence, Richard was now the pre-eminent member of the nobility. As Constable, he remained at the centre of court life, with responsibility for updating the rules for royal tournaments. He attended the sessions of Parliament between 1472 and 1475, along with the Parliaments of 1478 and 1483, appearing frequently at royal councils and at chapters of the Order of the Garter. In contrast to what Mancini had been told, royal charters attest to the fact that Richard was a regular presence at court, hardly the recluse that he had been made out to be. He remained close to his brother and the Yorkist dynasty's ambitions, both temporal and spiritual. Not only did Richard share in his brother's patronage of St George's Chapel, Windsor, selling off land to help fund the foundation, but he helped finance the founding of Queen's College, Cambridge, alongside Queen Elizabeth.

If Richard had really opposed his brother's execution, he was quick to reap the rewards of Clarence's sudden fall. Any regret or remorse that Richard felt about his brother's trial and execution did not prevent him taking full advantage of Clarence's demise, even while the latter was still imprisoned in the Tower awaiting sentence. On 27 November 1477, Edward granted Richard the lordship of Ogmore; the grant was a significant one since it anticipated the break-up of the Warwick inheritance and Clarence's death, upon which the alienation of the lands would have depended.[44] From the very start of proceedings, Richard had taken a part in planning his brother's trial. He had attended the council meetings of the previous winter, where Clarence's fate was discussed. He was also a constant presence at court during this time. On 9 November, Richard was present at a banquet where he did homage to Prince Richard, holding the prince's hand. As Constable, he had joined with the queen's brother Anthony,

Earl Rivers, in proclaiming the articles for the jousts that took place on 12 November. Richard also took advantage of his brother's incarceration to strengthen his own position. With Clarence's execution pending, formal recognition was now given of the enhanced status placed upon Richard and his family. On 18 February, the date of Clarence's death, Richard himself was appointed Great Chamberlain of England, restoring to the duke a title he had been forced to surrender as part of the original negotiations concerning the Warwick inheritance so bitterly fought over between the brothers. The next day, on 19 February, following on from the Act that had allowed Richard to alienate several manors from the Warwick inheritance for the purpose of establishing a religious foundation, the duke was licensed to found two colleges, at Barnard Castle and Middleham.[45] Richard was now the wealthiest landowner in England after the king himself. If fortune's wheel had turned for Clarence, casting him downwards, it had in turn raised Richard up to even greater heights.

4

A NORTHERN AFFINITY

Since inheriting the earl of Warwick's Neville lands in north Yorkshire and Wensleydale, Richard had begun to spend an increasing amount of time in the north, establishing his own northern power base centred on Warwick's lands. Richard took the remaining ties of service that belonged to the Neville retinue, fashioning it into his own image. After making his base at Middleham, he fostered the impression of a good lord by retaining Warwick's existing local office holders, such as Sir John Conyers, even going so far as to reward them with a pay rise.

The transition to becoming lord of the north, fitting seamlessly into Warwick's role, was further acknowledged with the birth of his son Edward, who was born at Middleham and took Warwick's title of earl of Salisbury in 1478. By marrying Warwick's daughter, Richard had converted his status from outsider to the natural lord of inheritance, consciously fostering Neville tradition. Richard established religious colleges both at Middleham and at Barnard Castle, possibly to act as a mausoleum for his family, and to reinforce the spiritual identity that now linked him with the Neville tradition.

Richard was more ambitious still. Soon he was looking beyond the confines of his Neville lands, with the aim of extending his lands and fashioning a northern power base the like of which had not been seen before. To Warwick's lordships of Middleham in Wensleydale, Sheriff Hutton in north Yorkshire and Penrith in Cumberland, he added the lordships of Barnard Castle in Durham and Scarborough in 1474, Skipton-in-Craven in 1475, and Clarence's lordships of Richmond and Helmsley in 1478. Many of his later acquisitions he obtained through exchange with other noblemen:

Skipton was traded with Thomas, Lord Stanley, for Chirk in Wales, while Scarborough was exchanged with the king, who wanted possession of Richard's property in Chesterfield and Ware.

While Richard was prepared to sell or trade much of the land he had been given by the king elsewhere in England, he always held on closely to the land that formed the basis of his northern hegemony. His power in the north was enhanced by his closeness to the king. No other nobleman could compete with the king's own brother, and soon Richard became the direct source to royal favour and grace. The city of York sought out his influence on a range of issues, to which Richard dutifully responded. In 1476, Richard was given presents, including six swans and six pikes, by a grateful corporation 'for his great labour' made to the king, 'for the conservation of the liberties of this city'.[1] The city appealed to Richard the following year, in October 1477: 'having a singular confidence in your high and noble lordship afore any other ... we humbly beseecheth your high and good grace to be a mean to the king our said sovereign lord ... in these premises, and we, your said humble servants, shall evermore pray to the single "almyfluent" god for your prosperous estate'.[2] Anything, Richard replied, 'that we may do to the weal of your said city we shall put us in our uttermost devour and good will by God's grace, who keep you'.[3]

Richard swiftly became acquainted with religious life in York, and in 1477 both the duke and his wife, Anne, formally joined the elite Guild of Corpus Christi, twenty-one years after his mother, Cecily, had been inducted into the order.[4] The festival of Corpus Christi, falling on the first Thursday after Trinity Sunday, was taken particularly seriously in York, with the guilds staging a huge cycle of mystery plays, with over fifty scenes acted out by over 500 performers. Starting at dawn, a procession of wagons wound through the streets of the city, each pausing to exhibit the individual drama acted out on the back of the cart: the shipwrights, fishmongers and mariners acted out the scenes from Genesis, while the goldsmiths decorated the crowns of the Three Kings. The following day, the procession of the Corpus Christi Guild would take place, moving from the Priory of the Holy Trinity to York Minster amid a dazzle of torches and lit tapers, crosses and banners. Regardless of status, every member of the guild was required to join the procession through the streets.

Apart from brief glimpses of her life in Richard's accounts, evidence of his wife Anne's existence during this period is hard to trace. As duchess, she should have accompanied Richard to important occasions of state, though she passes unmentioned in the heraldic accounts of the receptions. It seems that during this period, while Richard was not only campaigning in France in 1475, but fulfilling his role as warden of the West March, Anne was left to run her own household and at times take responsibility for ducal affairs. In 1475–6, the duke's councillors conveyed a message to the city of York from Anne herself, suggesting that she deputise for Richard in his absence, while in 1476 it was Anne alone who was admitted to the sisterhood of Durham Cathedral priory, which was dedicated to St Cuthbert and was the mother church for the Warwick lordship of Barnard Castle.[5]

There is also a surviving copy of a manuscript that we may be reasonably certain was shared between Richard and his wife: *The Booke of Gostlye Grace* by Mechtild of Hackeborn, written in the thirteenth century in Saxony by the sister of Gertrude, the abbess of a Cistercian community in Mansfield. The flyleaf of the book is inscribed with both the names 'Anne Warrewyk' and 'R Gloucestr', suggesting that the book was owned, and shared, jointly between husband and wife. Mechtild of Hackeborn's work was designed to demonstrate how one might preserve the health of the soul through prayer and self-discipline. Mechtild's work was very popular with the pious laity. The text focused on how members of the laity could make every day acts of remembrance to Christ, using simple means of expression; in particular, the work set out how touching one's fingers on the right hand could help join one's fingers to the Lord's, setting out specific examples of how, when 'stirred or tempted with pride', one should touch one's little finger and reflect 'on the meekness and on the subjection of thine God, and pray him that by his meekness thou may overcome all pride', while the thumb 'betokens the mightfulness of God, which is almighty', and divine protection against 'all adversities that comes to a faithful and true soul'; touching one's thumb with a finger represented the need to be 'strong in exercise of virtues and that thou withstand all vices manly and mightly'. The use of such private means of worship can possibly be witnessed in a copy of a later portrait of Richard, who wears rings on his right thumb, ring finger and little finger, while his left thumb and forefinger are poised to lift a ring from his little finger, suggesting that

Richard continued to use such acts of remembrance throughout his life.

There was good reason why Anne's presence remains shadowy during these years. It was around this time that Anne gave birth to their son, Edward. The first mention that a son had been born to the couple is in a deed dated 1 April 1477, in which Richard granted the lordship of Fulmer in Cambridgeshire, a manor that had formerly been the property of Elizabeth, countess of Oxford, to the president and fellows of Queen's College in Cambridge.[6] In return for the gift, it was agreed that the college would pray for the 'prosperous estates of Richard the said duke of Gloucester and dame Anne his wife, and of Edward their first begotten son earl of Salisbury with all such issue as God shall send betwixt them'. The bequest raises intriguing questions about Richard's own family life. It is clear that Richard and Anne intended on having more children if Edward was to be their 'first begotten': the queen herself had only just turned twenty, while Richard was twenty-four, so this is unsurprising, but indicates that the couple remained close, in spite of John Rous's later comment that they were 'unhappily married'. It has commonly been assumed that their only son, Edward of Middleham, was born in 1473; however, a separate chronicle collated by the monks at Tewkesbury Abbey, written around 1478, records how Anne was 'bore a son named . . . at the castle of Middleham, in the year of our lord 1476'. The name of the son has been left blank, but in the original manuscript the name 'George' has been inserted into the gap. This might suggest that Richard and Anne had a second son, who may not have survived long after childbirth, which would explain the specific reference to Edward as their 'first begotten' son in the Queen's College indenture. Alternatively, it could be that the blank space refers in fact to Edward himself, in which case he was three years younger than has commonly been assumed.[7]

Of course, there were other children Richard is known to have fathered, just not legitimate heirs with his wife. Little is known about the origins of John of Pontefract or Katherine, Richard's illegitimate daughter, though it seems from tracing back their ages that Richard must have sired the children perhaps in his teenage years, before his marriage to Anne. John of Pontefract was nearly old enough to obtain his majority in 1485, suggesting that he may have been born around 1471, though possibly later. Katherine, whom Richard married off in 1484, must have therefore been around fourteen at the time, suggesting she too was born around 1470. Though Richard would later publicly acknowledge his illegitimate children, indeed the records refer to John as the 'Lord Bastard', no evidence survives during Richard's early career to speculate any further.[8]

Richard's rise to power had been rapid, and at times ruthless. He had fought his brother Clarence for his wife's share of the Warwick lands, and won; even then, Richard had not been satisfied, going after his mother-in-law's Despenser inheritance too, before eventually succeeding, placing her under house arrest in one of his castles in the north while her lands were distributed as if she were dead. Richard was not prepared to allow anyone to stand in his way, particularly when it came to enlarging his landed estates. Similar treatment was meted out to the elderly and feeble countess of Oxford when he was granted the lands of her rebel sons, which did not include her own separate inheritance. The countess was taken into Richard's custody, where she was pressurised into surrendering her lands to which the duke had no legitimate claim. The countess had little other option. If she declined, Richard is supposed to have threatened that 'he would send her to Middleham there to be kept'. 'Wherefore the said lady, considering her great age, the great journey, and the great cold which then was of frost and snow, thought that she could not endure to be conveyed there without great jeopardy to her life.'

The king stood by, tacitly complicit in his brother's aggrandisement. In 1479, Sir John Risley visited the king while out hunting in Waltham forest. As their horses rode through the woods, while alone with the king Risley took the opportunity to ask for Edward's advice. Informing him that he intended to purchase from Richard the London property beside London Wall 'called the earl of Oxford's place', Risley requested 'his grace to give him his good council whether he might so surely do ye or nay'. Edward asked how the house had managed to come into Gloucester's hands. When Risley informed the king that the duke had 'come unto it by a release made' by the countess of Oxford, Edward replied, 'meddle not ye with the buying of the said place for though the title of the place be good in my brother of Gloucester's hands or in another man's hands of like might, it will be dangerous to thee to buy it and also to keep it and defend it'.

The king explained further, describing how the countess 'was compelled and constrained' by Gloucester 'to release and forsake her right in the said place'.⁹ Risley took heed of the king's advice and quickly lost interest in the property.

For all his undoubted loyalty, Edward understood, tolerated even, Richard's own independence, however violent. Even though the king must have known that once again history seemed to be repeating itself, with Richard transforming himself into yet another over-mighty subject like Warwick, this time with the entire north at his command, Edward considered it the lesser of two evils. As warden of the West March, combined with his vested self-interests in protecting his own landed hegemony, Richard's ambitions could be aligned with the royal policy of having a strong, outward-facing nobleman to defend the border with Scotland.

In contrast to the king, Richard, ever the hawk rather than the dove, craved military action. The taste for battle that he had acquired on the fields of Barnet and Tewkesbury had remained undiminished; consequently, the duke opposed and attempted to frustrate the peace that his brother had brokered with Scotland in 1474. When he was given the task as Admiral of investigating the looting of the Scottish ship *Le Salvator*, which had been wrecked off the coast of Bamburgh earlier in the year, nothing came of it, and in July 1474 the matter was removed from Richard's responsibility and instead handed to the charge of the ambassadors negotiating the Treaty of Edinburgh with James III. After the treaty was signed, Richard continued to frustrate the new concord by failing to hold the promised commissions or 'march days' on the borders to resolve disputes and order restitution for acts of piracy against Scottish ships. This left Edward IV suitably embarrassed, sending his chaplain and almoner, Alexander Lee, on an embassy in March 1475 to apologise to the Scottish king for the delay. On his journey north, Lee was instructed to 'take his way' to remind Richard 'of the king's pleasure in this party'. Clear instructions were sent to the duke, setting out the responsibilities that his brother expected him to fulfil. Additional instructions 'that toucheth the sea' ordered that 'bills of complaint' from Scots whose ships had been badly affected by English piracy be heard in front of Richard's lieutenants and deputies 'and there to have a full reformation and redress'. The final point, almost as a postscript, highlights Edward's simmering frustration at his brother's behaviour,

knowing that Richard had himself been behind some of the wrecking of
the Scottish ships himself: 'Item, where the king of Scots wrote to the king
for restitution of the despoil of two ships whereof the one was robbed by
the Mary flower etc, the king will that my lord of Gloucester be spoken
with in that party, considering that the said ship was his at that time.'[10]
Subsequently, Edward would not be prepared to allow his brother entirely
free rein and control of border fortifications such as Carlisle, appointing
his own stewards to maintain order and good government.

Tensions between Richard and longstanding northern noblemen, such
as Henry Percy, earl of Northumberland, whose family had traditionally
ruled much of the north-east for generations, would soon spill out into
conflict. In 1473, Richard began to seek recruits to his retinue, this time
from further afield, in Percy territory. In April, Richard managed to retain
Richard Knaresborough, a local tenant of the duchy of Lancaster. In
doing so, Richard brought himself into direct confrontation with Percy;
the earl was the principal landowner in the Honour of Knaresborough.
Matters came to a head on 12 May 1473, when the king's intervention was
needed in order for Richard and Northumberland to strike an agreement.
Northumberland was forced to capitulate, accepting Richard's supremacy.
He would become 'his faithful servant, the said duke being his good and
faithful lord, and the said Earl to do service unto the said duke at all times
lawful and convenient when he thereunto by the said duke shall be lawfully
required'. Richard, for his part, now promised to be Northumberland's
'good and faithful lord at all times, and to sustain him in his rights afore
all other persons'. Further agreement was struck that Richard would no
longer attempt to poach any of Northumberland's men, thereby allowing
the earl to maintain his independence without getting entirely subsumed
into Richard's orbit. The deal may have suited Northumberland, who understood there could be no fair bargain with the brother of a king, but it
marked the stage where Richard was now to be accepted as the true lord
of the north.[11]

Like any coalition, Northumberland's support was a vital component
of the settlement that bound northern society together, with Richard as
its figurehead. Largely the two men worked harmoniously; Richard and

Northumberland began to work closely together on local arbitration, while of the twelve men who served as sheriffs for Yorkshire between 1470 and 1483, six were retainers of Richard, while four were Northumberland's.[12] With Northumberland's loyalty confirmed, other members of the northern gentry sought to offer up their service to their new overlord. By extending his lordship and favour to those in need, Richard was determined to extend his power not just by accumulating land, but also a growing affinity of men, his retainers, to whom he paid fees from his northern estates. Many had served under the earl of Warwick, but Richard went much further. Creating a powerful connection of men who would serve his needs only helped to extend his authority even further into lands across the north.

Richard's lordship was an attractive prospect for many northern men seeking to benefit from his influence and power. Richard was a royal prince with access to royal favour. Men like Gerard Salvan from Durham would later petition the 'right high and mighty prince' to intervene on their behalf, asking the duke to send commandment to the sheriff of the bishopric to apprehend one Thomas Fishburn, whom Salvan accused of entering his home at Croxdale 'with force and arms . . . and there break and entered, and the same your orator would have feloniously murdered, and he might have had his purpose, which by the hand of God was laid apart'. Salvan requested that the duke arbitrate the case himself, while at the same time offering himself into the duke's service: 'I am a poor gentleman at my liberty, standing to take a master where I will and please, and I love none so well as you under God and the King. Wherefore I offer my service to your Lordship; and if ye will please to take me ye shall fine me true and at your pleasure, considering my true intent and service that I intend to do towards your good Grace, it shall please you to grant me a fee yearly; and your orator shall pray continually for the preservation of your princely estate.'[13] Sir John Henningham petitioned 'the right high and mighty prince my right and gracious lord the Duke of Gloucester' for permission and licence to obtain his wife's lands, 'in consideration of the true and faithful service . . . to the king and your good lordship done of your good grace, charity and right wiseness' for which John was willing to 'pray God for the confirmation of your good and gracious lordship long to endure'.[14] In his will, drawn up in June 1478, Sir John Pilkington requested

that his son Edward 'be had to my lord of Gloucester and my lord Chamberlain [William, Lord Hastings] heartily beseeching them as they will in
my name beseech the king his good grace that mine executors may have
the wardship and marriage of my said son and my land, paying to the king
500 marks'; appointing Richard and Hastings as his executors, Pilkington
further requested that 'I will that my lord of Gloucester have an emerald
set in gold, for which my said lord would have given me 100 marks'.[15]

Members of the northern nobility also sought to join Richard's wider
affinity, increasing his power and influence even further. Ralph, Lord
Neville, the nephew and heir of the earl of Westmorland, was the son of
John, Lord Neville, who had been killed at Towton, and had later been
attainted and had his lands confiscated. The attainder was reversed in October 1472, and Ralph was restored to his father's title and lands. In April
1475, Ralph was knighted, and subsequently entered Richard's service:
Richard himself later wrote calling on Ralph to 'do me now good service,
as ye have always before done'.[16] In Easter 1477, Ralph quit his claim to his
family's Yorkshire estates that his uncle had lost back in 1440 and were now
held by Richard. The ageing earl of Westmorland, at some point between
July 1477 and January 1479, then vested his lordship of Raby and a group of
manors in south-east Durham in his infant great-nephew, Lord Neville's
son, and a panel of feoffees, most of whom were Richard's councillors,
effectively placing the duke in control of the Westmorland inheritance.[17]
Richard was to be a frequent presence at the impressive castle at Raby from
November 1478, and used it as an official meeting place for his ducal counsel in the summer of 1480, meeting also with Bishop Dudley there twice in
the winter of 1480–81. Ralph Neville was not the only northern noble that
Richard managed to bring into his affinity. In June 1476, Richard signed
an indenture with the widowed Lady Scrope of Masham, who entrusted
the care of her sixteen-year-old son, Thomas, Lord Scrope, to Richard, to
'wholly be at his rule and guiding'. John, Lord Scrope of Bolton, Humphrey, Lord Dacre of Gilsland, Ralph, Lord Greystoke, and Henry, Lord
Fitzhugh of Ravensworth, all came into Richard's affinity, either voluntar-
ily or, realising that the king's brother would always have the upper hand
in the region, chose to resign themselves to their fates.

Richard had desperately hoped for military success in France in 1475. The duke's intention of winning martial glory on the continent is highlighted by his adoption of the white boar, or *sanglier*, a highly dangerous wild beast, whose ferocity and power made it one of the most difficult animals to hunt, as the insignia for his troops. When his father and brother Edmund were ceremonially reinterred at Fotheringhay in July 1476, Richard acted as chief mourner, overseeing the funeral arrangements for the cortège as it passed southwards from Pontefract. Mindful of his father's own military success in France during the Hundred Years War, he remembered in an epitaph laid at his father's new grave how in 1441 he had besieged Pontoise 'and drove away the French king'. The duke was desperate to emulate his father's glory. Two years later, in 1477, there seemed a brief opportunity for Richard to provide aid to his sister, Margaret of Burgundy, against the French, following the death of Charles the Bold; Richard sent men in support of his sister, while William, Lord Hastings, led an expedition of troops across the border from Calais. Yet Edward was unprepared to inter-vene and break the wealthy peace that he had signed with the French king, much to the disgust of many in the Yorkist establishment who considered his sister's honour and defence to be a chivalric imperative.

Instead, Scotland would become the arena for Richard's war. For sev-eral years, since the breakdown in a truce between the two countries in 1480, the duke had waited in anticipation of a Scottish invasion. As early as September 1480, Richard had expected to 'resist their malice', preparing troops for an invasion at the same time as paying for the defences of the West March out of his own pocket, repairing the city walls of Carlisle, and equipping the city with his own personal arsenal of cannon and crossbows. But the invasion never materialised. Edward continued to prevaricate over leading the invasion in person, raising a substantial subsidy from Parlia-ment for the proposed invasion in the winter of 1480; as late as January 1482, the king was still purchasing armour from France for his own per-sonal use. For Richard, the delays were punishing, both financially and on the morale of his troops. Without the king's presence, Richard knew that the southern lords and their retinues, those closely linked to the royal household, were unlikely to travel north. Supplies were running low, forc-ing Richard to make his own arrangements to purchase wheat, rye, peas and beans for basic subsistence in February 1482.[18] In the absence of war,

Richard chose to lead raids across the border, laying occasional siege to
Berwick: in August 1481, he had knighted several men at Hutton Field by
Berwick for their bravery.

Richard's perseverance had come not without cost, both financially
and personally. By 1480, he was already owed over £3,000 by the king in
arrears for his salary as warden of the West March; when his commission
was renewed for another ten years, he found the salary cut by over half,
down from £2,500 to £1,000.[19] Richard also had to tolerate his wages being
paid piecemeal; but by 9 March 1482 Richard was still owed 2,000 marks,
which Edward agreed would be paid 'at the feast of St John the Baptist
next coming'. Rather than make full payment to his brother, however, the
king ordered that the cost of a thousand bows sent to the duke from the
artillery in the Tower of London be taken from the amount, ordering the
Exchequer to 'retain in your hands of the said 2000 marks such and as
much money as the said bows in gross shall amount to'.[20] Several weeks
later, Edward deducted the cost of 500 sheaves of arrows from the final
total, again ordering the Exchequer to 'retain in your hands of the two
thousand marks foresaid such and as much money as the . . . said arrows
shall amount to'.[21]

Richard was feeling the cost of his Scottish incursions and the siege at
Berwick physically too. William Hobbes, the king's physician and sur-
geon, was sent with eight surgeons, at a cost of £13 6s, 'to attend upon the
Duke of Gloucester, in the King's service against the Scotch'. John Clerk
the king's apothecary, was paid £13 16s 9½d for 'divers medicines' to be
delivered to Richard 'of the king's gift, for the use of the said Duke in his
service against the Scotch'.[22]

Once again, it seemed that the prospect of war with Scotland had ground
to a stalemate, disappointing Richard's martial ambitions once more.
Then a breakthrough finally came in April 1482, with the surprise arrival
at Southampton of Alexander, duke of Albany, the exiled brother of the
Scottish king, James III. Albany appealed to the king for English assistance
to depose his brother. This presented a lasting solution to Edward's Scottish problem: regime change would allow him to place a pliant ruler on
the throne. This could be achieved, Edward hoped, by a short and precise

military campaign, rather than a drawn-out and costly war between two nations. The English war effort was immediately revitalised.

In June the treaty of Fotheringhay was concluded with Albany. Edward would recognise the duke as King Alexander and help place him on the throne. In return, once he had been established as king, Albany was to return Berwick to England, along with several other marcher castles. The duke was to do homage and fealty to Edward as his feudal overlord, end all Scottish alliances with France, and, in order to seal the agreement, marry Edward's daughter Cecily.[23]

There would not be enough time for the king to lead the invasion in person. If Albany's cause was to attract support, an invasion would need to be organised immediately. Richard would have to lead the English army on behalf of the king. On 12 June, only a day after the treaty had been signed, Richard was once again appointed as lieutenant-general in the north, and the campaign placed entirely in the duke's hands. The royal army under Richard's leadership marched immediately northwards, reaching York on 18 June. Preparations were now made for war. In total, Richard had been granted around £15,000, enough money to keep an army of 20,000 men in the field for twenty-eight days.[24] The war was to be fought at sea as well as on land, with £133 6s 8d being spent 'to pay the wages of divers fighting men upon the western sea, proceeding against the Scotch, according to the discretion of the said Duke'.

Scotland was to finally provide the nobility with the war that they had been denied in France; Richard's army was drawn from the retinues of noblemen across the country: the marquess of Dorset brought 600 archers from Warwickshire, Thomas, Lord Stanley, brought 3,000 archers and Lord Rivers promised 1,000 men.[25] The English army also contained a large number of mercenaries, with at least 1,800 Burgundian, German and Swiss troops travelling to the East March, led to the region by grooms and yeomen of the royal household.

The payments for a four-week campaign suggest that Edward had a clear objective and time scale by which to overturn James's rule. Richard arrived with his massive army at Berwick at the end of the third week of July. Facing them, the Scots had just 600 men garrisoning six towers on the borders. The Scottish king, attempting to assemble a force at Lauder, realised that he was hopelessly outnumbered. The town of Berwick swiftly surrendered, though the castle was prepared to continue to hold out for a siege.

Richard had a choice: to sit out the siege until Berwick fell, or to attempt the far grander plan of placing Albany on the throne. Then news reached him that the hapless James III had been arrested by his own Stuart half-uncles at Lauder, and forcibly taken back to Edinburgh. It seemed to Richard that he now had no option but to press his advantage: he would march to Edinburgh to place Albany on the throne.

On 24 July, Richard made knights or bannerets of forty-nine men; all but four of them northerners.[26] Then, leaving a small force behind surrounding Berwick Castle, Richard gave orders for the army to proceed straight to Edinburgh. After a march of thirty miles, Richard's forces entered the city unopposed. There they found the castle doors bolted shut; inside, James III was being guarded by the earls of Atholl and Buchan, who had possession of the royal seals. The earls flatly refused to negotiate. Instead, they were prepared to withstand a siege if necessary. Richard was in a dangerous position. Having marched thirty miles across the border into Edinburgh, he now risked being cut off and surrounded, vulnerable to attack from James's loyalists in the region. Albany's behaviour was equally worrying; when the duke announced that he would be prepared to enter into negotiations not for the throne but merely to secure the restoration of all his lands and offices that he had held before his flight in 1479, Richard 'suspected treason, not without cause'.[27] There was no other choice but to open up peace talks, which hurriedly took place within three days. While James III's councillors were prepared to offer Albany a full pardon for 'aspiring and tending to the throne', as well as confirming the restoration of his lands by an Act of Parliament, they were in no real position to honour the agreement, and, without access to the king, could hardly speak for James III himself. The chronicler Edward Hall later claimed that Albany swore to Richard in secret that in spite of any agreements that were reached with the Scottish lords, he would still promise to observe the terms of the treaty that had been signed at Fotheringhay in June.[28] Negotiations continued for the next two days, with Richard pressing for further concessions from the citizens, who were eager to be rid of the menacing English troops on their doorstep.

On 4 August, the provost of the city, together with the merchant community, swore an agreement with Richard, Albany and the earl of Northumberland, together with the earl of Argyll and the bishop of Dunkeld, that if the proposed marriage between Prince James and Edward IV's daughter Cecily, first agreed in 1474, did not take place, the money that Edward had paid towards his daughter's dowry would be refunded in annual instalments, at the city's expense. Given that Cecily had also been contracted to marry Albany, it was hardly surprising that Richard expected the proposed match between her and Prince James to fail, but his determination to ensure that the dowry was returned reflects the duke's desire to achieve the best possible outcome from what was becoming an increasingly dire situation. While Richard had taken care not to bind his brother's hands when it came to future diplomatic or military manoeuvres, his pragmatism came from his own experience in leading border raids of what could realistically be achieved in Scotland. Sensing that retreat would allow for greater gains to be made elsewhere, shortly afterwards he ordered his army to depart from the city, and on 11 August dismissed the larger part of his army. Rewards worth £350 were given to the duke's own retinue 'for their expenses in going from the town of Berwick to their own homes'. A further £595 was spent on 1,700 'fighting men' who were to be retained by the duke 'to accompany him in the war against the Scotch' for the next fourteen days.

Richard's withdrawal from Edinburgh was criticised by the Crowland chronicler, who wrote that the duke, 'having got as far as Edinburgh with the whole army without meeting any resistance, he let that very wealthy town escape unharmed'.[29] Richard was surely in a commanding position to dictate far better terms to the Scottish government; although he may have felt that he lacked instructions to do so following Albany's defection, Richard made no attempt to await further direction from the king as to the terms on which he should settle. Instead, Richard journeyed southwards and returned to the siege of Berwick, which had been left under the sole command of Thomas, Lord Stanley, apparently causing tension between the two men, since Stanley felt he had been left 'in great danger'.[30] With the Scottish garrison reluctant to fight on behalf of an imprisoned James III, who would be in no position to pay them, the castle at Berwick surrendered after a final siege on 24 August, 'though not without slaughter and bloodshed'.[31]

For the first time since 1463, Berwick had been re-conquered from the Scots. Edward was delighted, publicly thanking 'God, the giver of all good gifts, for the support received from our most loving brother, whose success is so proven that he alone would suffice to chastise the whole kingdom of Scotland'. Street parties were held and bonfires were lit in celebration as far afield as Calais, where every single gun on the city bulwarks 'and about the walls were shot for joy'. Edward was evidently overjoyed with the re-capture of Berwick, if only for the symbolic appeal of its repossession. He could not help but note that the castle, having been in the uninterrupted possession of our forefathers, whose just title having descended to us' had been lost by the Lancastrians 'before our coronation'. The king wrote as if Berwick's recovery was all part of the Yorkist plan, since 'we were bound to recover what was ours . . . A small chosen band therefore received the surrender of the town immediately on sitting down before it, though the same was entirely surrounded by impregnable walls. The citadel, however, because of its well chosen position and state of defence, was not taken until the rest of the army had returned; when, not without some slaughter and bloodshed, it was reduced.'[32]

Some could not help but whisper that the celebrations over Berwick had become a face-saving exercise to cover for the disappointment at failing to place Albany on the throne. For all the expense of raising an army, Richard had returned with little to show for his expedition. The Crowland chronicler was less than impressed at Richard's achievements. 'What he achieved in this expedition and what large sums of money, repeatedly extorted under the name of benevolence, he foolishly used up were amply demonstrated by the outcome of this business.' The chronicler considered Berwick's recovery a 'trifling gain', or perhaps more accurately, a loss (for the maintenance of Berwick costs 10,000 marks a year) that diminished the substance of the king and the kingdom by more than £100,000 at the time. King Edward was grieved at the frivolous expenditure of so much money although the recapture of Berwick alleviated his grief for a time.'[33] Others, too, were less than impressed with Richard's conduct and achieve-ments as leader of the Scottish campaign. Later that winter, it was alleged in York that John Lam had been overheard saying that 'the soldiers of this city were ill worthy to have their wages, for they did nothing for it but made whips of their bow strings to drive carriage with'. Lam denied the charge, but admitted that 'he heard some of their fellowship say that they did nothing else but waited upon the ordinance and carriage and over that he heard one of the soldiers say that he was so weary that he was fain to take off the string of his bow to drive his horse with'.[34]

While the Crowland chronicler exaggerated the cost of recapturing Berwick, nonetheless his point concerning the doubtful success of the Scottish campaign was valid. The English advantage had been lost, and nothing had been settled. Mostly this was Edward IV's fault: distant and indecisive, it was not until October 1482 that he decided to abandon his daughter Cecily's marriage with the heir of James III and drop plans for a marriage with Anthony, Earl Rivers, and Margaret of Scotland, yet after the recapture of Berwick he made no attempt to seek a new treaty with James III, and the truce was not renewed. By mid-November, it seems that Edward was determined to renew the war with Scotland, with writs being issued on 15 November to summon Parliament, the main purpose of which was to vote money for 'the hasty defence of the realm'. Yet Edward's relentless focus upon Scotland meant that he had taken his eye off conti nental affairs, allowing Louis XI to take full advantage of the diplomatic situation.

Events north of the border were soon overshadowed by the disastrous news on the continent. In March 1482, Mary of Burgundy died after falling from her horse. The new regent of Burgundy, Mary's husband, Maximilian I, pleaded with Edward to abandon his French treaty with Louis XI and support a Burgundian alliance instead, but once again Edward hesitated. By December, Maximilian had no choice but to cave in to pressure from the French, signing the Treaty of Arras in December. Mary's daughter, Margaret of Austria, was to be betrothed to the dauphin, Charles. For Edward, it meant the end not only of his long-cherished dream of marrying his eldest daughter, Elizabeth of York, to the dauphin, but also the end of his lucrative French pension. Louis XI had no need to buy off the English king any more, and the next instalment of the pension was never paid. Edward was furious, and, according to the Crowland chronicler, 'thought of nothing else but taking vengeance'; by February 1483, he was already committing himself to further action on the continent, rashly promising Brittany 4,000 archers to serve at English expense for three months if it could be stirred into action against Louis XI. Edward knew, however, that

he had been outplayed by the French king; 'the spirited prince now realised
that in the end he had been tricked by King Louis and was deeply troubled
and grieved'.³⁵ How different things might have been, some may have considered, if Edward himself had been prepared to defend his sister Margaret
of York after the death of Charles the Bold in 1477; if Clarence had instead
been married to Mary, by now the Burgundian territory would have been
in the hands of the house of York. Those who had pressed for military
intervention in support of Margaret, such as William, Lord Hastings, and
Richard himself, must have felt silently vindicated.

Still, Richard was feted as a national hero. Even his conduct at Edinburgh
was praised by the king for mercifulness and restraint. The day after Berwick's capture, Edward wrote proudly to Pope Sixtus IV, boasting that 'the
army which our brother lately led into Scotland, traversing the heart of
that kingdom without hindrance, arrived at the royal city of Edinburgh'.
There he had found 'the king with the other chief lords of the kingdom
shut up in a most strongly fortified castle, nowise thinking of arms, of war,
of resistance, but giving up that right fair and opulent city into the power
of the English'. Richard could have, the king wrote, 'instantly doomed the
same to plunder and flames', had not his 'compassion exceeded all human
capacity . . . The noble band of victors, however, spared the supplicant and
prostrate citizens, the churches, and not only the widows, orphans, and
minors, but all persons found there unharmed.'³⁶

Several months later, in February 1483, Parliament lauded Richard, 'the
very powerful prince' for his 'noble deed and act'.³⁷ Their unusual commendation heralded the passing of an Act, granting Richard his own personal
palatinate, carved out of the West March and south-western Scotland,
land which, the Act declared, the duke 'late by his manifold and diligent
labours and devoirs, hath subdued a great part of'. In return for a one-off
payment of 10,000 marks, Richard would now be left to his own devices.
Independent of the king for any further financial support, any land that he
subsequently conquered in Scotland would be his to rule.

The creation of the palatinate brought to fruition a long-cherished
dream of Richard's. The idea had been his own, a draft proposal of which
he seems to have presented to the king before the commencement of the

Scottish campaign. Richard's maddening rush to Edinburgh did, it seems, have a purpose: to demonstrate what might be possible for the future, and to set out the scope of his ambitions. For Edward, compromised as he was over continuing a war against Scotland when he was shifting his attention to another war against France, giving his brother carte blanche in Scotland was the most convenient means by which to continue to fight, at relatively little cost: for 10,000 marks, from which Richard would have to pay future wardens' salaries, Edward would be free to deal with France.

The symbolism of the palatinate outweighed the actual value of the lands. It was the first since Lancaster had been made a county palatine in 1351. Yet Richard's palatine status was restricted to Scottish territory only, where future conquest was by no means certain; clauses relating to the English northern lands in Cumberland were noticeably more restricted. Forfeitures for treason, which in a newly conquered territory were likely to be significant, were also reserved to the king, while wardships and marriages in Cumberland were also to be placed under royal control. It was clear that Edward IV was not prepared to surrender his position in the north-west entirely, but expected Richard to continue to act on behalf of the crown. For Edward, the creation of the palatinate and the gift of a lump sum of 10,000 marks may have seemed a high price to pay, but this had to be weighed against the savings that he would make in not having to pay the salary of the wardenship of the West March, now Richard's responsibility, that had run at 1,200 marks in peacetime and £1,000 during war.

In spite of the limitations on the palatinate, what mattered to Richard was that, above all, it provided him with an opportunity to create an inheritance, won on the battlefield, that for the first time would be truly his own. It did not seem to matter that the entire costs of the lands could potentially ruin him since he would no longer receive regular support from the crown, for he must have genuinely believed it was possible to carve a new livelihood out of conquest.

In reality, on Richard's part, it was nothing less than a desperate throw of the dice. His own finances had begun to falter. Already he was spending more than he was receiving in landed income. The establishment of Richard's two colleges at Middleham and Barnard Castle had placed him above

the noble families of the earls of Westmorland, the Nevilles, the Beau-
champs and even his own father, who had only founded one college each.
The limit of their ambition was a sensible one: even the richest magnates
could not afford the vast sums needed to pay the costs of a foundation
upfront; rather than bear the costs during their lifetime, they left their
executors to pay off their debts through a trust. In contrast, the scale of
Richard's own foundations and their huge endowments of 200 marks
for Middleham and 400 marks for Barnard Castle meant that the duke
was spending a capital value of around £8,000 on the projects. In order
to finance them, in 1478 Richard obtained permission through an Act of
Parliament to alienate six of his wife's Neville advowsons to the two colleges, while in 1480 he was forced to alienate six manors he had obtained
from the countess of Oxford to Middleham College. Richard made other
alienations, in effect donations, to other religious organisations: having
purchased Seaham rectory for £150, in 1476 Richard gifted it to Coverham
Abbey. Another three manors of the countess of Oxford were granted to St
George's Chapel in Windsor, while another manor, Fulmer, was given to
Queen's College, Cambridge.

The use of land to provide for religious foundations on this level, rather
than provide Richard with an income, is indicative of the duke's general
approach to his finances. Instead of his lands and lordships being used
for revenue, Richard chose to use the money for religious and political
purposes. Any revenue obtained from Middleham was spent on retaining
men in the local area, with Richard having increased the fees he paid in
order to retain loyalties. Already, by 1477, Richard was spending almost
all of the income that he received from part of his de Vere estates in East
Anglia, a total of nearly £400, on wages and his expenses, predominantly
on expensive cloths and furs, with an outgoing of £374. It was a similar
picture in Richard's lordship of Glamorgan, whose profits had dwindled
to £336 8s 5d, less than one third of what they had been during Edward II's
reign, of which Richard had committed himself to annual charges in payments of fees, wages and expenses amounting to £234 7s 11d, compared to
£166 15s 10d when the lordship was held by the earl of Warwick.[38] Certainly
the office of the warden of the West March would have cost more to run
and finance than the infrequent royal payments would have accommo-
dated for, with Richard already £3,000 in debt from money owed to him

by the crown. Other grants of land or agreements that Richard had entered into, including with Lady Hungerford, Lady Latimer and the countess of Oxford, saw Richard agree to take on considerable debts and expenses and to pay annuities on their behalf. In the absence of household accounts for the duke that would reveal his spending and revenue, it may be that Richard was drifting into a precarious financial position, spending more than his landed estate was raising.

Already Richard had been faced with some difficult choices in selling off land to raise cash. In October 1478, he sold the manor of Hoton Pagnell, near Doncaster, covering some 500 acres in the West Riding, to the king for £500, despite the fact that it resided in his northern patrimony that the duke was attempting to create.[39] Richard had only purchased the manor three years earlier for 500 marks.[40] It seems that Richard needed the money more than he was perhaps prepared to admit: in subsequent years, Richard would sell further manors, including Wivenhoe in Essex to John, Lord Howard, for 1,100 marks, South Welles in Romsey and other lands in Hampshire for £200, and the Fitzlewis lands in Essex worth 1,100 marks a year. Richard would stop at nothing to realise some additional cash. In Romsey, he sought to make a profit on the back of a dubious legal transaction.[41]

Richard, it seems, was beginning to struggle both financially and in performing his royal duties. On 28 February 1482, Edward wrote to his 'right trusty and entirely beloved brother' in his capacity as chief steward of the duchy of Lancaster north of the Trent. The king expressed his concerns that the honours and lordships belonging to the duchy had under Richard's control 'fallen in great decay' with the forests, woods and chases having been 'wasted as well by felling and carrying away of our timber and trees without our commandment or assent'. As a result, the forests were now 'destroyed and gone', along with the king's profits, 'to the hurt as well of us and of our tenants as decrease of our said game'. Richard, the king urged, was to ensure that the situation 'might be hastily redressed and reformed by good oversight of you and your deputies', which he accused his brother 'here before of long time hath been slothed and not done as to your office it belongeth with many other defaults herein not yet remembered right hurtful unto us'.[42]

The palatinate offered fresh hope and the potential for a new landed dynasty to be created. It was the culmination of more than a decade's work. Richard had created for himself a northern dynasty more powerful than the Nevilles had ever managed to achieve. Yet the stakes remained high. Richard's military power on the borders was dependent not on his salary as a warden, but on his retinue and his revenue as a northern overlord. The affinity that he had built up, a network of loyal supporters whose livelihoods were entirely dependent on the duke, was funded from the profits of his northern estates: Middleham and Sheriff Hutton in Yorkshire, Penrith in Cumberland and Barnard Castle on the Tees, along with the other lordships of Helmsley, Richmond, Skipton and Scarborough that he had also acquired. Everything rested on the security of his Neville patrimony.

And yet the security of Richard's Neville inheritance remained dangerously tenuous, dependent as it was on the teenage George Neville, the former duke of Bedford, whose survival was critical for Richard to enjoy his wife's estates as part of his inheritance. Richard's control of the lands remained perilous: if George were to die without an heir, Richard's own interest in the Neville estates would revert to just a life interest, with Richard in effect holding the lands for the rest of his life before they passed over to Lord Latimer as the next Neville heir.

In recent years, Richard had begun to take action to neutralise any threat posed by the Neville reversionary interest in his lordships of Middleham, Sheriff Hutton and Penrith. He secured a quit-claim from Ralph, Lord Neville, to ensure that no additional, even older, claim to the lands could be considered.[43] Richard was hampered in his efforts to remove the claims of the next in line to the Neville inheritance, Richard Neville, Lord Latimer, on his lands, since the young boy remained in the custody of Thomas Bourchier, the archbishop of Canterbury. Yet still Richard pursued other members of the family ruthlessly, obtaining quit-claims from Latimer's aunt, Katherine Dudley, in 1477 and his grandmother, Elizabeth, Lady Latimer, in 1480.[44] In an agreement drawn up on 20 March 1480 with the elderly widow, Richard revealed his intent: should the duke, 'at any time hereafter', obtain the custody of Lord Latimer, then he undertook to continue to pay Elizabeth an annuity of 300 marks, which she received from the archbishop, with Richard promising to continue to pay even if the archbishop cancelled his payment on account of her signing the agreement, which had come about through 'the desire and pleasure of the said duke'.[45] It seems that Richard had convinced Lady Elizabeth to support plans for Richard to secure the custody of her grandson, yet in the event Elizabeth died in 1481, with her estates reverting to the crown.

Richard had also successfully managed to secure the custody of the key figure of George Neville. Yet Richard had still to arrange a marriage for the young George, let alone ensure that he would produce an heir. All that Richard had worked for hung on the thread of George Neville's life.

For now, however, basking in the glory of his Scottish conquests, Richard could expect, regardless of the insecurity of his Neville inheritance, that he would remain a mainstay of the Yorkist dynasty for years to come. Having started out in life as a younger son, without any expectations of inheritance, Richard had already transformed his life beyond what he must have reasonably thought possible. He had done so by both accident and design, through marriage and through loyal service to the crown, but his determination to succeed at all costs remained the hallmark of Richard's early career. Yet Richard knew that his success was at best temporary. He had succeeded not as an over-mighty subject independent of the crown, but because he was a loyal subject of the king. His authority in the north was entirely dependent upon his position as the king's representative. All that Richard owned, he did so because of his brother: even his Neville inheritance, granted through his wife, Anne, had been partitioned only with the king's agreement. Now, with the creation of the palatinate on the Scottish marches, Edward had chosen to establish his brother as one of the greatest northern overlords the country had ever seen.

Upon his return to the throne, Edward IV had at first seemed to have learnt the lessons of the past: of the spoils of victory that he distributed after 1471, none went to the Woodvilles. Instead the family sought new avenues of influence and authority. The creation of Edward's son as Prince of Wales, duke of Cornwall and earl of Chester saw the establishment of a household and council for the prince. When the young prince was moved to Ludlow in 1473, his council was effectively given the task of running the Welsh government, led by the queen and the prince's governor, his maternal uncle Anthony, Earl Rivers. The Woodvilles therefore came to dominate the council, with their affinity formed tightly around the heir to the throne. The traditional interests of nearby magnates such as the duke of Buckingham, or the Stanleys in Cheshire, were to be subsumed into the council itself: Buckingham himself had to enter into an indenture and place Woodville protégés in key administrative positions, while Sir William Stanley had become steward of the prince's household by 1483. Through the instrument of the prince's council, the Woodvilles were able to exert power and authority that extended across nearly the entirety of Wales.

What mattered most, however, was possession of the person of the young prince himself. Edward was determined that his son grow up a paragon of virtue. Every moment of the prince's waking education was to reflect this; at dinner, he was to be read 'such noble stories as behoveth to a prince to understand and know', while 'at all times' the only topic of conversation 'in his presence be of virtue, honour, cunning, wisdom and deeds of worship'. In particular, there was to be no mention of any matter 'that should move or stir him to vices'. After breakfast, the young Edward was to be 'occupied about his learning', followed by 'all such convenient disports and exercises as behoveth his estate to have experience in'. Dominic Mancini had heard that while in Wales the Prince had 'devoted himself to horses and dogs and other youthful exercises to invigorate his body', while the Italian had learnt of 'the talent of the youth': 'In word and deed he gave so many proofs of his liberal education, of polite, nay rather scholarly, attainments far beyond his age', including 'his special knowledge of literature, which enabled him to discourse elegantly, to understand fully, and to declaim most excellently from any work whether in verse or prose that came into his hands, unless it were from among the more abstruse authors'.[46] John Rous also wrote how Edward had been 'brought up virtuously by virtuous men' and was 'remarkably gifted, and very well advanced in learning for his years'.[47] By exerting influence over the young heir to the throne, the Woodvilles hoped to secure their own political longevity.

As the prince's governor, the queen's own brother Anthony, Earl Rivers, had complete control over access to the young prince. Each morning, no man was to enter the prince's chamber 'except our right trusty and well-beloved the Earl Rivers, his chamberlain and his chaplains, or such other as shall be thought by the said Earl Rivers convenient'. While the prince ate at dinner, no one was to sit 'at his board' except 'such as shall be thought by the discretion of the said Earl Rivers'.[48] Perhaps most importantly, Edward granted that 'for the weal, surety and profit of our said son', full authority was to be granted to Rivers 'to remove at all times' the prince 'as the case shall require unto such places as shall be thought by their discretions necessary for the season'.[49] Rivers was given the opportunity to extend his authority over the young prince. On 25 February 1483, new ordinances for the household of Prince Edward were issued. For the first time the ordinances set down the names of the prince's chief household officers. The increase in the influence of the Woodvilles is striking. The names included Sir Richard Grey, Queen Elizabeth's second son by her first marriage, Anthony, Earl Rivers, and Richard Haute, the queen's cousin.[50] The new ordinances also declared that Edward was not to 'give, write, send or command any thing without the advise' of John Alcock, Richard Grey or Rivers. Significantly, an additional clause had been added insisting that if Rivers or Grey 'understand our said son of any unprincely demeaning or to deal contrary to these ordinances' then they were to 'forthwith show it in good manner unto himself to be reformed'; if the prince refused to 'amend' his behaviour, then they were to report to the king or queen.[51]

Rivers fully understood the power and influence he had been granted by the king. He was determined to use his position as the prince's governor to his own advantage. Among his surviving correspondence are letters dating from January 1483 that demonstrate how Rivers was planning to fill vacant parliamentary seats located in land belonging to the Prince of Wales and the young duke of York with his own men.[52] He also used his position to further the interests of the Woodville family. Another letter in his surviving correspondence concerned Rivers' attempt to give to Thomas, marquess of Dorset – the queen's eldest son from her first marriage – the office of deputy constable of the Tower, which Rivers had been appointed to in 1480.[53] In early March 1483, he wrote to his attorney Andrew Dymmock, explaining how 'my lord Marques and I be in a communication that he should have of me such interest as I have in the office of the Tower'; Dymmock was to sue the constable, Lord Dudley, on behalf of Dorset 'in that matter in all haste and send me word of their disposition'. His postscript read: 'Send me by some sure man the patent of mine authority about the lord prince, and also a patent that the king gave me touching power to raise people if need be in the march of Wales.'[54] It was clear that Rivers, residing at Ludlow with the Prince of Wales and charged with the possession of the young boy as his unofficial regent, was placed in an ideal position to exert his influence and authority.

Even with Prince Edward in their complete control, Queen Elizabeth could not help but embellish her family with royal favour. In 1474, she concluded a marriage between her eldest son from her first marriage, Thomas Grey, and Cecily Bonville, whose guardian was the king's chamberlain and close friend, William, Lord Hastings. Even Hastings would be caught out by the Woodvilles' tenacity. According to the marriage agreement, Cecily's inheritance was to be kept by the queen until she was sixteen, ostensibly to cover the 2,500 marks (£1,667) paid for the marriage, but in fact the cost was credited against Hastings's debts to the king, which would be written off to the exact amount, so the revenues were of immediate profit to Elizabeth. Hastings would not receive a penny. Created the marquess of Dorset, Thomas Grey steadily built up his power base in the West Country; he was also granted the lucrative wardship of Clarence's son, the earl of Warwick, while his own infant heir was betrothed to the daughter of the late duchess of Exeter, the king's sister, by her second husband. The Exeter estates themselves were not part of the inheritance, but nevertheless were settled on Dorset by an Act of Parliament in 1483. As a result the rightful heir to the estates, Ralph Neville, later earl of Westmorland, was cut out of his inheritance entirely.

The bending of the laws of inheritance had been a common feature of Edward's reign, particularly when it came to accommodating his own royal family, but the king was now twisting them to breaking point. In Wales, where previously William Herbert, the earl of Pembroke, had held sway as the king's lieutenant, his son and heir, sixteen years old in 1471, was stripped of part of his lands two years later, and in 1479 was forced to exchange his earldom of Pembroke for that of Huntingdon. His title and remaining Welsh lands were instead conferred upon the Prince of Wales, effectively granting them to Rivers, who continued to build up his power base in the country.

No member of the nobility nor their inheritance, it seemed, was immune from Edward's, and the Woodvilles', meddling. When, in January 1476,

John Mowbray, the fourth duke of Norfolk, earl of Nottingham and Warenne, died, he left an infant daughter, Anne, as sole heir to the duchy. She was immediately marked out as a bride for the king's second son, Richard, who had been born in August 1473 and created duke of York in May 1474. Even before the marriage had taken place, the young prince was given the title of earl of Nottingham in June 1476, followed by the dukedom of Norfolk in February 1477. To clear the path for his son's inheritance, Edward had been prepared to ride roughshod over the rights of the accepted heirs of the Mowbray inheritance, the descendants of the original first duke of Norfolk, William, Lord Berkeley, and John, Lord Howard. When Anne died in November 1481, a few days short of her tenth birthday, the laws of inheritance meant that her estates should have passed to Berkeley and Howard. Conveniently, Edward raised the issue of the crippling debts and bonds totalling £37,000 that Berkeley owed to the crown. These were written off in return for Berkeley surrendering his rights to the Mowbray inheritance; to make the transaction more palatable, Berkeley was also created Viscount Berkeley in April 1481. An Act in the January 1483 Parliament confirmed the arrangement, vesting the Mowbray inheritance in Duke Richard for his life, with reversion to his heirs and then finally to the heirs of the king himself. In effect, the entire rights of the dukedom and its lands had been sequestered into the royal family.[55] Berkeley may have felt that he had struck a reasonable bargain, but for the hardworking royal servant John, Lord Howard, the only recompense was to be a single manor; his royal master had silently disinherited him.

Edward's own wealth, particularly following the receipt of his French pension, combined with his increasing avarice, ensured that 'in the collection of gold and silver vessels, tapestries and highly precious ornaments, both regal and religious, in the building of castles, colleges and other notable places and in the acquisition of new lands and possessions not one of his ancestors could match his remarkable achievements'.[56] The king's building works at Windsor alone cost £6,572 in the years between 1478 and 1483, while at Nottingham Castle £3,000 was spent on refurbishing the building, adding a new tower and rooms with the latest glazed windows.

'You might have seen, in those days', the Crowland chronicler wrote, 'the royal court presenting no other appearance than such as fully befits a most mighty kingdom.' The sense of entitlement and exceptionalism, of the royal family detached from its nobility, the court and ordinary life, seems to have been an early trait of Queen Elizabeth, who made her own mother and sister kneel before her at dinner, not allowing them to sit until the first fish course had been served.[57] Yet the entire royal family was to be marked out as a separate caste in a new law passed in 1483, making it illegal for anyone but the king, queen and their relatives to wear the colour purple. The change was recognised by the Crowland chronicler, who noted how Edward's clothes, 'the costliest clothes very different in style from what used to be seen in our time', were lined with 'such sumptuous fur' and displaying the king, the chronicler observed, 'like a new and incomparable spectacle set before the onlookers' – a deliberately crafted image, one which reflected the increasingly, and perhaps to some dangerously, absolute monarchy that was forming at the Yorkist court.[58]

This sense of the court as a spectacle is underlined by the vivid account of the Italian Dominic Mancini's arrival in London in late 1482. Already in his fifties, Mancini was feeling his age. The 'damp cold' of the capital could hardly have agreed with a man born into a wealthy Roman family near the Via Lata. After Mancini had entered into the order of Augustinian friars, it was his friendship with a fellow Italian, Angelo Cato – a noted astrologer and later physician and councillor at the court of the French king, Louis XI, who had appointed Cato as archbishop of Vienne – that had led Mancini to take up residence in Paris. With Cato acting as his literary patron, it was here that Mancini enjoyed the company of a literary circle of friends; the city's printers had published one of the Italian's Latin verses in an anthology collected by a French professor the previous August, in which Mancini boasted of his talents as a 'most eloquent orator, a poet laureate and a palatine count'.[59]

Then, in the autumn of 1482 or early in 1483, Cato had contacted Mancini, requesting that he journey across the Channel. Exactly why Cato needed Mancini to travel to London is unclear, although the archbishop's influence in foreign affairs, providing Louis XI with the latest information concerning the gossip and movements within the royal courts of Europe, was extensive. Mancini's sudden arrival in London perhaps places the Italian in the role of an agent, acting at his patron's behest, and ultimately on behalf of the French authorities.

Now Mancini found himself in the city 'so famous throughout the world', its street stalls filled with goods heaped high: 'there are to be found all manner of minerals, wines, honey, pitch, wax, flax, ropes, thread, grain, fish, and other distasteful goods', the Italian observed, 'there is nowhere a lack of anything'.[60] In recent years, freed from the shackles of bitter civil war that had engulfed the country since the 1450s, England had grown increasingly prosperous. Nowhere could the accumulation of wealth and prosperity be better witnessed than at the court of Edward IV.

Edward seemed to have finally secured the future of the Yorkist dynasty. A nation divided had come to heal. Mancini observed how the king 'ruled England with great renown' and was 'very powerful'. Whether the Italian was able to gain access to the royal court, or had simply managed to glean some information from his contacts, he described how Edward was 'more favourable than other princes to foreigners'. The king appeared to have 'a gentle nature and cheerful aspect', he recalled, though 'should he assume an angry countenance' he could appear 'very terrible to beholders'. 'He was of easy access to his friends and to others, even the least notable', Mancini recalled. 'Frequently he called to his side complete strangers, when he thought that they had come with the intention of addressing or beholding him more closely. He was wont to show himself to those who wished to watch him, and seized any opportunity that the occasion offered of revealing his fine stature more protractedly and more evidently to on-lookers.' In particular, Mancini remembered how Edward 'was so genial in his greeting that if he saw a newcomer bewildered at his appearance and royal magnificence', the king would 'give him courage to speak by laying a kindly hand upon his shoulder'.

The king was now aged forty-one, and with seven surviving children from his marriage to his queen, Elizabeth Woodville, including two boys, his heir Edward, Prince of Wales, and Richard, duke of York, his confidence in his own authority was at its height. As the New Year arrived and the Christmas festivities at Westminster continued, the Crowland chronicler described how the king appeared 'dressed in a variety of the costliest clothes very different in style from what used to be seen hitherto in our time. The sleeves of the robes hung full in the fashion of the monastic frock and the insides were lined with such sumptuous fur that, when turned back over the shoulders, they displayed the prince (who always stood out because of his elegant figure) like a new and incomparable spectacle set before the onlookers. 'In those days', the chronicler continued, 'you might have seen a royal Court such as befitted a mighty kingdom, filled with riches and men from almost every nation and, surpassing all else, with the handsome and most delightful children born of the marriage.'[61]

Even Mancini could detect a sense that the entire spectacle was 'contrived'. Instead it seemed that these 'many performances of actors amidst royal splendour' had been simply put on 'so as to mitigate or disguise' the king's own 'sorrow', that in spite of his best efforts, nevertheless, 'he was never able altogether to hide it.'

As the king continued in his lavish lifestyle, so he repeated the mistakes that had cost him the crown in 1470, in his blatant favouritism towards Queen Elizabeth's Woodville kin. The monarch was expected to be the arbiter and protector of justice, yet Edward was clearly subverting the laws of inheritance for the personal gain of his wife's family. He could do so without challenge, for there was no longer any significant opposition to his reign; without Warwick or his brother Clarence opposing him, Edward knew that he could get away with anything that he wished. Only his brother Richard could have stood in his way, yet Richard himself had at the time been more than prepared to acquiesce in the bending of the law, and the use of parliamentary statute as a means to fix his own inheritance.

While Edward's own personal monarchy remained strong, the king's actions would not be a problem; yet they were undeniably storing up problems for the future. The disinherited, men such as William Berkeley, Ralph Neville or John, Lord Howard, would not forget the treatment that they had received at the hands of the king and the Woodvilles. The unpopularity of the queen's wider kin had only been entrenched by Edward, who sanctioned their actions and had placed his heir, Edward, and younger son, Richard, in their exclusive charge. If Edward was prepared to bend the laws of inheritance for the personal gain of the Woodvilles, what hope was there for the future, when one day Edward V would inherit his father's throne, ensuring that the Woodvilles retained their ascendancy?

For his brother Richard, Edward had been the most important figure in his young career so far. It had been Edward who had shaped Richard's own destiny; Richard had followed his brother into exile, and been handsomely rewarded for his service. Edward had allowed his younger brother to establish himself as an effective overlord of the north, replacing the vacuum of power left by the death of the earl of Warwick. No matter how great Richard's own ambition, it could only be fulfilled with the consent of the king. If Richard had cleverly and skilfully built up his power base, developing and shaping his estates and recruiting a retinue that presented his public face as a northern super magnate, Edward had permitted him to do so. Edward had permitted him, too, the luxury of running an expensive campaign in Scotland, appointing him commander-in-chief of an army 20,000 strong. It was here that Richard saw his future, an opportunity to carve out a destiny for his heirs. His plans for a palatinate demonstrate the scale of Richard's ambition; there were only three palatinates in existence, the last granted to John of Gaunt, and none were currently in noble hands. Yet once again Edward agreed to Richard's demands, placing him in the remarkably elevated position of being head and shoulders above the rest of the nobility. Richard had been loyal to his brother, though at times his independence of mind had tested the relationship between them; yet loyalty was not a virtue, it was a duty. Richard had sworn allegiance not only to his brother, but also to his heir, Prince Edward, in 1471. He had taken a different course to his brother Clarence, yet Edward must have known that, as a royal brother, Richard was powerful enough if he wished to cause equal difficulty. The rewards Richard received, whether in grants of land or in the support for his partition of the Warwick inheritance, only made Richard more powerful, stronger in terms of both wealth and military support. Yet Edward trusted his brother and his loyalty to the Yorkist dynasty; the consequences of that trust breaking down, the king must have considered, were too great, too awful, to contemplate.

PART TWO

PROTECTOR

5

'THE KING IS DEAD, LONG LIVE THE KING'

In contrast to the warrior-like figure that had conquered on the fields of Barnet and Tewkesbury, in middle age Edward IV had succumbed to the temptations of the court. 'In food and drink he was most immoderate', Dominic Mancini observed; 'it was his habit, so I have learned, to take an emetic for the delight of gorging his stomach once more. For this reason and for the ease, which was especially dear to him after his recovery of the crown, he had grown fat in the loins, whereas previously he had been not only tall but rather lean and active.'[1]

The Crowland chronicler, who seems to have had a window seat looking into the dynamics of power at the Yorkist court, was harsher still in his description of the king as a 'gross man so addicted to conviviality, vanity, drunkenness, extravagance, and passion' that 'in his own day he was thought to have indulged too intemperately his own passions and desire for luxury'.[2] Thomas More, writing years later, confirmed how Edward, who had once been 'of visage lovely, of body mighty, strong, and clean made', had in 'his later days' through an 'over-liberal diet' grown 'somewhat corpulent and burly', though 'nevertheless not uncomely'.[3] Edward's health seems to have declined in his final years: one later chronicler, Edward Hall, believed that Edward had contracted a malignant 'quartan' fever during his 1475 French expedition, a form of malaria from which he never recovered and which was aggravated by an excess of food. Yet it was a surprise to many when, around the time of the Easter feast, 'the king, neither worn out with old age nor yet seized with any known kind of malady, the cure of which would not have appeared easy in the case of a person of more humble rank, took to his bed'.[4] Mancini wrote that the king had been taken ill while out on a fishing trip on the Thames. Edward, 'being a tall man and very fat though not to the point of deformity', the Italian wrote, had 'allowed the damp cold to strike his vitals, when one day he was taken in a small boat, with those whom he had bidden go fishing, and watched their sport too eagerly. He there contracted the illness.'[5]

News leaked out from the court that the king was seriously ill, and unlikely to recover. On 7 April, at York, it was shown by the mayor how the previous day news had arrived 'that our sovereign lord the king is deceased and passed to God of whose soul shall God have mercy; where for my lord the dean desired my lord the mayor and all my masters his brethren to be this day afternoon at the Minster at the dirge of our said sovereign lord and to mourn at his mass'.[6] The news was premature. In spite of his worsening condition, Edward managed to turn his attention to the prospect of his young son's inheritance, seeking to heal old wounds at court.

William, Lord Hastings, now in his fifties, had been one of the king's most loyal companions at court. Having placed the teenage king on the throne in 1461, Hastings was to be a constant cornerstone of the Yorkist regime. Throughout Edward's reign, he occupied the office of chamberlain, a position that controlled access to the king. Hastings had also been granted the captaincy of Calais in 1471, just a year after the same office had been granted to Anthony, Earl Rivers. Both offices afforded Hastings the ability not only to control royal patronage, but also to command a large body of men, the largest standing garrison controlled by the crown. Hastings's relationship with Rivers was perhaps naturally strained, given their rivalry over Calais, but Hastings had also fallen out with the queen, who had grown jealous not only of 'the great favour the king bare him' but also for the fact 'that she thought him secretly familiar with the king in wanton company'.[7] Their mother's disapproval does not seem to have prevented her own sons, Thomas and Richard Grey, together with one of her brothers, Sir Edward Woodville, from becoming some of the principal 'promoters and companions of his vices', for it seems that Hastings had also begun a separate feud with Thomas Grey, marquess of Dorset, having quarrelled with him 'over the mistresses whom they had abducted, or attempted to entice from each other'.[8] Mancini described how the feud between Hastings and Thomas Grey had led 'the suborned informers of each' to threaten 'a capital charge against the other', while the Crowland chronicler noted that 'much ill will indeed had long existed' between Hastings and the Woodvilles.[9] Matters seemed to have got out of hand in August 1482, when one of Hastings's own men, John Edwards, confessed before the king and council that he had made false allegations against Dorset and Rivers while at Calais, but only because he had been 'in fear of his life' and of being placed in the 'breke' by his master.[10] The fact that copies of Edwards's confession were prepared, undoubtedly for circulation, suggests that the Woodvilles considered the matter serious enough to make capital out of it.[11]

Two days before his death, Mancini claimed, Edward had summoned and cajoled Hastings and Dorset to become 'reconciled' to one another; 'yet, as the event showed, there still survived a latent jealousy'.[12] The king also sought to revise his final will and testament, altering his previous testament that had been drawn up on the eve of his journey to France in 1475. Then Edward had appointed the queen to act as regent in the event of his death and the accession of his infant son. The Crowland chronicler wrote how 'on his death-bed', Edward had 'added some codicils thereto'.[13] Any revisions to his original will do not survive; however, it seems that the king did at some stage after 1475 make changes to his will, for the list of executors drawn up eight years previously does not match the list of executors who took charge of the king's goods after his death. Evidence that Edward did indeed add 'several codicils' to his will comes from a petition of the dean and canons of Windsor, who later recalled how the king, in the 'time of his sickness before his death' and 'having great remorse of conscience', 'right straightly charged by coporall oaths on a book' that Queen Elizabeth, together with the archbishops of York and Ely, 'and others to endeavour themselves to relief the said knights . . . surely to be helped and relieved in discharging of his conscience'.[14]

If the Windsor petition is correct, then it seems that the queen, Thomas Rotherham, archbishop of York, and John Morton, the bishop of Ely, had been witnesses to these final changes to the king's will. The Crowland chronicler, himself an insider at the king's court, wrote how Edward drew

up the alterations with his own salvation in mind: 'Those who were present at the time of his death bear witness to this; to them, especially to
those whom he left as executors of his last will, he declared, in distinct
and Catholic form, that it was his intention that satisfaction, in whole or
by voluntary composition without extortion, should be given to all men
to whom he was a debtor through some form of contract, fraud, extortion or for any other reason whatsoever . . . in consequence all his faithful
men were given hope that he would not be cheated of his eternal reward',
adding that 'long before his illness he made a full testament, as one who
had adequate wealth to discharge it, with many executors selected upon
mature consideration to do his will'.[15] The will Edward drew up in 1475,
before journeying to France, survives, indicating the extensive measures
the king had made for the payments of his debts, to provide for his younger
son, Richard, and dowries for his daughters Elizabeth and Mary of 10,000
marks each. His heir was to continue any grants he had made to 'divers
of our Lords as well of our blood as other and also Knights, Squires and
divers other our true and loving subjects and servants' who had 'faithfully
and lovingly assisted us and put them in the extreme jeopardy of their
lives, losses of their lands and goods in assisting us as well about the recovery of our Crown and Realm of England as other divers seasons and
times of jeopardy'.[16]

Even if Edward did add several codicils to his will, the surviving frame-
work of the 1475 document would have remained the same, along with the
expectation that all existing royal grants should be not only continued,
but that these rights of inheritance should not be tampered with as the
king's expressed final wish. Most of the will, however, was devoted to Edward's own elaborate designs for his new chantry at Windsor, with his
tomb as its centrepiece. He was to be buried 'low in the ground, and upon
the same a stone to be laid and wrought with the figure of Death with
a scutcheon of our Armour and writings convenient about the borders
of the same remembering the day and year of our decease'; over this a
vault was to be constructed, upon which would be built an altar and tomb
effigy 'of silver and gilt or at the least copper and gilt'. Already, perhaps
anticipating his demise, Edward had ordered thirty-three casks of touch-
stone, black marble from the Low Countries, for the construction of the
monument.[17]

The king's decline was clearly both sudden and unexpected, taking everyone by surprise. As the king's health worsened, key political figures remained absent from court. His brother Richard was stationed in the north, while his heir, Edward, Prince of Wales, remained at Ludlow, under the supervision of his maternal uncle, Anthony Woodville, Earl Rivers.

Edward IV died in the early hours of Wednesday, 9 April, at the Palace of Westminster, ten days after his illness had begun. Within hours of the king's death, early in the morning, Lord Audley and Lord Berkeley journeyed to the mayor of London upon the orders of the royal council, 'to show and give knowledge how that the King is past out of this present life this last night'.[18] They brought with them orders that 'for the safeguard of the city and in keeping of the peace' all officers of the city were to be summoned. Constables within the city were to be given 'commandment and charge to see the peace be kept every to their power, and not to provoke, do or cause any debate or strife with any stranger' while 'every person' was to 'be ready in harness if need should so require'.[19] The apprehension and uncertainty caused by the king's premature death is reflected in a letter by John Gigur, the warden of Tattershall College in Lincolnshire, to his patron William Waynflete, the bishop of Winchester, written on 19 April. 'I beseech you to remember', Gigur wrote, 'in what jeopardy your College of Tattershall standeth in at this day; for now our Sovereign Lord the king is dead we wete [know] not who shall be our lord nor who shall have the rule about us.'[20]

A meeting of the royal council was immediately called. Letters would need to be sent to Prince Edward, now Edward V, at Ludlow informing him of his father's death and at the same time ordering his household to make the journey to the capital, in order to be crowned. Regardless of the king's intentions, it was clear that no one was prepared for minority rule. Few had expected Edward to die at the young age of forty-one, leaving a twelve-year-old heir. While Edward V was four years short of his own majority and therefore too young to take the reins of government, he was old enough to possess a growing strength of feeling and opinion.

The new council seems to have been nearly an all-Woodville affair; the

Crowland chronicler described how the councillors met 'attending the queen at Westminster'. The king's treasurer, the elderly earl of Essex, had predeceased Edward IV by a matter of days, while the new king's uncle, Richard, remained at his estates in the north. William, Lord Hastings, remained a lone voice on the council in the capital, suspicious of the potential for the Woodvilles to seize power completely.

In spite of Edward IV's attempt to reconcile Hastings and the Woodvilles on his deathbed, it seems that Hastings's suspicions of the queen's kin lingered on. Hastings was hardly prepared for Rivers to arrive in the capital and dominate the king and country. As the king's chamberlain, Hastings feared for his own position. If the queen's family intended to control possession of the king, then they would need to appoint a more sympathetic chamberlain. Hastings's role as captain of Calais might also be under threat, especially since the position had been previously coveted by Rivers. 'He was afraid', the Crowland chronicler wrote, 'that if supreme power fell into the hands of the queen's relatives they would then sharply avenge the alleged injuries done to them by that lord. Much ill-will, indeed, had long existed between the Lord Hastings and them.'[21]

Hastings's first concern involved the number of men that Rivers was intending to bring with him, accompanying the king from Ludlow to the capital. Hastings feared the prospect of the Woodvilles seizing power simply through the number of armed men who might flood through the city gates upon the king's arrival. At a council meeting called shortly after Edward IV's death, the Crowland chronicler noted how 'various arguments were put forward by some people as to the number of men which might be considered adequate for a young prince on a journey of this kind. Some suggested more, some less, with other people indeed leaving to the judgement of him who is bound by no law the number of men which his faithful followers might bring.'[22] There were, however, 'more foresighted members of the council' present, who believed that 'the uncles and brothers on the mother's side should be absolutely forbidden to have control of the person of the young man until he came of age'. If the queen's relatives 'who were most influential with the prince' were allowed to bring with them 'an immoderate number of horse', then it would be impossible to bridle the Woodvilles' power. Hastings dug in and, continuing his argument, threatened that if the new king 'did not come with a modest force' he would 'rather flee' to Calais.[23] The reasoning was enough to persuade Queen Elizabeth, who, 'desirous of extinguishing every spark of murmuring and unrest', wrote to the king at Ludlow to arrive in London with no more than 2,000 men. Hastings had won the argument; 'the number was also pleasing to the aforesaid lord', the chronicler observed.[24]

If Hastings had been able to win over the council to take his initial concerns seriously, still the council was determined to have Edward V crowned as early as possible. A coronation date was set for the first Sunday of the coming month, 4 May. While the Crowland chronicler noted that the entire council was united on 'one consideration', that 'all who were present keenly desired that this prince should succeed his father in all his glory', still Edward was a child, who would need to rely on those close to him to rule and govern effectively. To crown the young king aged just twelve would be to declare him of age to rule. Edward was two years short of the expiry of his governorship as prince, and four years younger than the age of majority his royal uncles had attained. It was obvious that Edward was too young to rule alone, but, constitutionally, the very act of coronation would mean that there would be no need for a formal minority council or protectorate to rule on behalf of the king.

In crowning the young king, effectively declaring him 'of age', the Woodvilles would be able to dominate Edward from behind the scenes. It seems that there was growing disquiet that this was not what Edward IV had intended on his deathbed, when he added some final codicils to his will. Rumours had begun to circulate that the king had instead expressed his desire for his brother Richard, duke of Gloucester, to become Protector during his son's minority. Mancini had heard that Richard had been appointed Protector by the king in his will, or at least that 'men say that in the same will he appointed as protector of his children and realm his brother Richard'.[25] John Rous also believed that Edward's 'ordinance' had made Richard 'protector of England'.[26] If this was the case, the Woodvilles were determined to remove any possibility of Richard sharing power. Dominic Mancini believed that at the council meeting a discussion around the possibility of Richard becoming the king's Protector had also taken place:

Two opinions were propounded. One was that the duke of Gloucester should govern, because Edward in his will had so directed, and because by law the government ought to devolve on him. But this was the losing resolution; the winning was that the government should be carried on by many persons among whom the duke, far from being excluded, should be accounted the chief. By this means the duke would be given due honour, and the royal authority greater security; because it had been found that no regent ever laid down his office, save reluctantly, and from armed compulsion, whence civil wars had often arisen. Moreover, if the entire government were committed to one man he might easily usurp the sovereignty. All who favoured the queen's family voted for this proposal, as they were afraid that, if Richard took unto himself the crown or even governed alone, they, who bore the blame of Clarence's death, would suffer death or at least be ejected from their High estate.[27]

Mancini had heard from 'common report' that shortly after the council meeting had ended, William, Lord Hastings, immediately sent letters and messengers to Richard, reporting the council's decision. Advising the duke to 'hasten to the capital with a strong force', Hastings urged the duke to seize the king before reaching London. For his part, he warned Richard that 'he was alone in the capital and not without great danger, for he could scarcely escape the snares of his enemies', the Woodvilles, especially since 'their old hatred' had been aggravated by his friendship with the duke.[28]

Richard had remained at York, where he had organised a requiem for his dead brother, 'with an appropriate company, all dressed in mourning'. During the ceremony, 'full of tears', Richard took it upon himself to bind 'by oath, all the nobility of those parts in fealty to the king's son; he himself swore first of all'.[29] Receiving Hastings's message, Richard decided to act. The duke wrote the 'most pleasant' letters to Queen Elizabeth, consoling her and at the same time promising 'to come and offer submission, fealty and all that was due from him to his lord and king, Edward V, the first-born son of his brother the dead king'.[30] According to Mancini, who seems to have been able to read a copy of the letter, Richard also wrote to the council, declaring how 'He had been loyal to his brother Edward, at home and abroad, in peace and war, and would be, if only permitted, equally loyal to his brother's son, and to all his brother's issue, even female, if perchance, which God forbid, the youth should die. He would expose his life to every danger that the children might endure in their father's realm.' Richard also asked the council to take his own 'deserts into consideration, when disposing of the government, to which he was entitled by law, and his brother's ordinance'. In particular, 'he reminded them that nothing contrary to law and his brother's desire could be decreed without harm'.[31]

Richard seems to have been seeking what he believed was his right, as dictated by the late king's will. He had little reason to personally despise the Woodvilles. He himself had benefited from the queen's support in his dispute with his brother Clarence over the Neville patrimony ten years earlier, and they had mutually benefited from Clarence's demise, while he had established a good relationship with Rivers, who Mancini admitted was 'always considered a kind, serious and just man' who had 'injured nobody, though benefitting many'. Just a few weeks earlier, Rivers had sought to settle a local land dispute near his estates in Norfolk with his neighbour Roger Townshed, agreeing that the matter should be settled by the arbitration of the duke of Gloucester himself: it remains highly unlikely that Rivers would have agreed to appoint Richard to make an impartial judgement over his lands if he regarded the duke as his enemy.[32]

When the contents of Richard's letter were published, Mancini saw how it 'had a great effect on the minds of the people'. Already he had seen how the duke's popularity had stemmed from 'a belief in his probity'; now voices 'began to support him openly and aloud; so that it was commonly said by all that the duke deserved the government'.[33] Some in the council reportedly argued that the council should wait until Richard was present before any decision was taken, and that the decision should not be 'hurried through'. Without Richard's assent, they argued, 'the duke could only accede reluctantly, and perhaps might upset everything'. According to Mancini, to this the queen's son, Thomas, marquess of Dorset, replied, 'We are so important, that even without the king's uncle we can make and enforce these decisions.'[34]

Letters were sent by the council to the new king, Edward V, at Ludlow, which were received on 14 April. Two days later, the young king wrote to the borough of King's Lynn, ominously a Woodville stronghold, summoning their immediate presence in the capital for the king's coronation. The letter may have been issued in the new king's name, but had been clearly drafted for him, no doubt by Rivers, seeking the support of townships to assemble men to reach the capital as soon as possible.

With the Woodvilles still dominant, preparations for the new king's coronation continued. The city planned for his entrance into the capital, ordering that 410 citizens from fifty-two companies dressed in murrey gowns be ready on horseback, prepared to welcome Edward's arrival.[35] Three days later, with news of the king's arrival still forthcoming, the Mercers' Company ordered that thirty members be ready on horseback to receive the king, 'at such time as by the Mayor shall be commanded', in Hornsey Park, though a fine of forty shillings would be accepted if members were absent when they were finally called.[36] On 18 April a prayer was prepared for a convocation 'but it was not spoken at this time', remembering 'the new prince of excellent character and sweetest hope, our dread king Edward V, lady Elizabeth the queen mother, all the royal progeny', but with no specific reference to Richard himself as the king's Protector.[37] Meanwhile the queen, together with the court and council, proceeded to Windsor on 16 April to prepare for the late king's funeral, which took place four days later.

Edward IV's body had been laid upon a board at Westminster Palace, naked except for a loincloth, so that the lords, mayor and aldermen could gaze upon it, content that no foul play had been involved in his death. The body was then embalmed, wrapped in waxed linen and clothed, with a cap of estate on its head, and its feet shod in red leather, before lying in state for eight days at St Stephen's Chapel in Westminster, watched over by members of the household as requiem masses were constantly heard. On 17 April, Edward's body was placed on a bier and covered with a cloth of gold, to be carried into Westminster Abbey by fifteen knights and esquires of the king's body, his most trusted household men. The procession was led by the Chancellor, Archbishop Thomas Rotherham, nine bishops and two abbots, while before the bier walked Thomas, Lord Howard, carrying Edward's own banner. A parade of noblemen and the king's closest followers walked behind the procession, including Hastings and Thomas, Lord Stanley. A life-sized wooden image of the king, known as a 'similitude', had been constructed; this was now placed beside the bier, dressed in royal clothes and crowned, carrying an orb and sceptre, as the entire procession made their offerings in the abbey. The following morning, 18 April, the funeral procession left the abbey, leaving the capital via Charing Cross, before coming to rest overnight at Syon Abbey. On 19 April the procession carried on through Eton, where the bishops of Lincoln and Ely censed the corpse again, before arriving at Windsor and the dead king's new chapel dedicated to St George. That night the body was guarded by a company of nine lords and many from the king's household. On 20 April, final masses were celebrated by Archbishop Rotherham and the bishops of Lincoln and Durham, before offerings were made that would come to rest upon the tomb, including Edward's shield, sword and helmet. The controller of the household, Sir William Parr, clad in full armour and bearing a battle-axe head downwards as 'the man of arms' led the offerings of cloths of gold, before the coffin was lowered into the tomb. As custom dictated, the great officers of the household cast their broken staves of office into the grave, a sign that their service to their ruler had finally ended; the heralds did likewise with their coats of arms. Yet their service would continue afresh, and they were immediately presented with new coats, crying out, 'Le roy est vif! Le roy est vif!' The king is dead, long live the king: even Queen Elizabeth attended the funeral, not in her capacity as Edward's widow, but as the mother of Edward V.

With the old regime now buried, men eagerly anticipated the next. After Edward's funeral, the Crowland chronicler wrote: 'everyone looked forward to the eagerly-desired coronation day of the new king'.[38]

It was during his visit to York that Richard seems to have received a message from Henry Stafford, the duke of Buckingham, who had sent Sir Humphrey Percival to meet Richard.[39] If there was one member of the nobility whose support Richard believed he could count on, it was Buckingham. Dominic Mancini had learnt that the duke of Buckingham, 'since he was of the highest nobility, was disposed to sympathise with another noble: more especially because he had his own reasons for detesting the queen's kin'. 'When he was younger', Mancini explained, 'he had been forced to marry the queen's sister, whom he scorned to wed on account of her humble

origin.'[40] Buckingham may have been dissatisfied with his marriage to a
Woodville, though this had not prevented him from producing an heir. It
seems more likely that Buckingham's greatest grievance lay in the king's
treatment of his own inheritance, and in particular the landed estates of
Humphrey de Bohun, the earl of Hertford, who had died in 1373, yet whose
lands were inherited jointly by his daughters Mary, who had married Henry
IV, and Eleanor, who had married the youngest son of Edward III, Thomas
of Woodstock. The heiress of that marriage was Anne, the wife of Edmund
Stafford, 5th earl of Stafford – the mother of Humphrey Stafford, 1st duke
of Buckingham, and great-grandmother of the present duke. On the death
of Henry VI and his son, Edward, in 1471, the Lancastrian share of the inheritance should have been passed to the Staffords as sole remaining heirs.
Edward IV, however, was determined to claim the lands as his own, passing an Act of Attainder against Henry VI, leading to the forfeiture of his
lands to the crown. Unsurprisingly, with the lands providing an important
source of patronage, Edward remained stubbornly unwilling to overturn
the attainder on the lands or to allow Buckingham to enjoy what he must
have considered his rightful inheritance.[41]

It is unclear whether Richard or Buckingham made the first move to
contact the other, though Thomas More believed that soon after receiving
Hastings's messages warning him about the Woodville dominance in the
capital, Richard had contacted those 'whomsoever he perceived wither
at variance' with the Woodvilles, 'some by mouth, some by writing and
secret messengers', that 'it neither was reason nor in any wise to be suffered that the young king, their master and kinsman, should be in the
hands of custody of his mother's kindred, sequestered in manner from
their company and attendance'.[42]

Richard is not known to have had a close relationship with Buckingham
previously; Buckingham accompanied Edward IV on his 'great enterprise'
thirsting for military glory in France in 1475, yet like Richard had been
disappointed at the king's willingness to sign a peace agreement, returning to England early. The two dukes had also been acquainted with each
other during Clarence's trial, for which Buckingham had acted as the lead
member of the jury, pronouncing sentence upon the duke. Yet, for Richard,
Buckingham represented a branch of the nobility who viewed themselves
and their ancient lineage as distinct from the Woodville parvenus. It

was a distinction that Richard intended to exploit to the full if he was to secure the protectorship of the king, an office he considered to be his right.

The two dukes, having 'exchanged views', decided to both write to the young king as he prepared to depart from Ludlow, in order to discover what date he intended to arrive at the capital, and in particular what route his party would take, 'so coming from the country they could alter their course and join him, that in their company his entry to the city might be more magnificent'.[43]

Richard must have departed southwards for the capital soon after holding his vigil at York, and had left the city by 23 April.[44] The young king and his household meanwhile had yet to leave Ludlow by 23 April, where they celebrated St George's Day, 'concluding with a splendid banquet'.[45] Intending to set out towards London the following day, after receiving the dukes' messages Edward and Rivers apparently agreed to their request. The route of the royal train seems to have been deliberately altered to accommodate a rendezvous with Richard marching from the north. While the shortest journey to Westminster from Ludlow should have been to the south-west, through Worcester, Gloucester and Oxford, the royal party took a more northerly route. Crossing the Severn at Bridgnorth, the royal party may have stayed at Upton Cresset, before travelling via Stratford-upon-Avon, Banbury and Buckingham to Grafton Regis, Rivers' family seat in Northamptonshire.

By the time Richard had reached Nottingham on 26 April, it had been agreed that the two parties should meet at Northampton before marching into the city, a significant detour for the king and his entourage. The king's entourage reached Northampton early; instead of entering the city, Edward ordered that his retinue should be broken up and occupy the surrounding villages so that the city itself would be 'more convenient to receive his uncle', with the king himself moving to nearby Stony Stratford. Having had little previous contact with his uncle, Edward seemed determined to please Richard with 'extreme reverence'. While he remained at Stony Stratford with just a few household men, the king sent Anthony, Earl Rivers, and Richard Grey, the king's half-brother, to meet Richard at Northampton and 'to submit everything that had to be done to the judgement of his paternal uncle'.[46]

By the time Rivers travelled back to Northampton, both Richard and Buckingham had arrived in the city and had lodged at 'a very strong place belonging to the duke'. Rivers was met by Richard, according to the Crowland chronicler, with 'a particularly cheerful and merry face'; sitting down to dinner at the duke's own table, Richard and Rivers spent the meal 'in very pleasant conversation', afterwards 'passing a great part of the night in conviviality'.[47] Buckingham arrived mid-way through the evening, and as the night wore on the three men retired to their separate lodgings for bed.

Nothing could have prepared Rivers or Grey for what would happen next. At dawn, as the party prepared to travel to Stony Stratford for Richard and Buckingham to present themselves to the new king, Richard gave the sudden order that Rivers and his men were to be arrested. The Crowland chronicler believed the plan had been hatched between Richard and Buckingham late the previous night, after Rivers had gone to bed, yet the ambush must have been more premeditated than this: Mancini had heard how the two dukes had already arranged for the surrounding roads to be watched, preventing 'any one informing the young king of these happenings before their arrival'. Rivers and Grey were immediately taken north, to be imprisoned at Sheriff Hutton, Richard's castle in Yorkshire.

Richard and Buckingham rode at full gallop to reach King Edward before the news reached the king's household of Rivers' arrest. When they arrived, they immediately seized the king's chamberlain, the aged Thomas Vaughan, while orders were issued that the king's household was to withdraw from Stony Stratford and 'should not come near any places where the king might go, on pain of death'.[48] With the king now isolated, and his Woodville adherents removed from his presence, he came face to face with his uncle for the first time since he had been a young child. Going down on bended knee and baring his head, Richard explained to his nephew that he had been forced to take action 'to safeguard his own person because he knew for certain that there were men close to the king who had sworn to destroy his honour and his life'.[49] According to Mancini, who may have been able to gather his information from one of the king's own household staff, having saluted Edward as their sovereign, Richard and Buckingham 'exhibited a mournful countenance'. They explained to Edward how his father's death had been caused by his ministers, who had 'but little regard for his honour, since they were accounted the companions and servants of his vices, and had ruined his health'. They intended to remove the same ministers from the king, since 'a child would be incapable of governing so great a realm by means of puny men'.[50] Richard himself accused them of conspiring

> towards his own death and of preparing ambushes both in the capital and on the road, which had been revealed to him by their accomplices. Indeed, he said it was common knowledge that they had attempted to deprive him of the office of regent conferred on him by his brother. Finally, he decided that these ministers should be utterly removed for the sake of his own security, lest he fall into the hands of desperate men, who from their previous licence would be ready to dare anything. He said that he himself, whom the king's father had approved, could better discharge all the duties of government, not only because of his experience of affairs, but also on account of his popularity. He would neglect nothing pertaining to the duty of a loyal subject and diligent Protector.

Edward was not prepared to listen to his uncle. In a speech that must have taken Richard aback, the young king, 'possessing the likeness of his father's noble spirit besides talent and remarkable learning', replied that he had merely retained the ministers whom his father had recommended him, 'and relying on his father's prudence, he believed that good and faithful ones had been given him'. He himself had seen 'nothing evil in them' and instead 'wished to keep them unless otherwise proved to be evil . . . As for the government of the kingdom, he had complete confidence in the peers of the realm and the queen.' On hearing mention of Queen Elizabeth, Buckingham's patience snapped. 'It was not the business of women but of men to govern kingdoms', he is reported to have replied to the young king, adding curtly, 'if he cherished any confidence in her he had better relinquish it'. Instead, the king should 'place all his hope in his barons, who excelled in nobility and power'.[51]

Edward sensed he was fighting a losing battle. 'Perceiving their intention', the king decided to surrender himself into Richard's care, recognising that 'they were demanding rather than supplicating'.

In arresting Rivers and Grey, and seizing the king, Richard had transformed the political dynamic for ever. No one could have expected what had taken place at Stony Stratford: Rivers' and Grey's arrest had clearly come as a surprise to the earl himself, who only months before had been conducting friendly dealings with Richard. Arriving to dine with Richard and Buckingham, it is clear that Rivers did not suspect a thing. The consequences of the arrest were bound to reverberate across the country, for by his actions Richard had effectively pitched himself directly against the Woodvilles, opening up the potential for a new civil war. Yet it seems that this was a gamble which Richard had calculated he was willing to take. Above all, he believed that he had the dead king's wishes and right on his side. Loyalty to his brother seems to have extended even beyond the grave.

If Richard had made a miscalculation, it was that Edward V himself would recognise Richard's supremacy as his paternal uncle; perhaps he considered that the new king's loyalty would extend to his father's brother, just as Edward IV himself had recognised Richard's own importance as his only surviving brother. Edward V's defiance had demonstrated to Richard that he was wrong: the new king was himself a product of his Woodville kin; having been raised by Rivers and the queen's men, his loyalty lay first with them. The king's opposition to Richard's arrest of Rivers and Grey seems to have come as an equal surprise to Richard, yet it also demonstrated Edward V's own strength of spirit; he was hardly the vulnerable boy whom Richard had last seen at court in the early 1480s. Still, Richard must have considered, the king would come to be grateful for his efforts in securing his father's wishes. Richard fully considered it his legitimate responsibility as Protector to ensure that he had possession of the royal person. John Rous later wrote that Richard 'came upon him with a strong force at Stony Stratford and took the new king his nephew into his governance by right of his protectorship'.[52] The question here is whether Edward intended for his brother to be both the Protector of the Realm, and governor of the king's person, an office that in the past had been exclusively reserved for Rivers. By granting the protectorship to Richard, and the governorship of the king to Rivers, Edward may have considered that he had struck a sensible equilibrium of power that would allow both the paternal and the maternal sides of the new king's family to have an equal share in the responsibilities of government. Yet, in doing so, Edward had highlighted the weakness in the Woodvilles' authority: all that they had was the king's person. Richard also understood that the Woodvilles' power lay not in their own independent support base, for they had little if none at all, but in their possession of the king. With Edward in their hands, they were all-powerful; without him, they were nothing.

When news of Richard's seizure of the king reached the capital, panic ensued. 'The following night, when rumour of this had reached London', the Crowland chronicler wrote, 'Queen Elizabeth transferred herself with all her children into the sanctuary at Westminster.' 'In the morning', the chronicler recalled, 'you might have seen the partisans of one side and of the other, some sincerely, others dissimulating because of the confusing events, taking this side or that. Some collected their associates and stood by at Westminster in the name of the queen, others at London under the protection of Lord Hastings.'[53] The Chancellor, Archbishop Rotherham of York, was one of those willing to instantly take the queen's side, offering her the Great Seal, the possession of which would have given the Wood-villes the power to credibly raise men under its authority. Rotherham later seems to have had second thoughts about his rash actions, and managed to retain possession of the seal, perhaps when he realised that popular support for the Woodville cause in the capital was not strong enough to mount a challenge to Richard now that he had possession of the king. Mancini observed how when the news of Richard's and Buckingham's actions at Stony Stratford was announced, 'the unexpectedness of the event horrified everyone', yet when the Woodvilles attempted to raise an army and 'exhorted certain nobles who had come to the city, and others, to take up arms, they perceived that men's minds were not only irresolute, but altogether hostile to themselves. Some even said openly that it was more just and profitable that the youthful sovereign should be with his paternal uncle than with his maternal uncles and uterine brothers.'[54] Nevertheless, a 'sinister rumour' ran through the capital that Richard 'had brought his nephew not under his care, but into his power, so as to gain for himself the crown'. Richard wrote to both the council and the mayor, assuring them of his loyalty to the king. 'The contents of both letters were something after this fashion', Mancini reported:

He had not confined his nephew the king of England, rather he had rescued him and the realm from perdition, since the young man would have fallen into the hands of those who, since they had not spared either the honour or life of the father, could not be expected to have more regard for the youthfulness of the son. The deed had been necessary for his own safety and to provide for that of the king and kingdom. No one save only him had such solicitude for the welfare of King Edward and the preservation of the state. At an early date he and the boy would come to the city so that the coronation and all that pertained to the solemnity might be more splendidly performed.[55]

Richard's letter was read aloud both in the council chamber and in public. It had the desired effect: 'all praised the duke of Gloucester for his dutifulness towards his nephews and for his intention to punish their enemies'.[56] A surviving letter to Archbishop Bourchier of Canterbury, issued under Edward V's signet from Northampton though obviously penned under Richard's instruction, requesting the 'safeguard and sure keeping of the Great Seal of this our realm unto our coming to our city of London', indicates just how determined Richard was to reassure the council of his intentions. The tone of the letter was designed to appeal to the council's desire for unity, placating their fears of a takeover.

A surviving scrap of paper, upon which the new king, Richard and Buckingham had signed their names, with their accompanying mottoes, probably dates from these early few days, when Richard was attempting to win over the trust and friendship of his nephew. At the top of the parchment, Edward V has ascribed his name, followed by 'Richard Gloucester' and the motto, 'Lotaulte me lie', which translates as 'loyalty binds me'. Beneath Richard's signature, is the lavish signature 'Harry Buckingham' with his motto, 'Souvente me souvenir'.[57]

Other measures were taken to reassure the young king that his uncle had his best interests at heart, and was willing to indulge his wishes that some of those closest around him should be rewarded with royal favour. At St Albans, on 3 May, Edward sent letters appointing his chaplain, John Geffrey, to Pembridge parish church.[58]

Behind the scenes, however, even before entering the capital, Richard had begun to tighten his grip upon power. While Rivers and Richard Grey remained imprisoned, he was determined to act fast to weaken the Wood-ville threat that he must have realised might eventually pose a significant risk to his own position and security for the future. Immediately the illegal confiscation of Woodville lands began. On 2 May, a letter was sent out under the king's name to the farmers, tenants and inhabitants of lands in Woodham Martin, Essex, 'as Anthony Earl Rivers late had ... and to all other our officers, true liegemen and subjects hearing or seeing these our letters', that 'for divers causes and considerations us moving and by the advice of our most entirely beloved Uncle the duke of Gloucester' the lands had now been granted to Robert Bell, 'wherefore we will and charge you all and every of you that ye permit and suffer our said servant to occupy and enjoy the same lands and tenements without let or interruption as ye and every of you intend to avoid our grievious displeasure and answer unto us at your perils'.[59] The confiscations were being ordered by Richard himself, without the consent of the royal council as he now took matters into his own hands. Richard later observed that he had on 1 May 'given in commandment by a bill signed by our hand' to Thomas Stafford to occupy the property of Ludgarsale, 'and to do and exercise all manner things the same concerning by force of which commandment so given by our said bill'.[60]

On 4 May, Richard, Buckingham and Edward V entered London accompa-nied by 500 soldiers, where they were received with 'regal pomp'. Edward rode wearing blue velvet, while Richard, riding beside him, one observer noted, was dressed 'in black cloth, like a mourner'.[61] Thirty delegates from the mayor and aldermen of London and the city companies, clothed in murrey liveries, were each paid 13s 4d for the costs of their horses and har-nesses to ride to Hornsey Park to meet them; the Drapers' Company also sent thirty men, the Pewterers only five. Surviving company records reveal that the Goldsmiths spent 4½d on bread and drink at their hall as 'the riders were gathered to ride forth', with another 5d spent at Bishopsgate for 'a potell claret wine at their coming home'.[62]

Richard's determination to destroy the Woodvilles remained at the forefront of his mind even as he entered the capital in procession with the young king. 'As these two dukes were seeking at every turn to arouse hatred against the queen's kin, and to estrange public opinion from her relatives', Mancini recalled, 'they took especial pains to do so on the day they entered the city. For ahead of the procession they sent four wagons loaded with weapons bearing the devices of the queen's brothers and sons, beside criers to make generally known throughout the crowded places by whatsoever way they passed, that these arms had been collected by the duke's enemies and stored at convenient spots outside the capital, so as to attack and slay the duke of Gloucester coming from the country.'[63] Many men, Mancini observed, knew the charges to be false, 'because the arms in question had been placed there long before the late king's death for an altogether different purpose, when war was being waged against the Scots'. As a result, such mistrust only 'exceedingly augmented' the rumours that Richard himself coveted the throne.[64] Thomas More later wrote how Richard's men, as they made their way through the city, 'showed unto the people all the way as they went: "Lo, here be the barrels of harness that these traitors had privily conveyed in their carriage to destroy the noble lords withal."' Wise men, More wrote, were quick to reason that 'the intenders of such a purpose would rather have had their harness on their backs than to have bound them up in barrels', yet many of the 'common people' were apparently convinced, and clamoured for them to be hanged.[65]

After all the lords and city council, together with Richard and Buckingham, swore allegiance to the new king, Edward V was placed in the bishop of London's palace in the city, a public venue where the king would be both visible and accessible. John Rous wrote how Edward had his 'special tutor and diligent mentor in godly ways', John Alcock, removed from his household, 'like the rest', though he escaped imprisonment.[66] The young king was himself placed under guard, Mancini wrote, guarded in turn by Richard's and Buckingham's men, 'for they were afraid lest he should escape or be forcibly delivered from their hands'.[67] Buckingham was a constant presence. The duke was 'always at hand ready to assist Gloucester with his advice and resources', Mancini observed.

The same day Richard led his young nephew through the streets of the capital, elsewhere, on 4 May, George Neville died, aged just seventeen. His death may not have come as a surprise to Richard, who held the boy's wardship and probably had arranged for Neville to reside at one of his ducal households at Middleham or Sheriff Hutton. The consequences of the boy's death remained the same: Richard's tenure of the Neville estates in the north, essentially the entire power base that he had spent the past twelve years carefully cultivating, and from which the duke's new palatinate in south-west Scotland and Cumberland would be largely funded, was effectively no longer his. According to the terms set down in the division of the Warwick inheritance agreed by Parliament in 1475, George's death had reduced Richard's tenure from a hereditary one to a mere life estate: while Richard would for now be able to hold the lands as if a tenant, his son Edward would be unable to inherit them. Even Richard's tenure of the lands would not remain the same, for once the next male heir in line to the Neville inheritance, Richard, Lord Latimer, reached his majority in 1489, he would be entitled to reversions on the estates. Richard's own authority in these lands would be at risk of sharp decline, as his retainers would seek to have their own patents confirmed by Latimer.

The options available to Richard to address this sudden termination of his inheritance of the Neville estates were equally bleak. Even though the duke had managed to prevent a Woodville-dominated government from seizing the new king, and he himself was likely now to benefit as the king's paternal uncle and principal guardian, Richard could hardly expect that there would be any major alienations of royal property to the disinheritance of the crown during the young king's minority. Once the king was crowned, he would be able to form his own council, which was likely to witness the return of the Woodvilles, who would now have perfectly reasonable grounds to regard Richard as their enemy, and to oppose any increase in the duke's patronage. The marquess of Dorset even held the wardship and marriage of Clarence's son and heir, Edward, earl of Warwick, and would understandably most likely oppose outright any repartition of the Warwick inheritance. There was nothing, it seemed, that Richard could do to prevent his own life's work seemingly slip away from him.

It cannot be known whether Richard, riding into the capital with his nephew the king, understood the precariousness of his own situation. Yet, in less than a month, the duke had been forced to turn against his brother's own family in sheer desperation. Whether he genuinely believed that his brother had in his dying days chosen to make him Protector or not, Richard had no other option than to seize the only opportunity that could just guarantee his political survival.

6

'PROTECTOR AND DEFENDER OF THIS OUR REALM'

The arrival of the new king seems to have stabilised the fraught situation in the capital. By 8 May, John, Lord Howard, paid for men he had requested from his estates to be sent home.[1] The business of government under the new monarch continued as if uninterrupted. 'In his name the laws of the kingdom were enforced at Westminster and throughout the realm in the accustomed way. Coins were struck in his name, and all royal honours were paid to him as usual', wrote John Rous.[2] The mood seemed good; 'without fail, everyone hoped for and awaited peace and prosperity in the kingdom'. William, Lord Hastings, the Crowland chronicler observed, was 'bursting with joy over this new world'. Nothing had happened, Hastings asserted, 'except to transfer the government of the kingdom from two blood relatives of the queen to two nobles of the blood royal'. Moreover, this had been accomplished, 'without any killing and with only so much bloodshed in the affair as might have come from a cut finger'.[3]

Richard's recent letters to the council, combined with his track record of consistent loyalty to the royal dynasty that had seen the duke swear oaths of fealty to his nephew in 1471, 1477, and most recently in York and Stony Stratford, provided the reassurance that the duke's fidelity to his nephew the king and the new regime could hardly be doubted. Richard's insistence that all the lords and aldermen of the city of London should again take an oath of fealty to the king helped to win over any remaining resistance to his seizure of the young king; 'because this promised best for future prosperity', the Crowland chronicler wrote, 'it was performed with pride and joy by all'. In contrast, the behaviour of the queen and the Woodvilles had come close to the incitement of civil war. Dominic Mancini observed how they 'began collecting an army, to defend themselves and to set the young King from the clutches of the dukes', while the Crowland chronicler had noted with some concern how immediately after news of Richard's arrest of Rivers reached the capital, troops had begun to gather across the city.[4] Already the Woodvilles had made clear their attempts to raise armed resistance to protect their own interests; Richard, meanwhile, had provided reassurance, claiming to be acting in the best interests of the nation.

At a council meeting on 10 May it was decided that Richard would be appointed Protector of the Realm. In his receiving the office, contemporaries viewed Richard's appointment as being identical to the historical parallel of 1422, when, in the minority of the baby Henry VI, Humphrey, duke of Gloucester, had been made Protector. The Crowland chronicler described how Richard now received 'that solemn office which had once fallen to Duke Humphrey of Gloucester', indicating that Richard could only exercise 'this authority with the consent and good will of all the lords, commanding and forbidding in everything like another king, as occasion demanded'.[5] Richard may have been appointed Protector, but his role was to be cast almost in the original format as the Woodvilles had intended, as the first among equals on the council, though constrained in his own power by the council's ultimate authority to take decisions.[6] Richard quickly realised how constrained his powers as Protector would be.

At the same council meeting, he also discovered that his tenure as Protector would be limited to just weeks, rather than the years he might have envisaged by occupying the office until the king turned sixteen. The king's official coronation date was set for 22 June, with Parliament to be summoned for three days later, on 25 June. The arranging of the dates indicates that Parliament was to be opened by a king of full age, who had obtained his majority. There was no question that Edward V would not succeed to the full powers of his kingship. Evidence of the king's own sign manual, his signature represented by his initials, survives on seven warrants of the Great Seal: the fact that the king's signature was required indicates that not only was Edward V being inducted into government and taking an active role in the council's proceedings, or at least being made aware of council business, but it was also clear that the king was not considered a puppet ruler; his signature commanded an authority that seems to have been needed during Richard's protectorate.

Still, Richard was keen to stamp what authority he could on the royal council. New officers were quickly appointed. After his attempt to send the Great Seal to Queen Elizabeth, it was obvious that Archbishop Rotherham would have to be removed from his office as Chancellor. On 10 May, the archbishop was stripped of his office, reportedly after Richard had learnt that he had been the main 'champion' of the young king in previous council meetings, and, 'he supposed, would be faithful to Edward's heirs come what might'.[7] Rotherham was replaced by John Russell, the bishop of Lincoln, described by Mancini as 'a man of equally great learning and piety', who seems to have had initial reservations about taking on the role, being 'much against his will'. In spite of the king's royal sign manual being attached to a series of early instructions, Richard's dominance of proceedings is clearly evident, with the king acting as a cipher to the new Protector. A letter written on 15 May, 'at our city of London', had been signed by Edward, though it had been issued with 'the advice of our dearest Uncle the Duke of Gloucester protector and defensor of this our realm of England'; only as an afterthought were added the words above the line that had been written, 'and other lords of our council'.[8] On 19 May, Edward wrote to the keeper of the gaol at Nottingham Castle, Edward Holt, ordering him to relinquish his duties, 'upon pain of your allegiance', to be taken over by Robert Legh, 'for certain causes and considerations to us moving and by the advice of our most right entirely beloved uncle the duke of Gloucester protector and defender of this our realm of England during our young age'. This time there was no mention of the council, while the letter had been countersigned at the bottom by Richard himself.[9]

Richard began to exert more control over the young king's household. On 27 May, Richard's northern follower John Gunthorpe was appointed Keeper of the Privy Seal.[10] After briefly lodging the royal court at the bishop's palace at St Paul's, it was decided that the king would need to be transferred to more appropriate lodgings; according to the Crowland chronicler, discussions had being ongoing for several days in the council 'about the removal of the king to some other, more spacious place'. Some members of the council suggested the Hospital of St John in Clerkenwell, others Westminster; however, the proximity of the queen and her

daughters in sanctuary there would have made this location seem somewhat inappropriate. Buckingham suggested the Tower: it was secure and
was traditionally the location where kings resided before their coronation
procession to Westminster; certainly its rooms were viewed as a place
of security, rather than holding any of the sinister connotations that the
building would later come to represent. The duke's opinion, the Crowland
chronicler wrote, 'was accepted by all, even by those who did not wish it'.[11]

Richard's immediate priority was to limit the authority of the Woodvilles,
removing them from any chance of a return to power entirely. To Richard's astonishment, not only had Queen Elizabeth fled into sanctuary, but
other members of the Woodville family were still missing. He arrived in
the capital to discover that the queen's brother Edward Woodville had fled
to the south coast, preparing to sail a fleet into the Channel to combat
French piracy. Staggeringly, in a display of the Woodville dominance of the
council before Richard's arrival, Edward Woodville had been granted
£2,065 13s 4d for the wages for 2,000 men for two months, with an additional £856 13s 4d as a reward for the captains of two carracks that had not
previously been used, £226 7s 7d was also spent on ordnance to be brought
out of the Tower. Four hundred marks were also paid to the marquess
of Dorset for taking a thousand men to sea until Michaelmas.[12] In total,
these measures cost £3,670, absorbing all of Edward IV's cash reserves.
But Woodville had gone even further than this in amassing a fortune to
set sail with. Arriving at the south coast, Sir Edward Woodville also made
an indenture with the patron of 'the great carrack then lying at Hampton
Water' that Woodville would take a staggering £10,250 in English gold
coin from the boat, on the condition that Woodville and 'his friends in
England' should repay the money within three months.[13]

Woodville's intentions were patently clear. The money would help provide for the wages of any troops or mercenaries that he might need for
the future overthrow of Richard's protectorate, placing the Woodvilles
back in charge. For Richard, it presented an opportunity to claim that the
Woodvilles had stolen the dead king's treasure from the Tower to pay for
these enterprises. It was a convenient rumour that reached the ears of both
the Crowland chronicler and Mancini, who wrote how 'it was commonly

believed that the late king's treasure, which had taken years and such pains to gather, was divided between the queen, the marquess [Thomas, marquess of Dorset] and Edward'.[14] It was also untrue. If Richard had expected the Royal Exchequer to contain any such 'treasure', upon arriving at the capital to discuss the royal finances with the council, he was to be disappointed. The financial records show that Edward IV had left just £490 in reserve in his Exchequer, and £710 in his chamber coffers. This would not be enough even to pay for the dead king's funeral.

Nevertheless, any convenient fiction was welcome if it might help to discredit the queen's family. Richard was now desperate to hasten their fall even further. Richard still hoped to move against Rivers and Richard Grey. Having forcibly removed them to be imprisoned at his castle at Sheriff Hutton, the duke knew that they were hardly likely to forgive their arrest, and would seek revenge if released. Yet the coronation date approaching would mark the end of his own protectorship, when the new king, divinely appointed to rule, could order their release. If Richard was to avoid the recriminations that he feared could take place within just a few weeks, he would need to act fast. It was clear that Rivers and Grey would need to be removed altogether. Richard was willing to work through the traditional and accepted authority of the council to achieve this. He had hoped to persuade the council that they should be convicted 'of preparing ambushes and of being guilty of treason itself'. Convinced his authority as Protector would force the council to act, he was soon to be disappointed. The council refused to condemn Rivers and those of the king's household who had been arrested by Richard and Buckingham, since 'there appeared no certain case', arguing further that 'even had the crime been manifest, it would not have been treason, for at the time of the alleged ambushes he was neither regent nor did he hold any other public office'.[15] The council's decision represented a significant blow, not only to Richard's authority as Protector, but also to his hopes of removing the Woodvilles altogether before the king was crowned. Without their removal, upon Edward V's formal accession, Rivers and his Woodville associates would most likely be freed, able to seek their revenge against the duke.

Most pressing, however, was the need to prevent Edward Woodville sailing with his fleet across the Channel. With the council's permission, Richard was able to denounce Edward Woodville if he refused to disband his fleet, appointing 'a period of grace to allow for the return or desertion of officers of the soldiers and masters of the ships, who were under Edward's command'. If they refused, they would 'be proclaimed as outlaws, and he proclaimed that their goods were to be confiscated'. Meanwhile 'considerable rewards' were offered 'for anyone taking Edward alive or dead'.[16] Richard moved quickly to increase defences around the Solent. On 9 May William Berkeley was placed in charge of the Isle of Wight, while officials at Porchester Castle, where Woodville was constable, were sent orders to deliver the fortress to William Ovedale.[17] On 10 May, orders were given to Sir Thomas Fulford and John Halwell 'to rig them in all haste and to go to the Downs among Sir Edward and his company', no doubt in an attempt to try and entice the fleet away from Woodville. Four days later, on 14 May, further orders were issued to Edward Brampton, John Welles and Thomas Grayson 'to go to the sea with ships to take Sir Edward Woodville', carrying with them 'a clause to receive all that will come except the Marquess, Sir Edward Woodville and Robert Ratcliffe'.[18] The city of Canterbury even gave wine to Lord Cobham and other gentlemen sent by the king to arrest Woodville.[19]

   Caught up in the stand-off were two Genoese ships that had been lent to Edward Woodville by Genoese merchants, innocently under the impression that the ships had been requested by the government. The Genoese, hearing of the proclamation, realised that their own goods and ships were at risk. Yet if they refused to go to sea with Woodville, they also risked being plundered by his own troops. On each of their two ships Woodville had managed to place his own men, 'ones that by every kind of tie were most devoted to the commander'. It was only after the Genoese managed to get their English crew drunk enough and 'sodden' with wine, so that 'they now lay down upon the decks' or else 'wandered about overcome with drowsiness' that they were able to eventually trick them into going below decks, 'where they might rest agreeably', before calling up each soldier individually, to be 'trussed up with ropes and chains'. After the other Genoese ship had managed to overcome their English soldiers in a similar fashion as part of the 'joint plot', 'the Genoese began to sound trumpets and horns and hoisting the king's banners they announced that they would obey the protector and the council'.[20]

The success of the proclamation resulted in nearly the entire fleet returning to port. The Genoese merchant Johannes Ambrosius de Nigrono was rewarded with £384 7s 6d for unspecified services on 4 June, suggesting that the desertion of the ships had proved pivotal in destroying Woodville's fleet, with Mancini writing that 'the rest of the fleet followed the lead of the Genoese'. Woodville, however, managed to escape with two ships, most likely the *Falcon* and the *Trinity*, sailing for the Breton coast. On board, the treasure that he had amassed was never seen again.[21]

Edward Woodville's flight emboldened Richard to take further action against the Woodvilles. Confiscation of Woodville lands and property began in earnest, despite there being no legal grounds for their forfeiture. Richard may have faced resistance in council over the decision, which perhaps explains why he decided to issue orders for the confiscation under his own signet rather than in the king's name.[22]

It seems that, behind the scenes, Richard was beginning to come to the conclusion that he would need to take matters into his own hands if he was to limit the Woodvilles' power and prevent their full rehabilitation. Whether Richard had fully thought through the consequences of his actions is uncertain, but further confiscations were extended to cover the wider Woodville family, to be placed in the hands of Richard's loyal supporters. On 14 May, Ightham Mote in Kent, the property of the queen's cousin Richard Haute, who had been arrested at Stony Stratford, was seized by one of Richard's northern associates, Sir Thomas Wortley. Five days later, on 19 May, Robert Pemberton was ordered to seize the lordship of Wemington and to make an inventory of all goods and cattle to 'be put in surety to our behove'. The letter was given under Richard's own signet, while Pemberton was urged not to fail in his task, 'as ye will have our good lordship'. Two days later, Richard wrote to the tenants and inhabitants of the lordship of Thorpwaterfield, explaining that for 'certain considerations' the lands had been 'committed and granted to our entirely beloved cousin Francis Lord Lovell . . . we therefore on the king our sovereign lord's behalf', Richard's letter continued, 'command and on our own charge you and every of you that incontinent upon the sight hereof you do avoid yourself from the possession and occupation of any office there, and accept and take him as ruler, keeper and receiver of the same, and suffer such his servants as he will depute to have rule under him there'. The reward, Richard hinted, was that 'ye will have our good lordship', although, if the tenants refused, they would 'answer at your perils'.[23] By 28 May, rents from Rivers's lands were being paid directly into the Exchequer, while the next day a steward was appointed for the earl's lands in Norfolk.[24]

Former servants of both Edward IV and the queen were also involved in the confiscations of Woodville lands. Robert Pemberton, an usher of Edward IV's chamber and who had been appointed to one of his first offices, as a park keeper in Northamptonshire, by the queen in 1468, was now prepared to help seize Woodville land.[25] One of Edward IV's esquires of the body, Walter Hungerford, petitioned the crown for the annuity of twenty marks formerly in the possession of Edmund Haute.[26] John Cotington petitioned for the parkership of Whitemead Park within the forest of Dean, 'which office one William Slatter now gone to sea with Sir Edward Woodville late had'. In doing so, Cotington highlighted his future service to the king 'and unto the right high and mighty prince Richard Duke of Gloucester your uncle protector and defensor of this your realm'.[27]

These measures, no matter how illegal, were met with little resistance. There was every sign that the former household servants of Edward IV were more than prepared to tolerate the fall of the Woodvilles. Where land, money and power were involved, ties of loyalty grew thin. Just as they had accepted Richard's seizure of the reins of power as Protector, so were they prepared to accept the consequences of the duke's attack upon the king's maternal family.

In spite of the recent upheavals, Richard had felt no need to alter the new royal administration, with any changes confined to filling gaps left by the removal of the Woodvilles. In Edward V's royal household, Richard did not surround the young king with his own men: many of the king's servants, such as esquires of the body John Norreys and Walter Hungerford, and the usher of the chamber, Edward Hardgill, who had attended Edward IV's funeral, continued to serve the king. In his appointments, Richard seems to have been content to continue to reward men from Edward IV's own household, who were equally content to maintain their support of the Yorkist establishment. Edward V was placed in the care of former servants of his father's household, in a clear indication that Richard intended to preserve the status quo.[28] Aside from the confiscations of Woodville land, this meant that for Richard's own supporters there was little patronage for the duke to bestow upon them: in any case, the duke seems to have given most available grants to his dead brother's servants, rather than his own. Yet if Richard was content to maintain the royal household of Edward IV, this desire was outweighed by the massive grants that the duke was prepared to make to his leading supporter, Henry, duke of Buckingham.

Beginning with Buckingham's appointment as justiciar and chamberlain of both north and south Wales on 15 May, together with the constableship and stewardship of all royal land in Shropshire, Herefordshire, Somerset, Dorset and Wiltshire, and the power to array troops in the same counties, the duke was to be given the right during the royal minority to exercise all royal patronage throughout all areas. In effect, Buckingham was to be given quasi-regal status: even the chancellor of the earldom of March, now under Buckingham's control, was ordered to take his commands from the duke. The following day, on 16 May, a separate grant gave Buckingham the constableship, stewardship and receivership of the duchy of Lancaster's Honour of Monmouth, along with the duchy of York's lordship of Ludlow. In addition, the duke was appointed as constable and steward of Usk and Conway castles, and was to take possession of all the castles in north and south Wales, 'and as large fees, wages and rewards as William late earl of Pembroke deceased'.[29] The grant was accompanied with 1,000 marks, 'to have of us as our gift'.

At the same time, the duke was to be granted the 'power and authority by his discretion in our name for our defence and the defence of this our realm' with powers to 'assemble our said subjects defensibly arrayed' and to convey them 'unto such place or places and from time to time as shall be thought unto the same duke expedient'; the duke's 'great costs and expenses' were also to be paid.[30] The patent granting Buckingham the offices of chief justice and chamberlain in south and north Wales was specific that the power to appoint sheriffs in the region was conditional 'so long as the king's uncle Richard, duke of Gloucester, or anyone else shall be protector of the realm during the king's minority'.[31] Aside from his vice-regal powers in Wales, Buckingham was given 'the supervision and power of array of the king's subjects' in Shropshire, Hereford, Somerset, Dorset and Wiltshire.[32]

Importantly, all the grants ensured that Buckingham was able to take over every office of constable and steward of royal lands in Wales once they fell vacant. Richard's decision to establish Buckingham as a Welsh super-magnate can be partially explained by his need to immediately replace the vacuum of authority created by the Woodville-run council of the Prince of Wales, which had gone into abeyance with the accession of Edward V. But the timing of the grants, made over a succession of days in mid-May, suggests that a deal had been struck between Richard and Buckingham: the price of the duke's support for Richard's protectorate had been the establishment of his own quasi-regal fiefdom in Wales. The massive scale of the awards was recognised by contemporaries as highly unusual; John Rous observed that Richard 'gave all his treasure to Henry Duke of Buckingham'.[33]

It was a strategy that was not without its risks: while Richard had been careful not to alienate supporters of the previous regime, the grant to Buckingham of all royal offices yet to fall vacant was bound to alienate existing office holders, who would undoubtedly feel threatened by such a powerful vested interest.[34]

Surviving memoranda from the council meetings during the month of May indicate the royal council was getting on with the business of government, with the royal finances, defence of the realm and preparations for the coronation dominating discussions.[35] It was rapidly becoming clear that with Edward IV having left the royal finances virtually empty, the new government was going to struggle to remain financially solvent. The council had managed to scrape together an additional £1,016 from 'plate of silver coined within the Tower', selling an 'image of gold' to the London goldsmith William Sayles for £1,800, and wool worth £1,316 to the merchants of the Staple, yet Edward IV's funeral had cost £1,896 17s 2d.[36]

On 7 May, Richard, together with the duke of Buckingham, William, earl of Arundel, William, Lord Hastings, and Thomas, Lord Stanley, along with the archbishops of Canterbury and York, and the bishops of Bath and Wells, Chichester, Lincoln and Ely met at Baynard's Castle, the home of Richard's mother, Cecily, duchess of York, where it was decided that the archbishop would retain the seals of the late king, since the executors of

Edward's will were hesitant to act while the Queen remained in sanctuary. Meanwhile, custody of the king's jewels was given to William Daubeney, the clerk of the jewel house, and Richard Laurence and Rowland Forster, yeomen of the jewel house.[37] On 23 May, the archbishop wrote to the executors, including Hastings, Stanley and the archbishop of York, and John Morton, the bishop of Ely, stating that since the king's funeral expenses remained unpaid, he granted them power to sell certain of the king's goods to pay for the costs, after a proper valuation had been made by the archbishop's own valuers.[38]

The royal finances needed addressing urgently. Already the spiralling costs that the new administration had accrued had reached £5,514 2s 11d, which the executors of the dead king were expecting to be repaid 'in part of performing of his last will'.[39] To help make up the shortfall of the costs of running the royal court, Richard had spent £800 of his own money on the king's household 'during the time of his attendance about the most honourable person of the king'.[40] After Edward's death, the council had also agreed to send an extra 300 men to Calais; as a result the garrison had grown to 825 men. Already there were concerns for how the finances would be met. William, Lord Hastings, himself the captain of the garrison, was growing nervous about how his men were going to be paid. Advising his brother, Ralph Hastings, the constable of Guisnes, to 'hold content' with those men he already had stationed there, Hastings explained to Ralph that 'he cannot see well how the money can be gotten to content them'.[41] The merchants of Calais had already loaned £1,220 for the payment of the soldiers that had been sent to the town; however, they would expect to be repaid.[42]

Still, Richard was convinced that money needed to be spent urgently on the defence of the realm, particularly on the Scottish borders. On 10 May, Henry, earl of Northumberland, was appointed warden of the East and Middle Marches, a position with a salary of 2,000 marks, though the office was limited for a year's term, ending on 9 April 1484.[43] The appointment reflects Richard's own priorities in government; as someone who had spent several years fighting the Scots on the northern borders, had witnessed victory in Scotland and had been rewarded for his capture of Berwick, Richard was not prepared for the issue to slip off the agenda. As warden, Northumberland was given command of Richard's prized

Berwick, together with a garrison of 600 men, costing £438 a month in pay alone. A building programme was hastily ordered, to strengthen the fortress and increase its population by over 500 men. 'It was thought by the King's grace that there should be at least 120 houses made at Berwick this year', the council minutes recorded, costing £1,600, with an additional £1,000 to be spent repairing the walls and castle there.[44]

Edward IV's death had caused significant problems with the raising of taxation, which effectively could not be collected in the dead king's name; instead a new parliament needed to be called. On 15 May, the Mercers' Company expressed their concern that in spite of Edward IV's death, when all taxes previously passed should have been declared void, the collection of a subsidy on customs continued, while collectors 'in other ports busy them greatly to continue the execution of the office as they afore time used to do, and in no wise will suffer any goods to pass but if they have the subsidy'. It was evident to everyone that the only means by which financial stability could be restored would be through Parliament voting through the customs due to the new king. As a memorandum composed for the council revealed, 'the profits of the ports will draw but a little sum for the king's grace shall have no thing thereof but his custom only, for tonnage and poundage was granted no longer to the king but during his life natural'.[45]

Parliament would need to be summoned as soon as possible. On 13 May, writs were sent out, summoning Parliament to meet on 25 June.[46] Three days later, a writ was issued in the king's name calling for a convocation to take place, in order to address 'certain difficult and urgent matters closely concerning us and the state of our realm of England', a suggestive statement though this phrase had also been used in Edward IV's writ three months earlier.[47] On 20 May, letters were sent to sheriffs in each county ordering them to present those eligible for knighthood in London by 18 June so that they might prepare to receive the dignity at the coronation.[48]

Yet as the coronation date loomed ever closer, Richard began to grow increasingly nervous. He could not afford for his enemies to gain the upper hand once more. It was in Parliament's authority that Richard hoped to find a solution to the vexing question of the young king's authority and his own as Protector. If Parliament might confer the protectorship upon him until Edward had attained a reasonable majority, Richard would be able to continue in his current role.

This seems to have been the intended solution hinted at in a draft sermon for the opening of Parliament by the Chancellor, John Russell, who urged the commons, 'in the meantime, till ripeness of years and personal rule be ... concurrent together' in the young king, 'the power and authority of my lord protector is so behoveful and of reason to be assented and established by the authority of this high court'. For Russell, Parliament's approval of the continuation of the protectorship was 'amongst all the causes of the assembling of the parliament in this time of the year, this is the greatest and most necessary first to be affirmed'.[49]

It seemed that Parliament was being summoned principally for the purpose of enshrining Richard's continued protectorship in law, 'to be first moved for the weal of the king and the defence of this land'. Russell was convinced that Richard's authority was vital to preserve stability in the realm. The 'tutelage and oversight of the king's most royal person during his years of tenderness my said lord protector will acquit himself like to Marcus Emilius Lepidus twice consul of Rome'. Richard was 'next in perfect age of the blood royal' to continue in his position as the young king's tutor and Protector. Urging the assembled Parliament to grant Richard's protectorship 'as the ease of the people and the condition of the time requireth it', Russell imagined, and hoped, that 'the king our sovereign lord may have cause largely to rejoice himself and congruently sat with the prophet, to my said lord protector, his uncle here present ... Uncle, I am glad to have you confirmed in this place you be my protector.'[50]

It is clear from Russell's words that there was also to be a renewed assault on the Woodvilles during the Parliament. Using none too subtle a pun on Earl Rivers' name, Russell wrote that 'if there be any surety or firmness here in this world, such as may be found out of heaven, it is rather in the Isles and lands environed with water than in the sea or any great Rivers'. In contrast with the uncertain 'Rivers', Russell concluded that the security of the realm should be placed in the hands of 'the noble persons of the world, which some for the merits of their ancestors, some for their own virtues, been endued with great favours, possessions and Richesses' – another weak pun on Richard's own name. It was the true-born nobility, Russell argued, that 'may more conveniently be resembled unto the firm ground that men see in Islands than the lower people, which for lack of such in-ducement . . . be not without cause likened unto the unstable and wavering running water'.[51] Rivers and by inference the Woodvilles were base-born, while, Russell insisted, 'Nobelesse is virtue and ancient Richesse.'[52]

For Russell, parliamentary consent to the continuance of the protec-torship would not only allow for Richard to continue in the office after the king's coronation, but his office and authority would be strengthened, since the 'power and authority of my lord protector' would have been 'as-sented and established by the authority of this high court'. Russell's speech gives some indication of the wide-ranging powers that Richard would be expected to wield as Protector. Richard's planned role would extend far beyond that granted to Henry VI's Protector, Humphrey, duke of Glouces-ter, who had been denied the tutelage of the king. It was far from clear whether Russell's speech, and Richard's intentions for the future of his protectorship, would be backed by the royal council.

7

'THEIR SUBTLE AND DAMNABLE WAYS'

If the date of the coronation had been decided, there was still one significant obstacle to overcome before it might take place. Elizabeth Woodville remained in sanctuary with the king's younger brother, Richard, duke of York. It would be unthinkable for a coronation to take place while the royal family itself remained physically divided: as heir to the throne, the young Prince Richard would be expected to play a central role in the ceremony. Already Elizabeth Woodville's decision to take flight was causing the new government problems. On 7 May, when the executors of Edward IV's will had met at Baynard's Castle, they had been unable to carry out his bequests while so many of its legatees remained in sanctuary.[1] Richard tried his best to coax the former queen out of Westminster, going so far as to prepare a public oath on 23 May promising her safety that he was prepared to swear, along with the rest of the council and the archbishops of Canterbury and York, 'if the same lady wished to relinquish the privilege' of sanctuary.[2]

Mancini had heard that 'as the day [of the coronation] drew near', Richard had confronted the council, insisting 'how improper it seemed that the king should be crowned in the absence of his brother'. The young duke of York, Richard submitted, 'on account of his nearness of kin and his station ought to play an important part in the ceremony'. Mancini suggested that Richard had gone so far as to state that 'this boy was held by his mother against his will', and that the young duke should 'be liberated, because the sanctuary had been founded by their ancestors as a place of refuge, not of detention, and this boy wanted to be with his brother'. Mancini believed that the council had actually agreed to Richard's request, and that 'with the consent of the council he surrounded the sanctuary with troops'. The Crowland chronicler too observed that not only was 'the detention in prison of the king's relatives and servants . . . a great cause of anxiety, which was growing', but that others were beginning to voice their own concerns 'that the protector did not show sufficient consideration for the dignity and peace of mind of the queen'.[3]

Still, preparations for the coronation continued. On 5 June, letters were sent out in the king's name to fifty candidates whose incomes qualified them for knighthoods, ordering that 'we write unto you at this time, willing and nonetheless charging you to appear, prepare and furnish yourself to receive the noble order of knighthood at our coronation, which by God's grace we intend shall be solemnised the xxii day of this present Month, at our palace of Westminster'. Those receiving the letter were commanded 'to be here at our Tower of London iiii days afore our said Coronation' in order to have 'communication with our commissioners concerning that matter'.[4] On 6 June, a letter was read out at the council meeting at York, ordering for four citizens to be present for the opening of Parliament on 25 June.[5]

In London, Richard was joined at court by his wife, Duchess Anne, who had made the journey from the north to the capital in preparation for the king's coronation. He also sent a box of wafers to John, Lord Howard's house, for which his servant was rewarded with 20d.[6] Howard had long been an associate of Richard's. Despite an age gap between the two men of thirty-two years, they had worked together for over a decade. As early as 1469, Howard and Richard had met at Colchester, raising men together before joining the king's train to deal with the rebellion of Robin of Redesdale. In 1480, Howard purchased the manor of Wivenhoe in Essex from Richard, while in the years that follow several entries in Howard's household accounts reveal rewards to Richard's minstrels, trumpeters and players; in 1482, Howard even made a gift of seven crossbows of wood and one of steel to Richard. With Richard now Protector, Howard was a crucial ally and supporter of the new regime, and had already been rewarded with office for his efforts. The previous month, in a signal of his gratitude for being promoted to chief steward of the duchy of Lancaster south of the Trent, on 15 May, Howard's household accounts record how 'my lord gave unto my lord protector a cup of gold, and a cuer' weighing sixty-five ounces of solid gold.[7]

Four days later, on 9 June, Simon Stallworth, a member of the household of the new Lord Chancellor, John Russell, wrote to William Stonor in Oxfordshire, explaining how 'as for tidings since I wrote to you we hear none new'. The letter reveals that the coronation was being discussed; however, no communication with Queen Elizabeth in sanctuary at Westminster was now taking place. Her son, the marquess of Dorset, still a fugitive, seems to have managed to pass a message to the queen, for which the prior at Westminster had been reprimanded:

> The Queen keeps still [at] Westminster, my lord of York, my lord of Salisbury with other more which will not depart as yet. Where so ever can be found any goods of my Lord Marquess it is tayne [taken]. The Prior of Westminster was and is in a great trouble for certain goods delivered to him by my Lord Marquess. My Lord Protector, my Lord of Buckingham, with all other lords as well temporal as spiritual were at Westminster in the council chamber from 10 to 2 but there was not that spake with the Queen. There is great business against the Coronation which shall be this day fortnight as we say. When I trust ye will be at London and then ye know all the world. The king is at the Tower. My lady of Gloucester come to London on Thursday last.

There is no sense in Stallworth's letter of any change in the current situation; the coronation was still planned for a fortnight's time, while the remainder of the letter is concerned with the more mundane business of the payment of taxes and the issue of a dispute at Thame that Stallworth had managed to discuss with the Protector, indicating the level of minute detail with which Richard was now conducting government business.[8]

The surviving minutes of the council meeting on 9 June reveal that there was a discussion on the 'grounds for the coronation', including the expenses of the coronation that had been paid by the city, amounting to 1,000 marks, sent to the Guildhall on 2 May, covering half of the total 2,000 marks that had been set aside for the great wardrobe. It was clear that the council was struggling with the financial costs of making the books balance, especially with the new charges of 'the payment of the

wages of Berwick . . . which will amount to a great sum'. Then there was
the payment of the wages of 800 extra men at Calais. The situation was
hardly sustainable.[9]

The final memorandum noted how 'also it is to be remembered the
building of Berwick', one of Richard's pet schemes that he had been determined to push through, and which was already proving costly.

Few if any would have believed that the young king was the driving
force behind such expenditure. Richard was determined that the work not
only be commenced, but completed as soon as possible, even sending a
letter as Protector to Alexander Lee to 'put him in devoir to make up the
castle in haste most possible and lodging within the same'.[10] It seems that
Richard, having recently been granted his palatinate across the border,
was keen to resume the campaigning season in Scotland. The expenses of
the soldiers' wages for just the months of June and July were set to amount
to £915, and Richard was no doubt keen that their duties would extend
beyond a defensive capability.

To commit to another Scottish assault, however, would prove difficult at
the same time as maintaining a large presence at Calais: surviving financial memoranda drawn up that month estimated that there were currently
a total of 880 archers being paid six pence a day, which totalled £1,255 16s
for two months' pay.[11] Three hundred extra men had been sent to Calais for
eighteen days from 28 April to 12 May, though a decision had been taken
to continue to keep the men at the garrison until 7 July. An important clue
as to the significance of the Calais garrison can be found in the record of a
payment of £50 'paid for the costs of 300 men from Derbyshire to Calais'.[12]
For these were William, Lord Hastings's men, procured most likely from
the Honour of Tutbury in the county. It seems likely that beneath these dry
financial accounts lay a growing tension over the nation's foreign policy:
between Richard, on the one hand, who wished to pursue further military
action in Scotland, and Hastings, who may have wished for the Calais
garrison to be preserved at its extended size in order to protect against the
hostilities of the French.

There was no way that both Berwick and Calais could continue to
be funded simultaneously. A choice would eventually have to be made.
Perhaps it was disagreements over these costs, in addition to the 'great
business' of the coronation, that kept the council meeting running for four

hours. Or maybe Stallworth's cryptic comment that there was no one 'that spake with the Queen' at the meeting, indicated deeper divisions and tensions over the status of the Woodvilles in the run-up to the coronation less than a fortnight away. Certainly Stallworth's revelation that the marquess of Dorset's goods had been confiscated, and that the prior of Westminster was in 'great trouble' for acting as an intermediary between Dorset and the queen in sanctuary at Westminster, having had 'certain goods delivered to him by my Lord Marquess', suggests that Richard had managed to intercept some form of communication between Queen Elizabeth and her son, currently in hiding outside sanctuary.[13]

Yet something must have taken place at the council meeting to change Richard's mind. For the following day, on 10 June, Richard chose to put in motion a plan to destroy the queen and the Woodvilles for ever. Richard wrote a letter under his own private signet to the mayor of York, John Newton:

> The Duke of Gloucester, brother and uncle of Kings, protector, defendor, great Chamberlain, Constable and Admiral of England.
>
> Right trusty and well beloved, we greet you well, and as ye love the weal of us, and the weal and surety of your own self, we heartily pray you to come unto us to London in all the diligence you can possible, after the sight hereof, with as many ye can make defensibly arrayed, there to aid and assist us against the queen, her blood, adherents and affinity, which have intended and daily doth intend to murder and utterly destroy us and our cousin, the duke of Buckingham, and the old royal blood of this realm, and as it is now openly known, by their subtle and damnable ways forecasted the same, and also the final destruction and disinheritance of you and all other the inheritors of prosperity and honour, as well of the north parts as other countries that belong to us; as our trusty servant, this bearer, shall more at large show you, to whom we pray you give great credence, and as ever we may do for you in time coming fail not, but haste you to us hither.
>
> Given under our signet, at London, the xth day of June.[14]

It was just one of a succession of letters that Richard had begun to compose. The following day, he wrote in his own hand a private letter to Ralph, Lord Neville:

To my Lord Neville, in haste.

My Lord Neville, I recommend me to you as heartily as I can; and as ever ye love me, and your own weal and security, and this Realm, that ye come to me with that ye may make, defensibly arrayed, in all haste that is possible, and that ye will give credence to Richard Ratcliffe, this bearer, whom I now do send to you, instructed with all my mind and intent.

And, my lord, do me now good service, as ye have always before done, and I trust now so to remember you as shall be the making of you and yours. And God send to you good fortunes.

Written at London, xi of June, with the hand of your heartily loving cousin and master,

R. GLOUCESTER.[15]

Whether there was actually a genuine plot against the duke or not, both letters reveal much about Richard's own mindset. There is no indication that Richard had turned against the king himself; on the contrary, Richard's authority stems from the fact that he is the 'uncle and brother of kings', stressing his male descent to the crown. The comparison between the 'queen, her blood, adherents and affinity' and the 'old royal blood of this realm' suggests that Richard himself either viewed a factional conflict taking place at court, or equally recognised that he was able to exploit an already existing and common understanding that the Woodvilles were newborn, a caste apart from the traditional nobility. By making mention of the duke of Buckingham, Richard appealed not just to the fact that any quarrel was not just between himself and the Woodvilles alone, but the Woodvilles and the rest of the nobility, of which Buckingham could be considered to be the pre-eminent representative; mention of Buckingham's name also suggests that the duke was also complicit in Richard's sudden decision to turn against the Woodvilles.

Richard's suggestion that the queen had used some form of prophecy or magic, 'their subtle and damnable ways', and 'forecasted' his and Buckingham's death also harks back to earlier arguments employed against the Woodville family, most notably the accusations of witchcraft and prophecy surrounding Elizabeth's mother, Jacquetta of Luxembourg. While Richard's letter to Ralph, Lord Neville gives no explanation for why he should journey to the capital with an armed retinue – Richard no doubt expected Neville's loyalty without the need to justify his demands – the duke appealed to Neville's own safety, 'as ever ye love me, and your own weal and security'.

Why had Richard chosen to send the letters now? The duke must have calculated the time it would take for troops to assemble and then make the long journey from the north. The bearer of both letters, Richard Ratcliffe, did not leave the capital until 11 June, however, for he also took with him Richard's letter to Lord Neville, written the same day. York did not receive Richard's letter until Sunday, 15 June. It had the desired effect.

Shocked by Richard's assertion that he was under threat from a conspiracy organised by Queen Elizabeth, the city council at York agreed that, 'for as much as my lord of Gloucester good grace hath written to the city show that the queen and her adherents intendeth to destroy his good grace and other of the blood royal', Thomas Wrangwish, William Welles, Robert Hancock, John Hag, Richard Marston and William White, together with 200 horsemen 'defensibly arrayed', should ride to London. Ratcliffe had arrived with additional instructions from Richard, to be given by word of mouth to the city; these are revealed in the city's resolution that it would assemble its forces to arrive at Pontefract 'at Wednesday night next coming [18 June] there to attend upon my lord of Northumberland to go to my said lord of Gloucester good grace'.[16]

Either by some kind of prearrangement or by some understanding, the earl of Northumberland had arrived in the city several days beforehand.[17] As soon as he arrived, on 15 June, Ratcliffe must have taken the opportunity to pass on another letter, now missing, to the earl. Almost immediately Northumberland must have set off on a forty-mile journey on horseback to Hull, for on 16 June the earl approached the port with a 'proclamation ... of the behalf of my lord duke of Gloucester protector' that all men being between the ages of sixty and sixteen 'should be ready to attend of my said lord of Northumberland at Pontefract the morning after and Sunday then next as it were plainly contained in the said proclamation'.[18] The port's reaction was hardly enthusiastic: it was agreed that twelve men would be sent to Pontefract for the following Sunday [21 June], with each man to be paid 12d for twenty days. The 'proclamation' from Richard that Northumberland must have obtained from Ratcliffe suggests that Richard had already conceived that a northern army consisting of men from both

York and Hull, in addition to the private retinues of northern lords such as Neville, should gather at Pontefract on 21 June, three days later than had been initially planned.

There was no chance, therefore, that the army being gathered under the leadership of Northumberland and Ratcliffe would have reached London in time for the king's coronation. There would be enough time, however, for the northern army to arrive in the capital by 25 June and place pressure on Parliament to approve Richard's plans for the continuation of his protectorate. What is striking, however, is that Richard gambled everything on Northumberland accepting his plans and siding with him against the Woodvilles. In delegating the raising of an army to the earl, Richard seems to have known that Northumberland would have been present in York at the time of the arrival of his letters. Whatever message had been passed to the earl by Ratcliffe, Northumberland immediately agreed to Richard's demands; had the two men already come to some prearranged pact?

Even then, there was no guarantee that the army would materialise as planned. The city authorities in York assiduously began their preparations to gather men for the march to Pontefract. On 16 June, it was agreed that four assessors should be sent into every parish, together with four collectors of money and purveyors of horse, and that 200 soldiers in York and 100 soldiers from Ainsty should be mustered, with each soldier being paid 12d a day, though 'every soldier shall pay for his own jacket'. Aldermen were to wear jackets of silk and the captains jackets 'of chamlet' with a spare horse paid for by the chamber. Yet it was soon clear that the parish of St Saviour's was struggling to recruit men, being 'greatly impoverished', and so was allowed to send only two men.

Possibly due to this lack of enthusiasm, a second proclamation was issued in the city on 19 June, four days after the initial call to arms from Richard. Still dated by the reign of 'regis Edwardi quinti', the proclamation largely repeated Richard's letter to the mayor, but subtle changes in the wording of the text indicate the pressing need to raise men faster than was currently happening. Stressing that Richard 'straightly charges and commands that all manner of men in their best defensible array, incontinent after this proclamation made, do rise up and come up to London to his highness in the company of his cousin the earl of Northumberland, the lord Neville and other men of worship by his highness appointed', the language of the proclamation had become more urgent; instead of asking the citizens to 'aid and assist us against the queen', the proclamation now called on men 'to aid and assist him *to the subduing, correcting and punishing* of the queen'. Where, before, Richard's letter explained that the Woodvilles intended his and Buckingham's murder and destruction, as well as 'the old royal blood of this realm', this was now widened to include 'also the noble men of their companies'. 'Therefore in all diligence', the proclamation added as a rallying cry, 'prepare yourself and come up as ye love their honours, weals and sureties, and the sureties of yourself and the common weal of this said realm.'[19]

Still the city remained uncertain whether it was acting on behalf of Richard in his private capacity as duke of Gloucester or on behalf of the city itself, undertaking royal orders. These doubts caused further delays, until eventually, on 21 June, it was agreed the 'cunisaunce' of the duke of Gloucester should be carried to Pontefract, while every soldier arriving at Pontefract should wear the cognisance of the city, 'and then if the captains of this city think it to be done, every soldier of this city to wear the cognisance of the city and also the cognisance of my said lord of Gloucester'. Even with a week to prepare a band of soldiers to be at Pontefract for 21 June, York had still failed to assemble its men on time to depart the city, causing even further delays to the assembly of a northern army that Richard would have hoped to be marching southwards already.[20]

As the city authorities fussed over the details of what livery badges their soldiers should wear on the long march to the capital, the same day a writ arrived in the city, cancelling the Parliament due to assemble in four days' time, and instructing the sheriffs that 'it shall not need to any citizen to go up for the city to the parliament'.[21] Events in London, the citizens of York would soon learn, had taken a sudden and violent turn that had transformed everything.

Few could have known of Richard's letters ordering a northern army to assemble against the queen and the Woodvilles. No doubt Buckingham had been consulted by the duke. Yet there is a sense of urgency in Richard's letters which suggests that they had been penned in response to a development that had occurred around the time of the four-hour council meeting on 9 June, which suggests that Richard would have had little time to make his intentions known to other possible allies.

It was now only a matter of time until Richard's true intentions against the Woodvilles would become known. With his letters condemning the queen and 'her blood' now in the hands of Richard Ratcliffe galloping towards York, the duke's plot was laid. There could be no turning back.

8

'GREAT CONFUSION AND GREAT FEAR'

With the letters now dispatched, Richard had just a short window of time to secure support for his second coup. He recognised that he needed more than just Buckingham's support if he were to remove the Woodvilles entirely. Reaching out for Hastings's support once more seemed an obvious solution. As someone who had already calculated that the Woodvilles' ascent to power under Edward V would prove disastrous to his own interests, William, Lord Hastings, had been prepared to co-ordinate and aid Richard's and Buckingham's coup at Stony Stratford in late April. The Crowland chronicler reported how Hastings, 'who seemed to wish in every way to serve the two dukes and to be desirous of earning their favour', had been delighted at the establishment of Richard's protectorship, 'and was in the habit of saying that hitherto nothing whatever had been done except the transferring of the government of the kingdom from two of the queen's blood to two more powerful persons of the king's'.[1] According to Thomas More's later account, William Hastings and Richard were close friends, with More observing that 'undoubtedly the protector loved him well'.[2]

According to More, Richard used William Catesby to discover whether Hastings could be won over to his plan, while Dominic Mancini would later write how he believed Buckingham had been given the task of sounding out Hastings's loyalty. Catesby was a Leicestershire gentleman whose rise had seen him become a close associate of Hastings, but had more recently become linked to the duke of Buckingham. Catesby was already a steward of one of Buckingham's manors in Northamptonshire, and by March 1481 was one of the duke's feoffees.[3] In May, when Catesby had been appointed chancellor of the earldom of March, he had been placed under the orders of the duke of Buckingham. With his close links to Catesby, it seems possible that Buckingham could have used Catesby as an intermediary with Hastings.

According to More, Catesby, 'whether he essayed him or essayed him not', reported back how he had found Hastings 'so fast, and heard him speak so terrible words, that he durst no further break'. Catesby urged Richard to act to remove Hastings, believing he could not be trusted to support the Protector's next moves against the Woodvilles. For More, Catesby had his own agenda to pursue: with his estates located close to Hastings's new castle at Kirby Muxloe, Hastings's fall would prove too good an opportunity to 'obtain much of the rule that the lord Hastings bare in his country'.[4] Buckingham also had every reason to cast suspicion on Hastings, in order to gain possession of his duchy of Lancaster offices in the north Midlands. It is no coincidence that John Rous believed Richard had been 'strongly encouraged in these things by Henry, duke of Buckingham'.[5]

Beneath any self-interest that Catesby or Buckingham may have displayed, it seems that Hastings had indeed been growing increasingly suspicious of the direction Richard's protectorship was headed. More believed that 'the Lord Chamberlain of very trust showed unto Catesby the mistrust that others began to have in the matter', while, according to the Crowland chronicler, within a few days of Richard's arrival in the capital, Hastings had begun to have second thoughts: while Hastings had been 'extremely elated' at the transfer of power from the Woodvilles to the king's uncle, 'in the course of a very few days after the utterance of these words, this extreme joy of his was supplanted by sorrow'. The Crowland chronicler's view is supported by a later account by the Tudor historian Polydore Vergil, who described how Hastings 'when he saw all already thrown into confusion, repenting his action, brought together a gathering of his friends in the basilica of St Paul's for consultation'. While the gathering agreed that 'nothing good would come from such a beginning of assumed protection', they were willing to give Richard the benefit of the doubt, at least for the duke to justify his actions to the council. 'All the residue thought that there was no need to use war or weapon at all', concluding that they would 'tarry while duke Richard should come and declare what the matter was, why he had cast them who had the prince in government into prison'. Wanting to 'avoid variance and contention' amongst the nobility, they agreed that 'this resolution finally liked them all, because in appearance it stood with the profit of the commonwealth'.

Hastings seems to have placed himself at the head of the dead king's household men, who wished to see an immediate coronation and a seamless transfer of power to the young King Edward V as the best solution to continue the Yorkist dynasty. Richard had, according to Vergil, become aware of Hastings's desire 'to press and urge that Prince Edward at last should be crowned'. Mancini had heard how Hastings 'had been from an early age a loyal champion of Edward, and an active soldier', while Thomas Rotherham, 'though of humble origin, had become, thanks to his talent, a man of note with King Edward, and had worked for many years in the chancery'. John Morton, Mancini had been told, 'was of great resource and daring, for he had been trained in party intrigue since King Henry's time'.

It was the 'ability and authority of these men', Mancini had learnt, 'those who had been the closest friends of his brother, and were expected to be loyal to his brother's offspring', that had caused Richard to fear his position, considering that 'his prospects were not sufficiently secure' without their removal or imprisonment. Mancini wrote how Richard, through Buckingham, 'learnt that sometimes they foregathered in each other's houses'.[6]

For Richard, Hastings's power was equally disconcerting. It was perhaps for this reason that the duke had refused to grant Hastings any additional office aside from confirming his position as Master of the Royal Mint, while at the same time extending Buckingham's vice-regal powers into Wales. Nevertheless, Hastings's command at Calais had seen hundreds of additional soldiers join the garrison since Edward IV's death; already Hastings had threatened the Woodvilles, in April, by claiming that he would depart the country for Calais, and there was no reason why he might not carry out a similar threat again. Many of the new recruits had come from Hastings's own regional power base in Derbyshire, suggesting that he was strengthening his grip on the loyalty of the garrison. He had also begun to recruit to his own private retinue. On 13 May, Hastings signed an indenture with Thomas Green, recruiting him into his service. Green was to give Hastings 'faithful and true service during my life, in war and peace, with as many persons defensibly arrayed as I can or may make, whensoever I be by the said lord or any other in his name thereto required, at the costs of the said lord during my life.'[7] Amongst the entire nobility, Mancini believed, 'because of his generosity', Hastings's popularity was unrivalled.

Richard, too, admired Hastings; however, the latter's continued presence in the council posed too great a danger to the duke's own survival. Hastings had been a crucial ally in informing Richard about the Woodvilles' plans to secure the protectorship for themselves; without him, it is unlikely that Richard would have secured the king's person in time at Stony Stratford. Yet Richard had increasingly come to realise that Hastings's loyalties lay not with him, but with King Edward himself. Now Hastings, as much as the Woodvilles, sought to ensure that Edward V would be crowned as an adult king, dispensing with the need for Richard as Protector. Once he had realised that Richard's ambitions stretched beyond the confines of his own duty towards the Yorkist dynasty, it seems that Hastings had demonstrated his concern over the Protector's plans. Richard owed his success to Hastings, yet now he could no longer be sure of his future support. If Hastings could not be part of the solution, then he, too, Richard concluded, would need to go. 'Whether he feared his power or despaired indeed of being able to draw him to his opinion', Vergil concluded, 'he determined first to remove the man from the midst of the rest.'[8] 'Therefore the protector rushed headlong into crime', Mancini mused, 'for fear that the ability and authority of these men might be detrimental to him.'[9]

Richard must have known that, in removing Hastings, he would be crossing a divide, making a breach in the social and political order that could not be repaired. Yet he had no time to consider the consequences of his actions; he just had to act, and act fast. Already his letters to York and Lord Neville were travelling on horseback northwards; within days they would be read out, committing the duke to public warfare against the Woodvilles. Any delay in securing his position now might be fatal; faced with the possibility of Hastings turning back towards the Woodvilles in any oncoming civil war, Richard's own choices were narrowing by the day. No matter how illegal his future actions might be, the duke considered that he had no other option but to use his most convincing weapon, that of sudden surprise, paralysing his enemies before they might have the chance to take action against him.

First the trap would need to be laid. The Crowland chronicler reported how, on 12 June, Richard had ordered that the next day's council meeting would take place in two separate locations, dividing the council 'so that one part met in the morning at Westminster, and the other at the Tower of London, where the king was'.[10] The first meeting was to be chaired by the Chancellor, John Russell, while Richard would officiate over the second, which was to convene at around ten o'clock in the morning. Those invited included Archbishop Rotherham of York, Bishop Morton of Ely, Buckingham, Thomas, Lord Stanley, William, Lord Hastings, John, Lord Howard, 'and many others, whom he trusted to be faithful to him either by fear or favour'.

Polydore Vergil's manuscript version of his *Anglica Historica* provides the most detailed account of events, including the names of those who took part in Richard's coup, names which were later removed from the official printed version of the Italian's history. The day before the council meeting due to take place at the Tower, Richard ordered that Charles Pilkington, Robert Harrington and Thomas Howard, John, Lord Howard's son, and several other attendants should be placed secretly in the adjoining room to the council chamber, 'and ordered them, so that at a given signal, suddenly appearing they should surround him, who would sit with him, and should seize, from amongst the others, the lord Hastings and then should cut his throat'.[11]

No sooner had the council meeting begun than Richard struck. The earliest account of what occurred at the meeting comes from Dominic Mancini:

> One day these three [Hastings, Thomas Rotherham and John Morton] and several others came to the Tower about ten o'clock to salute the protector, as was their custom. When they had been admitted to the innermost quarters, the protector, as prearranged, cried out that an ambush had been prepared for him, and they had come with hidden arms, that they might be the first to open the attack. Thereupon the soldiers, who had been stationed there by their lord, rushed in with the duke of Buckingham, and cut down Hastings on the false pretext of treason; they arrested the others, whose life, it was presumed, was spared out of respect for religion and holy orders. Thus fell Hastings, killed not by those enemies he had always feared, but by a friend whom he had never doubted.[12]

Over time, a fuller picture of what had occurred behind the closed doors
of the council emerged. Polydore Vergil described how:

> with only God as witness, they meant to discuss serious matters between
> them. Richard, who was turning over in his mind another sadder business,
> addressed them thus: 'My lords, I have called you here today in this court
> solely in order to show you in what danger I stand. For I rest neither by
> night nor by day neither able to drink nor to take food, wherefore gradu-
> ally my blood and strength leave me, and likewise now all limbs are made
> thin as you see (he extended an arm) which evil certainly came to me from
> that woman Queen Elizabeth who poisoned me with her magic charms, by
> which malice I am dissolved.' To these words, as making little to the matter,
> when no-one gave answer, William Hastings, who loved Richard, and who
> was used to speak freely with him, answered that the queen deserved both
> to be accused and punished if it was found by the use of magic arts she
> had in any way harmed him. To this Richard said: 'I am lost, I say, by this
> woman's magic charms', to which William answered as formerly, namely
> that the queen should be punished if she had poisoned him with that evil.
> Then Richard, as he gave a sign for attacking to those who were lying in
> wait, said in a high voice: 'What then, William, if I am brought to ruin by
> your zealous reckonings?' Scarcely was this done when Charles Pilkington,
> Robert Harrington and Thomas Howard, who were lying in wait in the next
> chamber, immediately appeared and attacked on all sides, taking hold of
> William Lord Hastings and each presiding priest, York and Ely, and Lord
> Stanley.[13]

Hastings had no time to confess his sins. Immediately, 'without process
of any law or lawful examination', he was taken outside, 'unto the green
beside the chapel, and there, upon an end of squared piece of timber, without any long confession or other space of remembrance' was executed,
with his head cut off. 'And thus was this noble man murdered for his truth
and fidelity which he firmly bare unto his master', the *Great Chronicle*
noted.[14]

The author of the *Great Chronicle* believed that Thomas Stanley too
would have been killed, 'as the fame after went', if it were not for the fear
that Stanley's son, Lord Strange, would raise troops in Lancashire against
Richard. Set at liberty, Stanley escaped unhurt, except a cut to his face,

This arch-topped painting, copied from a prototype painted during his reign, is thought to be the earliest surviving portrait of Richard III.

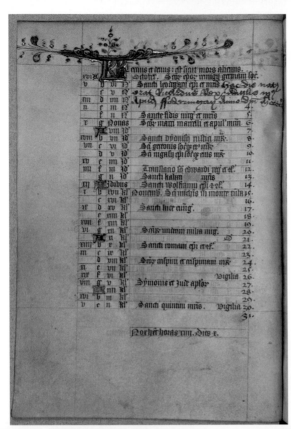

Left 'On this day was born Richard III.' Richard entered his own birth date, 2 October 1452, into the calendar of his personal Book of Hours.

Below Fotheringhay, Northamptonshire: Richard's birthplace, and the seat of the Yorkist dynasty. Richard's parents are buried in the Church of St Mary.

Middleham Castle, Yorkshire: Richard lived here while in the earl of Warwick's household in the 1460s. In 1471 the castle was granted to him and became his principal residence until he succeeded to the throne.

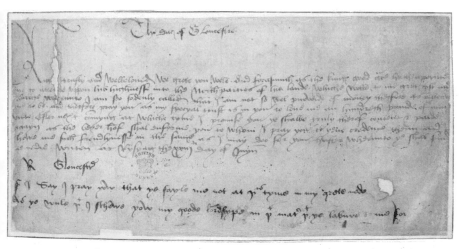

'Fail me not at this time in my great need': Richard's first surviving letter, dated 1469 and with a postscript in his own hand, requesting a loan for £100 from Sir John Say, under-treasurer to Edward IV.

Below Edward IV. He came to rely upon his younger brother Richard as a mainstay of the Yorkist dynasty.

Left The troublesome middle brother: George, duke of Clarence.

Right Edward enthroned atop Fortune's wheel, with his brothers ascending the spokes on the left-hand side.

Below Edward's controversial choice of bride: the widowed Elizabeth Woodville. The queen and her family's influence upon the king was resented by the nobility.

Above The queen's brother Anthony, earl Rivers, presents the first printed book in English to Edward IV, whose eldest son, the future Edward V, is at his side.

Yorkist supremacy in the civil wars was finally secured by two decisive battles fought within weeks of each other in spring 1471. At Barnet, Edward IV's rebellious Kingmaker, the earl of Warwick, met his death; while at Tewkesbury, Henry VI's heir, Edward of Lancaster, was killed, not without controversy. The sixteen-year-old Richard of Gloucester fought in both battles, leading Edward IV's vanguard. His success greatly enhanced his military reputation.

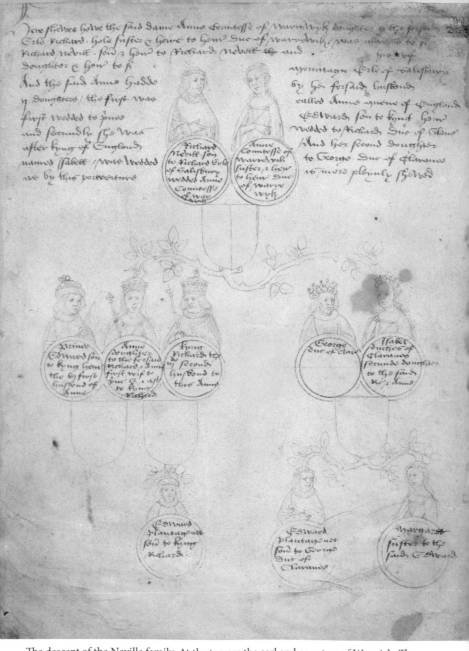

The descent of the Neville family. At the top are the earl and countess of Warwick. The middle branches show their daughters, Anne and Isabel. Anne is on the left, in-between her first husband, Edward of Lancaster, and her second, Richard of Gloucester. Below is Edward of Middleham, Richard and Anne's only surviving child. The right-hand branch shows Isabel, her husband George of Clarence, and their two children.

Left Edward IV's sons Richard of Shrewsbury, duke of York, and Edward, Prince of Wales, depicted in a stained glass window in Canterbury Cathedral, circa 1482. The following year marked the death of the king and the disappearance of 'The Princes in the Tower'.

Right The White Tower, in the grounds of the Tower of London. Edward V and his younger brother were last seen withdrawn into its confines.

Below This scrap of parchment represents an attempt by Richard and Henry, duke of Buckingham, to gain the confidence of the young king on 2–3 May 1483, shortly after seizing him. At the top is Edward's signature, 'Edwardus Quintus'; next inscribed is Richard's motto, 'Loyaulte Me Lye' ('loyalty binds me'); and underneath the broad sprawl of Buckingham's motto, 'Souvente Me Souvenir' ('remember me often'), and 'Harry Bokyngham'.

Left The Garter stall-plate of William, Lord Hastings. As a loyal supporter of the Yorkist dynasty, Hastings opposed Woodville control over Edward V. Yet he was brought down by Richard, who plotted his sudden execution on 13 June 1483, suspicious that Hastings' loyalty was ultimately to the young king, threatening Richard's own long-term security.

Below 'The fact of an enterprise': Richard's letter to Lord Chancellor John Russell on 29 July 1483 suggests opposition to his reign had already formed. Other sources indicate that an attempt had been made to free Edward V and his brother from the Tower of London.

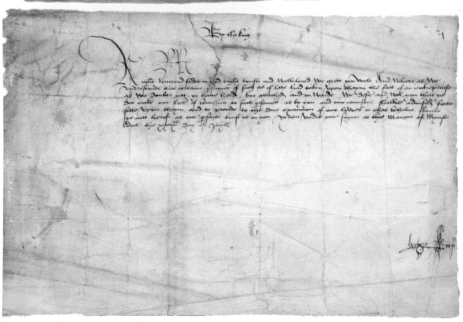

which had been 'rased with some weapon'.[15] Bishop Morton of Ely was placed in the custody of Buckingham at his residence at Brecon Castle, while Archbishop Rotherham of York was given over to the keeping of James Tyrell.

After Hastings's beheading, Vergil reported, 'all in the Tower shouted "Treason! Treason!" This shout went also throughout the city, the citizens and general populace believing the first words to be true and at the same time ignorant of that done within, began to repeat the shout.' Dominic Mancini may have even been present on the streets of London when, he wrote, 'the townsmen, who had heard the uproar but were uncertain of the cause, became panic stricken, and each one seized his weapons'. To calm the crowds, 'the duke instantly sent a herald to proclaim that a plot had been detected in the citadel, and Hastings, the originator of the plot, had paid the penalty; wherefore he bad them all be reassured. At first the ignorant crowd believed, although the real truth was on the lips of many, namely that the plot had been feigned by the duke so as to escape the odium of such a crime.' The proclamation, the text of which does not survive, contained the charge that Hastings, along with his accomplices, had planned to kill Richard and Buckingham at the council meeting, taking the king into their possession. Issued just two hours after Hastings's death, it was written on parchment in such a fine calligraphic hand that, according to Thomas More, 'every child might well perceive that it was prepared before'.[16]

Richard's actions against Hastings were almost an exact replica of those he had taken to secure the protectorship: an unexpected attack on his political rival, followed by a subsequent justification that claimed a conspiracy against the Yorkist state. Both were so unexpected because they went beyond the accepted political behaviour of the day. But was there any justification behind his sudden execution of Hastings? The traditional interpretation of events is that Richard had every reason to fabricate a charge against Hastings: if there really had been a conspiracy against Richard, his actions could be taken as self-defence; the duke could be the victim of circumstances thrust upon him, rather than the manipulator of events. Richard's attack on Hastings, and his claims of another plot against his life, was not only sufficient to justify Hastings's removal: now that the council had been persuaded, or cowed, into believing in a conspiracy against the Protector, they were prepared to back the duke's leadership in what seemed a full-blown political crisis. As the Crowland chronicler noted, 'with the rest of the faithful men expecting something similar these two dukes thereafter did what they wanted'. If Hastings had been planning a conspiracy against Richard, then it seems unlikely that he would have been taken completely by surprise at the council meeting. Still, in the absence of any official charges against Hastings, it is worth considering the evidence for a conspiracy against Richard, to understand whether other members of the council believed it to be true. Could there be more to the Hastings conspiracy than a trumped-up charge based on Richard's fear that Hastings had met with Morton and Rotherham in secret?

The charges of a conspiracy were believed by some at least. Whether persuaded by Richard's proclamation or not, one contemporary chronicle was confident enough to record how 'in the meantime there was divers imagined the death of the duke of Gloucester, and it was aspied and the Lord Hastings was taken in the Tower and beheaded forthwith.'[17] There were others who had been considered complicit in Hastings's manoeuvrings who were also immediately arrested. The king's secretary, Oliver King, later described how he had been arrested and 'grievously prisoned in the Tower by Richard . . . and put in jeopardy of his life'.[18] Meanwhile, his own property, which had included silver plate worth 500 marks, was seized by Richard's commandment and delivered to the London alderman Thomas Hill.[19]

Nor was King the only other person to be implicated in charges of a conspiracy. Archbishop John Morton had been arrested and placed in the Tower, though at a later date he was removed from the capital altogether and placed as far out of harm's way as possible, under house arrest at the duke of Buckingham's residence at Weobley on the Welsh border. A letter from his own university of Oxford, dated from late July, to Richard, urging his release, indicates that Morton's guilt went unchallenged. The university had hesitated to write to Richard, while 'we had any doubts about his future attitude towards your government and about what he was going to do'. Yet they were convinced, however, that Morton had erred 'through a human mistake, not through obstinacy, and has always sought your forgiveness for his fault'. Although Morton had already been punished, 'lightly in view of his faults', the university now prayed that Richard might 'change your mind and consider the man again and accord him the gift of your mercy'. There was no doubt that Morton had committed a wrong, but falling back upon classical allusions, the university argued that 'Sallust testifies that the Romans also considered it praise that they were more inclined to forgive than take revenge for injuries. If you wish to receive such great praise and glory, you will obtain it with ease if you are willing to embrace this man. By this excellent deed you will outdo and defeat the Romans themselves.'[20]

The case of John Forster is equally intriguing. In the Register of the Abbot of St Albans there is a note describing how 'William Lord Hastings suffered capital punishment, as his offences demanded (as it was stated) within the Tower of London'; on the following day, the register records, 'John Forster was committed to the Tower.'[21] John Forster later petitioned Parliament that on Saturday, 14 June, he 'suddenly was taken at Welde Hall' in Hertfordshire, 'by the servants and commandment' of Richard, 'and from thence with force and arms riotously was conveyed unto the Tower of London, and there kept and imprisoned as a prisoner in irons and fetters by the space of 40 weeks and more, having no meat neither drink for his sustenance from the said Saturday of his first bringing to the Tower till the Monday then next following ... whereby', Forster recalled, he 'was like to have perished, saving by God's preservation'.[22] Once again the hand of William Catesby is detectable in Forster's arrest; once more, self-interest seems to have played an important part in Catesby's motivations. According to the Register at St Albans, Forster released the office of steward of St Albans to William Catesby, 'in the hope of obtaining remission of his punishment' just two days after his arrest. The stewardship of the abbey, which had been held jointly by Forster and Hastings, had only been signed in February, but the new grant drawn up suggests that Hastings's share was to be ignored entirely, with Forster free to grant the office away. Catesby moved fast to secure the legal documentation for confirming the office, for the formal grant of the stewardship was made by the abbot on 1 August, while Forster was still imprisoned.[23] Forster remembered the occasion rather differently: as forty weeks in which he was 'menaced and threatened to be beheaded, attainted of high treason and also to forfeit and lose all his lands and goods' unless he paid Richard a thousand marks in money and jewels.[24]

But why was Forster arrested in the first place? And what role could he possibly have played in any conspiracy imagined by William, Lord Hastings? The link between John Forster and William, Lord Hastings, as joint stewards of St Albans Abbey is an important one, for it provides a link between Hastings and Elizabeth Woodville. Forster had been receiver-general of the queen's household since 1466. Though his position was now presumably defunct, this did not prevent him from maintaining contact with the queen when she was in sanctuary. A surviving account of Queen Elizabeth's expenses while she was in sanctuary reveal that, amongst other payments, including forty shillings for 'the king's coming', perhaps a reference to her son Edward V's arrival in the capital, and £4 to 'doctor Wrixham', possibly William Wrixham, canon of Hereford, and 13s 3d for 'the poor of chicksand', Elizabeth intriguingly made payment of £13 6s 8d to 'master forster'.[25] Could this be the same John Forster? If so, it suggests that Forster could have been a linking point between Hastings and the queen.

There were other ties between Hastings and the Woodvilles that would have raised Richard's suspicions. Hastings' stepdaughter, Cecily Bonville, the daughter of his wife Katherine Neville's first marriage, had married the queen's son from her first marriage, Thomas, marquess of Dorset, in 1474. It seems, however, that a shared mistress between the two men may provide the crucial link.

Thomas More's version of the events of 13 June makes an important addition to the tenor of Vergil's account, with Richard further accusing the queen of making 'counsel' with Edward IV's mistress Elizabeth Shore. King Edward, More related, would 'say that he had three concubines, which in three divers properties diversely excelled: one the merriest, another the wiliest, the third the holiest harlot in this realm, as one whom no man could get out of church lightly, but it were to his bed'. The merriest, however, 'was this Shore's wife, in whom the king therefore took special pleasure. For many he had, but her he loved.'[26]

Few in the council believed the fact that Queen Elizabeth would 'of all folk . . . make Shore's wife of counsel, whom of all women she most hated, as that concubine whom the king her husband had most loved'. More believed that Elizabeth Shore had struck up a new friendship, not with the queen, but with Hastings, describing how when Edward IV died, Hastings 'took her, which in the king's days, albeit he was sore enamoured upon her, yet he forbade her'.[27]

Shore's house was searched, and ransacked of all its goods worth over 3,000 marks. She was thrown into prison, while attempts were made to bring charges that she 'went about to bewitch him and that she was of counsel with the lord chamberlain to destroy him'. When these charges failed to convince, only then did Richard accuse her of sexual immorality, 'the thing that herself could not deny, that all the world wist was true, and that nevertheless every man laughed at to hear it then so suddenly so highly taken'.

Richard ordered Thomas Kemp, the bishop of London, to subject Shore to 'open penance, going before the cross in procession upon a Sunday, with a taper in her hand'. This she did, More later reported, with a countenance and pace so demure and womanly, that despite being stripped down to just her kirtle, she appeared 'so fair and lovely', blushing through the embarrassment of the spectacle, 'that her great shame won her much praise among those that were more amorous of her body than curious of her soul'.

Several months later, however, Richard would accuse Thomas, the marquess of Dorset, of 'holding the unshameful and mischievous woman called Shore's wife, in adultery'. This link between Hastings, Shore and Dorset is intriguing, and worth considering: immediately after reporting news of Hastings's execution, Mancini noted how Dorset had eluded the concerted manhunt by Richard's men. 'The duke learned from his spies', Mancini wrote, 'that the marquess had left the sanctuary, and, supposing that he was hiding in the adjacent neighbourhood, he surrounded with troops and dogs the already grown crops and the cultivated and woody places, and sought after him, after the manner of huntsmen, by a very close encirclement: but he was never found'.[28]

In a letter to Sir William Stonor, sent on 20 June, Simon Stallworth noted how Thomas Rotherham, John Morton and Oliver King 'are yet in the Tower', though he supposed that 'they shall come out nevertheless'. Men had been sent to search their London residences 'for sure keeping'; he suspected that 'there shall be sent men of my lord Protector's to these lord's places in the country. They are not like to come out of ward yet.' Immediately after referring to those arrested on 13 June, Stallworth continued: 'As for Foster [John Forster] he is in hold and men fear for his life. Mistress Shore is in prison; what shall happen her I know not.'[29] It seems that More was indeed correct in inferring that Elizabeth Shore had been involved with Hastings, just as it seems there must have been a link between John Forster and Hastings. The additional evidence of the timing of the marquess of Dorset's flight, together with the confiscation of his goods, suggests that Richard had discovered evidence that linked Hastings and Dorset, together with Elizabeth Shore and John Forster, in some form of association. Whether this was enough to convict Hastings in any court of law seems highly doubtful, but whatever secret messages had been passed from Hastings, via Forster or Shore, to Dorset, or indeed Queen Elizabeth, provided Richard with the pretext for launching his sudden attack.

Tellingly, however, Stallworth added in a final postscript to his letter how since Hastings's execution 'all the lord Chamberlain's men become my lord of Buckingham's men'.[30] If Buckingham had hoped to benefit from his rival's fall, his plan had worked. Both men were now free to act as they chose. 'In this way, without justice or judgement', the Crowland chronicler wrote, 'the three strongest supporters of the new king were removed and, with all the rest of his faithful men expecting something similar, these two dukes did thereafter what they wanted'.[31]

The change in the capital was immediately noticeable. 'Then great confusion and great fear attacked all men', Polydore Vergil later mused.[32] There certainly seems to have been a raised threat, for on 20 June 'it was showed the mind of the Mayor and Aldermen' that a watch was to be held at the Cheap, with seven fellowships taking their turn to stand guard. The state of alarm and confusion in the capital is well illustrated by a note written by the London merchant George Cely:

> There is great rumour in the realm. The Scots have done great in England. The Chamberlain is deceased, in trouble the Chancellor is disproved and not content. The bishop of Ely is dead. If the king, God save his life, were deceased. The duke of Gloucester were in any peril. If my lord Prince, God defend, were troubled. If my lord Northumberland were dead or greatly troubled. If my lord Howard were slain. De monsieur Saint John's.[33]

The final reference is to Sir John Weston, the prior of the Order of St John of Jerusalem, who was Cely's main source of information. It is clear that a great many rumours, mostly untrue, were flying around, though, interestingly, Cely and Weston both had bought into the rumour that Richard himself might be in 'peril'.

Still, men were prepared to believe that Richard was acting in the best interests of the king. 'Thus far, though all the evidence looked as if he coveted the crown', Mancini observed, 'yet there remained some hope, because he was not yet claiming the throne, inasmuch as he still professed to do all these things as an avenger of treason and old wrongs, and because all private deeds and official documents bore the titles and name of King Edward V. But after Hastings was removed, all the attendants who had waited upon the king were debarred access to him.'[34]

With the planned coronation of Edward V just a week away, events now moved fast. Richard's immediate priority was to secure the possession of the king's brother, Richard, duke of York, still in sanctuary with his mother, Queen Elizabeth, at Westminster. Already, Dominic Mancini wrote, Richard had 'with the consent of the council ... surrounded the sanctuary with troops'.[35] With Hastings dead, now the duke decided to act. The Crowland chronicler recorded how 'the following Monday they came by boat to Westminster with a great crowd, with swords and clubs and compelled the Lord Cardinal of Canterbury to enter the sanctuary, with many others, to allow her son Richard to leave and come to the Tower for the comfort of his brother', while Simon Stallworth noted how 'on Monday last was at Westminster great plenty of harnessed men there was the deliverance of the Duke of York to my lord Cardinal'. Under the date of 16 June in the household accounts of John, Lord Howard, is the ominous entry for '8 boats up and down from Westminster'.[36]

Archbishop Bourchier of Canterbury, together with John, Lord Howard, and the duke of Buckingham, argued that Queen Elizabeth and her children should 'return to the realm' and give up sanctuary, for which 'they gave both private and public faith'. When Elizabeth continued to refuse, instead they asked 'at least for her son Richard'. The choice of the aged Thomas Bourchier seems to have persuaded Elizabeth to finally relinquish her son, 'trusting in the word of the cardinal of Canterbury', Mancini wrote, who himself seems to have believed that there was 'no guile' behind Richard's motivations, and 'persuaded the queen to do this, seeking as much to prevent a violation of the sanctuary as to mitigate by his good services the fierce resolve of the duke'.[37] There was little else that Queen Elizabeth could do. She could see that Richard had 'herself besieged' in 'preparation for violence'. According to the Crowland chronicler, Elizabeth 'in words, assenting with many thanks to this proposal, she accordingly sent the boy' out of sanctuary. Elizabeth delivered her son to the archbishop, wrote one chronicler, 'by fair means, and for trust that the Queen had in the archbishop, which Bishop thought nor intended none harm'.[38]

The young prince was taken first to Westminster Hall, where he was met by the Chancellor, John Russell, 'and many lords temporal' along with the duke of Buckingham, who met him in the middle of the hall. He was then escorted to the door of the Star Chamber, where he was received by his uncle, Richard, 'with many loving words', Simon Stallworth wrote, 'and so departed with my lord Cardinal to the Tower where he is, blessed be Jesu Mercy'.

Richard's lodging in the Tower with his elder brother, Edward, 'did not arouse suspicion at that time' since kings and their close relatives were expected to make a formal procession from the Tower to Westminster the day before the coronation.[39] Nevertheless, 'after this', one London chronicler wrote, 'were the prince and the duke of York holden more strength and then was privy talking in London that the lord protector should be king'.[40] At the same time Richard ordered that his brother Clarence's son, the ten-year-old Edward, earl of Warwick, be brought to the city, where he was placed in the custody of his wife, Anne. For Mancini, it was an early sign as to Richard's intentions to seize the throne for himself: 'for he feared that if the entire progeny of King Edward became extinct, yet this child, who was also of royal blood, would still embarrass him'.[41]

The Crowland chronicler noted how, from the moment that Richard, duke of York, had been placed in the Protector's care, 'both these dukes showed their intentions, not in private but openly'.[42] Richard 'took off the mourning clothes that he had always worn since his brother's death', Mancini observed, 'and putting on purple raiment he often rode through the capital surrounded by a thousand attendants'. The public display, the Italian concluded, was intended to 'receive the attention and applause of the people as yet under the name of protector', but already it had been noted that 'each day he entertained to dinner at his private dwellings an increasingly large number of men'.[43] Thomas More later described how 'for little and little all folk withdrew from the Tower and drew to Crosby's place in Bishopsgate Street where the protector kept his household. The protector had the resort, the king, in manner desolate.'[44]

If Richard hoped that such displays of largesse would help to win around the hearts and minds of the public, the reaction of Londoners watching the spectacle was disquieting. 'When he exhibited himself through the streets of the city he was scarcely watched by anybody', Dominic Mancini wrote, observing the events unfold by the day, 'rather did they curse him with a fate worthy of his crimes, since no one now doubted at what he was aiming.'[45] Mancini wrote his account of these summer months when he had returned to France, finishing his text in December the same year, by which time he had an opportunity to reflect upon what had taken place. In retrospect, it was easy to see where Richard's actions were leading. Yet in the confusion of the present, uncertainty remained as to what exactly had happened to Hastings in the Tower; still Richard presented himself as the loyal uncle and Protector, determined to defend the king's interests. His letters condemning the Woodvilles had been written on behalf of the king; in an age when disinformation was more likely to be spread than accurate information, who could really have known what Richard intended, or what the consequences of his actions would be?

With both the king and his brother now safely in Richard's hands, the following day, 17 June, the decision was taken to cancel the summoning of Parliament, with writs of supersedeas being issued. No explanation was given for the cancellation. Parliament and the coronation were now officially postponed until 9 November, with the mayor and aldermen announcing to the city of London that the money collected for Edward V's coronation gift would be returned to the city's wards due to the postponement.[46] At New Romney, the corporation records show how there was 'paid for a message from Dover Castle, postponing Parliament and the Coronation'. The message arrived too late for the corporation, which had already sent John Cheyne 'riding to aid at the Coronation of King Edward V'; he must have just departed before the message had arrived, since the journey time between New Romney and the capital was at least two days.[47] Instead, the nobility were summoned from their estates across the country. Believing that they were being recalled to 'hear the reason for Hastings's execution' and to set a new date for the coronation, each arrived with his own sizeable retinues; instead they were ordered to 'retain a few attendants' and send home their servants and armed men to prevent the threat of looting.[48] Simon Stallworth wrote on 21 June how Edward, Lord Lisle, 'is come to my Lord Protector and awaits upon him', while the capital nervously awaited the arrival of troops from the north, adding how 'It is thought there shall be 20 thousand of my Lord Protector and my Lord of Buckingham's men in London this week, to what intent I know not but to keep the peace.'[49]

Nearly a fortnight had passed since Richard had composed his letters to the city of York and Ralph, Lord Neville, requesting their support against a Woodville conspiracy. Richard must have known on 10 June that his actions would set in train a series of events from which there would be no return. Yet it is unclear whether even the duke could have anticipated that within the next fourteen days William, Lord Hastings, would have been executed. Instead, it seems highly probable that Richard had been bounced into taking action sooner than he might have wished. The duke would have known that the northern army he had summoned would not arrive at the capital until 25 June at the earliest. As it happened, the earl of Northumberland and Richard Ratcliffe had not departed from Pontefract even by this date. Had Richard intended to wait until their arrival before springing his trap? As it happened, and events unfolded differently, the duke's hand was forced to take action much earlier than he must have hoped was necessary.

If the content of the Chancellor John Russell's draft sermon for the opening of Parliament is taken at face value, it seems that Richard's initial ambitions had been for the continuation of the protectorate. If so, Richard anticipated that he would face resistance from the queen and the Woodvilles that would need to be countered, hence his need to arrange a final attack on the queen and 'her adherents'. He had not bargained on William, Lord Hastings, choosing to take sides with the queen. When Hastings's links with Elizabeth Shore and the marquess of Dorset were uncovered, together with other links involving John Forster, Thomas Rotherham and John Morton, which suggested that Hastings had drawn increasingly close to the 'queen's party', Richard knew that he had to strike first, sooner than he had expected.

If the decision to execute Hastings was a knee-jerk response to what must have seemed remarkable news, it was also the catalyst for the sudden need to remove Richard, duke of York, from sanctuary, stripping the Woodvilles of any remaining power that they might have. Even then, Queen Elizabeth did not envisage her younger son Richard's fate when she allowed him to leave sanctuary in preparation for his elder brother's coronation; neither did the council, which allowed Richard to surround the sanctuary at Westminster with troops. Even the archbishop of Canterbury felt prepared to persuade the queen to hand over her son, doing so in good faith that they could still ensure that stability and order prevailed. Even after the coronation and Parliament were postponed, many in the council were still convinced that Richard's ambitions could not extend beyond the preservation of the Yorkist polity and the safe accession of Edward V. As late as 18 June, the young king was still signing warrants, while orders were issued for the appointment of men to gather food for the royal household for the next six months on 17 June.[50] Yet the business of government began to slowly wind down. In the signet office, the last document to survive is dated 11 June, while the last grants to pass the Great Seal took place on 14 and 15 June. The final date for any government business to be transacted under the name of Edward V was on the same date as Stallworth's letter, 21 June.[51]

9

'UNDOUBTED SON AND HEIR'

On Sunday, 22 June, crowds gathered outside St Paul's to listen to a sermon to be preached by Ralph Shaa, the brother of the mayor of London, Edmund Shaa. Both Richard and Buckingham had arrived to attend the spectacle, 'with a huge audience of lords spiritual and temporal'. Mancini wrote how Shaa in his sermon 'did not blush to say, in the face of decency and all religion, that the progeny of King Edward should be instantly eradicated, for neither had he been a legitimate king, nor could his issue be so. Edward, said they, was conceived in adultery and in every way was unlike the late duke of York, whose son he was falsely said to be, but Richard, duke of Gloucester, who altogether resembled his father, was come to the throne as the legitimate successor.'[1] Listening to the sermon preached by Shaa, who expounded the claim that 'Edward was not born of Richard duke of York, but from a certain other, who secretly knew his mother', few could believe what they were hearing. When Shaa continued his argument that 'no one could doubt . . . Richard is the true son of the duke, who by right should inherit his father's realm due to him, and since they were presently without a king, they wanted Richard the true royal child to become king', the crowd, 'at once astonished', began to turn against Shaa, 'and detested the great temerity of the orator, as others stood stunned at the strangeness and wonder of the thing, at the manner of madness; others feared for themselves, frightened by the terrible cruelty, as they were friends of the royal children, others judged the act to certainly mean the end for Edward's sons'.

Shaa's sermon was badly received by those listening; 'this sermon so discontented the greater part of the audience', one chronicler noted, 'that after this day [Shaa] was little reputed or regarded'.[2] Thomas More later wrote how Richard and Buckingham had ostentatiously made their way 'through the people and then stood to hearken to the sermon. But the people were so far from crying "King Richard!" that they stood as if they had been turned into stones, for wonder of this shameful sermon. After which, once ended, the preacher got him home and never after dared look out for shame, but kept him out of sight like an owl.'[3]

Richard's intentions were now clear, with Mancini noting that the sermon had been 'a special opportunity of publicly showing his hand'. Everyone now understood that he intended to claim the throne for himself. As one chronicler noted, 'it was declared by Dr Ralph Shaa brother to this mayor and proved by such reasons as he made there and then, that the children of King Edward were not rightful inheritors of the Crown, and that King Edward was not the legitimate son of the Duke of York as the lord protector was'; another wrote that it 'was declared at Paul's cross, that king Edward's children were not rightful inheritors unto the crown, but that the Duke of Gloucester's title was better than theirs'.[4]

Yet the argument used by Shaa, that Edward IV had been illegitimate, would soon be disposed of. The magnitude of the accusation, with Richard accusing his own mother, Cecily, of adultery, seems to have been ill thought through; certainly no one seems to have discussed it with Cecily herself. When she discovered what had been said at St Paul's, she was furious, forcing her son to reconsider his argument for succeeding to the throne. 'The common report was that Edward's sons had been called bastards, not Edward', Vergil wrote, yet this 'in every way is untrue, for Cecily . . . being falsely accused of adultery, complained (as it was said) in many places to many men, some of whom still live, of the great injury done to her by her son Richard'.[5] Instead, a new charge explaining the two princes' illegitimacy, and Richard's right to the throne, would need to be found.

For the moment, no one dared to challenge Richard. The fear of the approaching army from the north instilled a sense of paralysis in the capital. 'Armed men in frightening and unheard of numbers were summoned from the North, Wales and other districts within their command and power', the Crowland chronicler wrote. Yet the northern army, assembled under the leadership of the earl of Northumberland, Richard Ratcliffe and Ralph, Lord Neville, had still to depart Pontefract. Before they did, there was one last piece of business that needed to be dealt with.

Since their arrest on 30 April, Anthony Woodville, Earl Rivers, and Richard Grey, together with Edward V's chamberlain, Richard Vaughan, had been placed in separate prisons at Sheriff Hutton and Middleham. On 23 June, while still imprisoned at Sheriff Hutton, Anthony, Earl Rivers, drew up his 'last will', in no doubt that he was to 'bequeath my soul unto the great mercy of Jesus Christ, and to his dear mother our Lady Saint Mary, and to the glorious company of heaven'. He remained uncertain as to where the exact location of his death might be, requesting that 'if I die beyond the Trent' then he was to be buried beside St Stephen's College in Westminster; if not, then only his heart was to be interred there. Among the executors Rivers named were the Chancellor, John Russell, and William Catesby, while Rivers added, either with a hint of irony or perhaps with genuine forgiveness, that 'I beseech humbly my Lord of Gloucester, in the worship of Christ's passion and for the merit and weal of his soul, to comfort help and assist, as supervisor (for very trust) of this testament, that mine executors may with his pleasure fulfill this my last will.'[6]

It was not until the following day, on 24 June, that Rivers learnt that he was to be moved to Pontefract for his execution; while he had envisaged in the main text of his will that Richard Grey would still survive, now the extent of the Protector's revenge had revealed itself. If Rivers did not know of his and Richard Grey's fate until 24 June, this suggests that Richard had only issued orders for their execution after he had postponed the coronation. Written at the end of the document, almost as a coda, is a chilling clue to the sudden change of plan. Rivers added: 'My will is now to be buried before an Image of our blessed Lady Mary, with my Lord Richard [Grey], in Pontefract; and Ih'u have mercy of my soul.' John Rous later recalled a ballad that he had been told, which Rivers had supposedly written while facing his death at Pontefract Castle, in which the earl mourned the 'unsteadfastness' of the world, 'being of such wheeling'. 'Remediless', Rivers had come to terms with his 'woeful chance', and 'willing to die' could only add sardonically, 'welcome Fortune'.[7]

On 25 June, Rivers was executed at Pontefract, along with Richard Grey and Thomas Vaughan. Their 'chief judge' was the earl of Northumberland, while the Crowland chronicler believed that it had been Sir Richard Rat-cliffe, the 'chief leader and organiser' of the northern army, who had given the orders for their execution 'without any form of trial and in the sight of these same people'. Rous described how they were 'cruelly killed at Pon-tefract, lamented by almost all and innocent of the deed charged against them . . . the said lords were condemned to death as though they had in fact plotted the death of Richard Duke of Gloucester . . . for a thing they had never contemplated, the innocent humbly and peaceably submitted to a cruel fate from their enemies' butchers'. Rous later wrote that when Rivers' body was stripped, the earl 'was found to be wearing, at the time of his death, the hair shirt which he had long been in the habit of wearing against his bare flesh' and which was later hung in front of the image of the Blessed Virgin at the Carmelite Friars in Doncaster.[8]

Northumberland and Ratcliffe had presided over the execution of Rivers, Grey and Vaughan without any judicial process or trial. To do so, they must have been confident that they would escape any future recrimination if Edward V came to the throne; equally, they must have been confident that the man whose orders they were obeying would seek to protect their own interests, suggesting that once they had received the death warrants from the capital, perhaps sent as late as 18 June, they were also aware that now Richard intended to seize the throne for himself. Richard would remain resolute that Rivers deserved to die for his perceived treasons. Later, when granting Rivers' land to his supporter Roger Wake, Richard would describe the earl as 'our rebel Anthony Woodville'.[9] Whether Rivers himself had actively sought to undermine Richard seems highly unlikely; he had even agreed to march with the young king from Ludlow in April with a much reduced household of 2,000 men to dispel any rumours that he intended to unduly use force to establish a Woodville takeover. Rivers himself had been a popular man at court; even Dominic Mancini had heard reported that Rivers 'was always considered a kind, serious, and just man, and one tested by every vicissitude of life. Whatever his prosperity he had injured nobody, though benefiting many.'[10] Yet it was his influence over the young king, as Edward V's governor, that Richard most feared. For this reason alone, he would have to die.

Once the orders for Rivers' execution had been sent to Ratcliffe and Northumberland in the north, probably around 17 or 18 June, Richard must have understood that once the executions had been performed, there could be no turning back. If he was to secure his own preservation, he would need to seize the throne for himself. Having spent much of his protectorate working to continue the household of Edward IV, presenting himself as a beacon of stability, this sudden decision was the inevitable conclusion that Richard must have drawn if he was to escape the civil war and the kind of blood feud that he had witnessed during his younger years.

Richard's decision could not have been a carefully crafted plan. Instead it smacks of a rushed improvisation that had not been thought through. Justification for his intention to seize the throne would need to be found fast; in his haste, Richard clutched at any straw available. Ralph Shaa's sermon on 22 June attempting to set out the moral argument behind why Richard had a stronger claim to the throne than his nephew is a case in point. Not only had the same argument surrounding Edward IV's own illegitimacy been hinted at by the earl of Warwick in 1469, when it was scarcely believed, but the accusation itself created huge constitutional problems for the Yorkist monarchy. The house of York had always based its claims to the crown on its own assertions of legitimate inheritance in the person of Edward IV: through Parliament, it had legislated to ensure that its Lancastrian predecessors were no more than 'kings in deed not of right'. Suddenly, Shaa's assertions that Edward IV was in fact illegitimate would have thrown this entirely into doubt, potentially undermining the foundations of the entire dynasty. The fact that Richard had not even con- sulted his own mother, Cecily, in whose London residence at Baynard's Castle he had been staying, suggests that few could have known of Rich- ard's intentions.

There was one man who seems to have been guiding Richard towards the throne: the duke of Buckingham. One contemporary chronicle noted how Richard, 'with the instigation, advice, and aid of Henry duke of Buck- ingham', had 'himself crowned on fraudulent grounds', while, for John Rous, Richard had been 'strongly encouraged in these things by Henry Duke of Buckingham'.[11]

If Shaa's sermon had miscalculated, Buckingham was determined to resolve the situation. Two days later, on Midsummer's Day, Tuesday, 24 June, the duke came to the Guildhall, where in front of the mayor and 'a great multitude of citizens' he showed 'the title of the Duke of Gloucester, that he had unto the crown, exciting the people to take him for their king'.[12] According to the *Great Chronicle*, Buckingham made his oration, 'rehearsing the great excellency of the lord protector and the manifold virtues which God had endowed him with, and of the rightful title which he had unto the crown'. Buckingham's speech, the chronicler observed, lasted a 'good half hour' and had been 'so well and eloquently uttered and with so angelic a countenance, and every pause and time so well ordered', that men who heard the speech 'marvelled', claiming they had never heard a better speech. When the duke had finished, exhorting the crowd to 'admit the said lord protector for their liege lord and king', it was, however, only 'more for fear than love' that a 'small number' cried: 'Yea! Yea!'[13]

Mancini described a meeting of Buckingham and the lords, which may be the same meeting at the Guildhall. The duke's speech marked a departure in the argument used by Shaa that Edward IV, and by default his sons, had been illegitimate. Instead, a new line of attack against the legitimacy of Edward V had been found. Buckingham argued that 'it would be unjust to crown this lad, who was illegitimate, because his father King Edward on marrying Elizabeth was legally contracted to another wife whom the earl of Warwick had joined him'. Mancini had heard that Warwick had 'espoused the other lady by proxy . . . on the continent' on Edward's authority, most probably Bona of Savoy, the sister-in-law of the French king, Louis XI, who had been in contact with the earl during 1463–4 regarding a foreign marriage for the king.[14] Besides this, the duke argued, 'Elizabeth herself had been married to another, and had been ravished rather than espoused by Edward, with the result that their entire offspring was unworthy of the kingship.' As for the son of the duke of Clarence, Edward, earl of Warwick, he had been barred from the right of succession 'by the felony of his father'. Only Richard, Buckingham argued, with his 'previous career and blameless morals' a sure 'guarantee of his good government', remained as the inheritor to the crown, someone who 'could bear its responsibilities thanks to his proficiency'.

In questioning the legitimacy of Edward IV's marriage, rather than the dead king's own title, Buckingham attempted to construct a new argument for Edward V's deposition. That this should take place had already been decided. Richard and Buckingham just needed the best possible grounds for achieving their desired outcome. Yet Richard still remained hesitant.

Vergil believed that Richard intended to delay further his proclamation
as king, 'by reason of the fear of perils hanging over him from all sides';
however, he was persuaded by 'impatient friends' who 'urged him to take
the realm openly and cried out either he moved quickly or he withdrew'.
Still Richard wished for his title to be referred to the magistrates and
judges, arguing that rather than seizing the throne 'by force of assumed
domination', instead he might justify 'by considered opinion it could be
said to be done'.[15]

Buckingham's arguments may not have convinced those listening,
but for many they felt that they had little choice. After listening to the
duke's speech, 'the lords consulted their own safety'; it was fear rather
than through any sincere belief in any pretexts of legitimacy that made
their own minds up. 'Warned by the example of Hastings, and perceiving
the alliance of the two dukes, whose power, supported by a multitude of
troops, would be difficult and hazardous to resist', Mancini observed, 'they
saw themselves surrounded and in the hands of the dukes, and therefore
they determined to declare Richard their king and ask him to undertake
the burden of office.' Mancini described how the day after Buckingham's
address, though more likely on 26 June, the lords 'foregathered at the
house of Richard's mother, whither he had purposely betaken himself,
that these events might not take place in the Tower where the young king
was confined'.[16] A delegation of lords, both spiritual and temporal, and
commoners then presented Richard with a bill of petition, urging him to
take the throne.

The Crowland chronicler corroborates the fact that a bill, justifying
Richard's claim to the throne, had been 'put forward, by means of a sup-
plication contained in a certain parchment roll', explaining how 'King
Edward's sons were bastards, by submitting that he had been precon-
tracted to a certain Lady Boteler before he married Queen Elizabeth and,
further, that the blood of his other brother, George, duke of Clarence,
had been attainted so that, at the time, no certain and uncorrupt blood
of the lineage of Richard, duke of York, was to be found except in the
person of the said Richard, duke of Gloucester.' The chronicler described
how at the end of the roll, 'on behalf of the lords and commonalty of the
kingdom', Richard was urged 'to assume his lawful rights'. 'It was put
about then', the chronicler added, 'that this roll originated in the North

whence so many people came to London although there was no one who did not know the identity of the author (who was in London all the time) of such sedition and infamy.' The chronicler's doubts were shared by John Rous, who wrote how Richard had 'found a title to the crown to disinherit his lord the king . . . that is, not found but feigned it for his own advancement.'[17]

A copy of the petition survives in a bill that was presented to Parliament the following year, later formally named the *Titulus Regius*. It is not certain whether this version was in fact the same as the text presented in June 1483; nevertheless, it resembles the final, refined arguments justifying Richard's accession to the throne.

The preamble of the petition consisted of a general condemnation of the last years of Edward IV's reign, contrasting how in times past the kingdom had 'stood in great prosperity, honour, and tranquillity' when the king had taken counsel from 'persons of approved sadness, prudence, policy, and experience, dreading God, and having tender zeal and affection to indifferent ministration of justice, and to the common and politique weal of the land'. The immediate logic of the petition, no doubt written by men close to Richard, was to make a moral case for Richard's accession as a break with the misdeeds of his brother's reign, during which the laws of inheritance had been so perverted, and 'all manner of equity and laws laid apart and despised' that murder, extortion and oppression had been allowed to run rife, 'so that no man was sure of his life, land, ne livelihood, ne of his wife, daughter, no servant, every good maiden and woman standing in dread to be ravished and defouled'.[18]

Among the hyperbole, one constant theme peppered the petition: Edward IV's 'ungracious pretensed marriage' to Elizabeth, 'sometime wife to Sir John Grey'. This had been conducted 'of great presumption, without the knowing or assent of the lords of this land, and also by sorcery and witchcraft, committed by the said Elizabeth and her mother, Jacquetta, duchess of Bedford, as the common opinion of the people and the public voice, and fame is through all this land; and hereafter, if and as the case shall require, shall be proved sufficiently in time and place convenient'. It was on the legal basis of Edward IV's marriage to Elizabeth Woodville that the petition focused much of its attention. It condemned that marriage as being made 'privately and secretly, with edition of banns, in a private chamber, a profane place, and not openly in the face of the church'. And, further, it considered:

> how also, that at the time of the contract of the same pretensed marriage, and before and long time after, the said King Edward was and stood married and troth plight to one Dame Eleanor Butteler, daughter of the old Earl of Shrewsbury, with whom the said King Edward had made a pre-contract of matrimony, long time before he made the said pretensed marriage with the said Elizabeth Grey in manner and form aforesaid.[19]

As a result of the pre-contract, Edward and Elizabeth had 'lived together sinfully and damnably in adultery, against the law of God and his church'; the petition stated it now automatically followed 'that all the issue and children of the said king been bastards, and unable to inherit or to claim anything by inheritance, by the law and custom of England'. It repeated Buckingham's assertion that since George, duke of Clarence, had also been attainted of high treason, he had been barred from any claim to the throne. As a result, only Richard could claim to be the 'undoubted son and heir' of Richard, duke of York, and therefore the true heir to the English throne.

Echoing the initial accusations of bastardy placed upon Edward IV at Ralph Shaa's sermon at St Paul's on 22 June, the petition noted how Richard alone among his brothers had been 'born within this land, by reason whereof, as we deme in our minds, ye be more naturally inclined to the prosperity and common weal of the same', adding somewhat cryptically that, if necessary, 'all the three estates of the land have, and may have more certain knowledge of your birth and filiation'. The petition went on to praise Richard for his 'great wit, prudence, justice, princely courage, and the memorable and laudable acts in diverse battles which we by experience know ye heretofore have done for the salvation and defence of this same realm, and also the great noblesse and excellence of your birth and blood'.

Considering all these arguments, the petition concluded, 'we desiring affectuously the peace, tranquillity and weal public of this land' and its return to prosperity, as well as having 'singular confidence' in Richard's 'great prudence, justice, princely courage and excellent virtue', the petitioners requested that they had 'chosen in all that is in us and by this our writing choose you, high and mighty Prince into our King and sovereign lord, to whom we know for certain it appertaneth of inheritance so to be chosen'.

Once again, the official explanation for Edward V's illegitimacy had changed. Now an entirely new basis for disinheriting Edward IV's children had been found, this time centring not on a pre-contract with a foreign bride, but with Lady Eleanor Butler. Born Eleanor Talbot, she was the daughter of John, Lord Talbot, later 1st earl of Shrewsbury, who died on campaign in France in 1453. Her mother was Lady Margaret Beauchamp, the eldest daughter of Richard Beauchamp, 13th earl of Warwick; her mother's half-sister, Anne, was the wife of Richard Neville, 16th earl of Warwick, making Eleanor cousins with Isabel and Anne Neville. Eleanor, one of the couple's five children, was probably born around March 1436. Aged fourteen, she was married to Sir Thomas Butler, the heir of Lord Sudeley: Butler died in 1461, leaving Eleanor a childless widow. It is possible that Butler was killed fighting on the Lancastrian side that spring; after Edward had become king, he confiscated Butler's lands on the grounds that they had been granted by Lord Sudeley, still a committed Lancastrian, without royal licence. Eleanor appeared before the king to appeal the decision: Edward was nineteen and Eleanor was six years older when their meeting soon led to something altogether different. The Burgundian chronicler Commynes later claimed that Edward promised to marry Eleanor, 'provided that he could sleep with her first'.[20] Eleanor agreed, though not before Edward 'had made this promise' in the presence of the cleric Robert Stillington, 'and having done so, he slept with her'. In effect, Edward had entered into a pre-contract of marriage with Eleanor: a promise of marriage, followed by sexual intercourse, was all that was needed to create a binding contract recognised by the decretals of Pope Alexander III as having entered into a union that was valid. The only means by which Edward could have broken out of this pre-contract was if he had married any subsequent bride in a church and in public: something which he had conspicuously failed to do with his secret marriage to Elizabeth Woodville.[21]

If Eleanor hoped that the king might honour his promise, she was quickly disappointed. She may have gone to live with her sister Elizabeth, residing at Framlingham Castle in Norfolk, and became involved with the Carmelite Friary in Norwich, as well as giving bequests to Corpus Christi College, Cambridge. She died in 1468, aged only thirty-two; her death was certainly unexpected, for her sister and executrix was out of the country at the time.[22]

Years later Philippe de Commynes would write how the bishop of Bath and Wells, Robert Stillington, had 'revealed to the duke of Gloucester that King Edward, being very enamoured of a certain English lady, promised to marry her, provided that he could sleep with her first, and she consented. The bishop said that he had married them when only he and they were present. He was a courtier so he did not disclose this fact but helped to keep the lady quiet.' Stillington, having revealed to Richard the details of the pre-contract, then 'helped him a great deal in the execution of his evil plan'.[23] Much has been made of Stillington's role in revealing the so-called 'pre-contract', providing the final justification needed for Richard to seize the throne, yet what matters is not so much whether the pre-contract story were true or false, but whether people believed it to be true or not. Under canon law, the existence of a pre-contract would have presented a strong case for declaring the sons of Edward IV illegitimate. Edward had been in effect practising bigamy, and would have been seen as an adulterer. This rendered him incapable of marrying at any time in the future, since under canon law marriage was forbidden to a person who had been 'polluted' by adultery, when that adultery had involved a marriage contact. This had important implications for Edward's own marriage to Elizabeth Woodville. Having entered into a marriage pre-contract with Eleanor Butler, Edward was in effect committing adultery with Elizabeth, which then prevented him from legally marrying her.[24] Questions remain over whether Richard should have technically presented his case to a church court for judgement, but if he was acting on Stillington's advice, he possibly believed that the church's judgement would be behind him.

If Stillington had provided the material for the final version of the petition presented to Richard, justifying his claim to the throne, then it was also clear he was only furnishing Richard with additional, more detailed evidence for a claim he was already convinced he had. From the sermon preached by Dr Ralph Shaa at St Paul's Cross on 22 June, setting out Edward IV's own illegitimacy, to the final establishment of the claim that in fact it was Edward IV's children who were illegitimate due to the fact that Edward had been betrothed to another woman before his marriage to Elizabeth Woodville, it seems that there was no one clear version of why

Edward V was to be pronounced 'Edward the bastard'. Edward IV's play-boy reputation left enough latitude for other candidates to be found, but eventually the pre-contract argument would settle upon Eleanor Butler. The accusation was mere justification of a decision that had already been taken, and would have been taken anyhow: Richard had already resolved to secure the throne and depose his nephew.

What it is important to reflect upon is not necessarily the exact details of the pre-contract accusations and their validity in canon law, but the fact that contemporaries do not seem to have discussed in any great detail why the deposition should be taking place. As Mancini wrote, 'acts in the name of Edward V since the death of his father were repealed or suspended, seals and titles changed, and everything confirmed and carried on in the name of Richard III'.[25] It was this passive acceptance of Richard's accession that is most striking about his seizure of the throne, and the lack of resistance to what was considered a done deal.

Of course, both the Crowland chronicler and the text of the parliamentary petition could be later inventions: at the precise time of Richard's accession, the exact mechanism of Edward V's deposition might not yet have been finalised. Certainly the official records of the Exchequer remained vague about the legitimacy of Richard's title. When a writ dated 14 June in Edward V's reign was not able to be issued until after Richard had ascended the throne, the text of the grant explained that Richard 'as true and undoubted king of this realm of England by divine and human right' had taken 'the royal dignity and power and the rule and governance of the same realm for himself' from 'Edward the Bastard, formerly called Edward the fifth, king of England without just title exorcising and in possession of the government of the same realm, the royal dignity of the same and of the power, in the realm of England, from the same Edward legitimately having been removed by usurpation'.[26] In a separate document, a response to a letter from Lord Dynham, the governor of Calais, who wrote requesting what to tell his men who had sworn oaths of fealty to Edward V, Richard sent instructions on 28 June explaining that although 'such oath of allegiance' to Edward V 'was made soon upon the death of the said king Edward the iiiith to his son, not only at Calais but also in diverse places in England by many great estates and personages', they had been 'ignorant of the very sure and true title which our sovereign lord that now is, king

Richard the iiird, hath and had the same time to the crown of England'. In spite of the previous oath that they had sworn, 'now every good true Englishman is bound upon knowledge had of the said very true title, to depart from the first oath so ignorantly given to him to whom it appertained not'. Richard's 'sure and true title', the letter explained, 'is evidently showed and declared in a bill of petition which the lords spiritual and temporal and the commons of this land solemnly porrected [reached out] unto the king's highness at London the xxvith day of June . . .'[27]

Once Richard had formally accepted the petition declaring Edward V and his brother Richard illegitimate, the assembled group conducted him to the Palace of Westminster, walking on foot and followed by a 'great train' that included 'a great company of lords and gentlemen, with also the Mayor and the crafts'.

Richard himself rode on a specially provided saddle of rich crimson cloth of gold, 'wrought with nets and roses', together with a saddle for his swordbearer, indicating that the entire spectacle had been prearranged, and that the presentation of the petition was a mere formality, part of the display intended to demonstrate Richard's accession.[28] Two days later, Richard was able to boast to Lord Dynham at Calais how, 'notably assisted by well near all the lords spiritual and temporal of this realm', he 'went the same day unto his Palace of Westminster, and there in such royal honourable apparel within the great hall there, took possession and declared his mind that the same day he would begin to reign upon his people; and from thence rode solemnly to the cathedral church of London, and was received there with procession with great congratulation and acclamation of all the people in every place and by the way that the king was in that day'.[29]

Arriving at Westminster Hall, Richard put on his royal robes and, with a sceptre in his hand, formally took possession of the throne by sitting in the marble chair of the Court of King's Bench. Richard then informed the assembled judges that he intended to 'take upon him the crown' and would 'ministreth the law, because he considered that it was the chiefest duty of a king to minister the laws'. He ordered that the judges appear before him, while he spoke, 'commanding them in right straight manner that they justly and duly should minister his law without delay or favour', as one chronicler reported, 'justly and indifferently to every person as well to poor as rich'.[30] According to a later chronicler, with this 'pleasant oration as he could', Richard intended to 'win the hearts of the nobles, the merchants and artificers, and in conclusion all kind of men, but special the lawyers of this realm'. Determined that 'no man should hate him for fear', Richard 'declared the discommodity of discord, and the commodity of concord and unity'; at the same time he made a proclamation of pardon to 'all offences committed against him'.[31]

As proof of his new-found clemency, Richard ordered that Sir John Fogge should be brought before him. Fogge was a Woodville associate, and former household official of Queen Elizabeth, who had fled into sanctuary earlier in the year. In front of the gathered audience, Richard publicly took him by the hand, 'which thing the common people rejoiced at and praised', one commentator observed, 'but wise men took it for a vanity'. After he had given his address, Richard made the short walk across to the abbey, where at the church door he was met with a procession led by the abbot, who handed to him the sceptre of St Edward, which the king then offered up at the shrine of St Edward in the abbey.[32] Returning to Baynard's Castle, 'whomsoever he met, he saluted'.

The following day, at three o'clock, the council gathered in a room within the chapel of Baynard's Castle. There Richard, in the presence of Bishop Stillington of Bath and Wells, Bishop Courtenay of Exeter, Bishop Goldwell of Norwich, the duke of Buckingham, Thomas Stanley and John Gunthorpe, delivered the Great Seal enclosed in a 'bag of white leather' to John Russell, confirming his reappointment as Chancellor.[33] According to one chronicler, 'hasty provision' was now made for Richard and Anne's coronation, with the Keeper of the Great Wardrobe, Piers Curteys, receiving orders on 27 June to have materials and clothes for the ceremony prepared within six days. There was an enormous amount to do, not only in preparing the royal garments, but clothes for the entire procession of the nobility who would be involved in the ceremony. It was traditional for the king to issue special gifts of scarlet robes to knights and nobility attending the coronation; whereas Henry IV issued 2,895 ells (3,618¾ yards) to 611 people, only 522¾ yards of cloth were issued for Richard's coronation, an indication of the hastily arranged nature of the ceremony, which had to be planned within days not weeks.[34] Still, the total cost of the coronation would finally amount to £3,124 12s 3¾d, much of which would be spent on expensive cloths of gold, velvet and no fewer than 68,701 'powderings' of 'bogy shanks', a fur made of lamb's wool.

Within three weeks, Richard had gone from sitting in meetings of the council in early June as Protector, planning Edward V's coronation on 22 June, to ordering his own coronation as Richard III. Just twenty days had passed, yet the speed at which events had unfolded was breathtaking. Whether by design or whether he had felt he had no other option but to pursue the throne, by accident or ambition, by the influence of others or by his own individual actions, Richard had managed to secure the kingdom for himself, perhaps faster than any other king in English history. Within twenty days, Richard had not only turned every single acceptable political convention on its head, but had done so by departing entirely from his own self-image as the loyal brother and Protector, dumbfounding his contemporaries. Across his path to the throne, he had cut down some of the most influential and important members of the Yorkist nobility, the broken bodies of Hastings, Rivers, Grey and others testament to his ruthlessness. Yet Richard's success was not his alone; he had already recognised the part the duke of Buckingham had played in his accession, yet there were other members of the nobility who saw in Richard a means for their own advancement. They too, in due course, would expect reward. Meanwhile, thousands of northern men continued their march upon the capital, men whose own loyalties had been carefully cultivated by Richard as a northern overlord. Now they came southwards, not, as they had intended, to protect their lord from attack, but to witness his accession as king.

PART THREE

KING

10

'GOING IN GREAT TRIUMPH'

In advance of the coronation, security was tightly controlled. On 2 July, a proclamation was issued strictly forbidding any quarrels or violent behaviour, with a curfew being enforced, so that 'every man be in his lodging by x of the clock in the night', while no one 'other than such that his highness hath licenced' should bear arms, 'that is to say glaives, bills . . . long or short swords and bucklers' under pain of imprisonment.[1] Meanwhile the capital braced itself for the arrival of the northern army that was anticipated to reach the city at any moment. 'Armed men in frightening and unheard of numbers were summoned from the North', the Crowland chronicler wrote. The sense of foreboding had its antecedents in recent history, with a general suspicion amongst southerners bordering on paranoia about the savageness of their northern counterparts.[2]

This time, things would be different. The army was not that of an invading force; rather, it now represented the retinue of a king. On 3 July, the Mercers' Company recorded their preparations to receive 'the earl of Northumberland and the earl of Westmorland with many other knights, esquires, gentiles and commons now coming out of the North, to the number 10,000 men or more'. Noting how the two earls with their company currently 'doth hove and abode' in the field between London and Halywell, the mercers observed how Richard intended to ride out into the field and had commanded 'that the King's desire is to see all the said Company whole in their array'. Every member, the mercers concluded, should gather at the Leadenhall at eleven o'clock on 6 July, to travel to Bishopsgate and through the city 'set in a ray'.[3] John Stowe described the northern army, on his first sighting of it as it reached the capital, as 'meanly

apparelled, and worse harnessed'.[4] Mancini, who believed that Richard
had summoned the troops from his own estates and those of the duke
of Buckingham, since 'he was afraid lest any uproar should be fomented
against him at his coronation, when there would be a very great concourse
of people', described how Richard 'himself went out to meet the soldiers
before they entered the city; and, when they were drawn up in a circle on
a very great field, he passed them with bared head around their ranks and
thanked them'.[5]

After surveying his assembled army from Finsbury Fields, Richard returned to the city, processing along Bishopsgate, Leadenhall, Cornhill and
Cheapside, arriving at St Paul's to hear mass. As Richard made his journey,
he would have seen the 156 men from the city companies wearing specially
hired white harnesses who lined the route, on the orders of the mayor,
Edmund Shaa.[6] Returning to Baynard's Castle, Richard exchanged gifts
with his Duchess Anne, the future queen, who was busy in preparation
for the coronation in just three days' time; their joint coronation was to be
the first double coronation for both a king and a queen since the coronation of Edward II and Isabella in 1308. Anne had ordered a 'long gown of
purple cloth of gold, wrought with garters and roses' and lined with white
damask to be specially made for her husband, as 'the gift of our sovereign
Lady the Queen'.[7] In return, Richard gave Anne twenty-four yards of precious purple cloth of gold, twenty yards of which had been 'wrought with
garters', and seven yards of purple velvet, 'to our said sovereign Lady the
Queen for to have of the especial gift of our said sovereign Lord the King'.[8]

The next day, 4 July, Richard and Anne departed Baynard's Castle together for the Tower of London. Usually the journey was the occasion for
the monarch to pass by a multitude of pageants, plays and salutes from the
city companies, yet these were absent for Richard's coronation, no doubt
due to lack of preparation time. Instead it seems that the new king and
queen chose to be escorted to the Tower by barge on the river, possibly on
a freshly painted green and white barge, decorated with ostrich feathers
and a gold crown and white lion, bearing the royal arms.[9] After taking part
in the ceremony of creating new knights of the Bath, Richard was served
his dinner by the seventeen esquires chosen to be knights, before they
were taken away to be bathed. Since it was a Friday, only fish was served
that night, comprising a short menu of two courses of nine, then twelve

dishes, including salt fish, crabs, pike and gurnard for starters, then more elaborate freshwater fish dishes, including tench, bass, conger, salmon, perch, trout and a roast porpoise.[10] While the prospective knights were then to continue their evening at prayer, each with a lighted taper, until dawn, Richard and Anne would have departed to bed early, in preparation for more elaborate ceremonies the next day, as part of the vigil of the coronation. The following morning, Richard personally knighted those esquires who had stayed up until dawn; yet another dinner followed, with the newly created knights again serving the king two courses of thirteen, then fifteen dishes of fish. A large gathering must have been in attendance, for among other fish, 250 pikes, 600 plaice, 7,000 whelks and 1,344 salt eel were ordered for the dinner.[11]

Meanwhile, outside in the Tower grounds and on the streets of the capital, preparations busily continued, ready for the king and queen's procession that afternoon along the streets towards Westminster. The streets had been freshly swept and new gravel placed along the route, while behind the hastily erected barriers stood the city's companies in their best liveries, including the merchants of the Steelyard at Gracechurch, and the Goldsmiths' Company at the western end of Cheapside. 'Sights' had been constructed at certain points along the route, with stands of minstrels and singing children waiting in anticipation to greet the monarchs, while monuments such as the cross at Cheapside were freshly painted and gilded, as had been planned for Edward V's aborted coronation.

At one o'clock, the procession departed from the Tower. The nobility led the way, followed by the aldermen of the city clothed in scarlet, then the newly created knights of the Bath dressed in blue and white. Next came the clergy and officers of the king's household, the mayor, Sir Edmund Shaa, with the herald John Wrythe, the Garter King of Arms, immediately behind. Next followed the sword of state, commonly known as the 'king's sword', which was carried in its scabbard by Thomas Howard, the newly created earl of Surrey. To Surrey's right, his father, John, duke of Norfolk, rode as Earl Marshal of England; to his left, the duke of Buckingham, wearing blue velvet 'embroidered with the naves of carts burning in gold', rode as Lord Great Chamberlain.

Richard followed behind the two stalwarts of his regime, bareheaded as four knights carried a canopy of red and green baldachin, a richly embroidered silk threaded with gold that would have given the impression of shimmering in the sun. Four silver-gilt bells rang out on each of its corners, announcing the arrival of the king. Under his riding gown of purple velvet – the gift from his wife, Anne – heavily furred with over 3,000 ermine tails, Richard wore a doublet and stomacher of blue cloth of gold decorated with nets and 'pineapples'. On his heels were a pair of gilt spurs, while round his neck was a richly jewelled collar; on his left leg was a garter of the Order. Richard rode on a horse dressed in a trapper of purple cloth of gold, bordered with ermine sewn from 4,000 powderings. The saddle Richard sat upon was furnished with crimson cloth of gold wrought with nets, while his horse paced the route in a trapper of purple cloth of gold, bordered with ermine sewn with nearly 4,000 powderings. It must have been a dazzling sight, as the procession made its long and slow journey from the Tower to Westminster, stopping en route at recognised stages, including at Cheapside, St Paul's Churchyard, Ludgate, Fleet Street, Temple Bar, the Cross in the Strand and Charing Cross. At each of these stopping points, various 'sights' had been arranged for the king. With troops placed at 'suitable points' along the coronation route, Richard and the royal procession 'passing through the midst of the city attended by the entire nobility and a display of royal honours, with bared head he greeted all onlookers, who stood along the streets, and himself received their acclamations'.[12]

Behind the king and his footmen rode the king's henchmen, who included heirs to the most important noble families, including Lords Berkeley and Dacre, with the young Lord Morley being the highest in rank. Each wore crimson satin doublets under gowns of white cloth of gold; they were accompanied by their master, the Master of the King's Horse, Sir James Tyrell, who led the king's horse of estate, a riderless horse dressed exactly the same as the horse the king was riding, except that it carried the royal arms. Following on in the procession were another sixty knights and a hundred squires, the royal household riding while lesser ranks were on foot. Next came the queen's train, in a similar fashion to the king's household, except that their doublets were fashioned from crimson damask. Behind her chamberlain, the queen appeared, sitting among cushions in an open litter that was carried on poles between two palfreys trapped in white damask. Anne wore her hair loose over her shoulders, crowned with a circlet of gold, decorated with pearls and precious stones. Robed in white and gold, over her litter twelve knights carried a canopy decorated with bells; in the summer sun, robed in white and gold, with her train furred with ermine, Anne must have been one of the most striking features of the entire procession, 'a lady of gracious fame', one London chronicler who may have been present on the occasion declared.[13]

Anne was followed by three 'chares', four-wheeled carriages dressed in crimson and trimmed with gold, each bearing the royal arms, in which twelve noblewomen, the queen's ladies-in-waiting, sat in their gowns of blue velvet. A roll call of the wives of the supporters of the new regime, they included the new duchess of Norfolk and the countesses of Surrey and Berkeley, Viscountess Lovell, the two Ladies Fitzhugh, and Lady Scrope of Masham and Upsall, though curiously space was found for the wife of Thomas, Lord Stanley, Margaret Beaufort, the countess of Richmond, and mother of the exiled Lancastrian Henry Tudor, her son from her brief first marriage to Henry VI's half-brother, Edmund Tudor, perhaps as a demonstration that, with Richard's accession, the civil wars of the previous thirty years were considered but a memory.

The procession wound its way slowly through the streets of the capital, so that every man and woman might catch a glimpse of their new king and queen, interrupted by pauses as the new monarchs dutifully listened to the speeches, acts and singing that had been arranged for them at every prearranged station. At one station, the recorder of the city presented the king and queen with purses containing 1,000 marks and 500 marks, the city's contribution towards the cost of the coronation. Finally, arriving at Westminster Hall, Richard and Anne refreshed themselves with wine and spices, before returning to their chambers to change their clothes, then attending supper in the great chamber of the palace, with yet another banquet of fish, served in two courses of ten and thirteen covers. Finally, that evening, returning to his chamber, Richard took a ceremonial bath, lined with champagne-coloured cloth, to cleanse himself before his anointing.[14]

As the palace and the abbey worked through the night to finish the last-minute preparations for the following day, a small candlelit procession made its way from the Jewelhouse of the palace to the altar of Westminster Abbey. Carried in the hands of a bishop was a small golden vessel in the shape of an eagle, 'garnished with pearls of precious stones', that contained the precious holy oil of St Thomas Becket that would be used to anoint the king the following day. Placed upon the altar, the stage was now ready for its great performance.

The next morning, 6 July, Richard rose early, to be dressed by his Great Chamberlain, the duke of Buckingham, in his anointing garments, which included two sarcenet shirts, breeches and crimson hose that were attached to a crimson satin coat which went over the shirts. Anne was dressed by her ladies in a smock and kirtle, beneath a mantle of crimson velvet with a train. Once again she kept her hair loose, held 'conveniently in order' by a jewelled circlet of gold. At seven o'clock in the morning, Richard and Anne made their journey from Whitehall to Westminster Hall, to the king's bench, before the royal couple then walked barefooted to St Edward's shrine, in Westminster Abbey, accompanied by the nobility and the blaring of trumpets, clarions and the heralds of arms dressed in the king's coat of arms. First came the bishops wearing their mitres, the bishop of Rochester bearing the staved cross. Next were the coronation regalia, the earl of Northumberland carrying the blunted sword known as the curtana, unsheathed in his hand; Thomas, Lord Stanley, officiating as Constable, bore the mace; while the earl of Kent, standing to the king's right-hand side, carried the second sword, and Lord Lovell the third sword, to the left of the king. Then came the duke of Suffolk, bearing the sceptre, while the earl of Lincoln carried 'the cross with the ball', the earl of Surrey the fourth sword of estate, still in its scabbard, before the duke of Norfolk, who carried the royal crown in both hands. Richard followed, wearing 'robes of purple velvet', while the barons of the Cinque Ports carried a cloth of estate, a canopy of red and green baldachin fringed with Lucchese gold, over his head. The bishop of Bath and Wells, Robert Stillington, and William Dudley, the bishop of Durham, then followed on their side of the king, with the duke of Buckingham carrying the king's train, while holding aloft the white staff of his office as High Steward of England.

Next came Queen Anne, with the earl of Huntingdon bearing her sceptre, Viscount Lisle carrying an ivory rod, and the earl of Wiltshire holding the queen's crown. Walking between two bishops, Anne wore similar robes to her husband's, while her cloth of estate was carried over her by the barons of the Cinque Ports. The queen's train was carried by Margaret, countess of Richmond, followed by the duchesses of Suffolk and Norfolk, and the ladies of the queen, wearing the gowns of crimson velvet lined with white cloth of gold that had been gifts from the king.

The procession reached the west door of the abbey, before the royal couple proceeded down the aisle towards a specially created stage covered in red worsted at the abbey's centre, the centrepiece of which was the king's throne, St Edward's Chair. Choristers of the chapel royal chanted psalm 20, 'Domine in virtute', while the royal couple walked towards their thrones. Anne sat on the queen's throne, to the left of the king's and somewhat lower, while Richard stood by his. Facing in turn each of the four sides of the stage, towards the assembled audience, the archbishop presented Richard to the people, asking their assent to the coronation of 'Richard, rightful and undoubted inheritor by the laws of God and man to the crown and royal dignity of England', to which the audience dutifully replied with the traditional response, 'King Richard, King Richard, King Richard, yea, yea, yea'. Further anthems and psalms followed, of 'latin and prick song'. Richard was then led to the altar by the archbishop, where he made an offering of a pound of gold, before prostrating himself on cushions and returning to a chair facing the altar, while a brief sermon was given by an unnamed bishop. After the sermon had ended, the archbishop rose to put to Richard his coronation oath, for the first time in English.[15]

Next followed further ceremonies and litanies, culminating in the anointing and crowning of the king, using the holy oil of St Thomas Becket. Traditionally the ceremony was conducted with the assistance of the High Steward and Earl Marshal, yet it was the duke of Buckingham, the Great Chamberlain, who had the white wand of the Steward in his hand, rather than the official holder of the office, John, duke of Norfolk. Having created the king, Buckingham was determined that he alone should be in charge of his crowning, with the Great Wardrobe account recording Buckingham as 'having chief rule and devising of the ordinance' for the coronation. The duke helped Richard out of his robes, leaving him clothed in only his shirt and breeches. Once the garments had been loosened, the king knelt on cushions before the archbishop for the anointing.[16] Richard was then vested with the coronation regalia and royal vestments, including the great 'St Edward's cope' of black samite cloth of gold, woven all over with gold eagles. Richard was then seated in his chair at the altar, where the crown of St Edward was placed on his head by the archbishop of Canterbury, accompanied by the prayer, 'Coronet te deus'. The coronation ring, blessed by the archbishop on the altar, was then placed on the fourth finger of Richard's right hand. The king was then girded with the sword, which he offered at the altar before receiving it back, a sign that his strength and power should come from God. Gloves were then placed on Richard's hands in order for him to take delivery of the rest of the regalia, holding the sceptre in his right hand and the orb in his left. After a final blessing, Richard sat back in his chair and was kissed by the bishops in turn. Richard was then led to the throne of St Edward's Chair on the stage, where the bishops and nobles made their fealty and homage to the king, as Richard sat, the bishops of Bath and Durham helping to support the weight of the crown while the dukes of Buckingham and Norfolk, on either side of the king, supported the sceptre and the orb.

Anne's coronation as queen followed with a shorter ceremony, the anointing taking place only on her forehead in the shape of a cross and on her breast. After Anne had been girded with her own crown and coronation regalia, she was led to her throne accompanied by the duchess of Suffolk, curtseying before her husband the 'king's majesty' as she approached the stage. Mass was then observed, with both king and queen taking communion. Richard then offered up the crown of St Edward and his other sacred coronation relics at the shrine of St Edward, behind the high altar. Buckingham was on hand to help disrobe the king, to be clothed in robes of estate fashioned from purple velvet. Anne also changed into fresh robes, assisted by a gentlewoman of her chamber. The king and queen returned to the altar, where they were now crowned with lighter crowns, the 'Imperial crowns', and the coronation procession re-formed, returning to Westminster Hall, 'going in great triumph'.[17]

Richard and Anne returned to their chambers for a deserved rest, while the duke of Norfolk, as Earl Marshal, rode into Westminster Hall, clearing people out of the hall, the servants of the duke of Buckingham and the king excepted. Four large tables or 'boards' stretching the length of the hall were hastily erected, in preparation for the coronation banquet, which was to begin at four o'clock, with the formal entrance of the new king and queen, taking their places at the marble table of the King's Bench. Anne sat to Richard's left, while to his right was the bishop of Durham, who had been called to deputise for the seventy-nine-year-old archbishop of Canterbury, no longer able to stand the duration of the day's events. Dishes were served to the sound of trumpets, as they were carried in by the newly made knights of the Bath. Richard was served on a gold plate, Anne on a gilt plate, and the bishop of Durham on silver. Members of the nobility had been given ceremonial roles during the feast, with Lord Audley acting as the king's carver, while Lord Scrope of Upsall performed the duties of the king's cupbearer.

The banquet was intended to cover three courses, comprising seventy-five different dishes which were to be served to 1,200 'messes' – shared tables that would feed around 3,000 people in total. The surviving accounts detail the purchases for the feast that included thirty bulls, 140 sheep, 100 calves, six boars, twelve fatted pigs, 200 suckling pigs, eight hart deer, 140 bucks, and eight roe deer and fawns. In addition, the lower ranks in the hall would be treated to 288 marrow bones, seventy-two ox feet and 144 calves' feet. For the fish dishes, the caterer ordered 400 lampreys, 350 pikes, four porpoises, forty bream, thirty salmon cut into thin slices, 100 trout, forty carp, 480 freshwater crayfish, 200 cod and salt fish, another thirty-six other 'sea fish', 100 trench and 200 mullet. Poultry dishes included 1,000 geese, 800 rabbits and 800 chickens, with another 400 chickens 'to stew', in addition to 300 sparrows or larks, 2,400 pigeons, 1,000 capons, 800 rails (a large, fat bird), forty cygnets, sixteen dozen heron, forty-eight peacocks, eight dozen of both cranes and pheasants, six dozen bitterns, 240 quails, three dozen egrets, twelve dozen curlews and 120 'piper chicks' – probably young pigeons. To spice the dishes, twenty-eight pounds of pepper, eight pounds of saffron costing forty-eight shillings, twenty-eight pounds of cinnamon costing sixty shillings, four pounds of fresh ginger and twelve pounds of powdered ginger were employed, though the most popular seasoning seems to have been the sweet variety, with 150 pounds of Madeira sugar imported from Portugal, 150 pounds of almonds and 200 pounds of raisins making up the largest of the orders for spices in the kitchen. Dessert included 300 pounds of dates, 100 pounds of prunes, 1,000 oranges and twelve gallons of strawberries, decorated with 100 leaves of 'pure gold'.[18]

During the second course, the customary challenges began, following the time-honoured pattern of previous coronation banquets. Sir Robert

Dymock, the King's Champion, rode into the hall, riding on a horse trapped down to the ground with white and red silk. After making his obeisance to the king, a herald announced why he had come, 'declaring in all the hall if there be any man that will say the contrary why King Richard should not pretend and have the crown'. 'Anon every man held their peace for a while', one observer later recorded, 'all the hall cried King Richard and anon as they had so said the Champion cast down his gauntlet.'[19] Dymock then returned to the king, once again making his homage, while one of the lords brought him a covered cup of wine, from which Dymock drank, before casting the remainder on the floor and riding out, keeping the gilt cup in his right hand as his fee. Eighteen heralds then appeared on a stage in the hall, as 'one of them spoke certain words unto the King proclaiming his style'. After acclaiming the king's title three times, they departed.

The evening was growing late, and darkness had begun to descend. By the time it came to the third course, it was decided to abandon serving the desserts, 'saving only wafers and hippocras', while shortly afterwards 'great lights' of wax torches were brought into the hall, marking the end of the banquet, 'and when they were come into the hall anon the lords arose up and went to the King making their obeisance'. When this was finished, Richard and Anne rose from their table and departed for their chambers, 'and anon all the people departed and went their ways'.[20]

As the coronation banquet came to an end, looking around the hall at those who had attended the celebrations, Richard could have been forgiven for thinking with some relief that he had secured complete support for his accession. Almost all of the English nobility were present, in addition to over seventy knights, a third of whom had served in his brother's royal household. Having backed him as Protector, Richard must have considered, now they were prepared to pledge their loyalty to him as king.

The following morning, Richard dressed in a long gown of crimson cloth of gold, lined with green damask. The gown, and its colours, were to become one of his favourite styles of dress as king: later he had another three similar gowns made for him, including a gown of crimson cloth of gold in a checked pattern and lined with green satin, and two short gowns of crimson cloth of gold, one patterned with droops and the other with nets, but both lined with green velvet.[21] One of Richard's first acts as newly anointed king was to send back the coronation regalia for safe keeping, sending his newly appointed bishop of St David's, Thomas Langton, to deliver a precious ampulla, containing the holy oil of St Thomas with which he had been anointed, to the monks of Westminster Abbey. In an indenture made with the abbot of Westminster, the abbot was instructed to store the ampulla, described as an 'eagle of gold garnished with pearls and precious stones in which is closed the precious relic', until it might be required once more, when, upon the king's commandment, the abbot was to 'deliver again to the said king's highness whensoever it shall please him to ask it', though Richard ordained 'the same precious relic to abide and remain after his decease within the foresaid monastery'.[22]

For the government of the realm, it was business as usual. Even before his coronation, Richard had begun to reward those who had delivered him the throne. On 28 June, Francis, Viscount Lovell, one of Richard's close personal friends from his days in the north, was appointed chamberlain of the king's household, an important position that would see Lovell close by Richard's side at all times. William Catesby was confirmed as the chancellor of the earldom of March, created Chancellor of the Exchequer for life and was also granted the chamberlainship of the Exchequer, an office that had recently been held by Hastings.[23] John, Lord Howard, was created duke of Norfolk and Earl Marshal.[24] Two days later, on 30 June, Howard was also appointed steward to prepare for the king's forthcoming coronation.

John, Lord Howard's creation as duke of Norfolk, coming just days after Richard's accession, is a reminder that Richard had been able to build support for his removal of Edward V with the promise of righting perceived injustices committed by Edward IV. Self-interest drove men such as John Howard to support Richard as their king, against the Woodvilles, from whom they felt there would be little hope of redress. While claims that Richard himself had long harboured a hatred of the Woodvilles are false, this is not necessarily the case for those who were prepared to support Richard as an anti-Woodville alternative. In providing for the royal family and its Woodville relations over the later years of his reign, Edward had stoked tensions between the Woodvilles and the rest of the nobility, who had good cause to feel disenfranchised by the king's treatment of their own rights of inheritance in order to provide for his children and the queen's Woodville kin. One of the most egregious examples of this concerned the king's treatment of the Mowbray inheritance of the dukes of Norfolk, when Edward had co-opted the inheritance of the duke of Norfolk through the death of the child bride of Edward's son Richard, duke of York: Howard had effectively been disinherited in favour of the young prince. It is hardly surprising then that Howard became an early supporter of Richard's protectorate.

As early as 4 June, it seems that Howard was already lobbying for the possibility that Richard would reconsider the division of the Mowbray inheritance: on that day, Howard paid 20s to 'John Feeld for to have out certain writings of livelihood from my lord Berkeley', suggesting that the Mowbray inheritance was under discussion.[25] Less than ten days later, it would be Howard's own son, Thomas Howard, who would be one of the armed men who ambushed William, Lord Hastings, leading him to his death. For his support, Thomas was also created earl of Surrey. William, Viscount Berkeley, who had also been disinherited of the Mowbray inheritance by Edward IV and the Woodvilles, was another early champion of Richard's kingship, writing on 28 June requesting 'your most noble and abundant grace' as a 'humble and faithful subject'.[26] For his support, Berkeley would be created earl of Nottingham. Edward Grey, Lord Lisle's support for Richard had been noted in Simon Stallworth's letter of 21 June: on 26 June, the same day as Richard's accession, Lisle requested letters patent from Richard in a submission in which he described himself as 'your humble and true liegeman', adding how 'he shall ever pray to God for your most noble and royal estate'.[27] Lisle was now elevated in the peerage to become Viscount Lisle. Those northerners who had given their early support to Richard would also be later rewarded, with several grants issued highlighting the 'service done at great labour and charge, in particular about the acceptation of the crown and royal title of this kingdom'.[28] The earl of Northumberland, in supporting the provision of Richard's northern army, even went so far as to provide personally for five bucks and 100 shillings, which he gave to the soldiers from York, and would later be rewarded by Richard with the lordship of Holderness, 'in consideration of good gifts and laudable services to us both in our taking up of our reign and crown and in the defence of our kingdom of England against Scotland'.[29] Men joined Richard's cause not merely because they hoped that he would provide for their own self-interest; Richard himself stirred the ambitions of men, openly promising them rewards for joining his cause. 'And, my lord, do me now good service, as ye have always before done', he had written to Ralph, Lord Neville, on 11 June, 'and I trust now so to remember you as shall be the making of you and yours.'[30]

Appointments that had been made during his protectorship were swiftly confirmed. On 15 July, John Gunthorpe, appointed Keeper of the Privy Seal on 10 May by 'Edward bastard late called King Edward the Vth', who 'to his great cost' had yet to be paid, was finally reimbursed.[31] New commissions of the peace were issued, yet with the obvious exception of the removal of the Woodvilles and their associates, few changes were made. In Hertfordshire, where Elizabeth Woodville's possession of duchy of Lancaster lands in the county had resulted in a large number of Justices of the Peace with Woodville roots, including the executed Anthony, Earl Rivers, and Sir Thomas Vaughan and the still imprisoned John Forster, more sweeping changes were needed. While one local man, Richard Swanessey, was added to the bench, the new king chose to add three Yorkshiremen – Edward Goldsborough, Nicholas Leventhorpe and Richard Scrope, the brother of the king's close friend, John, Lord Scrope of Bolton – to the commission. The adoption of these northerners into the county, despite each having interests in the county either through marriage or land ownership, is striking, and an early sign of the king's desire to place loyalty to his northern followers above integration into local society.[32] Richard was determined to display that loyalty, above all else, would be rewarded.

The new king seemed to be in little doubt that he still commanded the loyalty of Edward IV's household men, despite his deposition of Edward V. In issuing new commissions of the peace on 26 June, even in Kent, the centre of Woodville influence, few changes were made to its membership, with Sir John Fogge, an ally of the Woodvilles whom Richard had been determined to conciliate, remaining on the commission. Two new members even included Sir John Guildford, a Woodville kinsman, and Richard Page of Horton, who had been an annuitant of Edward IV. In Wiltshire, a new commission of the peace issued on 20 July even included Lionel Woodville, Elizabeth Woodville's brother and the new bishop of

Salisbury, which Richard must have considered gave him a right to sit on the commission.[33]

Richard's intention seems to have been to establish himself as a king who would continue to operate as his brother had; he would rule as Edward IV would have done, as the head of a network of royal servants and a household that his brother had created. Richard's northern followers would remain within their local positions: there were a few opportunities for northern men to make the transition southwards, such as Sir Ralph Ashton, a northern retainer of Richard's who was appointed as a commissioner of the peace in Kent, but probably only because he had married into Kentish society only a few weeks previously.[34]

There would be further reward for those who had proved instrumental in gaining him the throne. On 13 July, Richard granted the duke of Buckingham his ultimate prize: the Lancastrian share of the Bohun inheritance, lands he had coveted for so long, the grant explaining that the award had been given for 'the true faithful and laudable service the which our said cousin hath in many sundry wise done unto us'. The agreement would need to be ratified by an Act of Parliament, with a promise that 'in our next parliament to be holden he shall be surely and lawfully by act of parliament' restored to the formal title of the lands, which had previously been partitioned by Henry VI.[35] Still, the duke was allowed to enter the manors immediately and start drawing an income from their lucrative revenues. A schedule attached to Buckingham's grant reveals that the thirty-eight manors, across eighteen counties mainly situated in East Anglia and southern England, represented a value of £1,100 annually. The lands also provided a significant resource of patronage, with hundreds of royal offices and positions in Essex and Hertfordshire being dependent upon the territory.[36] Further rewards were given to John Howard, now duke of Norfolk, including the power to array troops on behalf of the king in East Anglia, Cambridgeshire and the Home Counties on 16 July, and the office of Admiral on 25 July, together with a grant of forty-nine manors across East Anglia and other southern counties.[37]

Across the realm, recognising the opportunity to secure favour from the new monarch, some were swift to ingratiate themselves to the new regime. The inhabitants of 'your poor town' of Yarmouth wrote to Rich-ard, requesting their letters patent be granted, pledging that 'your said true liegemen and humble subjects shall ever pray to God for the continual preservation of your most noble and royal estate'.[38] It was to the rest of the country that Richard now looked to secure his authority as king, planning to depart from the capital on a summer progress that would eventually take him north to York.

On Saturday, 19 July, having spent the past six days at Greenwich, Richard departed from the capital by boat, intending to set out on a pro-gress of his new realm. His first destination was Windsor Castle, where Richard may have inspected progress on his brother's tomb within its two-storey chantry, set within the half-built chapel of St George that Rich-ard himself had contributed to. He was joined by his wife, Queen Anne, and John Howard, the new duke of Norfolk, whose household accounts record how 'my lord's grace departed to Windsor with the king', while Buckingham remained in the capital.[39] After spending four days there, the royal household journeyed towards Reading; Howard returned to London, while Anne remained at Windsor for the next few weeks.

While at Reading, Richard continued his policy of rapprochement in an attempt to appear a merciful king. A surviving agreement dated 23 July records that the king agreed he would be a 'good and gracious sovereign lord' to William, Lord Hastings's widow, Katherine, and her children, 'not suffering them to be wronged nor entreated contrary to our laws'. The king affirmed that Hastings would not be attainted, thereby protecting his heirs from confiscation of his lands, allowing them to 'have and continually enjoy such name, pre-eminence, interest, rights, possessions and inherit-ments as be descended from the same William'. Katherine would also hold all castles or manors that had been enfeoffed 'to the use of the said William the day of his death', aside from the manor of Loughborough, 'which to us and our dearest wife in her right belongeth'. Still Richard stood by his original charge that Hastings had sinned against him. Katherine and her heirs were to be pardoned for 'all offences and other things done by the same William to us or our progenitors'.[40] Other letters of pardon were sent to Hastings's brother, Sir Ralph Hastings, on 2 August.[41]

The following day, 24 July, Richard arrived at Oxford. Magdalen Col-lege had been given advance notice of the king's proposed journey, and on 22 July William Waynflete, the bishop of Winchester and founder of the college, came to 'oversee the condition of his college and the building of the same and also to receive honourably the most illustrious Lord King Richard the Third'. Richard was greeted outside the university by the chancellor of the university, where he was 'honourably received'. The chancellor was none other than Bishop Lionel Woodville, Queen Elizabeth's brother. Woodville had previously fled into sanctuary in May, certainly before 9 June. On 3 June, when new commissions of the peace were issued for Dorset, Lionel Woodville's name had been removed.[42] Yet by 26 June, the date of Richard's unofficial accession to the throne, Lionel Woodville was restored to the Dorset commission of the peace, and on 20 July was appointed to the commission for Wiltshire, a sign not only of Richard's determination to heal old wounds, but an indication also of the Woodville family's desire to be reconciled to the new king.[43]

Richard's visit to Oxford is well documented, and the Magdalen College accounts reveal that the king, after taking part in a procession, listened to a speech by Waynflete before staying overnight. Richard's royal train was accompanied by prelates and nobles, including the earls of Lincoln and Surrey, Lord Lovell, Thomas, Lord Stanley, Lord Audley, Richard Ratcliffe and John Alcock, the bishop of Worcester and the tutor to Edward V, 'and many other nobles who all stayed overnight in college'. On 25 July, the accounts continue, 'at the command and desire of the lord King', two 'solemn debates' were held in the great hall of the College. The account waxes lyrical about the generosity of the king, detailing Richard's gifts of venison and money to the disputants, before enthusiastically closing with the words, 'Vivat Rex in eternum' – 'May the king live for ever.'[44]

On 25 July, Richard and his entourage departed from Oxford's north gate for his royal palace of Woodstock. According to John Rous, during his visit Richard 'by popular request disafforested a great area of the country which King Edward IV his brother had annexed and incorporated in the forest of Wychwood under forest law, against conscience and to the public damage'.[45] Richard then journeyed to Minster Lovell, the residence of his close confidant Francis, Lord Lovell. So confident were the university authorities that the king's visit to Oxford had been a success that they decided to send a petition to the king at Minster Lovell on behalf of Bishop Morton of Ely, and a graduate of Balliol College, who had remained imprisoned since his arrest on 13 June in the Tower at the time of William, Lord Hastings's execution.[46]

Richard was determined to enjoy his summer progress, as the Crowland chronicler noted, 'wishing therefore to display in the North, where he had spent most of his time previously, the superior royal rank, which he acquired for himself'.[47] Richard departed Minster Lovell for Gloucester, where he stayed overnight, agreeing to a new charter for the town, 'because of the special affection which we bear towards the said town . . . considering the good and faithful actions of the said bailiffs and burgesses in causes of particular importance to us', awarding Gloucester with the freedom to elect its own mayor.[48] The king then journeyed on to Tewkesbury, where Richard may have paid his respects to his late brother Clarence's grave. Certainly Clarence was in his thoughts, for, on 4 August, Richard arranged for the remaining debt of 310 marks from a total loan of 560 marks owed by 'our late brother the Duke of Clarence, whom god pardon' to be 'full contented and paid'.[49]

On Friday, 8 August, Richard arrived at Warwick, where he was joined by his wife, Anne, who had been residing at Windsor Castle for the past two weeks. Warwick Castle had been one of Queen Anne's principal homes during her childhood. The royal family's arrival there marked not only a celebration of Richard's accomplishments, but the realisation that the Neville family had finally achieved the dream that Anne's father, the earl of Warwick, had been unable to obtain for his daughters: the throne. In celebration of the occasion, the Warwickshire monk John Rous presented the royal couple with two detailed rolls, filled with carefully drawn pen and ink drawings celebrating the ascent of the Neville family. In one of the rolls, alongside a drawing showing Richard and Anne crowned and wearing their coronation garments, Rous praised Richard effusively, writing that he was:

> The most mighty prince Richard by the grace of God King of England
> and of France and Lord of Ireland by very matrimony without discontin-
> uance or any defiling in law by heir male lineally, descending from King
> Harry the Second, all avarice set aside, ruled his subjects in his realm full

commendably, punishing offenders of his laws, especially extortioners and
oppressors of his commons, and cherishing those that were virtuous; by the
which discreet guiding he got great thank of God and love of all his subjects
rich and poor and great laud of the people of all other lands about him.[50]

But it was Anne, that 'most noble lady and princess', whose attention Rous
had sought to cultivate, the visit being the fulfilment of her true Neville
ancestry. She had been, Rous wrote in his manuscript, 'marvellously conveyed by all the corners and parties of the wheel of fortune and eftsone
[soon after] exalted again' after the death of her first husband, Prince
Edward, 'to the most high throne and honour over all other ladies of this
noble realm anointed and crowned Queen of England wife unto the most
victorious prince king Richard the Third', adding further, 'in presence she
was seemly amiable and beauteous and in conditions full commendable
and right virtuous and according to the interpretation of her name Anne
full gracious'.[51]

The scale of the celebrations can be glimpsed from the growing size
of the royal court that filled Warwick Castle.[52] Foreign ambassadors had
also begun to gather to pay their respects to the new king and queen.
It was at Warwick, Rous observed, that 'ambassadors from the King of
Spain came to the king for a marriage between the king's only son and the
daughter of the King of Spain'. Queen Anne brought with her a Spanish
envoy, Gaufridius de Sasiola, who arrived in England expecting Edward V
on the throne, but was determined that his journey would not be wasted,
and sought an audience with the new king. On 8 August, de Sasiola presented the official report that he had come to give, that the queen, 'my
supreme mistress', wished to 'have a good and firm peace' and to 'make,
enter into and establish with the said lord King good and firm leagues,
agreements and alliances'. If Richard wished to 'wage war' against France,
'for the recovery of his lands, lordships and possessions which appertain to
the crown of England', then Isabella was willing to lend him 'the use of all
her sea ports and the necessary victuals and arms at a low cost; and at sea
her ships, armed, for reasonable wages'.[53] Already Richard had appointed
Bernard de la Forssa, an experienced diplomat who had perfomed similar
missions for Edward IV, to journey to Spain. Fortunately, Forssa had yet
to sail, so Richard sent fresh instructions from Warwick indicating that

he was willing to negotiate a new treaty if Queen Isabella so wished.[54] To Elizabeth, the king replied, explaining how he had read the queen's 'very sweet and pleasant' letters, which were heard 'with joy and gladness'. 'For this we give your highness great thanks, the greatest we can possibly give. In case there is anything in our power that we can do for your highness to achieve a happy and auspicious outcome to this very great business', Richard requested that Elizabeth might accept Forssa's embassy, and 'urgently to hear him and give him credence'.[55]

During his progress, Richard also dispatched a series of diplomatic letters to the French king, Louis XI, informing him of his accession and willingness to maintain the current peace that had been agreed during Edward IV's reign. Louis wrote to Richard on 21 July thanking him for 'the letters that you have written to me by your herald Blanc Sanglier, and thank you for the news of which you have apprised me. And if I can do you any service I will do it with very good will, for I desire to have your friendship'. On 18 August, Richard replied, requesting that the French king intervene to prevent English ships being attacked by French pirates on the seas, jokingly ending his letter: 'I pray you that by my servant, this bearer, one of the grooms of my stable, you will let me know by writing your full intention.' Two days later, at Nottingham Castle, on 20 August, Richard wrote again to the French king, this time to make a particular, more personal, request. 'I have written to my servant Blanc Sanglier, now being with you, to make provision of certain wines of the growth of Burgundy and la Haute France, for myself and the queen my consort. I therefore pray you, my lord my cousin, that you will give order to your officers and subjects to suffer him to procure the said wines, and freely conduct them and pass into this my realm of England, without any disturbance or contradiction, and you will do me in this a very singular pleasure.'[56]

Other monarchs were also keen to make contact and establish diplomatic ties with the new king. On 16 August, James III of Scotland wrote to Richard proposing a truce for eight months, requesting that peace commissioners might meet on the border, or travel to England with an entourage of eighty persons.[57] Richard took a month to respond, and, refusing to comment on the specifics, agreed that an embassy might be sent to England.[58] If

Richard's interests in Scottish affairs seemed somewhat muted, for the
moment his concerns lay elsewhere, towards the Channel, and his relationship with France and Brittany. He had already sent Thomas Hutton
to deliver to Duke Francis II of Brittany a message of goodwill, explaining
that since King Edward's death 'folks of simple disposition' had taken to
the Channel to commit acts of piracy that had caused 'great trouble and
hindrance' in trade on both sides, though he hoped that 'a full reformation
of all attempts may well be had' through a treaty that Richard hoped might
be held in England in the near future. Hutton was also given instructions
to 'feel and understand the mind and disposition of the duke against Sir
Edward Woodville and his retinue, practising by all means to him possible
to ensearch and know if there be intended any enterprise out of land upon
any part of this realm.'[59]

On 26 August, Duke Francis sent his ambassador, George de Main-
bier, with instructions to inform Richard that in spite of an increase in
the number of English ships that have 'put themselves in warlike array
upon the sea, and have threatened to take and plunder the subjects of the
duke', which Francis requested Richard should do more to prevent, he was
willing to conclude an alliance after the meeting of the country's assembly
in September, 'for the great love and affection' he wished to show Richard.

Francis also had some important information to pass on to the king.
Since Edward IV's death, he revealed, Louis XI had on several occasions
requested that he send Henry Tudor, earl of Richmond, to the French
court, making 'great offers'. Nevertheless, Francis insisted he had 'given
him no inducement, fearing that the said King Louis would thereby create
annoyance and injury to some of the friends and well-willers of the duke'.
As a consequence, Louis had given 'great menaces to the duke of making
war upon him'. Without English aid, Francis surmised, he would be forced
to hand over Henry Tudor to the French, 'which he would be very loath for
the injury which he knows the said king Louis would or might inflict upon
the said king and kingdom of England'. The price for not handing over
Henry, Francis bargained, would be 4,000 archers, 'furnished with good
captains and a good chief', whose wages for six months would be paid for
by the king, an arrangement already agreed by Edward IV. In addition to
this, Richard should provide an additional two or three thousand archers,
if the duke required, which would be paid for by the duke himself. 'And

so doing', Francis indicated, he would be prepared to 'await the fortune of war, as it shall please God to send him, rather than deliver into the hand of the said king Louis the said lord of Richmond, or do anything prejudicial' to Richard and the English nation.[60]

As the son of Margaret Beaufort – grand-daughter of John of Gaunt – and Edmund Tudor – half-brother of the Lancastrian king Henry VI – the twenty-six-year-old Henry Tudor had a claim to the throne, albeit a dubious one. Yet for those Lancastrian exiles still holding out for their cause, Henry Tudor remained their best and only hope: after the crushing defeat of the Lancastrian army at the battle of Tewkesbury in 1471, Henry's uncle, Jasper Tudor, had realised that he needed to save his nephew's life, and flee the country together. Jasper had intended to set sail for France, presumably to seek refuge at the court of Louis XI. However, storms blew the ship off course, and after apparently landing briefly at Jersey, they landed at the small port of Le Conquet, on the westernmost point of the peninsula, in north-west Finistère, near Brest. Captured, Henry and Jasper were brought to the ducal palace of the Château de l'Hermine at Vannes, where Duke Francis II was residing. Jasper had 'submitted himself and his nephew to his protection'. The duke knew that the Tudors would be valued pawns in the diplomatic games he played between France and England. He received his new guests 'willingly, and with such honour, courtesy, and favour'. Treating them as if 'they had been his brothers', Francis pledged to protect both Jasper and Henry, allowing them to 'pass at their pleasure to and fro without danger'.[61] When Edward IV had heard the news of Jasper and Henry's escape and safe landing in Brittany, and hearing that they had been 'courteously received and entertained' by Francis, he was furious, 'which matter indeed he took very grievously, as though his mind gave him that some evil would come thereby'.[62] He sent secret messengers to Francis, promising great reward if he would hand over the earls. The tactic seems to have backfired: when the duke realised the value of his captives, 'that the earls were so rich a prey', he was determined not to release them. Understanding the advantage that possession of the Tudors had brought him, Francis knew that he would need to prevent their escape. He ordered that Jasper's English servants be removed, and his own men placed around the two earls, 'to wait upon and guard them'.[63] By October 1472, both Jasper and Henry had been taken to Suscinio, one of the duke's country residences, near Sarzeau on the Gulf of Morbihan. In early 1474, Francis decided to separate Henry from his uncle, placing Jasper in the fortress of Josselin, twenty-five miles from Vannes, and removing Henry to the chateau of Largoët, with its 144-foot-high, seven-storey, octagonal tower, known as the Tour d'Elven, that had been rebuilt in the 1460s and remained unfinished, hidden deep within a forest. For the next nine years, Henry Tudor would remain a prisoner there. Henry later told the chronicler Philippe de Commynes that 'since the age of five he had been guarded like a fugitive or kept in prison', though Duke Francis laid aside for his household the princely sum of £2,000, compared to just £607 10s for his Uncle Jasper.

Edward IV had done all he could to secure possession of Henry Tudor. Attempts to bargain for Tudor to be sent back to England in 1473 and 1476 both failed, though by 1482 it seemed that Henry's mother, Margaret, was prepared to countenance a deal with the king, securing a pardon for her son if he returned to England. Her attempts to lobby on behalf of her son were to continue into Richard's reign. On 5 July 1483, Margaret and her husband, Thomas Stanley, had met with Richard and his chief justice, William Hussey, at Westminster, where Richard gave his support to Margaret's claim to a ransom debt that she was attempting to obtain from the Orléans family in the courts in Paris. The following day, Margaret had played a prominent part in the coronation ceremony of the new king, bearing Queen Anne's train in the procession to Westminster Abbey and afterwards, alongside Katherine, duchess of Norfolk, acting as one of the servers at the banquet.[64] According to the Tudor chronicler Edward Hall, Margaret approached the duke of Buckingham shortly after Richard's accession, asking him to intercede with Richard on her behalf for Henry's return to the English court. In order to aid the chances that the king might accept Henry's return and subordination to the Yorkist regime, she proposed that Henry might take one of the Woodville daughters in marriage, the arrangement of which she would leave to the king, 'without any thing to be taken or demanded for the same espousals but only the king's favour'.[65]

At the same time, Duke Francis seems to have no longer felt bound to keep Henry and Jasper under such a close guard. By February 1483, Henry had returned to Vannes, where he was staying at the duke's residence of the Château de l'Hermine, though he was free to hear services at the local cathedral.[66] By the summer, Francis had given Henry and Jasper the freedom to travel across his dukedom, the news of which must have made Richard nervous.

Francis's threat to return Henry Tudor to France and into Louis XI's arms was somewhat muted by the sudden death of the French king on 25 August. John, Lord Dynham, wrote to inform Richard of the news. 'What direction shall be taken thereupon his decease with the Dauphin and that Realm is not yet known', Dynham reported back, though already he was concerned about the designs of Maximilian on the Burgundian towns controlled by the French. Already at sea 'the war is open between both realms', Dynham reported, while at Calais he had 'much to do to keep men still in peace here, for they would fain be in hand with the Frenchmen', adding, 'My lord it is thought here that the king should have a navy upon the sea to show himself as a king to rule and keep his streams betwixt this and Dover' in order to reduce piracy.[67] The death of the French king seemed to be a blessing; rather than follow Dynham's advice, Richard decided to take the opportunity to scale down military operations at Calais.

11

'THE FACT OF AN ENTERPRISE'

The royal progress continued to journey through the Midlands, resting at Coventry, at Leicester on 19 August, then at Nottingham Castle, where Edward IV had started a programme of remodelling the medieval castle with modern fifteenth-century quarters. It was to become one of Richard's favoured residences: the king had begun to consider the need to reinforce the status of his own lineage and the Yorkist dynasty as it now appeared. Already he had named his son Edward of Middleham to be Lord Lieutenant of Ireland on 19 July; at Nottingham, on 24 August, Edward was created Prince of Wales and earl of Chester, though curiously the traditional appointment as duke of Cornwall was omitted. Richard wrote to the archbishops how he had performed the formal ceremony, 'as the custom is by the girding of the sword, the handing over and setting of the garland on his head, and of the gold ring on his finger, and of the gold staff in his hand'.[1] Richard explained in his letter how he had chosen to elevate his son, 'having great care that, in the great anxieties which press upon us, those who are necessary to support us should not now seem to be lacking'.

The creation of his son Edward as Prince of Wales at Nottingham would be the prelude to a far greater and impressive ceremony that Richard had planned for his homecoming into his heartland, the city of York. The Crowland chronicler wrote how Richard was 'now desirous, with all speed, to show in the north, where in former years he had chiefly resided, the high and kingly station which he had acquired'. The day before Prince Edward's creation, on 23 August, Richard's secretary, John Kendall, had written 'in haste' from Nottingham to the mayor and aldermen at York, informing them that the king and queen had 'in all their progress ...

been worshipfully received with pageants'. Throughout the journey, the king's judges had sat 'in every place, determining the complaints of poor folk with due punishment of offenders against his laws'. 'I truly know the king's mind and entire affection that his grace bears towards you and your worshipful city, for your many kind and loving deservings shown to his grace heretofore', Kendall wrote, 'which his grace will never forget, and intends therefore so to do unto you that all the kings that ever reigned over you did never so much.' The city was advised, however, that it should plan to receive the king and queen, 'as honourably as your wisdoms can imagine', with pageants, 'such good' speeches, and 'clothes of arras and tapestry work' in the streets, 'for there come many southern lords and men of worship with them which will mark greatly your recieving of their graces'.[2]

On 29 August, the royal party – Richard, Queen Anne and Prince Edward – entered the city gates of York through Micklegate Bar, the gateway into the city upon which the heads of Richard's father, Richard, duke of York, and brother, Edmund, had been impaled after their defeat and death at Wakefield nearly a quarter of a century before. The entry had been carefully timed, chiming with the feast of the Decollation of St John the Baptist.[3] As the procession made its way through the city, the mayor, John Newton, made a speech welcoming the royal family and offered a gift to the king of 100 marks contained in a gold cup, and for the queen £100 in gold and precious plate, of which Miles Metcalfe, the city recorder and close acquaintance of Richard's, personally gave £100.[4]

The cathedral records at York tell how Richard entered the city, accompanied by the queen and the prince and 'many other magnates', including the earls of Northumberland, Surrey and Lincoln, Lord Lovell, Fitzhugh, Thomas, Lord Stanley, and his son George, Lord Strange, Lord Lisle and Lord Greystoke along with 'many others', including the bishops of Durham, Worcester, St Asaph, Carlisle and St David's. After being received by the city authorities outside the walls, Richard and the procession passed 'through displays and decorations' until arriving at the Metropolitan church of St Peter. Richard was 'honourably received' at the west door by the Dean and Canons, each wearing blue silk copes and 'sprinkled with holy water and censed', before entering the church to hear mass. Once the ceremony had finished, the procession left the church to stay in the archbishop's palace, where the royal family would reside for the rest of their visit.[5]

Two days later, Richard sent an urgent message to Peter Curtys, the Keeper of the king's Great Wardrobe, ordering that silks, satins, gowns and banners depicting not only the royal arms fashioned out of 'fine gold', but also St George, St Cuthbert, St Edward, the Trinity and Richard's own standard of the boar be immediately sent to York for another procession. In addition, forty banners for trumpets and four standards depicting boars were ordered, along with 13,000 cognisances or badges made of fustian 'with boars'.[6] The formal investiture of Prince Edward was set for Monday, 8 September, with the week leading up to the event occupied with the 'most gorgeous and sumptuous feasts and banquets', the Crowland chronicler observed, though he believed this was merely 'for the purpose of gaining the affections of the people'.[7]

On 8 September, the feast of the Nativity of the Virgin Mary, Richard and Anne, 'both crowned', returned in procession to St Peter's church, where in front of the lords and bishops, and with the high altar having been 'ornamented with silver and gilt figures of the twelve apostles and many other relics given by the Lord King', they heard mass with the bishop of Durham officiating, with the ceremony continuing until the evening. Returning to the bishop's palace for dinner, Edward was once again created Prince of Wales by Richard, 'in the presence of all'. For the Crowland chronicler, the occasion was nothing less than a second coronation. Prince Edward was created Prince of Wales, 'with the insignia of the golden wand and the wreath'. Richard, Anne and Edward then sat, 'so they say, crowned, for four hours'.[8] During the day of investiture, Richard not only conferred the honour of knighthood upon his son, but also knighted his nephew Edward, earl of Warwick, his illegitimate son John of Gloucester, and even Gaufridius de Sasiola, the Spanish envoy sent by Queen Isabella of Castille.[9] The Crowland chronicler was typically scathing about the entire display, accusing Richard of wasting money on nothing more than a vanity project. 'He had arranged splendid and highly expensive feasts and entertainments to attract to himself the affection of many people. There was no shortage of treasure then to implement the aims of his so elevated mind since, as soon as he first thought about his intrusion to the kingship, he seized everything that his deceased brother . . . had collected.' On the contrary, Richard's magnificent spending belied the fact that his expensive progress was already causing him financial difficulty. Payments for the royal household's expenses of £46 7s were taken from Elizabeth Woodville's Northamptonshire estates, while Richard had to borrow £100 from Furness Abbey on 9 September. Another £10 was lent by Thomas Metcalfe on 29 September.[10] For the moment, however, Richard was determined to enjoy his new-found status as king. Financial worries were certainly not reflected in the generosity of his progress. Thomas Langton, who had been consecrated as the bishop of St David's in Wales on 21 May, had accompanied Richard on his progress, and is listed as staying in Magdalen College with the king. Writing to the prior of Christ Church Cathedral at Canterbury from York at some point during September, describing the progress to date, Langton wrote how Richard 'contents the people where he goes best that ever did prince, for many a poor man that hath suffered wrong many days have been relieved and helped by him and his commands now in his progress. And in many great cities and towns were great sums of money give him, which all he hath refused. On my troth I liked never the conditions of any prince so well as his: God hath sent him to us for the weal of us all.'[11] Langton chose to turn to Latin for his next observation: 'Sensual pleasure holds sway to an increasing extent, but I do not consider that this detract from what I have said.' Langton's description of Richard as a generous and popular king is reflected by John Rous, who later wrote how 'The money which was offered him by the peoples of London, Gloucester, and Worcester he declined with thanks, affirming that he would rather have their love than their treasure.'[12] During July, Richard made an offering of 20s to our lady of Barking, and another offering of 6s 8d at Evesham, while £3 6s 8d was given 'to poor folks at our lady of Rumsivalle'.[13] While journeying through Doncaster, Richard ordered that a 'wife' alongside the road should be given 3s 4d. Only later would the Tudor writer Polydore Vergil cast aspersions on Richard's motivation for pursuing good deeds and works to attempt to win popularity and distract from this treatment of King Edward V and his brother, Richard, yet, regardless of the reason, even Vergil admitted that 'he repented his life of evil deeds and began then to show himself as another man, namely pious, just, gentle, polite, religious and generous, especially to the poor'.[14] In his giving, image mattered as much as reality. At every stage of Richard's progress, it seems that events were tightly orchestrated, as John Kendall's letter to the citizens of York reveals, with careful planning going into every public display. The intention, as Kendall made clear, was to present Richard in the best possible light.

Richard's northern progress, so soon after he had been crowned king, mattered. Not only did it demonstrate Richard's own confidence in his authority that he felt able to depart from the capital; it provided him with an opportunity to celebrate the foundation of his own dynasty, in his own image and among his supporters. The identity that Richard had forged over the past decade, that of his Neville ancestry through his wife and his northern patrimony, was not to be forgotten now that he was king; his journey to Warwick and then to York, the cultural centres of his and his wife's heritage, was meant as a homecoming, demonstrating that Richard understood where his power and influence really stemmed from. The message was simple: Richard would not forget his background. Nor could he afford to do so. Even as his progress continued, during the late summer and autumn months, back in the south there were increasing signs that Richard would soon be needing the support of his northern homelands once more.

Since Richard had assumed the throne, there had been little sight of the former King Edward and his brother, Richard, duke of York. The *Great Chronicle* of London recalled how 'the children of king Edward were seen shooting & playing in the garden of the Tower by sundry times'.[15] Dominic Mancini seems to have gleaned some information from one of the last men to have seen Edward V alive, his physician, John Argentine. With his stay in England almost finished, Dominic Mancini had managed to somehow make contact with Argentine, an early English humanist who had visited Italy in the 1470s and may have known Angelo Cato, Mancini's patron. Plausibly, Mancini may have arrived in England with letters of introduction, allowing him to gain such intimate access. Mancini recalled how:

> After Hastings was removed, all the attendants who had waited upon the king were debarred access to him. He and his brother were withdrawn into the inner apartments of the Tower proper, and day by day began to be seen more rarely behind the bars and windows, till at length they ceased

to appear altogether. The physician Argentine, the last of his attendants whose services the king enjoyed, reported that the young king, like a victim prepared for sacrifice, sought remission of his sins by daily confession and penance, because he believed that death was facing him ... I have seen many men burst forth into tears and lamentations when mention was made of him after his removal from men's sight; and already there was a suspicion that he had been done away with. Whether, however, he has been done away with, and by what manner of death, so far I have not at all discovered.[16]

Before Mancini could discover the fate of Edward V and his brother, he was recalled to France by his patron, Angelo Cato. 'These are the facts relating to the upheaval in this kingdom', Mancini wrote from his residence at Beaugency on 1 December that same year, 'but how he may afterwards have ruled, and yet rules, I have not sufficiently learnt.'[17]

Shortly before departing on his progress, on 18 July, Richard ordered that seventeen men be paid a total of £52 20d 'for their services done to our dearest brother the late king ... and to Edward Bastard late called king Edward the Vth'.[18] It marked the end of what had been a small royal household surrounding King Edward. The two boys, remaining in the Tower, were now alone.

With the king away from the capital, rumours and uncertainty, particularly surrounding the fate of the former King Edward V and his brother, had begun to grow. The Crowland chronicler reported that 'there was also a rumour that those men who had fled to sanctuaries had advised that some of the king's daughters should leave Westminster in disguise and go overseas so that if any human fate, inside the Tower, were to befall the male children, nevertheless through the saving of the persons of the daughters the kingdom might some day return to rightful heirs'. When this was discovered, Westminster Abbey 'and the whole neighbourhood took on the appearance of a castle and a fortress and men of the greatest strictness were appointed as keepers there ... over these men, as captain and chief, was a certain John Nestfield; he watched all entrances and exits of the monastery so that no one inside could get out and no one from outside could get in without his permission'.[19]

On 29 July, Richard wrote from Minster Lovell, to the Chancellor, John Russell, stating:

And whereas we understand that certain persons of such as of late had taken upon them the fact of an enterprise, as we doubt not ye have heard, be attached and in ward. We desire and will that ye do make our letters of commission to such persons as by you and our council shall be advised for to sit upon them and to proceed to the due execution of our laws in that behalf. Fail ye not hereof as our perfect trust is in you.[20]

It seems that something was afoot. Shortly after departing from London, Richard had granted the duke of Norfolk sole power to array troops throughout the whole of the south-east and East Anglia.[21] The Crowland chronicler reported how it was while Richard was on his progress that 'while these things were happening the two sons of King Edward remained in the Tower of London with a specially appointed guard', suggesting that the chronicler himself was confident that the two boys were still alive; however, 'in order to release them from such captivity the people of the South and of the West of the kingdom began to murmur greatly, to form assemblies and to organise associations to this end – many were in secret, others quite open – especially those people who, because of fear, were scattered throughout franchises and sanctuaries'.[22]

Contemporary records do not reveal exactly what 'enterprise' had occurred, nor who exactly had been imprisoned and for what cause. However, the Tudor antiquary John Stowe reported that shortly after the king's coronation 'were taken for rebels against the king Robert Russe serjeant of London, William Davy pardoner of Hounslow, John Smith groom of King Edward's stirrup, and Stephen Ireland wardrobe in the Tower, with many other, that they should have sent writings into the parts of Brittany to the earls of Richmond and of Pembroke, and other lords'. Stowe described how there had been rumours of a plot devised by the men who 'were purposed to have set fire on divers parts of London, which fire, whilst men had been staunching, they would have stolen out of the Tower, the prince Edward and his brother the duke of York'. Arrested and tried at Westminster, the four men were 'judged to death, and from thence drawn to the Tower Hill, and there beheaded, and their heads were set on London Bridge'.[23]

The account by Stowe may seem fanciful, especially since it is not repeated by any other contemporary chroniclers, nor do any indictments survive in the existing legal records, but the fact that some attempt was made to free the princes is also recorded by the French chronicler Thomas Basin, who reported that fifty Londoners had been involved in the enterprise, though only four men were executed, collaborating Stowe's account. Of the four men, only Smith can be traced, being listed among the grooms of the stable, though a John Smith is also named as 'one of the valets of our chamber' by Edward IV in 1482, who requested that his 'welbeloved servant' be paid an annuity of 6d a day, an annuity that remained unpaid by 22 May 1483.[24] He may also have been the 'master Smith' who had been discharged as one of the princes' servants on 18 July. Importantly, the Master of the Horse, the head of the stable and Smith's master, was John Cheyne who had refused to serve under Richard's regime.

No record of any executions has survived beyond the later accounts by Stowe and Basin, yet Richard certainly seems to have been informed of some kind of growing unrest ahead. On 9 August, payments were made for the manufacture and transporting of twenty-three Welsh bills and thirty glaives to Warwick.[25] On 13 August, John, Lord Scrope of Bolton, was given the 'rule, guiding and oversight' of the lordship of Gaynespark, Essex, 'that late belonged to our rebel John Welles'.[26] Tellingly, Welles was a half-brother of Margaret Beaufort, the mother of the exiled Henry Tudor, the earl of Richmond. Four days later, on 17 August, Nicholas Spicer, an usher of the royal chamber, was commanded to have 2,000 Welsh bills 'in all haste to be purveyed and made for us', with a royal signet warrant to summon as many blacksmiths required for the task.[27] The following day, a commission of *oyer et terminer* was issued to enquire into various treasons and felonies in London and the surrounding Home Counties, headed by the king's 'dearest kinsman' the duke of Buckingham.[28]

12

'CONFUSION AND MOURNING'

The royal progress remained at York until 21 September, having stayed for more than three weeks, longer than any stop on Richard's progress. From York, Richard travelled back to Pontefract Castle, where he remained for another two weeks, until 8 October. Richard continued to act as the benevolent king, making generous gifts almost daily. On 6 October, £40 was granted for the building of a church 'of our blessed lady' in the lordship of Barnard Castle in Durham.[1] On 10 October, Richard ordered that £5 be 'given towards the making of the glass window' at the monastery in Carlisle.[2] The same day, Thomas Wandesford, a former servant of Richard's father, the duke of York, was granted an annuity of 60s 10d 'towards his relief and sustenation now in his old and unwieldly age'.[3]

By Friday, 10 October, however, Richard suddenly decided to move southwards, travelling to Gainsborough before moving to Lincoln the following day.[4] This seems to have been in response to some kind of unrest taking place in the south. On 7 October, John Howard paid his servant Lenthorpe twenty shillings to ride into Kent to pass a message to William Schell, a member of his household; three days later, Howard sent another messenger into Kent, and on 11 October a third was sent to Rochester. By now Howard seems to have been made aware of an outbreak of unrest, for he then dispatched a force of more than seventy men to Gravesend. Howard himself was rowed up the river to meet the Chancellor, Bishop Russell, while at the same time the duke sent a letter to John Paston on 10 October, warning that 'the Kentishmen be up in the weald, and say that they will come and rob the city, which I shall let if I may'.[5] The capital prepared for the worst. The merchant Richard Cely recorded payment in his accounts for '2 bills of Normandy' and 'for 4 sheaves of arrows' under the heading 'in October anno '83, the time that great watches were kept in London'.[6]

Just over a fortnight earlier, on 22 September, Robert Morton was dismissed from the chancery. Morton was the nephew of John Morton, and he had succeeded his uncle as Master of the Rolls when John was appointed bishop of Ely. By 1479, Robert had himself been appointed archdeacon of Winchester, and in 1481 was made a canon of St George's Chapel, Windsor. The Morton family were well connected within the city. Another family member was a second Robert, a lawyer at Lincoln's Inn, who in 1478 had married Agnes, the widow of the alderman John Felde; Agnes was the sister of John Forster, the receiver-general of Queen Elizabeth from 1465. The connection between John Morton and John Forster suggests possibly that the initial Hastings conspiracy, or, at least, certainly those who had been connected to it, was being revived.

The same day as Morton's dismissal, a letter was sent to the sheriff of Southampton outlawing the retaining and use of liveries in the city, citing general concern about the recent increase in the practice which caused 'great division and jeopardy'.[7] The following day, 23 September, the queen's brother, Bishop Lionel Woodville, had his 'worldly' goods seized 'without delay', though they were to be 'safely put under sure keeping unto ye shall know our intent and further pleasure'.[8] Only the day before, Woodville had issued letters of his own to the abbot of Hyde regarding diocesan business; the matter involved a mundane transaction; however, what is important is that the letters pinpoint exactly where Woodville was residing when they were issued: Thornbury, in Gloucestershire.[9] It was here that Thornbury Castle, one of the duke of Buckingham's principal seats, was located. Woodville's presence here suggests that he was staying at Thornbury as a guest of the duke.

This crucial link between Lionel Woodville and Buckingham is as extraordinary as it is revealing. What was Lionel doing residing at one of Buckingham's residences? And why should Buckingham be involved in any dealings with the Woodvilles? In return for his support in seizing the throne, Richard had given Buckingham everything he could possibly want: lands, titles and office now made the duke the pre-eminent nobleman in the realm. Perhaps it was not enough for a man who was already comparing himself to Warwick the kingmaker, boasting as he handed out his livery, depicting Stafford knots, to former retainers of William Hastings, that now 'he had as many of them as Richard Neville Earl of Warwick had formerly had'.[10] The duke himself seems to have had royal pretensions. In 1474, he had obtained a heraldic decree which allowed him to display the arms of Edward III's youngest son, Thomas of Woodstock, duke of Gloucester, as his own. It was, as observers noted, 'a coat near to the king and of his royal blood'.[11] If it is impossible to discern Buckingham's motives, it is clear that if the duke had chosen to begin shady dealings with the Woodvilles, he had only chosen to do so suddenly, and in secret without the king's knowledge.

Richard did not suspect a thing. Thomas More recorded how the duke of Buckingham and Richard 'in fair manner departed' from Gloucester, and that the king 'both with great gifts and high behests in most loving and trusty manner departed at Gloucester'.[12] Buckingham was certainly back at Brecknock Castle by mid-August, for a letter written by him ordering a buck be delivered to John Isbury ends, 'given under our signet at our castle of Brecknock the 23rd day of August the first year of our sovereign lord king Richard the iiide'.[13] The Crowland chronicler believed that Richard, 'who never acted sleepily but incisively and with the utmost vigilance', soon discovered that the duke was planning to turn against him: 'this whole conspiracy was known well enough, through spies'. Yet, as late as 16 September the king had issued writs to receivers in north and south Wales ordering them to pay their accounts to the duke directly.[14] Even as late as 6 October, the sheriff of Hereford was still arranging to pay an annuity of £20 to Buckingham.[15]

There is evidence that Richard mobilised forces against the rebellion and in particular the threat of an invasion as early as 29 September.[16] For a while, Richard kept his knowledge of the conspiracy secret, deciding to 'dissemble the matter while he assembled an army' and to arrest Buckingham 'by guile'. According to Vergil, Richard 'summoned the duke to him by the most kindly letters and appointed the messenger, who carried the letters that he should persuade him with words of good omen to return to the royal court'. This Buckingham instantly refused. 'The duke answered the messenger that, for reasons of ill health, he was unable to come at present'. Richard would not take no for an answer, and summoned

Buckingham to court with 'threatening words': 'Then the duke openly answered that he would not come, and at the same time prepared for war and commanded the other conspirators elsewhere to make rebellion.'[17]

It was not until 12 October that Richard was prepared to face the truth. He wrote from Lincoln to John Russell, thanking him 'in our heartiest wise' for 'the manifold presents that your servants on your behalf have presented unto us at this our being here, which we assure you we took and accepted with good heart and so we have cause'. But Richard had not written merely to send a letter of gratitude to his Chancellor. He continued:

> And whereas We by God's grace intend briefly to advance us toward our rebel and traitor the Duke of Buckingham to resist and withstand his malicious purpose as lately by our other letters we certified you our mind more at large. For which cause it behoveth us to have our great seal here. We being informed that for such infirmities and diseases as ye sustain ne may in your person to your ease conveniently come unto us with the same. Wherefore we desire and nonetheless charge you that forthwith upon the sight of this ye saufly do the same our great seal to be sent unto us and such of the officers of our Chancery as by your wisdom shall be thought necessary.

The letter had been written in the neat and clear hand of the king's secretary, as would be expected of an official document from the crown, entitled 'By the King'. Yet Richard decided that, after his scribe had finished, he had more to say to impress upon the elderly Russell the need for urgent action. Instead of simply signing the document with his usual monogram in the top left-hand corner of the paper, Richard took his quill, and began to scribble furiously across the page, immediately after from where the letter had ended:

> We most gladly ye came yourself if ye may & if ye may not we pray you not to fail but to accomplish in all diligence our said commandment to send our seal incontinent upon the sight hereof as we trust you with such as ye trust & the officers pertaining to attend with it praying you to ascertain us of your news. Here loved be God all is well & truly determined & for to resist the malice of him that had best cause to be true the duke of Buckingham the most untrue creature living whom with God's grace we shall not be long till

we will be in that parts & subdue his malice. We assure you was never false
traitor better purveyed [provided] for, as bearer, Gloucester, shall show you.[18]

Intriguingly, on almost exactly the same date that Richard ordered the
seizure of Lionel Woodville's goods and the removal of John Morton's
relative Robert from the chancery, on 22 September, the king also wrote
to John Russell ordering for Parliament to be summoned under the Great
Seal for 6 November.[19] Russell began to prepare his address for the opening
of the new session, making mention of great men who 'be he never so
great' if 'that is most to be sorrowed, by unlawful assemblies and insurrections, putting not only the people but also the nobles to extreme jeopardy
and peril of life and lands ... such one, what so ever he be, is but as it
were a rotten member of the body', an oblique reference to preparations for
rebellion that had now been uncovered. If Richard was planning on using
Parliament to bring any adversaries to heel, the formal summoning of
Parliament on 22 September may have triggered preparations for rebellion
to have been brought forward, or possibly forced Buckingham's hand into
declaring for the rebels.

The man who had placed Richard on the throne, who had been his kingmaker, now intended to turn against him.

Buckingham's new alliance with the Woodvilles seems bizarre, and
undoubtedly stunned Richard, yet most sources are in agreement about
the reasons behind it. One chronicler described how 'many knights and
gentlemen, of Kent and other places, gathered them together to have gone
toward the Duke of Buckingham, being then at Brecknock ... which
intended to have subdued king Richard'. The chronicler was clear that
Richard had 'also put to death the ii children of king Edward, for which
cause he lost the hearts of the people. And thereupon many Gentlemen
intended his destruction.'[20] According to the Crowland chronicler, just
when 'the people round about the city of London' and in the counties of
Kent, Essex, Sussex, Hampshire, Dorset, Devon, Somerset, Wiltshire and
Berkshire 'began considering vengeance', there was 'public proclamation'
that the duke of Buckingham, having removed himself to Brecknock in
Wales, was 'repentant of what had been done', especially once 'a rumour

arose that King Edward's sons, by some unknown manner of violent destruction, had met their fate'.[21] And Robert Fabyan, writing in 1504, described how 'the foresaid grudge increasing, and the more forasmuch as the common fame went that king Richard had within the Tower put unto secret death the II sons of his brother . . . for the which, and other causes had within the breast of the duke of Buckingham, the said duke, in secret manner, conspired against him, and allied him with divers gentlemen, to the end to bring his purpose about'.[22]

It seems as though men were convinced that Edward V and his brother, Richard, had not only disappeared from view, but were now dead. From the outset, there had been endless speculation and comment as to how exactly the princes had died. None are conclusive, though taken together they reflect a fairly unanimous contemporary verdict that the princes were slain during Richard's reign, almost certainly in the summer of 1483. The *Great Chronicle* states that there were rumours still abounding after Easter 1484, commenting that 'much whispering was among the people that the King had put the children of King Edward to death'.[23] English sources from various regions came to the same conclusion. Robert Ricart, the mayor of Bristol, wrote in the calendar year for September 1483 to September 1484 that 'in this year the two sons of King Edward were put to silence in the Tower of London';[24] more precisely, in Colchester, on or around 29 September, Michaelmas Day, the town clerk, John Hervy, penned his end-of-year entry in the Colchester Oath Book, describing not only Edward V as an illegitimate king, but also as the 'late son of Edward IV'.[25]

On the continent, it was a similar story. Just a few days earlier, on 23 September, in the recently completed Sistine Chapel, Pope Sixtus IV held a mass for the dead 'for Edward, king of England'. Whether this refers to Edward IV or Edward V is debatable; however, regulations governing papal ceremonial stated that a requiem mass should be held as soon as the pope had received news of a royal death. Similar honours had been paid only ten days before on 13 September to Louis XI, after the pope had received news of the French king's death two days earlier. A delay of five months to perform a requiem mass for Edward IV seems unlikely, especially since Edward IV's death was known in Rome by 16 May, when a letter of condolence was sent from the papacy to Queen Elizabeth. Furthermore, news of Edward V's deposition had already reached the Vatican by 8 August, when a letter had been dispatched to Richard III. If Pope Sixtus believed that Edward V was dead by 23 September, one possibility is that he discovered the news from Angelo Cato, the Italian archbishop of Vienne, and Dominic Mancini's patron, who was an old friend and correspondent of Pope Sixtus.[26]

The fact of the princes' deaths seems to have been taken as an almost universal truth by most foreign commentators. On the continent rumour soon spread that Edward V and his brother had been killed, and was the topic of open discussion in France. Before his death in late August 1483, Louis XI was reported by Commynes to have believed that Richard had murdered his nephews, for which the French king considered him 'extremely cruel and evil'.[27] A genealogical roll, though dating much later, around 1513, also mentions that Thomas Warde, a chaplain to Edward IV, who had been sent to France in 1483 to collect the king's pension and was still in France when the king died, was at the French court when Louis was informed 'that Richard duke of Gloucester the protector had put his nephews to silence and usurped the crown upon them'.[28]

The linking of the news of the princes' deaths with Buckingham's sudden decision to rebel against Richard raises questions about Buckingham's own involvement in the affair. Did the duke already know of the princes' fate, or could he have been responsible for releasing the news that the princes were dead? A short Latin account of Richard's reign in the Bodleian Library describes how Richard, 'being afraid that his nephews might prevent him from reigning with the approbation of the kingdom', then 'first taking counsel with the Duke of Buckingham, as said, removed them from the light of this world, by some means or other, vilely and murderously . . . Alas, that such noble princes, heirs to so rich a kingdom', the short chronicle continued, 'should thus end their lives, innocent of any offence that merited such violence!'[29] The notes of a London citizen written around the same time stated that 'This year King Edward V, late called Prince of Wales, and Richard Duke of York his brother, King Edward IV's sons, were put to death in the Tower by the vise of the Duke of Buckingham' – in other words, on his advice or by his design.[30] Philippe de Commynes also believed that it was Buckingham who 'had put the two children to death', though in three separate other places in his *Memoirs* he places the responsibility on Richard, who 'had his two nephews murdered'.[31]

Another continental source, the Dutch *Divisie Chronicle*, written around 1500, suggests that the princes had possibly been murdered by Buckingham, though adding that 'some say' that Buckingham spared one of the children, 'which he had lifted from the font and had him secretly abducted out of the country'.[32] Nothing can be proved either way, for the clues provide no leads; nor can they be taken as conclusive evidence, apart from providing a sense of the foreboding conclusion that the fate of the two boys had already been sealed.

Years later, around 1508, Polydore Vergil wrote how Richard 'in truth did not hide the slaughter but after a few days allowed rumour of the boys' deaths to be spread abroad, so namely (it is to be believed) the populace, now no male heir of Edward lived, might bear the king good will'. If this was the case, Richard's actions seriously backfired. When news of the princes' deaths began to spread across the realm, 'all the people were filled with confusion and mourning . . . They ran in different directions all together, raging, certain that they would not have done such a thing. They cursed at the power of the cruelty, savagery and ferocity of the deed and especially bewailed that they were unable to avenge such an inhumane act.' In particular, the household men of Edward IV 'bore it impatiently', judging 'the common loss rightly knowing that a most barbarous tyranny had now invaded the state'. When Queen Elizabeth, still remaining in sanctuary, discovered the news of her sons' deaths she 'fell suddenly to the ground and lay for a long time half-alive'. The sound of her weeping and howling 'filled the religious house with noise', as, inconsolable, Elizabeth 'beat her breast' and tore out her hair.[33]

The existence of rumours, speculating as to the whereabouts of Edward V and his brother, Richard, duke of York, clearly fed on the removal of the two boys from public sight and their continued absence. It is noticeable that talk of the fates of the princes changed from the opportunity to rescue them from captivity, with the Crowland chronicler's observation that meetings were formed, 'to plan the princes' deliverance from captivity', with discussion even of moving the Yorkist princesses from sanctuary to the continent, in case any 'fatal mishap' should befall their brothers.[34] All this took place with a complete lack of knowledge as to what was happening behind the Tower walls: Dominic Mancini could report how 'many men' supposedly burst into tears at the mention of Edward V's name, 'and

already that there was a suspicion that he had been done away with', yet no
one really knew anything for certain.[35] It is only when mention of Buckingham is brought into the rumours that the 'common fame' turns from
rumours of plans to rescue the living princes into stories of the princes'
deaths by violence. But the change in direction and tone of the rumours
does nothing to prove either way that the princes were certainly dead, or
that Buckingham had been involved; we cannot be sure that the circulation of rumours during the summer and autumn of 1483 was not intended
to stir up public support for rebellion against Richard, playing on already
present fears and emotions.

The rumours can be threaded into a narrative, but what really matters is
not their content or veracity, but the fact of their existence at all. Both commentators, chroniclers and the public seem to have been overwhelmingly
affected by the thought that Richard would have not only struck down and
killed his own kin, but would have killed children. In a society scarred
by violence and civil war, moral boundaries still remained, limits beyond
which its members, even kings, could not stretch without consequences.

It is striking that, while Richard had been able to depose Edward V,
many if not most of Edward IV's household men had been prepared to,
perhaps temporarily, go along with the plan. Edward V would be replaced,
removed from the throne and placed in the Tower. Richard would rule,
ensuring the stability of the Yorkist dynasty; possibly, they considered
that when Edward V finally came of age, they could change their minds,
forcing Richard from the throne. For the moment, Richard's accession
had taken place in a swirl of brutal force. The threat of violence from the
descent of thousands of armed men from the north made it seem that
resistance to Richard's usurpation of the throne was impossible. Faced
with a choice of submission or inevitable destruction, most in Edward IV's
household chose to acquiesce in Richard's triumph. Few can have believed
the logic of Richard's, or Buckingham's, arguments that somehow Edward
IV's 'pre-contract' with a former love interest from nearly twenty years
ago would have ruled that the children of Edward IV were to be declared
illegitimate. Attempts to free the princes suggest that already by late July
preparations were being established to bring Edward V to the throne once
more.

Yet, once again, men seem to have underestimated the lengths Richard was prepared to go to defend himself. The very thought that Richard would have been prepared to kill his own nephews would have been an anathema in medieval society: children were to be honoured, as innocents themselves, as representations of Holy Innocents, the children slaughtered by Herod three days after the birth of Christ. Innocents' Day, 28 December, was regarded as a sacred day, on which people abstained from setting out on journeys or beginning new tasks, while the Massacre of the Innocents was frequently portrayed in medieval art. The most moving of the plays in the Corpus Christi cycles fixate also on the Slaughter of the Innocents. The disappearance of the two princes, and the rumours surrounding their deaths, stemmed from the moral shock as the reality gradually dawned that Edward and Richard would not be reappearing from behind the Tower walls. As the *Great Chronicle* noted, rumour superseded rumour, driving forward further rebellion, since 'when the fame of this notable foul fact was dispersed through the realm, so great grief stroke generally to the hearts of men, that the same, subduing all fear, they wept everywhere, and when they could weep no more, they cried out, "Is there truly any man living so far at enemity with God, with all that holy is and religious, so utter enemy to man, who would not have abhorred the mischief of so foul a murder?"'[36]

In the margin of the *Great Chronicle*, a reader paused to write, 'Innocentes, Mors Innocentium', as if in complete acceptance and agreement that an act of horrific and ungodly proportions had taken place. What exactly had happened, and who exactly had committed it, will remain disputed: what cannot be doubted is the overwhelming degree to which it was believed that Edward V and his brother were now dead, and that the responsibility for this lay with their uncle, their Protector, the nation's unexpected king.

The most telling reason that the rumoured deaths of Edward V and his brother were believed is in the sudden catapulting of Henry Tudor onto the political scene, as a potential replacement candidate for the throne. The Crowland chronicler wrote that 'all those who had begun this agitation, realising that if they could not find someone new at their head for their conquest it would soon be all over with them, remembered Henry, earl of Richmond, who had already spent many years in exile in Brittany'.[37] The author of the *Great Chronicle* believed that 'word sprang quickly of [Henry Tudor who] made speedy provision to come into England to claim the crown as his right, considering the death of King Edward's children, of whom as then men feared not only to say that they were rid out of this world'.[38] The Crowland chronicler wrote how Buckingham, having become 'repentant of what had been done' that he would be considered 'captain-in-chief of this affair', approached John Morton, the bishop of Ely, imprisoned at his residence at Brecknock, for advice. Morton suggested that the duke write to Tudor, 'inviting him to hasten into the kingdom of England as fast as he could reach the shore to take Elizabeth, the dead king's elder daughter, to wife and with her, at the same time, possession of the whole kingdom'.[39]

Polydore Vergil, basing his account on the testimonies of first-hand accounts told to him over twenty years later, told a similar story. At first, Morton, 'suspecting treason', refused to listen to the duke, yet 'when he saw that his mind was made up and in good faith he conversed freely with him . . . The duke disclosed everything to the bishop of Ely and informed him that the lines of Edward and Henry VI were joined by affinity, and thus at the same time this union might be restored to the realm . . . The manner was this, that Henry earl of Richmond who, it was reported, after the news of Edward's death, had been released by the duke of Brittany. They should send to him to come to the realm in all haste and to help him, if he would first promise on oath that, after obtaining the realm, he would take as his wife Elizabeth the eldest daughter of King Edward.'[40]

Morton agreed; yet it seems too much of a coincidence that the bishop in captivity was able to swiftly arrange for a servant of Margaret Beaufort, named Reginald Bray, to journey at speed to Margaret to inform her 'of all that had been decided'. It seems that Margaret Beaufort had already been plotting. 'After learning of the slaughter of Edward's sons', Vergil wrote, Margaret 'began to hope well, thinking it to be an act of God, as namely the bloodlines of Henry VI and Edward might be mixed', if her son Henry might be able to marry Edward IV's eldest daughter, Elizabeth.

First, however, Margaret would need the support of Queen Elizabeth in sanctuary. Surrounded by John Nestfield's troops as the queen was, it seemed an impossible task. But Margaret had a solution: her physician,

Lewis Carleon, she had learnt, had also treated the queen; few might suspect him, and he might be allowed to pass through the armed cordon to
converse with her. According to Vergil, Carleon 'did not delay approaching the queen'. Carleon, who must have known the queen's mind also,
chose to suggest that the plan had been devised by himself rather than
ordered by Margaret Beaufort, who as a former Lancastrian was still held
in suspicion. This was 'pleasing' to Elizabeth, who, believing the plot was
taking place at her own instigation, ordered Carleon to return to Margaret, living in Thomas, Lord Stanley's London house, with the message
that she should 'promise in her name that she would do her best to get
all the friends of her husband Edward to follow her son Henry, if now
he would swear, after obtaining the realm, to marry her daughter Elizabeth, or another of her daughters, if the first were to die, before he came
to the realm'. Having agreed to these conditions, Margaret then appointed
Reginald Bray to 'take charge of the conspiracy', ordering him 'as secretly
as he could' to 'draw others of the nobility to their side, who would be
able to help'.

Of course, Vergil's later account may have been written to provide
Margaret Beaufort with a central role in the conspiracy; Margaret, he
wrote, was 'commonly called the head of that conspiracy'. Yet Margaret's
involvement in the rebellion can be judged from the number of her kinsmen and servants who were to be listed among the rebels, including John
Cheyne, John Heron, Thomas Lewkenor and John Welles. Significantly, it
does seem that Lewis Carleon was implicated in the rebellion. In a surviving manuscript of his astrological tables, Carleon wrote that he had been
forced to redraw his work, since the original papers had been lost 'through
the pillaging of king Richard, while I was imprisoned in the Tower of
London'.[41]

Within a few days Bray had recruited former knights of Edward IV's
household, including Giles Daubeney, Richard Guildford, Thomas Rameneye, John Cheyne 'and many others', while Queen Elizabeth 'likewise
hastily made her friends partners of the deliberation'. Margaret employed
Christopher Urswick, a Lancastrian who had been recommended by
Carleon and who was described by Vergil as 'a priest of good character
and shrewd in setting things in motion', who, after taking an oath of
secrecy, made him her confessor and confidant. Urswick would be given

the task of travelling to Brittany to inform Henry Tudor of the conspiracy planned in his name. Yet just before Urswick was about to make his journey, Margaret learnt of Buckingham's intention to raise a rebellion against Richard. There was to be an immediate change of plan. Instead, Margaret ordered that Hugh Conway should travel to Brittany 'with a not inconsiderable sum of money', in order to disclose the plan, 'and to exhort him to return, and principally urge him to arrive in Wales, where he would find aid prepared'. Soon afterwards, Richard Guildford and Thomas Rameneye were also sent across the Channel to Brittany. When Henry had been informed of his mother's message, 'raised in spirits', he appealed to Duke Francis for help to make the journey to England. In spite of Richard's recent embassy under Thomas Hutton that had attempted to win back favour with Brittany, Duke Francis 'gave very willingly'.

Francis apparently remained resentful of Richard's decision to depose Edward V, who since 1481 had been pledged to marry his daughter Anne. The removal and disappearance of the young king had destroyed the careful plans for his own dynasty. He arranged for Tudor to be equipped with ships, money and men, in preparation for his invasion. At the same time, Tudor apparently received further letters from Buckingham, according to a later Act of Attainder, dated 24 September, urging him to invade. 'Meanwhile in England', Vergil wrote, 'the leaders of the conspiracy set in motion many things at the same time. Others held suitable fortified places with armed men, others prepared secretly for rebellion; others elsewhere were tensed and prepared to make war as soon as they knew Henry had arrived.' At the same time, John Morton sent secret messages to 'all who were raised in the hall of King Edward'.[42]

Richard continued to make his preparations to advance against Buckingham. He arranged for armed men to surround the duke's territory, 'held in readiness to pounce on all his domestic possessions as soon as the duke moved a foot away from his house'.[43] On 13 October, John Oter, a yeoman of the crown, arrived at York with a letter from the king, dated 11 October, to the mayor, aldermen and sheriffs of the city, describing how 'the duke of Buckingham traitorously is turned upon us contrary to the duty of his legiance, and entendeth the utter destruction of us, you all, and all other our true subjects that have taken our part, whose traitorous intent we with gods grace intend briefly to resist and subdue'. Requesting that 'ye will send unto us as many men defensibly arrayed on horseback' to Leicester, where Richard intended to muster his army by 21 October.[44] Similar letters were sent to Southampton on 13 October, requesting that the town send horsemen to meet him at Coventry on 22 October.[45] News of the outbreak of the rebellion in Kent could not have reached Richard by the time he had sent his letters; the king must therefore have committed himself to taking action against Buckingham beforehand.

Elsewhere, the king's closest supporters wrote letters, requesting immediate military support from members of the king's household. On 17 October, Francis, Viscount Lovell wrote to Sir William Stonor, a knight of the king's body who had loyally attended Richard's coronation several months previously, and would have been expected to rally instantly to the king's standard:

> Cousin Stoner, I command me to you as heartily as I can: for as much as it pleaseth the king's grace to have warned you and all other to attend upon his grace, and your company that ye would come in my cognisance and my company to come with you: and I am sure that shall please his grace best, and I trust shall be to your surety.
>
> Your heartily loving cousin Francis Lovell.
>
> Also cousin, the king hath commanded me to send you word to make you ready, and all your company, in all haste to be with his grace at Leicester the Monday xx day of October: for I have sent for all my men to meet me at Banbury, the Saturday the xviii day of October.[46]

Stonor did not reply. Instead he had chosen to join the rebels, who included Stonor's stepfather, Sir William Norreys, a close supporter of Edward IV. Sir George Browne was another knight of the body who had been close enough to the former king to be noted as one of those 'which wait most upon the king and lie nightly in his chamber'.[47] Now Browne wrote to his nephew by marriage, John Paston, with the cryptic message, 'Loyawlte Ayme', meaning 'loyalty I love', but which has been suggested as a conscious reference to Richard's own motto, 'Loyaulte Me Lye', with Browne signing off with the postscript, 'It shall never come out for me', suggesting that his own loyalty to Edward IV and his disinherited heirs would not be extinguished, at the same time as making a sardonic riposte to the new king's motto.[48]

A picture of an organised, concerted opposition was emerging. A riot had taken taken place at Gravesend Fair on 13 October, where it was described how one 'Bonting slew Master Mowbray with diverse others', possibly the same John Bountayn, the yeoman of the crown who had been sent by the duke of Norfolk to suppress the rebels but who instead joined their ranks at Maidstone. Another yeoman of the crown, William Clifford of Iwade, had been arrested by 15 October. Under the leadership of Sir John Fogge, Sir George Browne, Sir Thomas Lewkenor, Richard Haute and Sir John Guildford, the rebels assembled at Maidstone but were forced to disperse before regrouping on Penenden Heath, before marching through Rochester, reaching Gravesend on 22 October. The rebels then chose to move in a south-west direction for forty miles until they reached Guildford by 25 October. Meanwhile rebellion was spreading out across the country. There had certainly been an outbreak of trouble in Wiltshire by 17 October, when a servant of the sheriff of Cornwall carrying a file of returned writs had been confronted by Walter Hungerford and other rebels at Warminster and had his documents stolen.[49]

The rebellion has commonly become known as the Duke of Buckingham's Rebellion, yet this is misleading. In fact, few of the rebels had any connection or communication with the duke, who seems to have joined the rebellion when it had already gathered enough momentum to be viewed as a serious threat to the political order and Richard's kingship. From the start, however, a brief examination of some of those involved in the uprising indicates the serious challenge that Richard faced.

Evidence for who exactly participated in the rebellion and its precise timings has been skewed by the acceptance of a later Act of Attainder against the rebels, that not only ascribed the date of the risings to St Luke's Day, 18 October, as though the rebellion was co-ordinated to have been launched on a single day (incidentally the same date on which Henry Tudor was supposed to have set sail from Brittany to England), but also organised it into several geographic sectors, areas that in fact represented the regional commissions established by Richard on 13 November to enquire into the details of the rebellion. Outside of these artificial regional zones, there were other areas of dissent. Southampton seems to have taken up arms against the king, with its mayor later attainted for his part in the uprising. William Berkeley of Bisterne, the constable of the city, who was also indicted for rebellion, was present in the city on 8 and 21 October. Later the city decided to send a tun of wine to the king to appease him; nevertheless, Richard imposed an oath of fealty on the townsmen, and may have suspended the city's liberties.[50]

While the rebellion stretched out across most southern counties from Kent to Cornwall, there were three major centres of disturbances, taking place in the south-east, principally around Kent, but also Surrey and Sussex. The ringleaders were in fact former servants of Edward IV, his household men, many of whom had attended the dead king's funeral in April, and had initially been willing to serve under Edward V and Richard's protectorship. In Kent the rebel leaders included Sir George Browne, who had carried the banner of St George at Edward IV's funeral. Browne had entered the Yorkists' service under the influence of his stepfather, Sir Thomas Vaughan, who had recently been executed with Anthony, Earl Rivers, at Pontefract. Alongside Browne, Sir John Fogge of Ashford had been treasurer of Edward IV's household for seven years, and in addition to being a royal councillor had also been a councillor of the young Edward, Prince of Wales, since 1473. At Richard's accession, he had been singled out for pardon as part of Richard's conciliation strategy towards the Woodvilles – a strategy that had clearly failed. Another rebel ringleader was Sir William Haute, a first cousin of Queen Elizabeth Woodville, whose brother, Sir Richard Haute, had been one of Edward V's household men who had been seized at Stony Stratford and later executed at Pontefract in June. Sir Richard's son, also named Richard Haute, who had been a prominent jouster at the wedding celebrations of Prince Richard of York, joined his uncle in rebellion. In Surrey, the rebel leaders included Sir Thomas Bourchier of Barnes, a younger son of Lord Berners, who was a knight of the king's body and constable of Windsor Castle, and Thomas Fiennes, the second son of Richard Fiennes, Lord Dacre of the South, the chamberlain of Queen Elizabeth Woodville.

The second centre of rebellion focused on southern central England, where assemblies were planned at Salisbury and Newbury. Among the leading rebels were Sir William Berkeley of Beverstone, who had been an esquire of the body, constable of Southampton and Winchester; Sir William Norreys, a knight of the body since 1474; and Sir William Stonor, another knight of the body and former MP whom Queen Elizabeth had presented with a present of a doe to 'our trusty and well-beloved William' in 1481.[51] Sir Giles Daubeney was a former esquire and knight of the body who had served as sheriff in Somerset, Dorset and Devon, and Sir John Cheyne had been Edward IV's Master of the Horse. Other rebels had strong links to the Yorkist establishment, having served in the duke of Clarence's household: Sir Roger Tocotes had been steward of Clarence's Hampshire lands, while John Harcourt had been Clarence's receiver in the south-west. The Woodville influence in this region was also strongly represented by the young bishop of Salisbury, Lionel Woodville, and most likely also included Sir Richard Woodville.

The third focus of the rebellion was in the south-west, where rebels were to gather at Exeter, led by Thomas Grey, marquess of Dorset, and Sir Thomas St Leger. St Leger had been a loyal servant to Edward IV, a knight of the body and Master of the King's Hounds since 1478. Around 1472, St Leger had married the king's sister, Anne, duchess of Exeter: he soon tied his fortunes to the Woodvilles, betrothing his daughter by the duchess to Dorset, so that they might inherit the Exeter estates.

Combined together, the group of men that chose to rebel against Richard in the autumn of 1483 could hardly be considered a rabble of malcontents. Fear of losing their influence and position under the new regime might seem an obvious motive to rebel; however, Richard had been determined to ensure that those former servants of Edward IV willing to serve would not be made redundant: Sir Thomas Burgh, Sir Thomas Montgomery and Sir John Scott, trusted officials under Edward, all continued their seamless service under Richard. Richard had even gone out of his way to win the support of Woodville associates such as Sir John Fogge. Some of the rebel leaders had already benefited from Richard's largesse: Sir Thomas Lewkenor, Sir William Berkeley and Sir Thomas Arundel had all been made knights of the Bath at Richard's coronation. Sir William Knyvet was made constable of Castle Rising on 18 July, while Berkeley was confirmed as governor of the Isle of Wight as late as 27 July.[52]

While Richard paused at Leicester, he found time to consent to other grants, though perhaps with an eye on his own salvation during these uncertain times. On 22 October 1483, Richard granted the nunnery of Wilberfoss in York Meadows, worth ten marks yearly, to provide for a chaplain 'and for prayer for the good estate of the king and his consort Anne, queen of England, and his firstborn son Edward, prince of Wales, duke of Cornwall and earl of Chester, and for their souls after their death'.[53] The next day, on 23 October, just before he marched out of Leicester, Richard issued a proclamation against the rebels. The document began by suggesting that the king, 'remembering his solemn profession which he made at the time of his coronation to mercy and justice' had followed 'the same in deed' with his initial reaction on discovering news of the uprising. The king, the proclamation noted, 'first began at mercy in giving unto all manner persons his full and general pardon, trusting thereby to have caused all his subjects to have been surely determined unto him according to the duty of their liegance'. In particular, Richard was keen to underline the fact that as king 'in his own person, as is well known, hath dressed himself to divers parts of this his realm for the indifferent administration of justice to every person, having full confidence and trust that all oppressors and extortioners of his subjects, horrible adulterers and bawds, provoking the high indignation and displeasure of God, should have been reconciled and reduced to the way of truth and virtue, with the abiding in good disposition'.[54]

The moral and didactic tone of the proclamation may have at first seemed strange, especially the mention of adulterers, until its purpose was then revealed in the next paragraph, for there was one particular person for whom Richard had that reference in mind: 'This yet notwithstanding Thomas Dorset, late marquess of Dorset, which not fearing God, nor the peril of his soul, hath many and sundry maids, widows and wives damnably and without shame devoured, deflowered and defouled, holding the unshameful and mischievous woman called Shore's wife in adultery'. The other rebels, named as Sir William Norreys, Sir William Knyvet, Sir Thomas Bourchier of Barnes, Sir George Browne, John Cheyne, John Norreys, Walter Hungerford, John Rushe and John Harecourt of Staunton, 'without the king's authority have assembled and gathered his people by the comfort of his great rebel and traitor the late Duke of Buckingham,

and Bishops of Ely and Salisbury, intending not only the destruction of
the royal person of our said Sovereign Lord and other his true subjects,
the breach of his peace, tranquillity, and common weal of this his realm,
but also in letting of virtue and the damnable maintenance of vices and sin
as they have done in times passed to the great displeasure of God and evil
example of all Christian people'.

Richard promised that through the 'tender and loving disposition that
he hath and beareth unto the common weal of this his realm, and putting
down and rebuking of vices', any yeoman or commoner who was 'abused
and blinded' by the traitors and had already taken up arms, should 'not be
hurt in their bodies nor goods' if they withdrew from the 'false company'
of the rebels immediately 'and meddle no further with them'. Meanwhile
a price was to be offered upon the head of every rebel brought to the king
alive. Starting with the duke of Buckingham himself, Richard offered
£1,000 in money or £100 in land to 'whosoever ... taketh the said Duke
and bringeth him unto his highness'. For the marquess of Dorset or the
two bishops of Ely and Salisbury, 1,000 marks or 100 marks in land, for
each of the knights 500 marks or £40 in land.[55]

The machinery of government worked fast to distribute the king's messages demanding that men come to his aid. The Keeper of the Exchequer
sealed 1,862 writs between 30 September and 5 December.[56] Men across the
country mobilised fast.[57] 'People in this country be so troubled', Edward
Plumpton wrote to Sir Robert Plumpton on 18 October; men had received
commandments both 'in the king's name & otherwise', so, in the confusion, 'marvellously, that they know not what to do'. Lord Strange, he wrote,
'goeth forth from Lathom upon Monday next with 10,000 men, whether,
we cannot say'. As for the duke of Buckingham, he 'has so many men, as it
is said here, that he is able to go where he will, but I trust he shall be right
withstanded & all his malice, & else were a great pity'. Messengers, Plumpton observed, 'commeth daily both from the king's grace & the duke into
this country'.[58]

Buckingham seems to have left Brecon, heading north-east as far as
Weobley. Attempting to call the local gentry to him, the duke soon realised, however, that he had no support: even his own tenants refused to

back him, with some even sacking his residence at Brecon after his departure. Buckingham appears to have won the limited support of only a few men: the Act of Attainder names only John Morton, William Knyvet, John Rushe and Thomas Nandyke, described as a 'necromancer', but a Cambridge master of arts and an astrologer and physician.[59] Both Knyvet and Rushe had been indicted in Richard's proclamation of 23 October as acting alongside Dorset, John Cheyne, Walter Hungerford, George Browne and others. John Rushe was a London merchant who had links with the Woodvilles; as a deputy of customs at Yarmouth for the late Earl Rivers, Rushe was also a client of Margaret Beaufort, Lord Stanley and William Stonor. It is possible that he was the same John Rushe whose son Robert Rushe had been executed for his part in the plot to free Edward V and his brother from their confinement in the Tower.

If Buckingham was unable to attract many men to his standard, it seems that from an early stage the duke was attempting to win support from the Stanleys. He must have hoped that Thomas, Lord Stanley, would at least have given his support as Margaret Beaufort's husband. The duke may have also sought the support of the Talbots: during the minority of the earl of Shrewsbury, the head of the family was Gilbert Talbot, who seems to have fallen out of favour with Richard, having been dropped from the Shropshire commissions of the peace from the beginning of the king's accession. This could have been due to the family's links to William, Lord Hastings; Gilbert remained out of favour for the rest of Richard's reign. If Buckingham had managed to convince the two families to join the rebellion, he would have succeeded in surrounding the king as he marched west.

As for the Talbots and the Stanleys, both families refused to move. Their interests in the region had both been challenged by Buckingham's sudden arrival on the local political scene. Richard's grants to the duke had seen Buckingham establish himself as a major threat to the Stanleys' power base in north Wales and Cheshire, and the Talbots' traditional influence along the Welsh Marches and the north Midlands. Neither were prepared to allow the duke to extend his authority over them. Unlike in other areas, no former servants of Edward IV would join the duke in his rebellion; tainted by his association with Richard, Buckingham's own rising against the king seems to have been a late addition to the carefully planned sequence of risings elsewhere. His decision to rebel in fact did more to save Richard than if he had remained loyal to the king: with so few prepared to back him, even those hostile to the king, any organised opposition that might lead to a successful rebellion, attracting Stanley and Talbot support, was split. Buckingham's betrayal was the greatest blessing in disguise that Richard could have hoped for.

Richard continued his march southwards, as he sought to crush the rising early. By Sunday, 2 November, if not earlier, the king and his army had arrived at Salisbury, in the heart of the rebellion in Wiltshire.

Meanwhile, it was not until late October that Henry Tudor finally set sail from Brittany. One surviving document, signed by both 'Henry of Richmond' and Jasper Tudor, is dated 29 October, promising to repay Duke Francis a loan of 10,000 *livres tournois*, 'on the word of a prince'.[60] The bond suggests that Henry himself did not set sail until after that date, probably after receiving news that rebellion had already broken out prematurely.

It was a 'prosperous wind' that saw off the fifteen ships which accompanied Henry on his journey to England. Mid-voyage, however, the winds had transformed into a 'cruel gale' as a 'sudden tempest' scattered the fleet, each being separated 'from one way from another' so that some were blown back onto the Normandy coast, others into Brittany. Henry's own ship was 'tossed all the night long with the waves'. As dawn broke and the wind calmed, the chalk cliffs of the south coast and the haven of Poole Harbour came into view. Shaken by the storms and their sleepless night, in the gloom of morning light the devastating impact of the storm was revealed: only Henry's and one other vessel had made it through the night. As the ships drew up closer to the shore, there was worse news to come. The shoreline was 'beset with soldiers' from Richard's army. Henry commanded that no man should land until the rest of the fleet had time to regroup. In the meantime, he sent across several men in a single skiff to the shore to find out the identity of the guards. Navigating the boat out to within speaking distance of the soldiers who, encouraging them to land, called out that they had been 'sent by the Duke of Buckingham to escort Henry to the camp, which he had nearby with his flourishing army, so that

Richard is depicted twice in the Rous Roll, described as a 'most mighty prince'. He all but disappears from a version of the roll made after his deposition, where he is mentioned only as the husband of Anne Neville.

Warwick Castle, the seat of the Beauchamp family, from which Anne was descended. The couple returned here in triumph during the king's progress of August 1483. It was here that John Rous may have presented them with his roll, praising Richard's virtues.

Above The illuminated initial of a charter granted by Richard III in 1484. Above the royal arms with the boar supporters is Richard's motto.

Above John, Lord Howard. Howard's support for Richard's usurpation was rewarded with the duchy of Norfolk. He loyally served the king, and led the vanguard of Richard's forces into battle at Bosworth.

Left William Catesby, one of Richard's loyal dependants, whose support was crucial in Richard's seizure of the throne.

On learning of the duke of Buckingham's rebellion, on 12 October 1483, King Richard dictated this letter to his Chancellor, John Russell, requesting the Great Seal be sent to him at Lincoln. Richard added the lengthy and emotional postscript in his own hand, declaring his determination 'to resist the malice' of 'the most untrue creature living'.

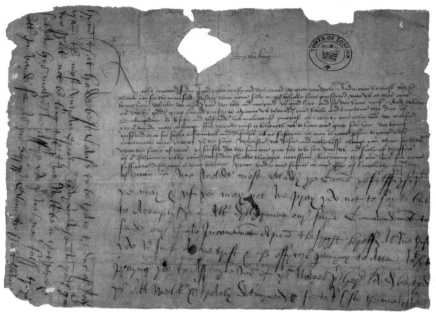

Above A later copy of a drawing of the young Henry Tudor. Forced into exile after the battle of Tewkesbury in 1471, aged just fourteen, Tudor's own claim to the throne was weak. Yet after the disappearance of the Princes in the Tower, he became the choice of dissident Yorkists to replace Richard III.

Below Elizabeth of York, the eldest child of Edward IV and Elizabeth Woodville, was considered an ideal bride for Henry Tudor. Yet after the death of Richard's queen in 1485, rumours swirled that the king planned to marry his niece Elizabeth himself.

Richard's final surviving letter, dated 11 August 1485, informing Henry Vernon of the arrival of Tudor from France, four days previously. 'God be our guide, we be utterly determined in our own person to remove in all haste goodly that we can or may.' Vernon was to provide men 'horsed and harnessed' in all haste, 'upon pain of forfeiture unto us of all that ye may forfeit and lose'.

The boar symbol of Richard III on a silver gilt badge. It was likely to have been worn by a high-ranking supporter at Bosworth.

A collection of thirty-four cannon balls discovered at the site of the battle.

The golden badge of an eagle with a snake in its mouth, discovered at a separate location, possibly near the windmill where the duke of Norfolk was captured and Richard's vanguard defeated.

A leader of the rebellion against Richard in 1483, Sir John Cheyne fled to Brittany to join Henry Tudor, returning to fight at Bosworth. He came into direct combat with the king, who reportedly struck him with such force that he came off his horse.

As Henry Tudor's stepfather, Thomas, Lord Stanley, came under repeated suspicion from Richard, yet he remained too powerful to challenge. Stanley's inaction at Bosworth, despite leading a force of several thousand men to the battle, may have been the result of Richard holding his son in captivity, or the tactics of a seasoned trimmer. Either way, his refusal to join the king's forces was decisive.

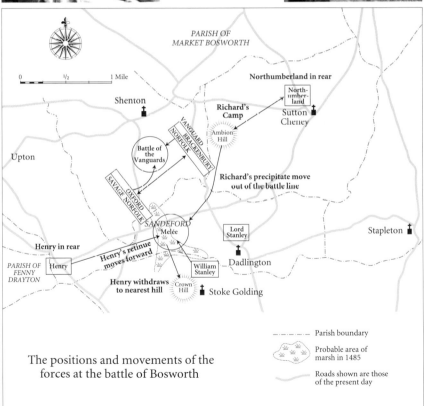

The positions and movements of the forces at the battle of Bosworth

The critical moment of the battle occurred when Lord Stanley's younger brother Sir William ordered his troops to charge on Richard III, resulting in his death. Having been declared a traitor by Richard days before Bosworth, Sir William had nothing to lose.

The gravesite of Richard III, discovered in August 2012 under a car park on the site of Greyfriars. The hands had evidently been tied.

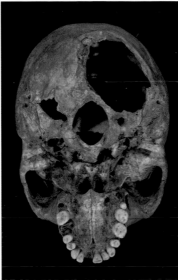

Above Wounds inflicted on Richard's skull include a fatal blow to the back of his head that sliced through the bone, and a puncture wound at the top of the skull. In total, ten wounds to the skeleton have been identified.

Below The bones of Richard III clearly demonstrate a curvature of the spine known as scoliosis.

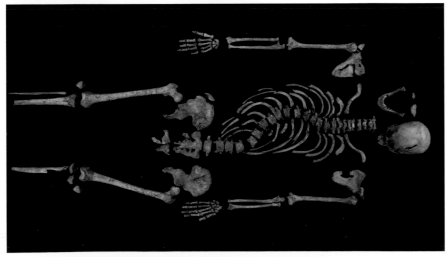

Left This portrait in the Royal Collection at Windsor seems to have been copied from a contemporary original. Richard's right shoulder has been heightened to suggest the humpback. His lips and eyes are narrowed to hint at villainy.

A Tudor depiction of Richard with a broken sword, symbolising his defeat and failed monarchy. The left – not the right – shoulder is humped in keeping with John Rous' descriptions. An X-ray reveals that the king's left arm was originally shown greatly shortened. This was later painted over.

they could join forces and pursue the fleeing Richard'. Henry suspected a trick. He was correct, for by now Buckingham was in Richard's hands.[61]

The storms had not only hampered Buckingham's efforts to gather a force of men; he had struggled to find a place to cross the River Severn. It rained for ten days, causing the river to burst its banks and become a raging torrent. For years afterwards, 'the Great Water' would be remembered as a time of death and devastation. The floods were noted in most contemporary chronicles as occurring precisely around the time that Buckingham would have been seeking to raise the standard of rebellion. On 15 October, the chronicle of Bristol's mayor, Robert Ricart, noted that there was the 'greatest flood and greatest wind at Bristol and in the county there abouts that ever was seen'; another local chronicler recorded how that same evening there 'was the greatest wind that was ever heard of, which caused a wonderful great flood . . . which bore away houses, corn, cattle and drowning above 200 people'.[62] Richard would later note 'how of late through sudden rages and tempests of the sea great parts' of Somerset, particularly in the lordship of Brean, 'was drowned and pisshed by inundation of waters', and 'inhabitants of the lordship there were put to great danger, fear and loss as notably it is known'.[63] Another chronicler also recalled how, that evening, 'the moon being then eclipsed at the swelling of the seas gave but little light, appearing of divers colours', with streaks of red, blue and green appearing around the moon during its eclipse, until 'at the top a little light appeared' and the moon 'waxed clear again'.[64] There is a modern explanation for this, for there was a total eclipse of the moon on the night of 15 October, when it was also a full moon. The total eclipse lasted from 11.47 p.m. to 00.32 a.m., which could have had an additional effect on the high tides.[65] Buckingham could have hardly had any worse fortune.

When Buckingham, who had withdrawn to Weobley, the home of Walter, Lord Ferrers, together with Morton, realised that he was 'hemmed in', he decided that there was only one course open to him. Changing his attire, apparently 'he was finally discovered in the cottage of a certain poor man because the supply of provisions taken there was more abundant than usual', though it seems that the duke was betrayed by his servant Ralph Bannister.[66] Upon his arrest, Buckingham was handed over to Sir James Tyrell, who accompanied the duke on the road to Salisbury, where he was

interrogated. Revealing all about the conspiracy, including naming his
associates, the duke had hoped that through his confession 'he would be
able to speak with Richard, which he urgently asked for'. Yet there would
be no final meeting between the king and the man who had secured him
his crown. Buckingham was executed in the marketplace at Salisbury
on 2 November, All Souls' Day, 'notwithstanding the fact that it fell on a
Sunday'.[67]

13

'TRUE AND FAITHFUL LIEGEMEN'

Confiscations of the rebel estates began immediately.[1] Just as quickly, rewards were parcelled out to ensure the loyalty of the men whose support Richard was now desperately dependent upon. On 2 November, Thomas, Lord Stanley, described as 'our right trusty and well beloved counsellor', was granted Buckingham's former lordship and castle of Kimbolton in Huntingdonshire, a sign of Richard's relief that Thomas, Lord Stanley, and his brother, Sir William, had chosen the king's side over Margaret Beaufort.[2] Richard was desperate to keep the family firmly on his side. Sir William Stanley was rewarded with the office of chief justice of north Wales on 12 November; Thomas Stanley was granted the office of constable, worth £100 a year, on 18 November, as well as Buckingham's manor of Thornbury in Gloucestershire. Other grants to the family followed, 'for the singular and faithful service which they have hitherto done to us not only in favouring our right and title ... but also in repressing the treason and malice of our traitors and rebels'.[3] There were rewards too for those who had brought the duke to his knees. Buckingham's captor, Ralph Bannister, was granted the manor of Ealding in Kent, together with a yearly reward of £4 and the keepership of Rochester castle for 'the taking and bringing of our said rebel into our hands'.[4]

Other loyal members of the nobility, on whom Richard was now increasingly reliant, would also in time be rewarded for their support. On 30 November the earl of Northumberland was appointed Great Chamberlain.[5] The earl was further rewarded with the lordship of Holderness, formerly belonging to Buckingham, and the important constableships and stewardships of Dunstanburgh and Knaresborough, an important sign that Richard's own regional conflict around Richmondshire with the earl had now come to a close. On 1 December, Northumberland was granted a large parcel of manors in Kent, Essex, Devon, Dorset, Somerset, Suffolk, Gloucester and Wales, 'for special causes us moving'.

On the following day, 3 November, Richard marched towards Exeter. Passing through Dorset on his journey, Richard arrived at Poole Harbour to be informed that Henry Tudor had landed at the harbour, but had by now chosen to hoist his sails and return to Brittany. It would later be remembered how the king, perhaps in celebration, having ordered the repair of a quay wall, 'promised large things to the town'.[6]

Richard's decision to journey through Devon and to arrive at Exeter took the city officials by surprise, 'such as sudden that all things could not be so provided in such honourable manner as they would'.[7] The king was met at the gates of the city by the mayor and the brethren of the city in their finest array. The recorder of the city made a 'congratulatory' oration, for which he was rewarded with a scarlet gown. After the recorder had finished, the mayor delivered his mace to Richard, along with the keys of the city gates and a purse containing 200 nobles. Richard replied 'very thankfully' and with 'very good speeches' returned the keys and mace to the mayor. He was then led in procession to the bishop's palace, where he was lodged and 'very bountifully entreated' with a full spread of meat and plate 'sufficient for the king and his whole train'. The king asked the household staff what had become of the bishop, 'saying he was a wily prelate and had made him good cheer'.[8]

The prospect of any further uprising was over. News of Buckingham's execution seems to have resulted in the immediate collapse of the rebellion. 'Overcome by fear', Peter Courtenay, the bishop of Exeter, Dorset and other rebels, 'or as many of them as could find ships in readiness', fled to Brittany. Others chose to 'lay low' in hiding, under the shelter of friends and later in 'the protection of holy places'. Most managed to flee across the sea, but not before declaring Henry Tudor as 'alter rex' at Bodmin on 3 November. John Cheyne and Giles Daubeney, having fled southwards, made their escape to Brittany with an Exeter rebel, John Halwell, on a boat belonging to Stephen Calmady of Devon.[9] Thomas St Leger was not so fortunate: 'upon a sudden', he was captured before he could take flight and beheaded at Carfax in the city. 'To save his life innumerable sums of money had been offered', the Crowland chronicler wrote, 'but in vain.'[10]

The duke of Norfolk was sent to Bodiam Castle in Sussex, to mop up the remaining traces of rebellion. The rebels had locked themselves inside the castle; it took two weeks of besieging the walls to force their surrender. In late November, at Gloucester, 'evil disposed gentlemen' had assaulted the king's officers, leaving the constable of the town 'beaten and grievously maimed . . . thereby in despair of his life as it is to us showed to our full great displeasure'.[11] In Kent, the archbishop of Canterbury struggled to collect rents from his lands there, requiring Richard to send a letter to the tenants that since the archbishop had been accepted 'into the good favour of our grace', failure to pay would be met by 'our high displeasure at your uttermost peril'.[12] In a proclamation sent into the county, Richard again attempted to pacify the Commons by suggesting that his 'true subjects' had 'been abused and blinded' by the rebels; when they understood their treasons, 'since have well and truly behaved . . . for the which the king's grace standeth and will be to them good and gracious sovereign lord'. A further appeal was made to seize the rebels Sir John Guildford, Sir Thomas Lewkenor, Sir William Haute, William Cheyne, Richard Guildford and Reginald Pympe, with a reward of 300 marks or £10 in land upon their heads, 'and great thanks of the king's grace'. It was underlined that anyone harbouring or lodging any rebels in their house, or providing comfort to them after the proclamation had been issued, were to be taken as rebels themselves. Men were also to refrain from stealing the goods and cattle of any rebels, but instead to show them to commissioners appointed by the king, 'and they that so truly will show it shall be well rewarded, and they that do the contrary shall be punished according to the law'.[13]

On 9 November, Richard rode into London, where he was met by the aldermen and citizens wearing 'violet clothing' beyond Kennington, and taken to the Great Wardrobe at Blackfriars, where he was lodged.[14] In a sign of the king's nervousness that further uprisings might take place, he did not surrender the Great Seal to the Chancellor until 26 November.[15] Meanwhile, searches were made for rebels who had gone into hiding, with Richard ordering a review of whether sanctuaries such as at Beaulieu Abbey were in fact legitimate.[16]

In the aftermath of the rebellion, it is hardly surprising that a cloak of suspicion shrouded the royal court. There was a heightened state of security

surrounding the king, with new locks added to Richard's chamber doors.
It seemed that there were now few families Richard would be able to trust.
Indirectly, the rebellion had touched many of the southern noble fami-
lies, leaving the king uncertain over whose loyalty exactly he held. Few
were spared from his paranoia; after years of service to the crown, John,
Lord Audley, whose brother Thomas had been counted among the Dorset
rebels, was removed from the commissions of the peace in the south and
Midlands. Robert, Lord Poynings, whose relative Edward was attainted for
his part in the Kentish uprisings, was also indicted, while Richard, Lord
Dacre, the father of the rebel Thomas Fiennes, was removed from the commissions of the peace, as were Thomas, Lord Lawarre, in Southampton
and Sussex and John, Lord Berners, in Essex. Though many later recovered
Richard's confidence, Richard's sweeping suspicions even caused him to
wrongly confiscate the lands of Sir John Donne, the brother-in-law of
William, Lord Hastings, who was able to clear his name by autumn 1484
yet would never regain his offices at Calais.[17] Even in his own government
departments, Richard did not feel secure. On 22 November, Richard Bell
was stripped of his office as a clerk of the privy seal. Bell was replaced by
Richard's 'trusty servant' Robert Bolman, for his diligent service 'specially
now in this our great Journey'.[18]

Not only had the rebellion lasted for nearly a month, it had encompassed
a far larger geographical area than the later Act of Attainder was keen
to suggest. One contemporary London source described the rebellion as
affecting 'Kent to St Michael's Mount'.[19] While Richard had been fortunate
that it had been crushed before any serious armed confrontation was able
to occur, it was undeniable that the rebellion had shaken Richard's new
regime to its foundations. These were not disaffected outsiders, but the
very opposite: revolt had taken place in the very heart of government, the
king's household itself. Of the ninety-eight men later named in an Act
of Attainder, over a third were in Edward IV's service; the total number
may even be nearer half. Five of Richard's own yeomen of the crown were
attainted, while an additional four were hanged at Tyburn for treason.
Thirty-three rebels had been justices of the peace, with ten having been elevated by Richard himself. Three, John Trefry in Cornwall, John Wingfield
in Norfolk and William Berkeley in Southampton, were even sheriffs, vital
linchpins of law and order in their regions. Others had recently received

royal grants from Richard just weeks before, including Walter Hungerford and Sir Thomas Arundel.[20] Almost all of the men whom Richard had been able to rely upon being deployed against Sir Edward Woodville in May 1483 now chose to join the rebel forces.[21]

Above all, the rebellion was a rising whose heart lay at the centre of the former household of Edward IV. Of the dead king's esquires of the body, twenty-four were from the south, of which eleven rebelled; of the remaining thirteen, five had already been removed from the commissions of the peace by Richard in the summer of 1483, while two more would rebel the following year.[22] Of the king's knights of the body, six of the ten knights who represented southern counties chose to rebel.[23] The devastating collapse in the structure of authority in the southern counties is revealed in the striking fact that 48 per cent of those knights and gentlemen who served as sheriffs in fourteen southern counties from Cornwall to East Anglia between 1478 and 1482 joined the rebellion.

Richard's victory had been, the Crowland chronicler dryly noted, 'over an enemy without a battle', yet the costs of raising an army had come at 'no less expense than if the armies had fought to hand'.[24] Richard was forced to approach the lending markets in the capital for help. The merchant Richard Gardener lent the king 100 marks 'upon a pledge of a salt of gold with a cover ... garnished with silver and precious stones' that belonged to Richard. The mayor and aldermen of London lent a further £100 after Richard pledged to them 'a coronalle of gold garnished with many other great and rich jewels'.[25] According to the *Great Chronicle*, the loans were not so much requested as required: 'he instanced them himself ... to lend unto him certain sums'.[26] Richard was even forced to sell 275 pounds and 4 ounces of silver and gilt plate, including seven pots, five bowls, twenty-four platters, twenty-two dishes and twenty-one saucers worth £550 13s 4d sold to the goldsmith Sir Edmund Shaa on 23 December.[27] Nevertheless, Richard spent a further £764 17s 6d for 'certain plate ... for our year's gifts against Christmas last past and for other jewels' that had been purchased by Shaa 'and delivered to our own hands'.[28]

As Christmas approached, Richard was in a generous mood. On

3 December, Richard directed that £100 be paid 'unto our welbeloved servants the grooms and pages of our chamber . . . for a reward against the
Feast of Christmas next coming'.[29] On 8 December, Richard granted an
annuity of twenty marks to Joan, the late wife of John Malpas and later
John Peysmersh, 'for her good service to the king in his youth and to his
mother the duchess of York'.[30] The wife of one of the king's rebels, Alexander Cheyne, Florence, was taken 'into our protection, safeguard and
defence', with her lands and goods protected, 'for the good and virtuous
disposition that Florence . . . is reputed to be of'.[31]

These were not isolated cases. Richard made various donations and
annuities, both to individuals and institutions. At the Epiphany celebrations on 6 January, at a banquet sitting crowned at Whitehall, Richard
gave the mayor and aldermen of London a gold cup 'garnished with pearls
and other precious stones' to be used in the chamber of the Guildhall.
Displayed at the following council meeting a week later, it was also declared 'how the King, for the very great favour he bears towards this City,
intended to bestow and make the borough of Southwark part of the liberty
of the City, and also to give £10,000 towards the building of walls and
ditches around the said borough'.[32] Yet the grant of such a huge sum of
money never arrived; nor did the city authorities ever remind the king of
his lavish generosity that night, perhaps suggesting that they recognised
the king's mood and actions may have been influenced by something other
than the Christmas spirit.

As the Christmas and Epiphany celebrations drew to a close, on 10 January Richard journeyed to Canterbury, at the heart of the recent rebellion.[33]
Richard's visit had a sole purpose: to restore order and leadership to a
county destabilised by rebellion and the desertion and flight of the rebels,
many of them prominent members of the local gentry. While at Sandwich
on 16 January, the sheriffs in Kent were ordered to gather all men between
the age of sixteen and sixty to appear in person and swear an oath of loyalty to the king. The text of the oath underlined that not only were men
to swear on the Holy Evangelists that they would be a 'true and faithful
liegeman' to the king, but that they also 'in his cause and quarrel at all
times shall take his part and be ready to live and die against all earthly

creatures', especially 'to the resistance of and supressing of his enemies, rebels and traitors if I shall any know'.[34]

Other oath-swearing sessions were carefully co-ordinated, orchestrated by the king's northern favourites, including Sir Marmaduke Constable, William Mauleverer, Sir Ralph Assheton and Sir Thomas Bourchier of Leeds. This was a prelude to the king's decision to establish an entirely new network of trusted supporters, mostly northerners, in the county, effectively implanting a new gentry class in the region.

No longer would Richard be prepared to trust his brother's men. From now on, Richard was determined to move out of his brother's shadow, appointing his own men, mostly from his trusted ducal affinity, to confirm his authority. Just eleven of Edward IV's knights would now remain in Richard's service, and only two south of the Thames.

Richard was also faced with the difficulty of restoring royal authority to those regions affected by the rebellion. With many of the rebels having been the mainstays of local law and order, local government in these areas now faced a vacuum of power that needed to be filled urgently. This was particularly pressing over the question of the local military command of counties whose leading local figures had fled abroad to join Henry Tudor: Richard needed to restore the structure of local government and the raising of levies if he was to ensure that he would be able to effectively face any future opposing force.

He was forced to rely increasingly on a small number of men whom he felt he could trust, men who had long been in his service in his ducal household. Yet, in doing so, Richard excluded those whom he desperately needed to build relations with and harness their support. Instead, he only alienated them further: those who had remained loyal to the king during the rebellion of 1483 in their own local areas saw little material reward for their loyalty. In Devon, Richard gave away land valued at around £1,400, yet of the nineteen men who were granted land, just four were local to the area — and between them they received just £180.[35]

The northern nobility did especially well from the transfer of land. Richard, Lord Fitzhugh, gained lands in Somerset, Dorset and Wiltshire worth nearly £140 per annum, while Ralph, Lord Neville, was given the Somerset estates of Giles Daubeney and the countess of Richmond worth £200 per annum. Yet conclusions that Richard had enacted a wide-ranging

plantation of the south by northerners is wide of the mark. On first ap-
pearances, the northerners William and Halnath Mauleverer, appointed
to offices in Kent and Devon, had existing family connections in the areas
that they were granted lands, with Halnath having been appointed sheriff
of Cornwall as far back as November 1470. On thirty-five occasions during
Edward IV's reign, so called northerners were given offices in the southern
counties of Cornwall, Devon, Somerset, Dorset and Wiltshire, including
the Yorkshireman Sir Roger Tocotes, one of those attainted in 1484.[36]
Henry Bolingbroke had in 1399 also drawn heavily on his own northern
estates of the duchy of Lancaster and was dependent on the backing of
northern lords such as the earls of Westmorland and Northumberland.

The men placed in the south were often second-born sons, with no
inheritance to secure their futures in their northern home counties. Without the commitment or tie to their family and estates, Richard carefully
selected men whom he recognised would give the attention to their new
inheritances carved out especially for them by the king. By 1484, these
newcomers accounted for a third of all new sheriffs, and south of the
Thames they represented two thirds. Richard's aim was to re-create the
household network that Edward IV had assiduously cultivated; his supporters were to be the king's own intelligence gatherers, acting as his eyes
and ears.[37]

The introduction of his northern supporters into southern society could
hardly have been expected to be considered a popular measure. 'What
great numbers of estates and inheritances were amassed in the king's
treasury in consequence!' the Crowland chronicler wrote. 'He distributed
all these amongst his northerners whom he had planted in every part of
his dominions, to the shame of all the southern people who murmured
ceaselessly and longed more each day for the return of their old lords in
place of the tyranny of the present ones.'[40]

While Richard passed his Christmas in lavish celebration, at Vannes
Cathedral, hundreds of English exiles, many of them rebels who had managed to escape across the Channel and into Brittany, gathered to hear a
solemn ceremony. Having managed to eventually make his journey in his
battered ship back to Brittany, Henry Tudor had 'much lamented' when
he was informed of the news of Buckingham's execution. Tudor's heart
had been lifted, however, on his discovery that the marquess of Dorset,

together with a 'great number' of English gentlemen, had arrived shortly before him and remained at Vannes. Henry 'rejoiced wondrously'; meeting with Dorset and the English exiles for the first time, there was 'much mutual congratulation made'.[39] The exiles would now be joined in their common cause: determination to overthrow Richard.

Neither Henry nor the marquess and his Yorkist followers could deny their families had fought on opposing sides of the civil war; Henry Tudor was of undoubted Lancastrian descent, the royal family many had bitterly fought to overthrow. Yet, with everyone suspecting the death of Edward V and his brother Richard, the Yorkist exiles had no other choice: Henry would have to be their candidate for the throne. A compromise, they argued, would nevertheless still need to be found, in the form of Elizabeth of York, whom Margaret Beaufort had previously argued might marry her son in order to effect a union between the two rival houses, ensuring that the house of York and its lineage remained intact. It was at Vannes on Christmas Day 1483 that Henry, upon oath, promised that 'so soon as he should be king he would marry Elizabeth, king Edward's daughter'. His men then swore him homage, 'as though he had been already created king', pledging that 'they would lose not only their lands and possessions, but their lives, before ever they would suffer, bear, or permit, that Richard should rule over them'.[40]

14

TITULUS REGIUS

Richard would need parliamentary authority to legalise the arbitrary grants he had already made of rebel lands to his supporters, many of which had been made in tail male, permanently alienating the lands, instead of giving them temporary custody. This had been done without taking the correct inquisitions, threatening to put at risk the rights of those who had claims on the land. Parliament would need to be summoned, providing Richard and his regime with the legitimacy that he desperately needed.

Already, on 9 December, writs had been served for Parliament to meet at Westminster on 23 January. In January, the Great Wardrobe supplied cord, ribbon and 500 lattice nails for the hangings in the Parliament chamber, in preparation for the state opening of Parliament. Richard's Parliament robe, made from crimson velvet furred with ermine sewn with 6,000 powderings of bogy shanks, was specially designed with a pattern of golden lions, though the fur of the kirtle, mantle and hood was recycled from an old robe of blue woollen cloth made for Edward IV.[1]

Having already had to draft two sermons for the previously aborted parliaments, the Chancellor, John Russell, now took the parable of the lost coin from the Book of Luke as the basis of his opening speech. In the parable, a woman is elated when she tidies her house to find a silver coin she thought she had lost: Christ equates this to the joy felt by angels at a sinner's repentance. Russell explained how 'that one coin, the tenth, had been lost from the most precious fabric of the body politic of England and that to hunt for it and find it would require the king and all the lords spiritual and temporal to be very assiduous and diligent during this parliament', concluding that 'after the finding of the tenth coin, which signifies perfection, our body politic would endure gloriously'.[2] The message to those listening to Russell's sermon would have been clear: the new regime would be determined to be a break with the old, and was equally determined to put its own house in order.

The purpose of the Parliament, which only sat for twenty-seven days, until 20 February, was threefold: in the shadow of Buckingham's rebellion, Acts of Attainder needed to be passed against rebel estates, legitimising their confiscation; Richard had to legitimise his own royal title in Parliament; and he sought to gain the support of his subjects with legislation designed for popular appeal. It is no coincidence that Richard was also the first king to publish in English Acts passed during the Parliament, allowing for a wider circulation of their contents.

Everything was calculated to please. Richard was careful to distance himself from what he viewed as the greed of his brother's reign. During the Parliament, Edward was accused of having been 'of such ungodly disposition and provoking the ire and indignation of our lord God, such heinous mischiefs . . . were used and committed in the realm among the subjects'.[3] Richard was determined to move out of his brother's shadow. In a highly unusual move, despite being short of money, Richard chose not to request any direct taxation from Parliament. Refusing to collect a tax of the tenth and fifteenth granted in Edward IV's Parliament, he was, however, prepared to collect the subsidy levied on foreign merchants, something he had done as Protector. Instead, the first of the common petitions passed during the Parliament was an Act 'to free the subjects from benevolences'.

The legislation was clearly designed to demonstrate how Richard, in contrast to his brother, wished to present himself as a king ruling on behalf of the people, not merely ruling over them. Richard sought consciously to undermine at every opportunity his brother's legacy, even if the long-term financial consequences of limiting the king's authority to raise money were being ignored. The Act described how 'the commons of this his realm, by new and unlawful inventions and inordinate covetousness, against the law of this realm have been put to great thraldom and importable charges and exactions, and in especial by a new imposition named a benevolence, whereby divers years the subjects and commons of this land against their wills and freedom have paid great sums of money to their

almost utter destruction'. Men had been forced to 'break up their households and to live in great penury and wretchedness, their debts unpaid and
their children unpreferred', while others – 'to the great displeasure of God
and to the destruction of this realm' – had resorted to cancelling obits and
masses for the souls of their ancestors, 'as they had ordained to be done
for the wealth of their souls'. The Act now set out that the king's subjects
'and the commonalty of this his realm' were 'from henceforth in no wise
be charged by no such charge, exaction or imposition called benevolence
nor by such like charge', while outstanding payments owed were to be 'an-
ulled for ever'.[4] A second common petition called for the revoking of an
Act passed in the previous Parliament which ensured that the king was to
retain the royal rights wardship within the duchy of Lancaster, regardless
of whether lands had been enfeoffed. Though Richard recognised that the
Act as it stood was 'to his great profit', nevertheless it would be to 'the great
hurt and thraldom of his subjects'. Richard therefore agreed to annul the
Act, 'having more affection to the common weal of this his realm and of
his subjects than to his own singular profit' in order that 'his said subjects
stand and be at their liberties and freedom in like form as they were before
the making of the same acts'.[5] This was almost certainly done under Richard's initiative: at a time when Richard was seeking popular support, the
need for popularity took precedence over the king's need for money.

Six of the sixteen statutes further attempted to reform the criminal
justice system, in a bid to win popularity. 'An act for bailing of persons suspected of felony' ensured that those arrested and imprisoned 'for suspicion
of felony, sometime of malice and sometime of light suspicion' and who
currently were unable to apply for bail 'to their great vexation and trouble' would now be allowed to apply to a Justice of the Peace to seek bail.
This was a natural extension to legislation passed in 1461. For Richard, the
adoption of the petition was an easy item of legal reform, for which a campaign had been ongoing for several years. Alongside this Act, 'An act for
returning adequate jurors' sought to raise the standard of a jury by raising
the qualification for service. Other Acts passed protected a felon's goods
from being seized until he had been convicted, and imposed restrictions
on local officials who dealt with disputes arising at fairs and markets, in an
attempt to crack down on abuses of privilege, while existing laws relating
to land and property susceptible to fraud were also reconsidered.

Another series of bills, concerned with regulating trade and manu-
facturing, had a deliberately xenophobic quality to them, designed to
appeal to the English mercantile classes. The fact that no fewer than five
statutes were passed to protect English traders from foreign competition
was a clear demonstration of the king's desire to befriend his financial
backers. Anti-'alien' Acts had previously been a feature of many medieval parliaments, with Italian merchants the main targets. Now Richard's
Parliament re-enacted two anti-alien Acts of Edward IV's first Parliament,
in addition to new legislation. Foreigners were blamed for everything
from the loss of English jobs to the excessive cost and poor quality of imported bowstaves, apparently caused by the 'subtle means' and 'sedicious
confederacy' of the Lombards. Several protectionist measures first introduced by Edward IV, including the prohibitions on the import of silk and
laces, were confirmed, with the measures being extended to a wide range
of goods manufactured by leather and metal workers. 'God Save King
Richard', the Pewterers' Company recorded in their accounts, no doubt
in jubilation.[6] Foreign merchants were also to be forced to spend their
profits on English goods, in an attempt to deal with an increasing shortage
of silver, caused by merchants taking their profits out of the country in
cash. Regulations were introduced preventing corruption in wine and oil
sales, with barrels to be 'gauged' by the king's gauger, to ensure correct
volumes were being sold. There was also to be a crackdown on the fraudulent finishing of cloth, though by 25 October this rushed Act had been
found to be 'hurtful' and sheriffs were ordered to make a proclamation
lifting all penalties that had been imposed by the Act.[7] The fact that Richard gave his assent to a range of Acts reflecting the powerful xenophobia
of the London merchant community suggests that, rather than acting
from a position of strength, the king was desperate to win support for
his new regime, particularly after the rebellion in the autumn, regardless
of the cost.

The centrepiece of the Parliament was the passing of the *Titulus Regius*,
an Act certifying Richard's claim to the throne. The Crowland chronicler
described how the king's title was to be discussed and 'corroborated' in
Parliament, 'even though that lay court was not empowered to determine
on it since there was a dispute concerning the validity of a marriage'.
Nevertheless, the chronicler wrote, 'it presumed to do so and did so on

account of the great fear affecting the most steadfast'.[8] The preamble of the
Act also suggests that there remained some uncertainty surrounding the
legitimacy of Richard's own title. It explained how:

> Where late heretofore, that is to say before the consecration, coronation
> and enthronement of our sovereign lord King Richard III, a roll of parch-
> ment, containing in writing certain articles of the tenor underwritten, on
> the behalf and in the name of the three estates of this realm of England,
> that is, the lords spiritual and temporal, and of the commons, by many and
> divers lords spiritual and temporal, and other nobles and notable persons
> of the commons in great multitude, was presented and actually delivered
> unto our said sovereign lord the king, to the intent and effect expressed at
> large in the same roll; to which roll, and to the considerations and instant
> petition comprised in the same, our said sovereign lord, for the public weal
> and tranquillity of this land, benignly assented.

Yet since none of the people who presented the roll, despite representing
the 'three estates', had been assembled 'in the form of a parliament . . .
divers doubts, questions and ambiguities' had been 'moved and engendered in the minds of diverse persons'. Parliament was therefore needed
to ratify the petition, 'removing the occasion of doubts and ambiguities'.[9]

The petition presented to Richard in June 1483, or at least the 'tenor of
the said roll of parchment', was then printed in full, describing in detail the
failure of Edward IV's government, before setting out the explanation of
the king's pre-contract with Eleanor Butler, and 'pretensed marriage' with
Elizabeth Woodville, so that 'it appeareth evidently and followeth that all
the issue and children of the said king [have] been bastards, unable to
inherit or to claim anything by inheritance'. Once the text of the petition
had been rehearsed, the Act explained how Richard's title was both 'just
and lawful, as grounded upon the laws of God and nature, and also upon
the ancient laws and laudable customs' of the realm. 'Yet, nevertheless,
forasmuch as it is considered that the most part of the people of this land
is not sufficiently learned in the abovesaid laws and customs whereby the
truth and right . . . may be hid, and not clearly known to all the people and
thereupon put in doubt and question', the Act explained, reasoning that
'the court of Parliament is of such authority, and the people of this land of
such nature and disposition' that any declaration made by the three estates

of the realm assembled in Parliament 'maketh before all other thing, most faith and certainty; and the quieting of men's minds, removeth the occasion of all doubts and seditious language'. The Act therefore pronounced that Richard was the 'very and undoubted king of this realm of England . . . as well by right of consanguinity and inheritance as by lawful election, consecration and coronation'. Finally, it was agreed that 'the high and excellent Prince Edward, son of our sovereign lord the king, be heir apparent'.[10]

Though the assertion of the new king's title was undoubtedly the main business of the Parliament, as it had been previously for Henry IV in 1399 and Edward IV in 1461, the Act is not presented as the first item of business; rather, in the Parliament roll it appears after the grant of tonnage and poundage, granted on the final day of Parliament, 20 February. It suggests that Richard was keen to give the impression that the issue was being kept at arm's length, to which he then 'benignly assented'. It is understandable that Richard would want to distance himself from the statement of his claim to the throne, especially when the main argument for his usurpation had been that his brother's marriage had been bigamous, and that Edward IV's children had been bastards; this was a matter for the church courts, not Parliament to decide, a fact not lost on the Crowland chronicler.[11]

The longest piece of legislation on the surviving Parliament roll was the Act of Attainder, stripping the duke of Buckingham and the rebels of their lands and estates. Richard's sense of betrayal is still evident in the Act's preamble, declaring how the 'great and singular movers, stirrers and doers of the said offences and heinous treasons' included 'Henry, late Duke of Buckingham now late days standing and being in as great favour, tender trust, and affection with the king our sovereign lord, as ever subject was with his prince and liege lord'.[12]

The Act of Attainder followed the traditional pattern of complete forfeiture of the lands of those attainted and the disinheriting of their heirs, with protection for their wives' lands. Yet there were significant differences between Richard's treatment of the rebels, compared to the actions his brother had previously taken. The total number of people attainted, 103, was greater than in any single Act of Attainder in Edward IV's reign and for the first time included the ecclesiastical estates of three bishops:

'So many great lords, nobles, magnates and commoners', the Crowland chronicler wrote, 'were attainted that we nowhere read of the like even under the triumvirate of Octavian, Anthony and Lepidus.'[13] In addition, Richard had already taken possession and confiscated many of the estates even without parliamentary approval. Perhaps because of this, there was no use of a suspended attainder which would come into effect if an individual failed to make their submission to the king: for Richard, many of the rebels' treasons would be permanent. Of course, negotiations had already been going on over who should be included in the Act: several men who had been listed among the rebels in the commissions of arrest issued in November 1483 now escaped attainder through having secured a pardon. Throughout the course of the Parliament, negotiations continued over the fate of certain rebels, leading to some confusion in the Act itself, with men on the initial list of rebels not being attainted later on in the legislation, as men or their families bought their pardons.[14] Fourteen rebels took active steps themselves to secure a pardon from the king in the following five months. Several weeks later, Richard drew up a list of eight rebels still in sanctuary at Beaulieu Abbey, whom he was prepared to give one final chance, marking their names out in his own hand in a 'book of exception' that was given to Edmund Chaterton.[15]

In order to convince Richard of their changed ways, many attempting to seek a pardon agreed to live under imposed restrictions as proof of their good behaviour. Edward IV had begun to adopt a system of bonds and recognisances, in which groups of men were made to stand surety for the good behaviour of offenders, often their family relatives, friends or associates. In return for significant sums of money paid upfront, former rebels or offenders of the crown would be allowed to go free, but only if their bail money had been paid first. Richard adopted this system of suspended penalties with zeal. The friends standing surety for the former rebel Thomas Leukenor were made to pay 1,000 marks with a pledge that Leukenor would be of good and true bearing towards the king and his heirs, and serve him both in peace and war when required; for Sir Richard Woodville and Sir William Berkeley, the price was 2,000 marks each. Often Richard was determined to add specific conditions to the bonds, tightening his control over his subjects. Leukenor was forced to reside with the king's treasurer, Sir John Wood, 'until the king's pleasure was known on his behalf'; Nicholas Gaynesford was not allowed to enter Kent[16] while William Berkeley agreed to live in a place appointed specially by the king.[17] Knyvet later claimed he had only managed to secure his freedom by paying 700 marks to the king and 100 marks to the queen, at the same time as agreeing to hand over four manors to the king, including the castle of New Buckenham in Norfolk. Richard was not the only beneficiary of the deal, for Sir James Tyrell was also to be given a manor and land. Knyvet later claimed that Richard had pledged to pay £300 for the land, but had failed to do so.[18] While a pardon could not lift the Act of Attainder passed against them, or restore them to their forfeited lands, it would at least bring a reprieve from the death penalty and allow their families 'to receive or cherish' them with food, which 'shall not by occasion thereof' result in the king's 'displeasure or indignation'.[19] Yet the restoration of estates was a different matter: only six out of the twenty-eight pardoned rebels would receive a royal grant. One of the few rebels to regain some of his land was Walter Hungerford.[20]

Aside from the Act of Attainder, other bills sought to punish offenders. Revoking an Act passed in the January 1483 Parliament that had allowed the duchy of Exeter lands to be granted to Thomas Grey, the preamble of a new bill went out of its way to present Thomas St Leger, who had been executed at Exeter, as a villain who had persuaded Edward IV 'by great labour' to accept an Act passed in 1467 that settled the Exeter lands on the heirs of Anne, duchess of Exeter's body rather than the daughter she had by Exeter, adding that the duchess's daughter by Exeter 'lived by short time after' the passing of the Act. The tone of the Act was to smear St Leger with deliberately passing an Act to benefit his own daughter with the duchess, yet that daughter was not born until 1476, nine years later.

In addition to St Leger and the duke of Buckingham, Henry Tudor's mother, Margaret Beaufort, was singled out for her role in the rebellion. Margaret herself was accused of 'assenting, knowing and assisting Henry late duke of Buckingham and his adherents in compassing and doing treason'. The Act also set out how Margaret had provided financial assistance to her son, Henry Tudor: 'Forasmuch as Margaret, countess of Richmond, mother to the king's great rebel and traitor, Henry earl of Richmond, hath of late conspired, confederated and committed high treason against our sovereign lord the King Richard the third, in divers and sundry ways, and in especial in sending messages, writings and tokens to the said Henry, desiring, procuring and stirring him by the same to come into this realm and make war against our sovereign lord . . . Also the said countess supplied great sums of money, as well within the city of London as in other places of this realm, to be employed to the execution of the said treason and malicious purpose.' Yet Richard, 'of his grace especial, remembering the good and faithful service that Thomas Lord Stanley hath done and intendeth to do to our said sovereign lord, and for the good love and trust that the king hath in him, and for his sake, remitteth and will forbear the great punishment of attainder of the said countess, that she or any other so doing hath deserved'.[21]

Richard's decision to exempt Margaret from a full Act of Attainder, confiscating her estates, was hardly an act of charity. Even if Richard had wished to pass an attainder against Margaret, the fact that her marriage settlement in 1472 guaranteed the earl a substantial income from her estates made it too dangerous for Richard to go down a route that could threaten his fragile relationship with Stanley. Yet the king's commensurate punishment was equally harsh.[22] Margaret was to forfeit her right to all titles and estates, with all her properties being re-granted to her husband. The material change may have been small, but for Margaret the significance could hardly have been greater. For a woman who fiercely guarded her independence, not to mention the protection of her only son's rights and inheritance, she was being reduced to the status of a humble wife, dependent entirely upon her husband and his survival. Her estates were now granted to Stanley for life in tail male, preventing them from ever being inherited by her son. By allowing the lands to be re-granted after Stanley's death, Richard had in effect cast Margaret into a positon of being already dead to the king. Her rights to her mother's Beaufort inheritance were also cancelled, while lands that Margaret might have hoped to be given to Henry were granted away to others.[23] The king's council also decreed that Stanley was to 'remove from his wife all her servants, and to keep her so straight with himself that she should not be able from henceforth to send any messenger neither to her son, nor friends, nor practice any thing at all against the king'.[24] Later her confessor, John Fisher, recalled how: 'Albeit in King Richard's days she was oft in jeopardy of her life, yet she bore patiently all trouble in such wise that it is wonder to think it.'[25] Still, many were surprised that Thomas, Lord Stanley, had not only evaded punishment but had received a reward; 'it went very hard', Vergil observed, 'that Thomas Stanley was not accounted amongst the number of the king's enemies, by reason of the practices of Margaret his wife'.[26]

A final Act on the roll, placed among the common petitions though it was nothing of the kind, ordered the forfeiture of all royal grants of lands or revenues to Edward IV's widow, Queen Elizabeth, or, as she was now known, 'late wife of Sir John Grey', which 'for certain great causes and considerations touching as well the surety of the most royal person of the king', the grants of land 'whatsoever made at any time to Elizabeth, late the wife of Sir John Grey, knight, and late calling herself queen of England' should be declared null and void from 1 May 1483, the date when Richard had first ordered the queen's and the Woodville assets to be seized.[27] The lands included a large part of the duchy of Lancaster in southern England, which Richard had initially promised to the duke of Buckingham on 13 July, but now the king would retain for himself: Edward IV's will had enfeoffed some of the land, though Richard simply ignored the terms of the will, making no attempt to revoke it.

Over the past few months, Queen Elizabeth had been urged 'by frequent intercessions and dire threats' to allow her five daughters to leave sanctuary. She finally relented, but not without forcing Richard to swear an oath, promising her daughters' security and a number of specific conditions. Richard agreed. On 1 March, Richard made a public statement, declaring:

> that if the daughters of Dame Elizabeth Gray late calling herself Queen of England, that is to wit Elizabeth, Cecille, Anne, Kateryn and Brigitte will come unto me out of the Sanctuary of Westminster and be guided, ruled and demeaned after me, then I shall see that they shall be in surety of their lives and also not suffer any manner hurt by any manner person or persons to them or any of them in their bodies and persons to be done by way of ravishment or defouling contrary to their wills, nor them or any of them imprisoned within the Tower of London or other prison, but that I shall put them in honest places of good name and fame, and them honestly

and courteously shall see to be found and entreated and to have all things requisite and necessary for their exhibition and findings as my kinswomen.

And that I shall do marry such of them as now be marriable to gentlemen born and each of them give in marriage lands and tenements to the yearly value of 200 marks for term of their lives and in likewise to the other daughters when they come to lawful age of marriage if they live and such gentlemen as shall hap to marry with them I shall straightly charge from time to time lovingly to love and entreat them as their wives and my kinswomen, as they will avoid and eschew my displeasure.[28]

The declaration also promised a yearly sum of money to the former queen. The entire agreement is shrouded in the suspicion on Elizabeth's part that Richard had the potential to undertake all the deeds that she now hoped to prevent on oath. For her part, the agreement was an act of cynical realism in a situation to which she could see no end. For the time being at least, Richard was king of England, with no immediate change likely. Having been stripped of her lands and available assets, she was running out of money in sanctuary. In striking a deal with Richard, at least she could ensure that her daughters would be provided for, while she would have a sizeable income of 700 marks, equating to £466 13s 4d a year, an annual income that would allow her to maintain her noble lifestyle.

Soon after Elizabeth Woodville had agreed to deliver her daughters from sanctuary, the Crowland chronicler described how 'by special command of the king there were gathered together in a certain downstairs room near the corridor which leads to the queen's quarters, almost all of the lords spiritual and temporal and the leading knights and gentlemen of the king's household, the chief amongst whom seemed to be John Howard, whom the king had recently created duke of Norfolk. Each person subscribed his name to a certain new oath, drawn up by persons unknown to me, undertaking to adhere to the king's only son, Edward, as their supreme lord, should anything happen to his father'.[29]

The Crowland chronicler deliberately assimilates events to make the oath-swearing, taking place not in one of the state rooms but in a back room down a corridor, appear shady. In reality, Parliament had ended on 20 February, while Queen Elizabeth had left sanctuary with her daughters on 28 February, leaving no opportunity for the oath to be sworn in public.

The oath-swearing was likely to have been modelled on the oath that Richard had taken back in July 1471, when he swore loyalty to Edward IV's son, an oath that had also been taken outside of Parliament. Yet Edward IV, and Henry VI before him, had both used Parliament to confirm the prince's possession of his estates: while Edward of Middleham had been created Prince of Wales and earl of Chester at York the previous autumn, it seems unusual that there was no formal acknowledgement of his creation; nor was he granted any associated estates with his creation as Prince of Wales: Richard as king would continue to hold the entire royal patrimony.[30]

15

'THEIR SUDDEN GRIEF'

Richard continued to bestow his generosity upon those who were willing to legitimate the new royal family. On 2 March, Richard agreed to grant the royal heralds a residence at Coldharbour with a licence worth £20 a year to find a chaplain to celebrate a daily divine service 'for the good estate of the king, his consort Anne and his first born son Edward, prince of Wales'.[1] On 5 March the prior and canons of the cathedral church of St Mary, Carlisle, were granted two tuns of red wine 'for use in their church, that they may pray for the good estate of the king and his consort, Anne, queen of England, and for their souls after their death and the souls of the king's progenitors'.[2] Two days earlier, William Husse, the chief justice of the King's Bench, was also given a licence to found a chantry 'for the good estate of the king and his wife Anne' worth £20 a year.[3]

Richard also continued to look favourably upon those he considered in need. He was shown the plight of Edmund Philpot, a bricklayer from Twickenham whose house and all his goods were 'suddenly burnt to his utter undoing'. Richard, 'having respect with compassion to the piteous case and infortune' of his situation, issued a licence on 7 February 1484 urging 'such well disposed people as of their devotion and charity' to give alms to help Philpot build a new house.[4]

On 7 March, Richard granted to Katherine Mountferaunt 'on account of her poverty' £20.[5] Similarly, on 10 March, he granted to Margaret, the wife of John, earl of Oxford, and the daughter of Richard's uncle, the late earl of Salisbury, the sum of £100 a year.[6] Thomas Sadland of Shrewsbury, who on account of 'his good service to the king's father in England and Ireland and to the king' was given an annuity of £8 on 2 April.[7]

While the royal court was still residing in the capital, Richard sat on his throne in the Star Chamber at the palace of Westminster. In front of him, he had ordered that his justices be gathered together in one room. Assemblies of the justices and serjeants-at-law were not uncommon, particularly when difficult chancery or common law cases needed further exemplification or advice. Yet those present in the room would have understood that this was no usual gathering: for a king to summon them was almost unprecedented. Unlike his audience at Oxford University, when the king sat for hours listening to the disputations between students at Magdalen College concerning moral philosophy, rewarding each side for their rhetorical efforts, this time Richard had arranged for his justices to meet him to discuss certain points of law. He had several questions that he wished to ask them, or, rather, to understand their expert opinions on the law. In establishing his dedication to justice, Richard was following closely in his brother's footsteps. In October 1462, Edward himself had even sat in person as judge in the marble seat of the King's Bench, trying cases of rape. In doing so he was demonstrating his royal duty as dispenser of justice; in April 1463, Bishop Neville opened Parliament with a sermon, taking as its theme, 'Let those who judge the land prize justice'.

For Richard, the administration of justice, something he had placed so much weight upon in previous proclamations, was in itself the essence of kingship. He took a strong interest in ensuring justice was performed, no less than his brother had done before him. Examples of Richard's interference, or rather insistence that the due process of law be followed, are rife. On 22 February, Richard wrote to the justices of the peace in Warwickshire how 'grievous complaint hath been made unto us on the behalf of our poor subject', one Robert Dalby, who had complained to the king that his manor of Bockhampton had been seized by Robert Worsley. Richard sent Dalby's petition to the justices, ordering: 'wherefore we willing the administration of justice in that behalf and also trusting in your wisdoms, learning and indifferency will and desire you if it be as surmised that ye see our said subject put in the peacible possession of the said manor'. Essentially, the king had merely passed the complaint to the local justices to investigate the matter.[8] As Richard stated openly in front of the audience assembled before the justices at Star Chamber, it 'is the King's will to wit, to say "by his justices" and "by his law" is to say one and the same thing'.

Richard's own understanding of the duties of a king, in particular the role of a monarch as law maker and upholder of justice, was central to the ideal of good government and good kingship. In his letter of instruction to Thomas Barret, the bishop of Enachden in Galway, Ireland, written later in the year, Richard gave further insight into his own philosophy of the duty and role of a king. It was the responsibility of 'the king's grace' to 'in no wise will our holy mother church to be wronged, but shall maintain it in every behalf as justice and right requireth. And over that to see that no manner robberies or extortions be suffered to be committed amongst any of the king's subjects, of what estate so ever they be; them so offending utterly to be punished according with the king's laws.' It was also important that 'by the passage of the common high ways the king's subjects may be assured to go and pass without unlawfully letting'. The doer of all these actions, Richard believed, 'may appear and be named a very justiciar as well for his proper honour and weal as for the common weal'.[9] As Sir John Fortescue neatly summed up in his *De Natura*, 'to fight and to judge are the office of a king'.[10]

Yet Richard seems to have been at times compromised when it came to upholding the duties of his office, and perhaps his own natural inclination, to secure 'rest and peace and quiet among all our liege people'. While his official pronouncements condemned the seizure of forfeited land and the dangers of undermining the laws of inheritance, stating his personal commitment that he was 'utterly determined all his true subjects shall live in rest and quiet, and peaceably enjoy their lands, livelihoods and goods according to the laws of this his land, which they be naturally born to inherit', the reality at times could in fact be an entirely different story.[11] The case of Richard's servant, Richard Pole, highlights the king's partiality towards his own men in legal cases. Pole had married the widow of John Stradling, with whom she had a son, Edward. The wardship of the child had been granted by Edward IV to Richard Fowler; after Fowler's death, with the king's permission, his widow passed the wardship on to Henry Danvers. As the young boy's stepfather, Pole wanted Edward's wardship for himself, and in April 1483 seized the boy. Danvers appealed to the law courts for help, and had managed to secure a hearing for his case by June 1483, yet a year later, in July 1484, Richard had agreed to grant the wardship to Pole, in consideration, the grant read, of his 'true and thankful service'.[12] Later it was claimed that both young Edward and his mother were murdered.[13] It is perhaps hardly surprising that in 1485 a London attorney, William Crouch, publicly attacked the king for the poor quality of the king's justice, only to find himself soon accused of having used seditious language.[14]

In early spring, Richard decided to make a progress northwards. By Tuesday, 9 March, he and Queen Anne had reached Cambridge, where they were warmly welcomed with a present of fish worth £6 5s, while the king's minstrels were rewarded with a payment of seven shillings.[15] The university had already benefited significantly from his patronage as duke, ever since his first endowment of fellowships at Queen's College in 1477; now Richard was prepared to make an even more lavish donation, granting £300 towards the building of the church at King's College, while several manors in Buckingham and Lincoln were to be granted to Queen's College, and its president, Andrew Doket, received an annuity of £100.[16]

During the visit, Richard also took the opportunity to expand on his own religious beliefs and concerns, writing a circular letter to all the bishops across the country on 10 March, declaring that 'amongst other our secular business and cures, our principal intent and fervent desire is to see virtue and cleanness of living to be advanced, increased and multiplied, and vices and all other things repugnant to virtue, provoking the high indignation and fearful displeasure of God, to be repressed and annulled'. First, this meant that an example needed to be set. This was to be 'perfectly followed and put in execution by persons of high estate, pre-eminence and dignity' in order that this would 'enduceth persons of lower degree to take thereof example, and to ensue the same'. The instructions continued:

We therefore will and desire you and, on god's behalf inwardly exhort and require you, that according to the charge of your profession you will see within the authority of your jurisdiction all such persons, as set apart virtue and promote the damnable execution of sin and vices, to be reformed, repressed and punished accordingly after their demerits, not sparing for any love, favour, dread or affection, whether the offenders be spiritual or temporal. Wherein ye may be assured we shall give unto you our favour, aid and assistance if the case shall so require and see to the sharp punishment of the repugnators and interrupters hereof if any such be. And if ye will diligently apply you to the execution and performing of this matter ye shall not only do god right acceptable pleasure, but over that we shall see such persons spiritual as been under your pastoral cure nor otherwise to be entreated or punished for their offences but according to the ordinances and laws of holy Church.

If any complaint 'or suggestion be made unto us of you', then the king was determined that the case be heard by the ecclesiastical court of the archbishop of Canterbury. The letter ended: 'thus proceeding to the execution hereof ye shall do unto yourself great honour and unto us right singular pleasure'.[17]

The timing of the letter, written while Richard reflected in the company of Cambridge ecclesiastics, suggests that it had been written with the audience of his present company in mind, a statement designed to please. Yet Richard's letter is still nonetheless remarkable in its tone and content. In contrast to his brother Edward, Richard's understanding of monarchy seems to have been to take a direct interest in the morality of his subject's souls. Already several of Richard's proclamations had touched upon the issue of sexual morality, making mention of the marquess of Dorset's relationship with Elizabeth Shore. Here, Richard had chosen to make the correction of morals a centrepiece of his kingship, with his talk of 'cleanness of living' now to be at the 'principal intent' of his business. Whether Richard could practically achieve this was a different matter; his intention for any complaints to be managed by the archbishop of Canterbury's court suggests that he was willing to leave the practicalities to others. Rather than being simply politically inspired, Richard's concern for the church seems to have stemmed from a personal sense of mission for correction and self-improvement.[18] Richard also seems to have displayed a genuine love of theological scholarship. On 26 February, Richard agreed that his 'well beloved' scholar, John Bentley, would be granted an exhibition of four pounds annually to study at Oxford, citing 'our charity and for the increase of virtue and cunning'.[19] He surrounded himself with graduate scholars, with a marked preference for Cambridge graduates, many of whom were also steeped in the new humanist learning of Italy. In May 1483, Richard had appointed Dr Thomas Langton to the vacant see of St David's: Langton, a northerner from Appleby in Westmorland, had been a student at Pembroke Hall, Cambridge, who had studied at Padua and Bologna, where he had taken a doctorate in canon law. Several months later, when the palatine see of Durham became available, he promoted another northerner. John Shirwood was the son of a town clerk of York and had been a protégé of Archbishop Neville of York, who had appointed him archdeacon of Middleham. Shirwood had studied at Cambridge and in Italy, being proficient in both Latin and Greek, and was one of the most distinguished humanists of the day. Richard thought highly enough of Shirwood to recommend him to the pope to be appointed a cardinal. John Gunthorpe, the dean of Wells, appointed Keeper of the Privy Seal in May 1483, was another Cambridge graduate whom Richard sought to promote; a former warden of King's Hall, he had studied in Ferrara and was a talented Greek scholar.[20] In September 1483, Richard appointed Thomas Barowe as Master of the Rolls; a northern Lincolnshire clerk who had been educated at Eton and in canon law at Cambridge, Barowe had been Richard's chancellor while he was duke, pointing to the fact that many of these northern, Cambridge-educated scholars must have been introduced to Richard before he became king. Perhaps Barowe, who was described at Cambridge as 'to his mother the University a great and faithful lover', knew Gunthorpe and Langton from his days at King's Hall, and introduced them to his master.[21] Alternatively, this close-knit circle of scholars, with remarkably similar backgrounds, came together as the result of the patronage of George Neville. Yet it seems that the king himself took an active and personal interest in ensuring he was surrounded by scholars who reflected his own religious tastes. Richard selected as his private chaplain John Dokett, another scholar at Eton and King's College, Cambridge, who like Langton had studied at Padua and Bologna, and had become a

doctor of canon law. Dokett had even written a commentary on Plato's
Phaedo; he was most likely a relation of Andrew Dokett, the president of
Queen's College, Cambridge, which benefited significantly from Richard's
patronage.[22]

Since Henry Tudor's return to Brittany, Richard had been determined that
the duchy would be made to pay the price for its sheltering and supporting
him. On 18 December, Thomas Wentworth had been appointed captain of
the fleet 'set unto the sea to reconnoitre the fleet of our enemy of Brittany'.[23]
The mayor and aldermen of London were ordered to seize all Breton property and ships. A fierce naval war raged in the Channel between the two
countries. Already no letters passed between Calais and London, because
'the search was so straight', the merchant William Cely complained, as
Richard's agents kept a close watch on Henry Tudor's movements: 'we
could have no conveyance of no letters to London by no manner man'.[24]

The safety of the seas would remain a significant problem for Richard
for months to come, yet Richard's tactics worked. The spoils of confiscation and piracy against Breton ships began to pour into English ports.
Duke Francis, by now fearing that the increase in English naval activity
was merely the prelude to a seaborne invasion of his duchy, summoned
all his subjects who owed military service and ordered all residents on
the coast to maintain a constant watch for English ships.[25] Richard was
set on targeting not just the Bretons: on 12 February, he issued orders that
'certain of our ships of war' should be provisioned 'to resist our enemies
the Frenchmen, Bretons and Scots'. In his new-found confidence, Richard
seemed to be inviting war on three fronts. In spite of the desire of the
Scottish king, James III, for peace with England, his having sent peace
missions in August and November, Richard remained determined to press
ahead with a policy of peace achieved only through military action.[26]

On 18 February, the king sent letters to the gentry throughout the
country, declaring that 'we be fully determined, by God's grace, to address us in person with host royal toward the party of our enemies and
rebels of Scotland, at the beginning of this next summer', and sending
out a command that 'you dispose you to serve us personally in the said
voyage, accompanied and apparelled for war, according to your degree'.[27]

The campaign was planned for 1 May, with recipients of the letters to join Richard in Newcastle at the end of that month.

James III realised by now that any hope of a truce was pointless. On 24 February the Scottish Parliament issued commandments for all able-bodied men to be prepared to join James 'for the defence of the Realm', while preparations began for the raising of an army to besiege Dunbar in May, prompting Richard to order the castle's refortification.[28] By late March, Richard had commissioned four ships 'to do service of war upon the sea in the north parts'.[29] Richard's own personal view of war against the Scots had been shaped by the years he had acted first as warden of the West March, then as lieutenant-general of the king's army.[30] It seemed that Richard was convinced he needed to end the incessant border raiding and recriminations through one final war.

In preparation, Richard wrote on 11 March to King Charles VIII of France, urging his 'very dear cousin' that his ambassador, Thomas Langton, was to visit the French court, in order to 'explain to your majesty in our name certain matters concerning us'.[31] Langton himself was granted a 'special mandate' to 'treat, communicate, agree and conclude' a truce 'or abstinences from war both by land and sea'.[32] Langton would not arrive at the French court for several months, however, by which time he was too late.

Already Richard's naval operations had terrified the French into believing that the English were about to launch an attack. In response, they had already reached out for allies, including the Scots. On 13 March, James III concluded with a French embassy a reconfirmation of the 'auld alliance', restating their old agreement for mutual assistance if either country were attacked by the English. In their desperation, on 5 April 1484, a French delegation, led by three councillors of Charles VIII, arrived in Brittany promising support for a new English venture under Henry Tudor. In reality, the French king hoped that another invasion would distract Richard's naval fleet from the damaging piracy that was affecting French ships, at the same time as potentially weakening any prospect of English support for Francis against a French invasion of the duchy. The offer was too generous for Francis not to suspect that the French had their own agenda, but, nevertheless, work began on preparing a small fleet with French support, a flotilla of six ships from the ports of Morlaix, Saint-Pol-de-Léon and Brest, carrying 890 men. Richard's foreign policy and its aggression towards both France and Scotland was proving to be solely to Henry Tudor's benefit.

Already rumours had begun to circulate that the exiled rebels planned to land in England, 'together with their leader, the earl of Richmond', whom they 'had sworn fealty, as to their king', hoping that 'a marriage would be contracted with King Edward's daughter'. 'The king was better prepared to resist them in that year than he would have been ever at any time afterwards, not only because of the treasure which he had in hand', the Crowland chronicler believed, 'but also because of the specific grants made and scattered throughout the kingdom.' In order to buy their loyalty, the nobility were rewarded by the king with a succession of annuities; over the next two months, a stream of grants ensued.[33] Over the next eighteen months, over sixty annuities and grants of land for life were issued, costing the king easily over £1,000 a year. Richard relied heavily on his own northern lordships to make up the balance. At Barnard Castle, the king granted away £143 from an annual revenue of £300; at Middleham, new grants of land and annuities cost the lordship £400, and at Sheriff Hutton £350. It has been estimated that three-quarters of the value of Richard's Yorkshire lordships had been alienated or was being consumed by fees and annuities.[34]

Richard had also 'found time for the defence of his territories', planning a fresh network of communications, which would ensure that any news of landings on the coast would be instantly relayed back, following 'a new method, introduced by King Edward at the time of the last war in Scotland, of allocating one mounted courier to every 20 miles; riding with the utmost skill and not crossing their bounds', the messengers were capable of carrying 'messages 200 miles within two days without fail by letters passed from hand to hand'. In a letter written by Richard in April, the king revealed that 'we have appointed and ordained certain of our servants to lie in divers places and towns betwixt us and the west parts of this realm, for the hasty convenience of tidings and of all other things for us necessary to have knowledge of'. If any royal servant needed a horse 'for their hasty speed to or from us' they were to be provided with 'ready money', while if they happened to be travelling at night, they were to be supplied with guides.[35] In addition, Richard had 'provided himself with spies overseas, at whatever price he could get them, from whom he had learned almost all the movements of his enemies'.[36] In preparation for either his military ventures or defence of the realm, payments were granted for cannon, gunpowder and ordnance, as well as carpenters and gun makers.[37]

News of Tudor's activities had also prompted Richard to increase his diplomatic overtures. On 28 February 1484, Richard wrote to the pope, offering 'our most humble commendation and most devout kissing of your holy feet'. He had planned to 'inform your holiness before this of our assumption of the rule and crown of this our kingdom', but was forced to delay any correspondence, explaining that 'this indeed was in our mind, and we would most willingly have done so, had not the unexpected perfidy and evil conspiracy of certain people hostile to us, to loyalty and their oath prevented us from conveniently doing this'. Now Richard sent Thomas Langton with messages to the papacy, whom he described in a separate letter on 10 March as 'our very dear and most faithful counsellor and spokesman who knows the secrets of our heart'.[38]

On or around 9 April 1484, a year since Edward IV's death, Richard's son and sole heir, Edward, Prince of Wales, died at Middleham Castle, having been 'seized with an illness of but short duration'. He had not even yet entered his teenage years, though he was considered old enough to have been summoned for the opening of the Parliament earlier in the year.[39]

Only glimpses of Edward's life can be gleaned from the surviving accounts at Middleham for the previous year; he had made a journey to the abbeys of Jervaux, Coverham, Wensleydale, Fountains and Pontefract, where he had made offerings of 15s, 20d, 2s 6d and 4s, while a chariot had been constructed to take him from York to Pontefract after his coronation as Prince of Wales. Other purchases included a book of hours, covered in black satin, and a psalter, a gown of grey cloth, 6s 8d, to 'Metcalf and Peacock for running on foot beside my lord prince', probably when he was journeying in his chariot, and 100 shillings for the wages of Jane Colyns, who must have been the prince's official maidservant.[40] Other items that must have belonged to the prince included an illuminated manuscript of the popular military treatise *De Re Militari* by Vegetius, decorated with the English royal arms surrounded by two boars and, at the bottom of the page, a griffin, Edward's insignia as earl of Salisbury, suggesting that the manuscript had been specially commissioned for the young boy in preparation for his forthcoming military education.

Now, the king's only son and heir, the Prince of Wales, was dead. Richard and his wife, Anne, were devastated. The news came clearly unexpectedly, for they were still both residing at Nottingham Castle when it was broken to them: 'On hearing news of this, at Nottingham . . . you might have seen his father and mother in a state almost bordering on madness, by reason of their sudden grief.'[41] Settling the final payments for the prince's household as it was eventually wound up, Richard continued months later to refer to Edward as 'our dearest son the prince'.[42]

Edward's death meant that Richard and Anne were childless; the king no longer had an heir. For the security of the dynasty, Richard would need to nominate his heir apparent. 'Not long after the death of the prince', John Rous wrote, 'the young Earl of Warwick, Edward, eldest son of George, Duke of Clarence, was proclaimed heir apparent in the royal court, and in ceremonies at table and chamber he was served first after the king and queen', yet possibly realising that the young earl, as Clarence's son, might be considered to have a stronger claim to the throne than Richard himself, in spite of his father's attainder, Richard changed his mind, with Warwick being 'placed in custody and the Earl of Lincoln was preferred to him'.[43] John de la Pole, the earl of Lincoln, was the son of John de la Pole, the duke of Suffolk, and Richard's elder sister Elizabeth; technically, Lincoln could claim a line of descent through the female line that was stronger than Richard's own claim to the throne, yet, obviously, running through the male line, Richard's own dynastic claim remained supreme. Yet to acknowledge his heir through the female line must have raised concerns. Already Edward, earl of Warwick, had been first recognised as heir, having the strongest direct male descent of the Yorkist dynasty; such open acknowledgement had meant that once Warwick had reached his majority, he could justifiably claim that his male descent was stronger than Lincoln's. At the same time, the female children of Edward IV, led by Elizabeth of York, might at some point in the future be able to argue that their own claims, and those of their children, would surpass that of the de la Pole line. The danger for Richard in meddling with the Yorkist line of succession, dependent itself on recognising the value of the female line of inheritance, was that it might open a possible minefield of claims in the future. Moreover, the appointment of Lincoln as his designated heir only highlighted how Richard's own family dynasty hung by the thread of Richard's own life; with no other children, men might consider who else to turn to if they believed Richard's reign was under threat.

His son's death seems to have left Richard reeling with grief. His plans to invade Scotland in less than a month's time were put on hold while the king remained with his wife at Nottingham Castle for the rest of the month. The threat of an invasion by Henry Tudor meant that Richard could not risk a Scottish campaign when his army and northern followers were now needed to defend southern England. Richard was prepared to consider changing his policy of war on two fronts. On 13 April, he extended the first olive branch of peace by agreeing to pay £150 compensation to a Rouen merchant who had been affected by English piracy.[44] The same day, he instructed a herald to wait at Berwick for Scottish ambassadors until 15 May.[45] If the Scottish ambassadors arrived and were prepared to accept a truce, Richard would proclaim a truce throughout the borders until 31 October. Back in February, Richard had signalled his intention in a letter to arrive at Newcastle on 1 May, to lead an army northwards against the Scots. This muster was now cancelled, as both the king and queen recovered from their grief at Nottingham.

By the end of April, Richard's attention turned once more to his intended northern progress. On Tuesday, 27 April, Richard departed from Nottingham, heading first to Doncaster overnight, before arriving at Pontefract on Thursday, 29 April. By May Day, Richard was in York; the royal progress then moved northwards, to Middleham on Wednesday, 5 May, staying for three days before departing for Barnard Castle on Sunday, 9 May, and on to Newcastle on Thursday, 13 May. By Friday, 14 May, Richard had reached Durham. On 16 May, St Brendan's Day, Richard gave offerings of 11s 11½d to the cathedral at Durham. It was a token offering; however; the king supplemented the donation with the gift of the robe he had worn during the recent sitting of Parliament, described as being 'of blue velvet wrought with great lions of pure gold – a marvellous rich cope'.[46] Richard stayed in the city for several days before beginning to make his way back down southwards, visiting Rievaulx Abbey on 20 May, Scarborough Castle on 22

May, and Sheriff Hutton on 24 May, where Richard may have paid a visit to the grave of his son.[47] On 27 May, while at York, Richard ordered the receiver at Middleham to pay the friars of Richmond 12 marks 6 shillings and 8 pence for the saying of 1,000 masses for Edward IV.[48]

After a brief stay at York, Richard spent the next two weeks until Saturday, 12 June, at Pontefract. It would mark a prolonged stay in Yorkshire for the king, who remained in the area, residing at castles in Pontefract, York and Scarborough, until 23 July.[49] Richard took the opportunity to reward his northern homeland with several grants, bestowing unprecedented privileges upon its corporations: Hull, Beverley, York and Newcastle received significant financial concessions, while Scarborough was established as a county and Pontefract a borough.[50] Already earlier in the year Richard had granted Kingston upon Hull the freedom to ship goods and merchandise, wool excepted, free from payment of any customs for the next twenty years, 'in consideration of the poverty of the town and the expenses which they have sustained in journeying to Scotland and in other places at the king's pleasure and for the relief of the port of the town'.[51] Similar measures would be granted to York, remitting the city from payment of its tax, with Richard 'remembering and calling unto our mind the great zeal and tender affection that we bear in our heart unto our faithful and true subjects the mayor, sheriffs and citizens of our city of York of long time past', now 'for many causes and also understanding that notwithstanding our great liberality and graces late shown unto them by us for the profit and welfare of the said city'.[52]

To the disappointment of northern noblemen such as Henry, earl of Northumberland, or Ralph, earl of Westmorland, who may have hoped to fill the vacuum of power left by Richard's absence from the north, Richard's accession as king had if anything strengthened his hold over the region. For Northumberland, the agreement he had reached with Richard as duke in 1474 no longer applied: Richard was free to recruit the earl's men into royal service if he so wished. He willingly chose to do so: five Percy retainers who had been knighted by Northumberland during the Scottish campaign received grants from the king, including his brother-in-law Sir William Gascoigne, Christopher Ward, who became Master of the Hart Hounds and sheriff of Surrey and Sussex; and Sir Marmaduke Constable, who was appointed steward of Tonbridge in Kent. These appointments had the effect of removing Northumberland's men from the north altogether, hollowing out his retinue, and eroding the very principle of loyalty that the earl's noble status depended upon.

As king, Richard also commanded the duchy of Lancaster lordships, a rich source of patronage which Richard now used to bolster the retinue and ducal power structure he had built up during the 1470s. It was in the Honour of Knaresborough, a duchy of Lancaster lordship where Northumberland was steward, that the earl would find his influence most curtailed; now Richard himself was the duke of Lancaster, he was free to act as he wished. Northumberland and his men retained their offices, yet Richard soon granted new annuities from the lordship to his own men.

If Northumberland had hoped that Richard's accession might enable him to become the king's deputy in the region, he was to be disappointed. Richard's ducal council had been formally headed by his son, the association of the council with the prince giving it a status that helped keep law and order in the region. With Edward's death, however, Richard needed to re-establish the council's authority by placing the next in line to the throne, the king's designated heir, at its head. As the king's eldest nephew and heir, John de la Pole, earl of Lincoln, would be expected to lead the council, though he would do so explicitly on behalf of the king. Lincoln was an outsider, whose family's estates lay mostly in East Anglia and the Thames Valley. For Richard this was a positive advantage, for it meant that Lincoln, having no independent interests or conflicts of loyalty in the region, would be able to act for the king alone.

The new council was in effect a continuation of the ducal council that Richard had operated in the area for years as duke of Gloucester. It was to act as the final arbiter in local disputes, at the same time as providing a means of redress and access to justice for local communities. Before handing over its leadership to the earl of Lincoln, Richard set out careful regulations to ensure that the council remained impartial in its function. 'First the king will that no lord nor other person appointed to be of his council for favour, affection, hate, malice' should speak in the council, while any lord sitting on the council with any conflict of interest was to leave his seat 'during the time of the examination and ordering of the said matter unless he be called, and that he obey and be ordered therein by the remnant of the said council'. No matter 'of great weight or substance'

was to be discussed or ordered unless the earl of Lincoln was present, together with two commissioners of the peace. All letters were to be signed
by Lincoln's own hand, with the words *'per consilium Regis'* beneath, in the
presence of the council. The council was to spend a quarter of the year at
York, 'and oftener if the case require', where it would 'examine and order
all bills of complaints'. If the council became aware of 'any assemblies
or gatherings made contrary to our laws', they would have the power 'to
resist, withstand and punish the same' without recourse to the king, while
those arrested should be committed to the nearest gaol or castle.[53]

Richard was determined that, as a royal council, Lincoln's household
would be tightly managed, with the king dictating every last detail of its
operation. Lincoln himself was ordered to reside permanently at Sandal
Castle, a residence of the duchy of York rather than one of Richard's Neville
properties, in an attempt to make the establishment of the council appear
as neutral as possible. Richard ordered the building of a new tower at the
castle on his visit there in June, and later a new bakehouse and brewhouse
were built. A series of ordinances drawn up by the king for the household
in the north ordered how 'the hours of God's service, diet, going to bed and
rising and also the shutting of the gates' were to be performed 'at reasonable time and hours convenient'. Arrangements for breakfast were to be
strictly controlled in particular, with Lincoln and Lord Morley appointed
to attend one breakfast table, members of the Council of the North at another table, while 'the children' were to dine 'together at one breakfast'.
Security was kept tight, with the Treasurer ordered to have possession of
the keys of the gates while the household was at dinner and supper. No
servant was to depart without the Treasurer's permission, while no boys
were to be admitted to the household. Liveries of bread, wine and ale were
strictly controlled, being 'measurable and convenient and that no pot of
livery exceed measure of a potelle', 'my lord and the Children' being the
only ones excluded from the arrangement.[54] While residing at Sandal, the
earl was to behave more like the king's servant than his appointed heir.

16

'DEFEND ME FROM ALL EVIL'

It was during Richard's journey to Yorkshire that the king was visited by the Silesian knight Niclas von Popplau, who later recorded his travels to England, providing us with the only detailed contemporary description of life at Richard's royal court.

In spite of his recent troubles – the death of his son, and the persistent memory of rebellion and betrayal – Richard presented a court that was lavish, cultured and generous. Popplau had been impressed at the quality of the singing in the king's chapel, something which Richard carefully cultivated. On 28 March, Richard agreed to pay Sir John Perty an annuity of ten marks, 'and so from thenceforth yearly during the king's pleasure' Sir John was to 'sing for the king in a chapel before the holy rood at Northampton'.[1] Later in the year, 26 September, while at Nottingham, Richard gave authority for John Meloynek, one of the gentlemen in his chapel, 'knowing also his expert ability and cunning in the science of music', to 'take and sieze for us and in our name all such singing men and children being expert in the said science of music as he can find and think sufficient and able to do us service'.[2] Lighter entertainment was provided by minstrels, of which Richard had his own travelling troop since his days as duke of Gloucester, though as king he was able to attract performances from abroad, with passports being granted to Conret Suyster and Peter Skeydell, minstrels from the duke of Bavaria.[3] Other forms of entertainment included hunting, with Richard owning thirty-six running dogs and nine harriers. Richard wrote to 'our dear and welbeloved', the widow Elizabeth Russell, about the condition of Streynsham Park in Worcester, having been informed that 'by means of excessive hunting the game within the said park is greatly diminished and wasted'. 'We desiring to have the same replenished and kept for our disports against our resorting to those parts', Richard ordered that no man regardless of his status was to be allowed to shoot or course in the park.[4] Other animals were kept for amusement, with John Brown being appointed 'master guider and ruler of all our bears and apes to us appertaining'.[5]

Richard's fondness for jewels was such that orders were sent that all imports of precious stones were to be first reserved for the king's purchase before being offered to the open market, with a licence issued to Louis de Grymaldes to bring 'a diamond and other gems or precious stones' into any port in the country, 'to the intent that if they be for our pleasure we may have the sale thereof before all other'.[6] The merchant George Cely would later bequest to his brother Richard 'the jewel which I had of King Richard', a red spinel ruby described as 'a jewel with a balas and fine pearls hanging thereby' which was worth £100.[7] Richard sent to John Dawn, 'treasurer of our household in the north parts', several parcels of plate, including a cup of gold with a sapphire in the top, a 'goblet of jasper garnished with gold pearls and stones', three pots of silver emblazoned with coats of arms on the lids and six silver bowls. Hugh Brice, the mayor of the city of London, was given 'a cup of gold garnished with pearls and precious stones' as a gift 'to the use of the commonality of the said city'.[8]

The king's tastes in clothing could be equally expensive, as the wardrobe accounts testify: Richard Gowle alone supplied Richard and Anne with silks worth nearly £200 in 1483, while John Pickering sold Richard clothes with a value of more than £1,000 during the same period.[9] Payments were made in October 1484 to the comptroller of the port at London for nineteen 'pieces of fine Holland cloth' worth £61 4s 9d, and other 'certain clothes of velvet and silks' worth £16 18s 4d 'for us and to our use'.[10] The following January, an additional £50 5s 4d was spent on 'certain clothes of velvet satin and chamlet' as well as marten furs and bog shanks for 'our right trusty and right entirely beloved brother' John, duke of Suffolk.[11]

A sense of Richard's understanding of the importance of dress can be gathered from his instructions in September 1484 to the bishop of Enachden, which were to be related to the Irish earl of Desmond. Richard was determined that, in becoming the king's liegeman, Desmond should not only swear an oath of loyalty 'and be ready to live and die against all earthly creatures and utterly endeavour me to the resistance and suppressing of his enemies, rebels and traitors', but also gave particular instructions that Desmond was to abandon 'the wearing and usage of the Irish array and from henceforth to give and apply himself to use the manner of the apparel for his person after the English guise, and after the fashion that the king's grace sendeth unto him, as well of gowns, doublets, hose and bonets'. Richard even sent Desmond two long gowns, one cloth of gold and the other velvet, two doublets, one velvet and the other fashioned from crimson satin, three shirts, three pairs of hose in the different colours of scarlet, violet and black, and two bonnets. A collar of gold 'of his devise' weighing twenty ounces and worth £30 was also sent to the earl, which the bishop was to deliver 'in most convenient place and honourable presence'.[12]

Richard's instructions to Desmond also reveal a personal side to the king, in which he sent his condolences for the death of the earl's father, who had been murdered, it was alleged, in February 1468 by the earl of Worcester acting on behalf of the Woodville family, merely for facing up to Edward IV and declaring that his marriage was an unsuitable one. Richard recalled in his message 'the manifold notable service and kindness' that Desmond's father had given to 'the famous prince the duke of York the king's father at diverse seasons of great necessity in those parts to his great jeopardies and charges done'. Richard expressed his sympathy and 'inward compassion' that, although he was only 'then being of young age' when Desmond's father had been 'slain and murdered by colour of the laws within Ireland by certain persons then having the governance and rule there, against all manhood, reason, and good conscience', he understood how the earl must feel at the loss of his father, for 'the semblable [similar] chance was and happened since within this realm of England, as well of his brother the duke of Clarence as other his nigh kinsmen and great friends'.[13] It was obvious that, in spite of his intention to keep his true feelings 'inward', Richard was inviting a comparison between the deaths of Clarence and the earl of Desmond's father, with the inference that the Woodvilles lay behind both men's deaths.

Other letters written during the year hint at a compassion that extended even to his sworn enemies. In an undated letter, Richard wrote to his Chancellor, John Russell, revealing that it had been 'showed unto us' that the solicitor-general, Thomas Lynom, having been sent to interview

Elizabeth Shore, still imprisoned at Ludgate on Richard's orders, had been 'marvelously blinded and abused with the late [wife] of William Shore' and now was in a relationship with the prisoner.[14] Earlier in the year, on 29 January, Richard had rewarded Lynom with the manor of Colmouth in Bedfordshire, noting how 'we trusting in your truth, diligence and discretion'.[15] Now, Richard wrote, Lynom had seemingly taken the opposite course, and remarkably had become betrothed to Elizabeth Shore, and 'hath made contract of matrimony with her as it is said, and entendeth to our full great marvel to proceed to the effect of the same . . . We for many causes would be sorry that he so should be disposed', Richard informed Russell:

> Pray you therefore to send for him, and in that ye goodly may exhort and stir him to the contrary. And if ye find him utterly set for to marry her and none otherwise will be advertised, then if it may stand with the law of the church, we be content the time of marriage [be] deferred to our coming next to London that upon sufficient surety found for her good abearing ye do send for her keeper and discharge him out of our said commandment . . . committing her to the rule and guiding of her father or any other by your discretion.[16]

From Pontefract on 3 June, Richard found time to write to his mother, Cecily, duchess of York, informing her that her servant, a Wiltshire gentleman named William Collingborne, was to be removed from his post, though he had secured a replacement, to whom the king requested Cecily 'to be good and gracious lady . . . I trust he shall therein do you good service, and that it please you that by this bearer I may understand your pleasure in this behalf.'[17] Several months earlier, he had granted Cecily a lavish grant of the customs of wool; in recompense for grants totalling £689 6s 8d yearly that had been made by Edward IV, but 'of which she has received no payment', Richard had generously given his mother permission to ship 775½ sacks of wool for the next two years, then reduced to 258½ sacks 'until the king shall provide her for life with the sum' that she had been promised, an enormous grant that must have been worth thousands of pounds.[18] Richard's affection for his mother in his letter is obvious. Not only does the king recommend himself 'as heartily as is to me possible'; Richard went further to request from his mother 'in my most humble and effectuous wise of your daily blessing, to my singular comfort and defence in my need', adding, perhaps somewhat poignantly, though implying that both mother and son had not been in contact for some time, 'Madam, I heartily beseech you that I may often hear from you to my comfort,' Richard wrote to inform Cecily: 'And I pray god send you the accomplishment of your noble desires.' It was signed: 'with the hand of your most humble son, Ricardus Rex'.[19]

Surviving letters and accounts provide us with momentary fragments of Richard's life as king; those written in his own hand, or dictated by him, bring us as close as is possible to the public persona. But what of his private thoughts? One of Richard's most treasured possessions would have been his illuminated Book of Hours, produced around 1420, though several prayers have been added to the work, suggesting that the collection had been chosen and then enhanced for the king's personal use and tastes. It is tempting to read back into many of the prayers the king's own voice speaking to us, highlighting his personal fears and ambitions. A prayer to St Michael in Richard's Book of Hours begins, 'O St Michael the archangel of God, defend me in battle that I perish not in the terrible judgement'.[20] In a litany added to the book, the idea of the just crusade is highlighted: 'Let us pray almighty ever loving God, in whose hand are all the rights of kingdoms, come to the help of the Christians and let the peoples of the heathen who trust in their fierceness be destroyed by the power of your right hand.'[21] Special prayers in Richard's Book of Hours include to Ninian, George, Christopher, Joseph the Patriarch and Julian, although only the prayer to Ninian has been added for Richard personally:

> O God who has converted the peoples of the Britons and the Picts by the teaching of St Ninian, your confessor, to knowledge of your faith, grant of grace that by the intercession of him by whose learning we are steeped in the light of your truth, we may gain the joys of heavenly life. Through Christ our lord. Amen.

As patron saint of the West March towards Scotland, St Ninian was perhaps an unsurprising choice of saint for Richard to venerate; however, it demonstrates the efforts that Richard was making to ensure that he would become integrated into northern society. Yet the king's northern piety ran more than skin deep. Six years earlier, in July 1478, Richard had established his college at Middleham, providing for six priests whose stalls would especially venerate Saints George, Katherine, Ninian, Cuthbert, Anthony and Barbara. The preamble to the Middleham foundation gives an insight not only into Richard's own piety, but also the duke's understanding of his own complex and varied journey through a life already very much lived. In a sense it reads like a confessional, of a man grateful for his sudden rise in the world, in the knowledge that his own fortunes have come at the expense of others.

'Know ye that where it hath pleased Almighty God, Creator and Redeemer of all mankind', the text began, 'of His most bounteous and manifold graces to enable, enhance and exalt me His most simple creature, nakedly borne into his wretched world, destitute of possessions, goods and inheritaments, to the great estate, honour and dignity that He hath called me now unto, to be named, knowed, reputed and called Richard Duke of Gloucester.' God's 'infinite goodness', Richard proclaimed, had not only endowed 'me with great possessions and of gifts of His divine grace' but had also managed to 'preserve, keep and deliver me of many great jeopardies, perils and hurts'.[22]

The statutes also give detailed instructions for services, which mostly followed the traditional Catholic ceremony, although specific details bespeak a strong northern element to the devotions. The 'anthem of Saint Ninian confessor' was to be sung, with the Latin colet, 'Deus qui populous Pictorum et Britonum'. The feast days of St George and St Ninian, Richard declared, were to be marked out by the foundation to be 'served as principal fests, when so it their days fall, and also Saint Cuthbert day in Lent, and Saint Anthony day that falls in January, be served as principal in likewise.'

In establishing the foundation at Middleham, Richard was clearly considering his own mortality and the salvation of his soul. Nevertheless, the foundation was to pray for the souls of himself and his wife jointly, further underlining Richard's mission that the foundation was to follow in the footsteps of his Neville inheritance. Richard's instructions concerning the conduct of the six priests at the foundation are also striking for their tone and concern for moral behaviour. No minister was to 'haunt tavern or other unhonest place or person at any time' or be allowed to 'lie out of the College' during night time, without the permission of the dean. If any priest or clerk 'use at any time in ire any inhonest or slanderous words against his fellow, his superior or inferior', he was to be fined two pence from his wages each time. And perhaps attesting to the casual violence that remained largely accepted in fifteenth-century society, Richard further commanded that if any priest 'draw violently a knife, he shall pay of his said wage at every time so doing four pennies, and if he draw blood he shall pay of his said wage as much as the dean . . . shall reasonably deme him to pay'.[23]

The statutes designed for Middleham bear a striking resemblance to those drawn up the previous year in Richard's grant of land to Queen's College, Cambridge, in order to employ four priests who were 'well learned and virtuously disposed as doctors of divinity, bachelors, opposers or masters of art' as well as 'being priests of ability' who would 'proceed to be doctors and to preach the word of God'. Each of the priests would be paid £8 a year, and again would pay particular attention to the honouring of St Anthony, St Ninian and St George, reflecting Richard's own personal religious preferences not only for traditional saints such as St George, but northern saints such as St Ninian of Whithorn, Galloway, who had converted the Picts to Christianity, and who came to symbolise the claims of the diocese of York over south-west Scotland.[24]

The grant gives the impression that Richard was a man whose piety was both genuine and well versed in the liturgical details set out in the Middleham statutes, which reserved to the duke the sole power to revise and adjudicate on any disputed interpretation of the statutes. Richard's choice of saints is idiosyncratic and reflects at the same time the personal piety of the duke, which must have been heartfelt. Among the total list of thirty-five saints whom Richard had expressed 'such saints as that I have devotion unto', the choice of five native saints can be explained through Richard's northern connections: St Wilfrid of Ripon and St William of York were celebrated Yorkshire saints, while even the rather obscure Gloucestershire martyr St Alkelda had been included, no doubt since the parish church of Middleham had been dedicated to her memory. Both St Anthony and St Ninian, who appear in the Middleham statutes and the foundations of Queen's College, Middleham and Barnard Castle, were also painted on the stalls of Carlisle Cathedral during Richard's time in the north. Perhaps tellingly, the legend of St Anthony recalled how the saint had lived in the desert 'twenty-four years and more without any company

but the wild boar'.²⁵ It was the boar that was the only beast which refused
to threaten Anthony, despite the orders of the devil, and it may be this
religious connotation that inspired Richard to take up the symbol of the
white boar for his insignia. The surviving copies of the Duke Richard's
books suggest that he maintained a strong religious interest; alongside
his copy of the *Visions of Matilda* and his verse Old Testament, unusually
Richard owned a copy of Wycliffe's translation of the New Testament.²⁶
Other glimpses of Richard's piety can be witnessed in his donation of £40
in 1472 and 1473 to the repair of the impoverished church at Coverham,
a Neville foundation near Middleham, while in 1474 he presented a bell
to the fraternity of shipmen in Hull, to hang in the chapel of the Trinity
Guild, and gave a contribution to a window depicting the Last Judgement
at Great Malvern, where the duke was lord of the manor.²⁷

Richard's active religious faith, his relationship with God, and his belief
in the power of prayer can also be seen in a prayer specially added to his
Book of Hours. The beginning is missing, but among the requests that
Richard would have incanted are the following passages:

> deign to establish and confirm concord between me and my enemies. Show
> to me and pour out on me the glory of thy grace. Deign to assuage, turn
> aside, extinguish and bring to nothing the hatred they bear towards me ...
>
> Jesus Christ, so of the living God, deign to free me, thy servant King
> Richard from all the tribulation, grief and anguish in which I am held, and
> from all the snares of my enemies, and deign to send them Michael the
> archangel to my aid against them. Deign, O Lord Jesus Christ, to bring to
> nothing the evil designs which they make or wish to make against me ...
> O most gentle Christ Jesus, by all these things, to keep me thy servant King
> Richard, and defend me from all evil and from my evil enemy, and from
> all danger, present, past and to come, and free me from all the tribulations,
> griefs and anguishes which I face ...

In these words, one can almost sense Richard's own personal struggle
against his perceived enemies, whether they were the French, the Scots,
Henry Tudor and the English exiles, or the experiences of a king, facing
rebellion and grieving over the death of his son, who now sought solace in
prayer. Yet Richard's prayer for deliverance from his enemies should not
be taken as a text exclusively reserved for the king's own struggles during

his reign. Victory over one's enemies is just one of the militaristic themes
of many of the psalms: another prayer in the manuscript seeks protection
from the 'good angel' against all enemies, 'visible and invisible'.[28] Nor is
Richard's prayer by any means unique, for the text itself was already over
a hundred years old. Richard's sister, Anne, duchess of Exeter, owned
a prayer book containing the same prayer, while it was copied into the
primer of Alexander, Prince of Poland, in 1491. It is from this text that we
can perhaps deduce the rubric to Richard's prayer, which is missing in the
psalter. It reads: 'Whoever is in distress, anxiety or infirmity or has incurred the wrath of God, or is held in prison, or has experienced any kind
of calamity, let him say this prayer on thirty successive days and he must
be without mortal sin. It is certain that God will hear him completely,
that his trouble turn to joy and comfort – and this is proven by many
persons.'[29] The closing paragraph of the prayer, with its thanks to God 'for
all the gifts and goods granted to me because you made me from nothing and redeemed me out of your beauteous love and pity from eternal
damnation' is also strikingly similar to the tone of the foundation charter
for Middleham, with its references to Richard as a 'most simple creature,
nakedly born into this wretched world, destitute of possessions' who had
been raised to 'great estate, honour and dignity'.[30]

That Richard viewed himself as a man chosen by God, and as someone who could identify his own fate through the Old Testament kings, is
reflected in the inclusion of a rare prayer to Joseph, the youngest son of
Jacob, who usurped his eldest brother's birthright, in which direct comparison is made with Richard:

> O God who gave wisdom to the blessed Joseph in the house of his Lord
> and in the presence of Pharaoh and freed him from envy and hatred of
> his brother but also raised in honour, I pray to you Lord God Omnipotent
> that similarly you deliver over your servant Richard from the plots of my
> enemies and to find grace and favour in the eyes of my adversaries and all
> Christians.[31]

What use Richard made of these prayers, or how often he sought to repeat
them, cannot be known, though the king considered the work important
enough to take with him even when staying in his royal tent, where it
would eventually be discovered.

17

'COMMOTION AND WAR'

While Richard remained in the north, the sea war against the Scots had continued in earnest, becoming Richard's principal concern in the months of June and July. From his base at Scarborough, he co-ordinated the activities of 'our army now being upon the sea'. Further orders for military weapons and guns to be sent north were issued.[1] According to the Crowland chronicler, 'near the town and castle of Scarborough', where Richard resided between 27 June and 11 July, 'in the same maritime theatre he had remarkable success against the Scots', despite the fact that 'he had lost to the French some ships and two of the toughest captains Sir Thomas Everingham and . . . John Nesfield' in a naval battle near the Scarborough coast.[2] The Scots' siege of Dunbar had also failed due to Richard's ability to keep the fortress supplied by sea; since he was only likely to keep an army in the field for a month at most, James III desperately needed to sue for peace.[3] Richard was more than prepared to oblige. On 21 July, James wrote to Richard, stating that he had been informed by an English embassy led by 'your familiar squire' Edward Gower that Richard wished for an Anglo-Scottish truce, to be sealed with a marriage alliance.

The news that Richard was prepared to abandon his hostilities towards Scotland had come as a bitter blow to the Scottish exiles, James III's erstwhile brother, Alexander, duke of Albany, and James, the forfeited 9th earl of Douglas.[4] With Richard preparing to come to terms with James III, in desperation the two men launched a raid into Scotland. It was to prove a disaster. On 22 July, Albany and Douglas were routed at Lochmaben in Dumfriesshire by a small army of local lairds. Douglas was imprisoned while Albany fled back to France, where he would be killed a year later fighting in a tournament in Paris. For the Crowland chronicler, the debacle and defeat at Lochmaben countered English successes on the seas, admitting that 'in that same summer . . . they inflicted no less destruction upon us, for the Scottish fugitives . . . besides many Englishmen . . . fell into their hands'.[5]

James III would have preferred to negotiate a peace rather than a truce; however, the Scottish terms, which included the return of Dunbar and Berwick, towns that had been hard won by the English, were unrealistic. Berwick itself had been the only prize gained from Richard's invasion into Scotland in 1482, significantly improving England's defences against that nation. It was unlikely that Richard would ever give up these towns unless forced to do so. The Scots embassy arrived at Nottingham Castle on 12 September, led by James III's trusted secretary, Archibald Whitelaw, where they were met by Richard, surrounded by an impressive number of advisers. Whitelaw opened with a lengthy Latin oration, filled with classical allusions, which he delivered in front of the king for at least half an hour. Whitelaw clearly expected Richard to understand the compliments that he now poured effusively upon him. First the secretary listed what he believed to be Richard's greatest virtues, namely his humanity, courtesy, liberality, loyalty, justice, his greatness of heart and a wisdom that had instilled in him a kindness that was directed to everybody. Next, Whitelaw thought it best to praise Richard's military virtues, including his experience, courage, authority and good fortune. In doing so, Whitelaw compared Richard to Tydeus, who had been the bravest warrior at the siege of Thebes, in spite of his small stature. 'Never before had nature dared to encase in a smaller body such spirit and such strength', Whitelaw related, adding 'in his small body the greatest valour held sway', possibly reflecting on Richard's own small stature.

Neatly, Tydeus's own emblem was that of a boar also. It was this image of the boar that Whitelaw continued with in his oration when extolling the benefits of peace, with a quotation from Vergil which described a boar peacefully roaming the mountains: 'so long as rivers flow into the sea . . . so long as the wild boar delights in the mountains . . . your honour, your name and your glory will survive for ever'. Aside from the allusion to Richard's own insignia and behind the diplomatic flattery was the clear point that Richard, having won all possible laurels, had no need for war.

Contrasting the horror of war, which 'gives the country a frightful aspect',
Whitelaw explained how 'in peace God is worshipped particularly because
He is the provider of peace; strong and effective justice prevails, every
virtue and good government flourish'.[6]

Eventually a three-year truce was concluded; however, no long-term
peace could be accepted by the Scots without the return of Dunbar and
Berwick, which Richard absolutely refused to countenance. It seems likely
that Richard himself conducted the negotiations over the truce; the Crowland chronicler admitted that the agreement was drawn up 'as the king
desired' on 'those matters which seemed to require particular attention'.[7]
With his own relationship with France deteriorating rapidly, Richard urgently needed to secure his northern border, and maintain a peaceable
truce for the immediate future. On 23 September 1484, letters were issued
ordering that no subject, no matter 'what estate, degree or condition they
be', should make war by land or sea against the Scots, 'under pain of death
and of all they may forfeit'.[8]

During the summer, before the visit of the Scottish embassy, Richard
abruptly chose to return to the capital. His decision seems to have been
influenced by unrest in the south, with the growing threat once more of
rebellion. That summer, James Newenham 'lately confessed certain great
treasons by him and others conspired and done'. On 6 July, while at Scarborough, Richard issued letters of commission to Lord Scrope, the mayor
of Exeter and seven gentlemen, 'to sit, hear and determine upon the said
treason and to proceed to the execution and judgement against the offenders according to their demerits'.[9] Later the same month, Scrope was again
instructed to investigate the treason of Richard Edgecombe of Cotehele,
John Lenne of Launceston and several other men who had apparently
conspired to send 2,000 lb of tin worth £31 13s 4d and broadcloth valued
at £15 to two of the exiled rebels, Robert Willoughby and Peter Courtenay,
the bishop of Exeter. Edgecombe was indicted for planning to send Lenne
to Brittany with the cash; both men having been declared rebels intending
'the destruction of the crown', Edgecombe's lands and goods were seized;
however, he managed to escape to join the exiles in Brittany.[10]

More threatening was the discovery of the treason of William

Collingborne, the servant of Richard's mother, Cecily, who had been removed from her household by the king only the previous month. According to a later indictment, Collingborne and 'other false traitors to the king' had on 10 July 1484, 'in the parish of St Botolph, Portsoken ward, falsely and treasonably imagined and contrived the death and destruction of the lord king and the subversion of his realm of England'. Collingborne had apparently 'excited, moved and urged a certain Thomas Yate, offering him £8 to go to foreign parts across the sea in Brittany to speak there to Henry, once calling himself earl of Richmond, Thomas, formerly marquess of Dorset, and John Cheyne, esquire, and other traitors, rebels and great enemies of the lord king'. Yate urged them to return to England around the feast of St Luke, 11 October, 'with all their power, and to say that, if they should return to the port of Poole in Dorset'. Collingborne would arrange to meet them there, 'together with the people of the realm, and make insurrection and war against the king, and that the whole realm would join them'. The indictment asserted that 'They also urged John Cheyne to go to the king of France and tell him that his ambassadors were being deceived, and that the king of England will not keep his promises, except to postpone the war between them from the winter to the spring so that he can prepare his forces, and also to advise the king of France that he should assist the traitors.' Eight days later, on 18 July 1484, in London, in the parish of St Gregory the Pope in Farringdon, Collingborne 'gathered together other traitors and rebels, and imagined and contrived the death and destruction of the king through war, commotion and discord between the king and his subjects'. As the indictment described:

> And to achieve that false and nefarious aim, Collingborne and others, on the said 18 July, falsely and treasonably wrote and made various bills and writings in rhymes and ballads ('in rittimis et balladis') containing mutterings, seditious speeches and treasonous incitements, and having made them, on the same day placed and publicly fixed them to various doors of the cathedral church of St Paul in London, to move and excite those king's lieges reading and understanding the bills and writings to make and levy commotion and war against the lord king, against their due allegiance, to the final destruction of the lord king and the subversion of his realm of England.[11]

The actual text that Collingborne had pinned to the door of St Paul's was not recorded by the indictment, though it was not missed by the author of the *Great Chronicle*, who recorded the rhyme that had been 'fastened upon the Cross in Cheap and other places of the city':

> The Cat, the Rat, and Lovell our dog,
> Ruleth all England under a Hog.

The chronicler knew exactly what the cryptic verse meant, explaining how the Cat and the Rat stood for Sir William Catesby and Sir Richard Ratcliffe, while Lovell was Francis, Viscount Lovell, who between them 'ruled this land under the king which bare a white boar for his cognisance'. 'For the devisers of this rhyme, much search was made', the chronicler noted, with 'sundry accused to their charges', before eventually William Collingborne was arrested and imprisoned, awaiting trial for treason.[12]

The rhyme evidently hit a raw nerve, exposing as it did the influence of Richard's councillors on the king. Even as far away as Durham, the prior, Robert Ebbchester, had written to Richard Redman, the bishop of St Asaph, describing how Sir Richard Ratcliffe had come to him bringing witnesses to show that he had a grant of a vicarage that had been agreed by his predecessor, requesting that Ebbchester ratify the grant. 'Whereupon with the advise of my brethren', Ebbchester continued, 'considering the great rule that he beareth under the king's grace in our country' he had agreed to Ratcliffe's demands.[13] Having already been appointed Chancellor of the Exchequer and served as speaker in Richard's Parliament, William Catesby occupied the supreme position within the royal council. Already in December 1483, Thomas, Lord Stanley, had paid him an annuity of five marks 'for his good will and counsel past and to come'; other rewards of both office and land were soon to follow, which Catesby was swift to accept. Lord Dudley made him a steward of his manor of Rugby with a fee of ten marks, while the archbishop of Canterbury appointed him bailiff of Pagham and the Abbey of St Mary's Combe with a fee of two marks.[14] All three men had been richly rewarded over the past year. William Catesby had been given lands in Warwickshire, Northamptonshire, Leicestershire and London worth £273 a year, with a rent payable to the king of only £20.[15] Sir Richard Ratcliffe, the younger son of a Cumberland esquire, was granted lands in the south-west worth 1,000 marks (£666 13s 4d), for which he had to pay an annual rent to the crown of £50. Lovell, who had only reached his majority in 1477, had known Richard since childhood, having grown up in the earl of Warwick's household. Though his family estates were based around Northamptonshire and Oxfordshire, Lovell remained a dutiful follower of Richard's, being knighted by the duke in August 1481 during the Scottish campaign. The following June, Lovell had intended to journey south to attend the king, when he had heard that Richard 'and such other folk of worship as hath any rule in the said north parts' were to be sent north to fight the Scots. Out of loyalty, Lovell felt obliged to stay. When Richard became Protector, Lovell was appointed chief butler of the royal household; upon Richard's accession to the throne, he was created chamberlain of the household, a position which required constant and close contact with the king. In addition to several annuities worth at least £64, Lovell was granted rebel estates in Oxfordshire and Berkshire worth a total of £400 a year, for a rent of just £30 a year. All three men held highly influential positions in Richard's government, for which they were amply rewarded, yet to single out Catesby, Ratcliffe and Lovell risks glossing over the many other supporters of Richard's regime who profited handsomely from acquiescing with the king's rule. Over the course of his reign, Richard would give away or 'alienate' lands worth £12,000 a year to his close-knit group of supporters, many of them already part of his ducal retinue, receiving just £735 15s in return from reserved rents. Other families were also massive beneficiaries from Richard's patronage, not least John Howard, the duke of Norfolk, and his son Thomas, earl of Surrey. In August 1484, Surrey was granted £1,100 a year from the revenues of the duchy of Cornwall, nearly half of the entire net revenue of the duchy, while as late as 28 February 1485 Norfolk was granted thirty-five lordships and manors.[16]

The other reason for Richard's return to the capital was to oversee the reburial of the Lancastrian king, Henry VI, whose corpse Richard now ordered to be exhumed from its grave at Chertsey Abbey, to be reburied at St George's Chapel, Windsor. Over the past decade, Henry's final resting place had become a shrine for visiting pilgrims, spurred on by an increasing number of supposed miracles, the first being dated to as early as 1481. By moving Henry's remains to Windsor, Richard hoped that the revenues from the growing cult of the saintly king would be able to be put to better use in funding the chapel, which had been founded by Edward IV and to which Richard had already contributed significantly. The body apparently smelt 'very pleasantly scented', a sign of his holy properties; it was 'certainly not from spices', John Rous observed, 'since he was buried by his enemies and butchers'. Leafing open the corpse's shroud, it was found to be 'for the most part' uncorrupted, 'the hair in place, and the face as it had been except it was a little sunken, with a more emaciated appearance than usual'.[17] When the vault of the tomb was opened in 1910, however, Rous's claim was found to be completely untrue. Not only were the bones found wrapped in fabric, and placed inside a wooden box, measuring just over three feet in length, ten inches wide and nine inches deep, and sealed with a sliding top panel; the wooden box had then been placed in a lead casket, not much larger in size, that had been soldered shut, before finally being enclosed in a full-sized wooden coffin, fastened with bands of iron. The intention was clear: that it would seem to those present at the reinterment that the king's intact body was being laid to rest. The entire cost of the translation of the remains, recorded in the accounts of the College of Windsor, was £5 10s 2d.[18] Later, John Pigot, the abbot of Chertsey, would claim that Richard had ordered the tomb of Henry VI to be broken up despite the vociferous protests of the monks, yet this was countered by the dean of Windsor, Christopher Urswick, who claimed that the exhumation had been made with the approval of the abbot, who had in fact insisted on opening the tomb himself. Interestingly, Richard himself was present at Windsor on 19 August, having made the journey from Westminster. It seems that the king had timed his visit to coincide with the translation of the Lancastrian king's remains.[19]

Richard was determined not to remain in London for long. After a stay of barely two weeks, Richard was back in Nottingham on 26 August in preparation for the visit of the Scottish embassy and the signing of the truce. Richard's arrival at Nottingham marked another lengthy stay away from the capital. Apart from a five-day stay at Tutbury Castle between 22 and 26 October, Richard would remain at Nottingham for nearly three months, departing for London on 4 November.[20]

Now that a truce with Scotland had finally been arranged, Richard recognised that he would need to deal with the threat that Henry Tudor and the English exiles in Brittany posed. A truce with Brittany had already been arranged on 8 June, to take effect from 1 July and to last until April 1485.[21] This was a welcome relief to naval shipping in the Channel, as well as to Duke Francis, who had feared an imminent English invasion. Now peaceful relations between the two countries had been restored, once again Richard tried to coax the duke into handing over Henry Tudor.

The presence of Tudor and the 400 English exiles in the small walled town of Vannes was becoming oppressive, as tempers often flared in the tense atmosphere of uncertainty and fear.[22] Richard sent messengers to Francis, promising him the yearly revenues of the confiscated lands belonging to Henry and his exiles if he agreed to place them in custody. When the messengers arrived, they found the aged Francis unwell, 'by reason of sore and daily sickness'. The duke was also suffering from a failing mind. Instead they were received by Francis's chancellor and chief minister, Pierre Landais, 'a man both of sharp wit and great authority'.[23] Resented by several Breton nobles, Landais was in need of allies. He had reached out to France, forming an alliance with Louis, the duke of Orléans, who was currently in a power struggle with his cousin Anne of Beaujeu over the control of the young French king, Charles VIII, and the running of the kingdom. Orléans was seeking to create a grand coalition with England and Burgundy's ruler, Maximilian of Austria, along with French nobles and Brittany to attempt to topple Anne and her government. What both Landais and his ally Orléans needed was for Richard to agree to support an invasion of France, in return for which Landais would arrange for Henry Tudor to be handed over.

For Richard, the opportunity to help lead a joint offensive against England's longstanding enemy was too good to miss. On 11 August, in a proclamation prohibiting piracy against all nations, significantly the French were excluded.[24] Two days later, on 14 August, letters were sent informing recipients that the king had been 'credibly informed that his adversaries of France' intended to launch an attack on the Calais pale, 'for whose malice to be mightily resisted, his highness hath made and daily is making great and notable punishment sufficient with God's mercy to break all their purpose'. Ordering for all subjects in the Cinque Ports and 'other places of the sea coasts' to provide ships 'to serve the king when need shall be', Richard commanded that everyone was to:

> Make themselves daily ready in their persons with their ships, guns, artillery, arms and victuals and other things necessary to the war so that as soon as any certainty of assigning the king's town of Calais or any other place within the pale, there shall be notified unto them by the king or his council, they fail not to assist his royal person, his lieutenants and deputies in manner and form afore . . . and as they be bound to do at such times as kings of England make their voyage unto France upon pain of forfeiting . . . .. Letting them wit that the king that is prince which for the defence of this realm and all the possession of the crown of England is disposed to employ his own royal person as far as any king that hath done in years past to the encouraging of his faithful subjects and confusion of all his enemies.[25]

It certainly seemed that Richard was serious enough about military involvement against France. Around the same time, Richard offered Brittany between 4,000 and 6,000 archers, the offer being made through the Burgundian agent, 'le petit Salazar', Juan de Salazar, a Spanish captain who was in Duke Maximilian of Austria's service.[26] No archers were for the moment provided, but news soon reached the French court in September of a rumour that 6,000 English archers were soon to arrive in Brittany. Everything now centred on securing possession of Henry Tudor.

Henry himself remained at Vannes in August and into September, for on 15 August and 8 September 1484 he is recorded in the cathedral accounts as having attended mass there, making small offerings of alms.[27] Four days later, there appears in the same accounts an offering from 'le grand escuier d'Engleterre' – most likely Sir James Tyrrell, Richard's Master of the Horse, whose arrival in the town suggests that the net was closing on Tudor.[28]

Richard's plans to capture Tudor were just days away from being finalised. It was John Morton, the bishop of Ely living in exile in Flanders, who being informed 'from his friends out of England' about Landais's negotiations with Richard, managed to get notice to Henry of the trap that was being laid around him. His agent, Christopher Urswick, who had travelled to join Morton in Flanders, met Henry at Vannes, where he passed on the message, advising him to 'get himself and the other noble men as soon as might be out of Brittany and into France'.[29] Henry immediately sent Urswick on to the French court to request Charles VIII's permission to enter into France. Two days later, around 1 October 1484, Henry himself left Vannes, accompanied by five servants, on pretence of visiting a friend. He would not return. When he had travelled five miles outside the city, he turned off the highway into a nearby forest. Stopping to change his clothes into those of a common servant, he then rode straight across the border and into France. Landais had been finalising plans to send a number of specially chosen men under 'trusty captains' to seize Henry when he first heard news of Henry's escape. Immediately he sent out men on horseback in pursuit, with orders that if they could overtake Henry they were to arrest him and return him to Brittany. Yet, upon their arrival, they discovered that Henry had crossed the French border 'scarcely an hour before'.[30]

For the 400 Englishmen remaining at Vannes, their future seemed a terrifying prospect. Having no knowledge of Henry's flight, when they discovered what had happened 'they were overcome with such fear that now they despaired for their safety'. Yet when Duke Francis discovered what had happened, ignorant of his treasurer's plans to seize Tudor, he was aghast. He had always been consistent in his support of the exiles, and it was at the very least a matter of honour that their welfare should be taken care of. In compensation, he rewarded Sir Edward Woodville, Sir John Cheyne and Edward Poynings with a gift of 100 *livres tournois* each, as well as one *livre tournois* for each of the 408 exiles still stationed at Vannes. The cost of their lodging was also paid by the duke in recompense, totalling 2,500 *livres tournois*, while the duke offered free passage for the English exiles into France.[31]

Meanwhile, the French king, Charles VIII, was at Montargis when he was informed on 11 October that Henry had arrived in his kingdom. Charles was evidently delighted with the arrival of his new guest. On 3 November, he wrote how the English were 'in marvellous and grand division' over Tudor.[32] The following day, a commission was given to lodge 400 of Tudor's supporters in Sens, sixty kilometres to the east of Montargis, while on 17 November the French council authorised a payment of 3,000 *livres tournois* to Henry, declaring, however, that it was 'for this time only'.[33]

18

REBELS AND TRAITORS

Henry Tudor's defection to France had been an unmitigated disaster for Richard. Yet Tudor's immediate prospects remained wafer thin. There seemed little chance that France would be able to spare any forces for his cause, with its Flemish cities now at war with Maximilian of Austria. If anything, Henry's flight had removed the immediate need for English military or financial aid to Brittany. Yet Henry Tudor's escape and survival now came to dominate Richard's foreign policy, as the king was determined to quash any threat that this possible usurper and his band of exiles might pose.

By the autumn of 1484, a new cycle of rebellion and unrest had broken out. Christopher Colyns was ordered to command two ships, the *Carrigon*, with 200 soldiers on board, and the *Michael of Queenborough*, with 100 soldiers, between October and November at a cost of £129 4s 2d.[1] On 9 October, Richard was presented with the confessions of three merchants from the West Country who had been arrested and taken to Exeter, 'which have lately aided our rebel Sir Robert Willoughby and other being in Brittany'. Once again, commissions were issued under John, Lord Scrope, 'for whose punishment in fearful example of others'.[2] Richard seems to have been genuinely frightened that a new rebellion was on the horizon. Orders were given to the earl of Arundel that no one was to fit out a ship for sail without making bonds of security that it would not be employed against the king's friends or subjects.[3] Around the same time, a writ was to be sent to Edward Berkeley, 'to show why he might not answer us of 1,000 marks by him forfeited of recognisance for the misbehaving of our rebel Sir William Berkeley'.[4] Sir John Ferrers was also bound by a recognisance of 500 marks, to 'henceforth keep duely our peace', and ordered not to depart more than a mile out of the walls of the city of London. Lord Lisle and Sir James Lawrence were also bound under recognisances 'that they should not pass our city of London or a mile about the same unto such time as ye should have from us otherwise in commandment'. Both bonds were cancelled in early December, 'for certain causes and considerations us moving be content that they shall depart at liberty'.[5]

In the capital, tensions between traders and foreign merchants seem to have also erupted. The official figures recorded in the Exchequer seem to point to England's trade with the continent slipping into an economic recession. Between October 1482 and September 1485, the number of wool sacks exported fell to an average of 5,283 sacks, compared with an average of 8,064 sacks in the decade previously, and 8,742 sacks between October 1485 and September 1490.[6] The most severe drop in exports took place in the north-eastern ports, with Boston shipping just 883 sacks in 1484–5. As a result, the staplers and clothiers seem to have been competing for a diminishing supply of wool, which resulted in a proclamation being issued in October 1484 that no one was to 'buy or bargain any wool not shorn before the Feast of St Bartholomew [24 August], except to make cloth within the realm', preventing the staplers from undermining clothiers by making advance purchases of wool before it had the chance to be woven into cloth.[7] Orders for the 'restraint to continue both for strangers and the King's subjects' were discussed at the Guildhall in front of the mayor of London on 27 August 1484, while on 3 October it was noted how the mayor 'divers times had communication and moved to forgo going to fairs'.[8] On the Tuesday before 21 October, a crowd of 'many simple disposed persons of divers crafts', including shearmen, fullers and cappers, gathered at the Guildhall, calling for the mayor to return wool that had been shipped to Calais, 'with much crying and matter of grief and complaint, simple and rudely than uttered'. The alderman Edmund Shaa, on behalf of the mayor, agreed that no more wool would be shipped, nor would ships already filled with wool be allowed to depart until 'the coming of the King to the town, at whose coming then the Mayor and Aldermen would help to show their grief, and beseech and pray the King's grace to see a remedy to their comfort'. The crowd remained unconvinced, however, and 'with a great cry and shout' departed. The mayor and aldermen sent messengers to the men, who replied that they believed the words had been spoken 'under a cloak' merely to allow the foreign ships carrying wool to set sail. Making their way to the harbourside, they began to take down the sails of the wool ships and forcibly remove woollen cloth from the ships. Fearing a riot, the mayor ordered that an armed force be sent to the harbour, at which point the rioters 'departed and fled'. The city remained on tenterhooks. The Mercers' Company recorded how the mayor ordered every man to 'be ready in his harness', prepared 'to come forth when so ever he be called', while servants were to be prevented from going 'unto any congregation or assembly' and the loan of harness was to be strictly prohibited.[9]

Amid this unrest, on 2 November, the trial of William Collingborne took place at the Guildhall. The trial was intended to demonstrate the consequences of rebellion against the king, even if it had involved pinning rhymes to the door of St Paul's and around the capital. Collingborne was brought before the justices at the Guildhall by the sheriffs, where he denied all charges. The following day, Friday, 3 November, the jury declared a guilty verdict, pronouncing their sentence that Collingborne 'be taken to Newgate gaol, and from there dragged through the city to Tower Hill, hanged there upon the gallows, cut down to the ground while living, his innards to be taken out of his belly while living and burnt, and his head removed, his body to be divided into four parts and his head and quarters to be placed wherever the king should decide'.[10] The Londoner Robert Fabyan described in his *Chronicle* how a new pair of gallows was specially constructed for Collingborne, who, after he had hanged 'a short season' from its rope, was 'cut down, being alive, and his bowels ripped out of his belly and cast into the fire there by him'. All the while, Collingborne remained conscious until, according to Fabyan, the executioner 'put his hand into the bulk of his body'. 'O Lord Jesu, yet more trouble', Collingborne managed to cry out. They were to be his final words; he died shortly afterwards, 'to the great compassion of many people'.[11]

If Henry Tudor had managed to slip through the net and escape to France, Richard was not prepared to allow any further mistakes to occur. News reached him through his network of spies that Henry and the English exiles, their confidence raised from their arrival at the French court, were planning to rescue the Lancastrian earl of Oxford, John de Vere, incarcerated since the 1473 rebellion at St Michael's Mount in Hammes Castle, one of the forts on the Calais pale. Oxford, who had fought against Richard at the battle of Barnet thirteen years earlier, had been a formidable military commander and a devout follower of the Lancastrian cause. He also had his own personal reasons for hating Richard, who had confiscated his mother's estates and left her almost destitute, as he later complained, 'by heinous menace of loss of life and imprisonment'. If the earl was prepared now to support Tudor's cause, Richard recognised that any plot needed to be foiled if he was to prevent Tudor from gaining a major publicity coup as well as a dangerous new ally. On 28 October, William Bolton, a yeoman usher of the royal chamber, was dispatched from Nottingham Castle to Hammes, carrying with him personal letters from the king to Sir James Blount, captain of the castle there, ordering Blount to hand over his most celebrated prisoner 'in all goodly haste' to Bolton, 'and to see him surely conveyed to the sea side'. Blount was not to depart until the earl had been 'shipped'.[12] Sir Robert Brackenbury, the constable of the Tower, was also sent to Dover, in preparation to meet the earl and escort him to the Tower.[13]

Bolton was too late. Not only had Oxford escaped from Hammes, but he had done so with the assistance of Blount and John Fortescue, the gentleman porter of Calais, who as sheriff of Devon and Cornwall in the 1470s had been responsible for first arresting the earl. Blount had left the garrison and its seventy-three men in the hands of his wife, with orders for the castle to be defended against any future attack. Oxford, Blount and Fortescue fled immediately to Henry Tudor's exiled court, now residing at the Ile-de-France. Meeting the earl, Henry was 'overwhelmed with extraordinary joy', Polydore Vergil later wrote, 'wherefore because of the coming of the earl of Oxford rejoicing above all measure he began to hope better of his affairs'.[14] The arrival of Oxford, together with Sir James Blount, gave Henry Tudor for the first time not only substantial military reinforcements that would help persuade the French government that his cause was worth supporting; it also gave him the confidence that he could claim the throne in his own right, no longer as a puppet ruler propped up by the Woodvilles.

When Richard discovered the news of Oxford's escape, he 'bewailed' being 'greatly disturbed that distinguished men, whose influence was strong among the people, inclined with such eagerness towards Henry'.[15] More alarming, however, was the defection of Sir James Blount, a member of the king's own household, raising Richard's doubts over the loyalty of his own establishment and making himself even more mistrustful of those outside his own close-knit circle.

News of Oxford's escape and the defection of the Hammes garrison was serious enough for Richard to immediately depart from Nottingham Castle on 4 November, reaching Westminster by Wednesday, 10 November.[16] By now, news had reached the king of yet another rebellion on the Essex coast. On 2 November, John Risley of Colchester, his servant, William Coke of Lavenham, Sir William Brandon and his sons William and Thomas, Sir William Stonor and others launched an armed rising in Colchester. The rebels then seized a boat at East Mersea, escaping to join Tudor in France.[17] The rebellion had been planned for some time, with money being raised in London for the enterprise; the pewterer Everard Newchurch later informed Henry Tudor that he lent £13 to Sir William Brandon 'to go to do your good grace service beyond the sea'.[18] The rebellion seems to have extended into Hertfordshire, with Ralph Penne of Aldenham suffering forfeiture of his estates, while another gentleman, Robert Clifford, was pardoned the following April for his involvement in the rising, but only after earlier promising to inform the royal council of any news or information which he might obtain that affected the king.[19] Meanwhile, Robert's brother Roger had been arrested in the south-west, with the Exeter records mentioning that he passed through the city as a prisoner.[20] It all pointed to the potential for a revolt on a far wider scale, while Richard would not have failed to notice that many of the rebels involved had close connections with the earl of Oxford's household and Essex estates, suggesting some degree of co-ordination had been planned to chime with the earl's escape. While the Essex rising may have been small by comparison to the rebellion of the previous autumn, most worrying for Richard was the fact that new rebels close to the royal household had chosen to become involved. John Risley was an esquire of the king's body, who had been rewarded with land in Hampshire for his service against the rebels the previous year.[21]

Richard was sufficiently alarmed to decide to travel to the south coast in person, in an attempt to shore up royal authority along the coastal areas of the Channel vulnerable to invasion. He first journeyed to Dartford, then Rochester Castle the following day, before arriving at Canterbury on 17 November.[22] It seems that the king ordered that his illegitimate son, John of Pontefract, be sent over to Calais, possibly to join John, Lord Dynham, in organising a siege of Hammes Castle, for which Dynham would spend £500 of his own money.[23] Richard attempted to win back Blount to his side, offering him an initial pardon on 17 November, and again on 30 November, promising to protect all the offices that had been granted him by Edward IV if he returned to the fold.[24] John Morton also received an unsolicited pardon, this time issued uniquely under the Great Seal, less than a fortnight later.[25] Richard's overtures for peace were ignored.

Elsewhere, the king's officers doused out any remaining flickers of rebellion. While Richard was absent from the capital, on 17 November 1484, assembling a band of armed men wielding swords and daggers, one of the king's own knights of the royal body, Sir Gilbert Debenham, broke into the rebel Sir William Brandon's London residence in Southwark, and with 'force and arms' seized £100 'and took it away contrary to the king's peace'.[26] The practice of confiscation of land gave Richard's own household servants and followers a power which they wielded with a brutal lack of restraint. William Finch, who was in the service of Robert Morton while in exile with Henry Tudor in Brittany, later described how, when he returned 'in his coming home from Brittany' he was tracked down by 'the servants of the said King Richard' and 'not only beaten and maimed . . . as it appeareth as well on his hands as other parts of his body, but also all that he had was taken from him . . . Through the which he was and is sore impoverished and so indebted.'[27]

Several months after his attack on Brandon's house, Debenham was once again on the rampage, this time attacking the possessions of Thomas Fastolf in January 1485 on what seems to have been his own private act of revenge. Worryingly, Debenham was accompanied by John Waynflete, the serjeant-at-arms. It seemed as though, with a taste for power that their offices and royal authority brought them, Richard's men were beginning to cross the line and descend into violent abuse of their office.[28] Yet Debenham's behaviour did not prevent Richard from employing him to keep the peace at Harwich, where Richard remained nervous that a rebel invasion might still be planned, sending a commission to the bailiff and constables of Harwich in late December, 'to aid and assist Sir Gilbert Debenham and Philip Bothe in the keeping of the said town and to resist rebels if they arrive there'.[29] Whether Richard was simply unaware of Debenham's private abuse of his position, or if he chose to turn a blind eye to such events, his toleration of violent and illegal behaviour seems to stand in stark contrast to his profession of love for the 'administration of justice' just a year earlier, or his impartial treatment of members of his own retinue who had committed offences during his time as duke of Gloucester.

Yet Richard had no other choice. Ever since Buckingham's rebellion, with the defection of a large number of the Yorkist royal household overseas, men whom the Yorkist dynasty had depended upon for maintaining law and order in their localities, Richard had been forced increasingly to rely instead upon a dwindling band of supporters to prop up his kingship. His authority rested on the shoulders of men such as Debenham, for without them, in the face of an ever-growing threat of invasion by Henry Tudor, Richard must have known that his kingship would be nothing.

As winter settled upon the country, Richard was becoming preoccupied to the point of fixation with addressing the threat of Henry Tudor. On 5 December, he wrote to the city of York, apologising that he had no time to consider their application for a royal clerk: 'for certain urgent causes we have not granted the said licence unto our said servant, but the same have deferred unto after Christmas'.[30] Whether through his spies, scouring the country for evidence of activity by Tudor and his accomplices, or through the open publication of Henry Tudor's letters that seem to have been flowing into England on a regular basis, Richard ordered a fresh crackdown on anyone receiving any information or letters from the rebels. On 6 December, Richard wrote to the mayor of Windsor that he had been 'credibly informed that our rebel and traitor now confederated with our ancient enemies of France by many and sundry ways conspire and study the means to the subversion of this our realm and of unity amongst our subjects' by 'sending writings by seditious persons which counterfeit and contrive false inventions . . . and rumours'. Their intention, Richard believed, was to 'provoke and stir discord and division betwixt us and our lords', which, the king was keen to stress, 'be as faithfully disposed as many subjects can suffice . . . We therefore will and command you straightly', the letter continued, that in addition to 'eschewing the inconvenients abovesaid . . . You put in your utmost devoir if any such rumours or writings come amongst you, to search and enquire of the first showers and utterers thereof, and them that ye shall so find you do commit unto your ward and after proceed to their sharp punishment in example and fear of all other, not failing hereof in any wise as ye intend to please us, and will answer to us at your peril.'[31]

Whatever messages passed across the seas during the winter, one letter survives, copied down alongside Richard's own letter, suggesting that the mayor had been vigilant in obeying the royal commands. The author purports to be none other than Henry Tudor himself, and the document a circular letter to his 'good friends and our allies', in which he states he has been 'given to understand your good devoir and intent to advance me to the furtherance of my rightful claim due and lineal inheritance of that crown'. As if recognising that his own flimsy claim to the throne would not be enough, Tudor's appeal to any potential supporters centred also on the man he hoped to replace, calling 'for the just depriving of that homicide and unnatural tyrant which now unjustly bears dominion over you . . . I give you to understand that no Christian heart can be more full of joy and gladness', the letter continued, 'than the heart of me your poor exiled friend who will upon the instance of your sure advertisement, what powers you will make ready and what captains and leaders you get to conduct, be prepared to pass over the sea with such forces as my friends here are preparing for me, and if I have such good speed and success as I wish according to your desire, I shall ever be most forward to remember and wholly to requite this your great and most loving kindness in my just quarrell'. In a clear sign that the letters had been part of an active recruiting drive through a network of secret messengers sent across the Channel, a postscript read: 'I pray you give credence to the messenger of that he shall impart to you.' The letter noted that it had been 'given under our signet'; signed with the regal monograph, 'H.R'.[32]

Just a year earlier, in October 1483, he had avoided the use of the royal style, instead using his traditional signature, 'Henry de Richemont'.[33] Now, for the first time, Henry was setting out his own right to rule, and his claim to the throne. To claim the crown formally even before he had set foot in

England was a bold and unheard-of step. Neither Henry Bolingbroke in 1399 nor Edward IV in 1471 had made their intentions known, asserting that they simply wished to be restored to their dukedoms instead. It seems that the price for French support had been for Henry to declare his intention to usurp the throne, causing maximum possible disruption to English affairs; in his letter of 3 November to Toulon, Charles VIII had boasted of the English divisions that he was now determined to exploit. Henry, he wrote, had arrived in France, 'in order to recover the realm of England from the enemies of France'; Henry's own claim to the throne rested, the letter continued, on him being the younger son of Henry VI.[34] This was patently false, but Charles VIII and his guardian, Anne of Beaujeu, needed a propaganda coup to bolster their flagging regime against the criticisms of Louis, duke of Orléans. With growing fears that Richard III would join forces with Brittany and Burgundy against France, the arrival of Henry Tudor offered an opportunity to not only hold England to account, but to turn the tables on the Orléanist faction. Few of the general French population would have known of Henry Tudor's true origins, but the news that the government had secured possession of a Lancastrian heir to the throne would certainly have resonated.

With news that Tudor and the French were sending letters calling for Richard's deposition into the country, military preparations would be stepped up, beginning with the issuing of a commission of array on 8 December for all counties. Detailed instructions to commissioners for gathering and inspecting every man and their weapons were issued, with commissioners instructed first to 'thank the people for their true and loving dispositions showed to his highness the last year for the surety and defence of his most royal person . . . exhorting them so to continue', before ensuring 'they be able men and well horsed and harnessed and no rascal, and to endeavour them to increase the number by their wisdoms and policies if they can'.[35] The commissions of array coincided with the publication of a proclamation, condemning Henry Tudor and the rebels as if they were an extension of the rebellions that had taken place the previous autumn.[36] The rebels had taken as 'their captain . . . one Henry late calling himself Earl of Richmond', who through his own ambition and 'insatiable covetousness' and being 'stirred and excited' by the rebels, 'encroacheth upon him the name and title of Royal estate of this Realm of England, whereunto he hath no manner, interest, right or colour as every man well knoweth'. The news that Henry was currently in French hands would be used to full effect, castigating the earl for taking financial support from England's oldest enemies. Richard warned that Henry had struck a deal with France, who had 'bargained with him' to give up all claims that the kings of England had 'and ought to have' to the French crown, as well as forfeiting the English possessions of Calais, Guines and Hammes.

Beside this 'greatest . . . shame and rebuke that ever might fall to this land', Richard warned that Henry and the rebels 'intended at their coming to do the most cruel murders, slaughters, robberies and disinheritances that ever were seen in any Christian Realm'. In order to prevent these 'inestimable dangers' and to ensure the king's rebels 'may either be utterly put from their said malicious purposes or soon discomfited if they enforce to land', Richard commanded that every one of his subjects:

> like good and true English men to endeavour themselves and all their powers for the defence of themselves, their wives, children, goods and inheritances against the said malicious purposes and conspiracies which the ancient enemies of this land have made with the king's said rebels for the final destruction of the same land as is aforesaid. And our said sovereign lord as a well willed diligent and courageous prince will put his most royal person to all labour and pain necessary in this behalf for the resistance and subduing of his said enemies, rebels, and traitors to the most comfort, weal and surety of all and singular his true and faithful liegemen and subjects.[37]

At the same time, a separate proclamation declared how 'the king's grace willeth that for the love that he hath for the ministration and execution of Justice for the common wealth of this realm . . . if any person findeth grieved of murder, manslaughter, extortion, oppression or any other injury or wrong contrary to justice, done by any officer or any other person' they were to 'show it to the king's grace and according to Justice and his laws they shall have remedy'.[38] The timing of the proclamation, coinciding with the king's attack against Tudor, was hardly subtle. Regardless of its noble statements and professions of justice, it more than suggests that, above all, Richard viewed such statements and their intent principally as a means by which to secure popular support.[39]

Meanwhile, Richard continued his negotiations with Brittany. By 20 December, Duke Francis II agreed to send an embassy to England to discuss the extension of the truce. On 2 March, this was finally agreed, with an announcement that the arrangement would last until 1492. To the French, England's renewal of the Breton truce appeared a direct threat to France's own security, while many believed that an English attack was now a real possibility. It seemed that France was also on the brink of civil war: in January 1485, Louis of Orléans formally announced his intention to liberate Charles VIII from his sister, Anne of Beaujeu. At the same time the worsening situation in the Netherlands was proving an increasing distraction for the French government: since the death of Mary of Burgundy in 1482, the Flemish towns of Ghent, Bruges and Ypres had been running the country in the name of the infant archduke, Philip, refusing to accept the regency of Philip's father, Maximilian of Austria. With the Flemish towns adopting a Francophile policy, there were potential major gains to be had. In November and December 1484, armies were raised on both sides, with war breaking out in January 1485. It was hardly surprising that Henry Tudor's mission would no longer be viewed as an immediate priority by the French. According to Vergil, Richard 'understood from making investigations that Henry was wearying of begging the French for aid to be gone, was gaining nothing and making no progress'. The news came as a comfort, yet Richard was taking nothing for granted. 'So as not to be unprepared for attack', Vergil wrote, 'he commanded the nobles living around the sea coast, and chiefly the Welsh to keep watch so that the approach to the kingdom would not lie open to his adversaries.'[40]

It was during the Christmas celebrations of 1484 that Edward IV's daughters, Elizabeth, now aged eighteen, and Cecily, fifteen, were allowed to take part in the court festivities. Elizabeth made an instant impression. According to the Crowland chronicler, Elizabeth's conduct was among the 'things unbefitting' and 'evil examples' which should not sully 'the minds of the faithless': 'There are many other things besides, which are not written in this book and of which it is grievous to speak', yet the chronicler admitted that 'nevertheless it should not be left unsaid that during this Christmas feast too much attention was paid to singing and dancing and to vain exchanges of clothing between Queen Anne and Lady Elizabeth, who were alike in complexion and figure. The people spoke against this and the magnates and prelates were greatly astonished.'[41] The chronicler's censorious comments may reflect his own ecclesiastical background, writing for a monastic audience, yet they also point not only to the lavish nature of Richard's court, but also to the striking observation that Elizabeth of York and the queen should have been seen as close. Only the previous year, Richard had effectively disinherited Elizabeth when he had declared her brothers illegitimate; if this was the case, why should Elizabeth be allowed to share the rich silks of gold and purple traditionally associated with royalty? To observers, comparing the queen and Elizabeth together, they seemed so alike as to be disconcerting; what else was being reported upon, those 'evil examples' that the chronicler spoke of, it is impossible to know. Yet it was from this moment that rumours surrounding Elizabeth's own position at Richard's court had begun to swirl.

The welcoming of his nieces to court was just one part of Richard's strategy of reconciliation with the Woodvilles and their supporters. Elizabeth Woodville and other English exiles had supported Henry Tudor's attempt to seize the throne on the condition that he marry Elizabeth of York, a concession that they had been so insistent upon that Henry had been forced to swear an oath the previous year. Now Henry's declaration of his claim in writing, basing it on lineal descent, suggested that Tudor was prepared to base his claim to the throne not on marriage to Edward IV's daughter, crowning her rightful queen, but on his own Beaufort descent, meaning nothing less than a Lancastrian restoration to the throne. The arrival at Henry's exiled court of the Lancastrian earl of Oxford, who had never recognised the Yorkist dynasty, must have been equally concerning. Richard was quick to recognise the Woodville discomfort at Tudor's new positioning. In an effort to destabilise the English exile community, who were principally from the Yorkist establishment and entirely unwilling to countenance a wholesale Lancastrian restoration, Richard was prepared to extend the offer of pardon to former rebels now willing to come back into the fold. On 12 January 1485, the queen's brother, Richard Woodville, and Sir John Fogge bound themselves to the king in a recognisance for the sum of 1,000 marks to 'bear themselves well and faithfully'. Their pardons followed in February and March, along with a pardon for the Woodville kinsman and rebel Richard Haute.[42] During the first five months of 1485, several other former rebels were persuaded to accept Richard's authority, and accepted pardon, including Reginald Pympe, Roger Tocotes, Amyas Paulet and William Ovedale.[43] Robert Radcliffe, who had been an early supporter of Edward Woodville and had previously been declared a traitor by Richard as Protector, was also welcomed back and rewarded by Richard in April.[44]

Encouraged by the treatment of her daughters, Queen Elizabeth also seems to have been in contact with her exiled brother, Edward, and son, Thomas, urging them to defect from Henry's camp. Thomas, marquess of Dorset, had found himself sidelined after Oxford's arrival, and increasingly despondent at the lack of enthusiasm of the French government to support their cause. 'Not expecting any good to come from Henry's approaches', and having been in contact with his mother, he became 'enticed by rewards and many promises from Richard'.[45] Dorset chose to desert Henry's camp in Paris, and fled in secret, his destination Flanders, where he intended to board a boat to return to England. When Henry learnt of Dorset's flight, he became 'greatly disturbed in mind', in particular since the marquess had been a close confidant, and 'privy to all their deliberations'. Henry had to act fast to prevent Dorset from betraying his plans to Richard. Men were sent out 'in all directions' to pursue the marquess: eventually he was captured by Humphrey Cheyney and Matthew Baker, 'taking a short cut through a field', who placed Dorset temporarily in custody in Lyon Castle.[46]

Still a slow drip of rebels continued to cross the seas to join Henry's exiled community. The rebel William Berkeley of Beverstone had been pardoned in March 1484, after his uncle, Edward, and brother-in-law, John, Lord Stourton, had put up a bond of 1,000 marks for his good behaviour. By the end of the year, however, Berkeley had chosen to flee to Henry, leaving his own family to foot the bill.[47] Others included John Mortimer, an esquire of the king's body, while Piers Curteys, the Keeper of the King's Great Wardrobe, who had worked assiduously to prepare for the king's coronation, forfeited both his land and office to take refuge in sanctuary.[48] Tudor was also being supplied with money and goods from several London merchants, with the draper William Bret purchasing six 'curas called harneys', twelve pairs of brigandines and twenty-four sallets for £37.[49]

Richard would celebrate Christmas at court in confident anticipation that he would be able to crush any future rebellion by Henry Tudor in the forthcoming year. At the feast of Epiphany, 6 January, Richard appeared wearing the royal crown, and took such a prominent role in the festivities taking place in Westminster Hall, it seemed as if he was re-creating 'his original coronation'.[50] The same day, Richard was taken aside to hear the latest report from his spies, who had sent back new information from the continent. They brought back news that Henry Tudor and the English exiles abroad were planning an invasion, which would now take place that summer. 'Without any doubt, his enemies would invade the kingdom or make an attempt, as soon as the summer came.'[51] Richard's initial reaction was not what had perhaps been expected. 'He wanted nothing better than this', the Crowland chronicler reported, 'since it might well be thought that it would put an end to all his doubts and misfortunes'.[52]

19

'GRIEF AND DISPLEASURE'

Shortly after the Christmas festivities, the Crowland chronicler wrote how Queen Anne 'fell extremely sick'. As her illness 'increased more and more', Richard chose to sleep in separate apartments to the queen.[1] According to Vergil, Richard 'desired the death of his wife Anne, which in any way he decided to accelerate'; however, the king feared that, in doing so, he might 'offend opinion . . . when he believed he had engendered goodwill in the people'.[2] Instead, the Italian believed, Richard chose to alienate his wife slowly and subtly: 'First he abstained from their conjugal bed and at the same time now and again complained to everyone, and especially to Thomas Rotherham, archbishop of York, whom a little before he had released from custody, that she had not given birth.' Rotherham believed that it was a sign that 'the queen would not live long', feeling confident enough to tell his own friends.[3] Rotherham seems an unusual confidant for Richard to divulge such personal information, especially given that he had been removed from office for handing over the Great Seal to Elizabeth Woodville, but perhaps it had been Richard's intent to ensure that news of his wife's demise should deliberately reach Woodville circles as part of a planned attempt at public disinformation about the queen's health.

Vergil believed that the king himself 'took care to start a rumour, from an unknown source, among the people concerning the death of his wife the queen, so namely either the woman being affected with anguish by the rumour had fallen into sickness, and perished, or he could judge how the people would perceive it'. When Anne discovered that the rumour of her imminent death was 'spreading among the people', determined to discover the cause, 'she approached her husband, sad and weeping lamentably, and asked him why he wished to be free of her'. Richard replied 'consolingly' and 'bade her be of good cheer'.[4]

Vergil's highly partisan account cannot be corroborated; however, the Crowland chronicler observed that after 'the queen began to be seriously ill', her sickness 'was then believed to have got worse and worse'; as a result, Richard 'was completely spurning his consort's bed' having 'judged it right to consult with doctors'.[5] This seems a more likely account of the real situation: Anne had fallen seriously ill, possibly with an infectious disease such as tuberculosis, on account of which the king was forced to sleep in separate chambers, only driving further rumours that Richard intended to leave the queen and marry another.

By now, rumours had begun to spread that the king had expressed an unlikely interest in marrying his own niece, Elizabeth of York. 'It was said by many that the king was applying his mind in every way to contracting a marriage with Elizabeth either after the death of the queen, or by means of a divorce for which he believed he had sufficient grounds. He saw no other way of confirming his crown and dispelling the hopes of his rival', the Crowland chronicler later observed.[6]

An inscription found in the copy of the French prose *Tristan*, which had once belonged to Richard, is that of Elizabeth's own signature and motto, 'sans removyr, Elyzabeth': previously Elizabeth had signed herself 'Elizabeth the Queen's daughter', which suggests that at the time of signing the book, she was unable to call herself princess. Did Elizabeth borrow the book from her uncle, or did Richard give her the book himself? Another inscription among the books of the royal library is more intriguing still. At the end of the book, a French verse translation of Boethius's *De consolation philosophiae*, Elizabeth has signed the book not with her own motto, but with Richard's own, 'Loyaulte Me Lye', although in spite of her careful handwriting, Elizabeth made an error in writing 'loyaulte' and was later to insert the letter 'y' over the word. Scribbles throughout the work, in a fifteenth-century hand, show a particular interest in the changing nature of fortune. Perhaps in making use of her uncle's motto, Elizabeth had re-signed herself to her own change in fortune, accepting Richard as king.[7]

Another piece of evidence is a transcript of a letter, apparently written by Elizabeth of York to John, duke of Norfolk, in February 1485, which was shown to the antiquary George Buck by the earl of Arundel in the seventeenth century. According to the letter, the contents of which were summarised by Buck, Elizabeth 'being very desirous to be married', had written to Howard that she knew how much 'the king her father much loved him, and that he was a very faithful servant unto him and to the king his brother then reigning, and very loving and serviceable to King Edward's children':

> First she thanked him for his many courtesies and friendly offices and then she prayed him as before to be a mediator for her in the cause of the marriage with the king, who, as she wrote, was her only joy and maker in this world, and that she was his in heart and thoughts, in body and in all. And then she intimated that the better half of February was past and that she feared the queen would never die.[8]

On first impression, the letter, if taken at face value, seems to corroborate the rumours circulating around the court, that Richard and Elizabeth were close before his wife had died; yet closer inspection of Buck's work reveals that Sir George made significant additions to the first draft of his original notes, including, crucially, the words 'in the cause of the marriage'. Written without the later additions, it can be read that Elizabeth 'prayed him to be a mediator for her to the king', which hardly implies that marriage was on the cards.[9] Even if Buck made his revisions in good faith, the words 'the cause of the marriage with the king' need not specifically have to refer to a marriage to her uncle, but instead could plausibly refer to Richard's negotiations on her behalf to marry her to another eligible bridegroom. Already Richard had married her younger sister Cecily off to Ralph Scrope of Upsall, a younger brother of Thomas Scrope, Lord Scrope of Masham; Elizabeth expected that, according to Richard's declaration the previous year, he would soon arrange her marriage. It is perhaps this sense of anticipation that can be read into the letter, if the original did indeed exist.

On 16 March, Queen Anne died at Westminster, her death in the morning occurring ominously, as was noted by the Crowland chronicler, 'on the day when the great eclipse of the sun took place'.[10] There is no record of what grief Richard suffered, though surviving records reveal that the king,

in the final days of the queen's life, seems to have taken to hunting with hawks, a distraction from the realities of life and the burden of his office. On 8 March, John Mountguy, Sergeant of the King's Hawks, was ordered to 'purvey and take at price reasonable in any place' within the realm falcons and hawks 'as by him shall be thought convenient for the king's disports'.[11] Three days later, John Gaynes was granted a passport 'to go into the parties beyond the sea with four persons in his company to purvey hawks for the king', while, on 27 March, Walter Bothnam was sent into Wales and the marches, again with a mission to 'provide and take at price reasonable ... all manner other hawks such as he shall think necessary for the king's disports'.[12]

Queen Anne's illness and death seem to have prompted Richard to contemplate his own mortality, in spite of the fact that he was only thirty-two, with his thoughts returning to the establishment of foundations in his name. In particular, at his planned foundation at York, the costs of the wages of a hundred priests remained unpaid. On 2 March 1485, Richard wrote ordering that 'wherefore we not willing our said priests to be unpaid of their wages, seeing by their prayers we trust to be made more acceptable to God and his saints, will and straightly charge you that ye do content and pay' to the church officials at York 'all and any sum of money which hath grown or hereafter shall grow'.[13] The following day, in a letter to the Exchequer, two weeks before Anne's death, payments were made 'to the household of our most dear wife the Queen'.[14] Still, Richard saw fit only to bury Anne at Westminster Abbey, 'by the south door that led to St Edward's Chapel', rather than at any of her Neville family mausoleums at Bisham, Warwick or Tewkesbury or her own colleges of Barnard Castle, Middleham and York, with a funeral costing only a few hundred pounds, though the Crowland chronicler described how Anne had been buried 'with honours no less than befitted the burial of a queen'.[15]

Richard had already begun marriage negotiations for a new bride across the seas. While the negotiations remained secret, allowing rumours surrounding his relationship with Elizabeth of York to murmur on, they demonstrate that Richard, no doubt anxious to secure his own dynasty with a male heir, was clearly looking elsewhere for a bride. On 22 March, Richard wrote from Westminster how 'we have at this time by the advise of our council advised and appointed our trusty and right wellbeloved Sir

Edward Brampton . . . to pass out of this our realm unto the parts of Portugal', where he was to be sent on ambassadorial duties, 'to do as we have commanded him on our behalf'. For his journey, Brampton was given 100 marks.[16] His mission was to negotiate a marriage for the king; Richard's intended bride was Joanna of Portugal, the daughter of King Alfonso of Portugal. The Portuguese Council of State recommended that the king's sister accept the projected English marriage, in particular 'for the concord in the same kingdom of England that will follow from her marriage and union with the king's party, greatly serving God and bringing honour to herself by uniting as one the party of Lancaster, and York, which are the two parties of that kingdom out of which the divisions and evils over the succession are born'.[17] It would later be reported that the Portuguese council had been anxious to accept the marriage suit as soon as possible, for they openly feared that otherwise Richard 'could marry the Infanta Dona Isabel of Castile, and make alliance with those kings. If the marriage to the Infanta Joanna was not progressed swiftly enough, they warned, 'the sovereigns of Castile may give him their eldest daughter as his wife', noting with some alarm that 'it suits the king of England to marry straight away'. It would later be reported how King John 'bullied and brow beat' Joanna into submission, employing her aunt, Philippa, 'to try more feminine means of persuasion'.[18]

In fact, Brampton had not just come to negotiate a marriage for the king; he arrived with letters proposing a double marriage. Not only would Richard marry Joanna, to act as a sweetener for the Portuguese, but Brampton also offered Elizabeth of York's hand to John II's cousin, Manuel, duke of Beja. The contemporary observer Alvaro Lopes de Chaves wrote three years later how this was sold as a 'marriage between the daughter of King Edward of England . . . and the Duke of Beja', while Brampton had arrived 'to swear the betrothals and commit the Princess Joanna in marriage'.[19]

Meanwhile in London it was reported that there was 'much simple communication among the people by evil disposed persons contrived and sown to the very great displeasure of the King showing that the queen as by consent and will of the King was poisoned for and to the attend that he might then marry and have to wife lady Elizabeth'.[20] According to the *Great Chronicle* of London, 'after Easter' there was 'much whispering among the people that the king had put the children of King Edward to death, and also that he had poisoned the queen his wife, and intended with a licence purchased to have married the elder daughter of King Edward. Which rumours and sayings with other things have caused him to fall in much hatred of his subjects as well as men of good behaviour as of others. But how so the queen were dealt with, were it by his means of the visitation of God, she died shortly after . . . which was a woman of gracious fame.'[21]

Richard called a meeting of the council, where he was forced to 'make his excuses at length, saying that such a thing never entered his mind'. Some were not convinced, the Crowland chronicler observed, especially those 'at that council who knew well enough that the contrary was true'. They included Richard Ratcliffe and William Catesby, to 'whose opinions the king hardly ever dared offer any opposition'. Both remained resolute that the marriage would not take place, not least for their own self-interest. 'It was supposed by many, that these men, together with others like them, threw so many impediments in the way, for fear lest, if the said Elizabeth should attain the rank of queen, it might at some time be in her power to avenge upon them the death of her uncle, Earl Anthony, and her brother Richard, they having been the king's especial advisers in those matters.' Ratcliffe and Catesby confronted Richard at the meeting and 'to his face' told him that the 'people of the North' would rise in rebellion if he were to marry Elizabeth. To emphasise their point, they brought with them 'more than twelve' doctors of divinity to tell him that the pope would not grant a dispensation to such a close blood relative.[22]

Richard needed to take action to dispel rumours of his marriage from spreading any further. On 30 March, in the great hall of the Hospital of St John of Jerusalem, in front of the mayor and aldermen of the city, and 'many of his lords and of much other people', Richard gave an outright denial of the accusations. His 'grief and displeasure' clearly evident, according to the account given in the minutes of the city's Acts of Court, the king declared that 'it never came in his thought or mind to marry in such manner wise nor willing or glad of the death of his queen but as sorry and in heart as man might be, with much more in the premises spoken'. Richard then 'admonished and charged every person to cease of such untrue talking on parcel of his indignation'. Any person caught spreading 'any of this foresaid untrue surmised talking' was to be arrested and punished by the mayor. According to the Crowland chronicler, the king spoke in 'a clear, loud voice' and 'carried out fully the advice to make a denial of this kind – as many people believed, more by the will of these councillors than by his own'.[23] Richard decided to take further action against the rumours, sending letters to be read out across the country. A letter written by the king on 5 April was read to the council at York two weeks later, describing how 'divers and seditious and evil disposed persons both in our city of London and elsewhere within this our realm' had daily sown 'seed of noise . . . against our person and against many of the lords and estates of our land . . . some by setting up of bills, some by messages and sending forth of false and abominable language and lies some by bold and presumptuous open speech and communication one with another'.[24]

Whether the rumours surrounding Richard's plans to marry his niece were true or not, what matters is that they were believed, even by close members of his council such as Richard Ratcliffe and William Catesby, to the extent that the king, extraordinarily, had been forced to publicly deny them. The fact that Richard had been forced to make such a submission not only demonstrates the remarkable sway that Catesby and Ratcliffe had on his own judgement, but also the striking dependence that Richard placed on his Neville connection.

Rumours of Richard's plan to marry his niece Elizabeth soon reached the continent, where news of Queen Anne's death had already added to the suspicions. During the spring of 1485, Henry Tudor had departed for Rouen, before arriving at Harfleur, where, at the mouth of the River Seine, he began to prepare his invasion fleet. Believing the rumours to be true, Henry, 'suddenly seized with anxiety', communicated his fears to the earl of Oxford that 'if Richard were to marry the eldest daughter of Edward he would not be able with honour to take any other of the sisters and however if he did not do so he feared that all Edward's friends would abandon him'. Oxford agreed; instead both men decided that another marriage alliance should be investigated, 'as a way of having honour which could be a protection in such a crisis'.[25]

Henry looked to reach out to old friends. In particular he remembered those connections that he had fostered at an early age while he had grown up in the household of William Herbert, earl of Pembroke. Henry remembered the earl's daughter, 'of marriageable age whom Henry, nurtured in the earl's hall, knew well and loved'. Henry now sought to make a separate alliance with Walter Herbert and Henry, earl of Northumberland, who was married to another one of the Herbert sisters. Vergil related how 'as soon as he could he sent Christopher Urswick to Scotland, pretending that he meant him to go another way, by means of trusted messengers, to treat for a new marriage alliance with Henry earl of Northumberland to whom one of Walter's sister was married'. Yet Urswick's mission was to prove a failure. 'When Christopher set off he found no-one in Scotland to whom he would dare give the order to the earl' and he was forced to return to Henry 'with his mission unaccomplished'.[26]

'While everything was uncertain', Henry also took into his confidence Richard Fox, 'a man distinguished both for good character and good ability', to discuss the invasion plans should any proposed marriage alliance fail to materialise. Both men agreed that 'it would for the good of all to hurry things along'.[27] Henry had decided to return to his ships on the Seine, when he received a message from John Morgan that if he arrived in Wales, he would be welcomed by Rhys ap Thomas, John Savage and 'a not inconsiderable sum of money' that had been gathered by Reginald Bray.[28]

Good news was also forthcoming from the French government. Under pressure from what seemed a growing threat of the build-up of the English navy in the Channel, Charles VIII and his advisers resolved to give final backing to Henry Tudor to launch an invasion upon England. On 4 May an *ordonnance* was presented to the Estates, seeking further financial assistance in order to help Henry Tudor.[29] Shortly afterwards, Henry would receive an additional 40,000 *livres tournois* – around £4,400 – to support his invasion. Yet only a first instalment of 10,000 livres was to be paid immediately. There is no evidence that the rest of the money ever arrived, as the Beaujeu regime had intended to provide Henry with enough money to start his preparations for an invasion, but no more. Eventually, a further 30,000 livres were obtained in a loan taken out at Paris on 13 July, though Henry was forced to leave Thomas, marquess of Dorset, and John Bourchier, Lord Fitzwarin, behind as hostages as surety for the loan. The choice of Dorset and Fitzwarin as pledges was an entirely deliberate ploy on the part of the French; for if Henry's invasion attempt failed, the possession of the only two Yorkist lords in his army represented their best chance of getting their money back.[30] Meanwhile, Henry Tudor continued to gather together an army of men, mainly mercenaries from the disbanded military camp of the Pont-de-l'Arche that had been established by Philippe de Crève-coeur, Seigneur d'Esquerdes. There is no evidence that Esquerdes ever joined Tudor's army himself; instead it would be the professional soldier of fortune, Philibert de Chandée, who had no connection to the Beaujeu government, who would be entrusted with leading Henry's mercenaries. It was hardly promising; Commynes summed up the French support as 'a little money from the king, and some three thousand of the most unruly men that could be found and enlisted in Normandy'.[31]

Throughout all this, Richard's preparations for the defence of his realm had been intensifying. On 13 January, Richard's loyal henchman, Sir James Tyrell, having been sent to Flanders during the winter to seek out assis-tance from Maximilian of Austria and Burgundy, had been appointed to take command of Guisnes Castle, while preparations were made to ship a force from Dover to Calais. The same day, a commission was sent to all knights, squires and gentlemen in Cheshire, 'showing that the king hath deputed the lord Stanley, the lord Strange and Sir William Stanley to have the rule and leading of all persons appointed to do the king service when they be warned against the king's rebels'. The men were to be ready to assist the Stanleys, with 'all the power that they can make . . . if any rebels arrive in those parts'.[32] On 15 January, £140 6s was spent on over 3,000 bowstaves, to be sent to Southampton, while orders were sent out for the purchase of several ships for the king's fleet.[33]

Richard was still struggling to deal with the situation at the Hammes garrison, whose men had now pledged their loyalty to Henry Tudor. Early in the New Year, Richard ordered that the garrison be placed under siege with 'war machines' sent from Calais; however, when those inside the castle discovered the king's men approaching, messages were sent to Tudor's camp with requests for military support. Soon the earl of Oxford along with Thomas Brandon and 'many other warriors' returned to Hammes to assist the beleaguered garrison. Positioning themselves not far from the castle, Brandon and thirty men managed to enter the castle via a nearby swamp, and once within its walls were able to drive their attackers away, while the earl of Oxford 'was no less energetic as he attacked from behind'.[34] The earl's assault proved enough for those inside the castle, led by Thomas Blount's wife, to be able to escape the siege from Richard's forces. Vergil wrote how many, 'leaving the castle, returned with his company safe to Paris and Henry'.

Even those who had not rebelled were to find themselves blamed for the debacle. The Essex knight Thomas Montgomery, an established supporter of the Yorkist household, had been rewarded with land in Essex valued at £412 in February 1484, at the same time as being appointed Master Forester and Steward of the King's Forests.[34] During the illness of Lord Mountjoy, the lieutenant of the Guisnes garrison, Montgomery, had been deputised as lieutenant; it seems that Richard held Montgomery partly to blame for what had happened over the debacle of Oxford's defection, for shortly afterwards Montgomery was removed from his post while the Essex lands he had been granted were instead transferred to an endowment for Richard's projected royal chapel of St Mary in the London church of All Hallows by the Tower.[36] The loyalty of Lord Mountjoy, the elder brother of Thomas Blount, was also in question, despite the fact that he was already seriously ill. On 22 January, Mountjoy was replaced by Sir James Tyrell. Tyrell already had important responsibilities keeping order and maintaining royal influence in Wales, yet now he was to be immediately sent to Guisnes, with officials in Glamorgan being ordered simply to 'accept [him] as their governor and leader as he hath been heretofore, notwithstanding that the king sendeth him to Guisnes'.[37] As for a replacement for Blount at Hammes, it would not be until mid-May 1485 that Thomas Wortley, a Yorkshire knight of the body to whom Richard had previously entrusted responsibility for forfeited Stafford estates in the north Midlands, would be sent to command the garrison there.[38]

But it was at Calais that Richard envisaged the greatest need to change leadership. Its governor, John, Lord Dynham, like James Blount, had been appointed under the previous regime by William, Lord Hastings; while Dynham had been prepared to accept Richard's accession, his letter to the king in late June 1483, querying the validity of the oaths the garrison had sworn to Edward V, had hardly endeared him to the king.[39] Dynham had taken an active role in besieging Hammes against Oxford, paid out of his own funds, though this was not enough to win back Richard's confidence, with the king possibly blaming failure of the siege on Dynham personally. Richard realised that he could not remove Dynham altogether, without the fear of recrimination and further defections from a garrison still loyal to the memory of Lord Hastings; instead he chose to create a level of command above him.

On 4 March, Richard appointed John of Gloucester, his illegitimate son, captain of Calais. Described in many surviving records as simply 'the Lord Bastard', in the patent detailing his appointment Richard described him as 'the most notable our dear bastard son ... whose disposition and natural vigour, agility of body and inclination to all good customs, promises us by the Grace of God great and certain hope of future service'.[40] Payments were also authorised on 3 March for the 'costs and expenses of all those that shall be assigned by our commission ... to resist or subdue our rebels or enemies', while the Master of the Ordnance was to be paid 'for all manner habiliments of war by sea and by land for the defence of this our realm and for the resistance of our rebels and enemies'.[41]

The military preparations were not without their costs. The Crowland chronicler observed that Richard was already struggling financially, with the king 'beginning to run very short'.[42] Richard was fully aware of the perilous state of the royal finances. Despite having an income of around £25,000 and the greatest landed income of his predecessors due to the scale and size of the attainders he had been able to pass as a result of Buckingham's rebellion, by now Richard had granted away over £12,000 of lands, with just a total of £735 in rent being paid back into the royal finances. The collapse in the wool trade had seen his revenues fall further, but it was the administration of the crown's estates that Richard was particularly concerned to attempt to reform. Late in 1484, a 'remembrance' for the 'hasty levy of the king's revenues growing of all his possessions' had been drawn up. Aside from recognising the delayed debts owed to the crown, the need for yearly audits of lordships by surveyors and greater efficiency in collecting customs, the document highlights the concerns facing Richard. Many lordships and manors, the remembrance noted, have been 'committed to divers persons ... by the which the king's woods and his courts with other casualties been wasted and lost to his great hurt'.[43] Allowances that had been granted for the repair of castles and manors had frequently been mis-spent, while the lordships themselves were failing to bring in the revenue expected. At the same time, there was concern that 'lords, knights and esquires, many of them not lettered' had been made stewards of the king's lands in several counties, where they had taken for themselves 'great fines and rewards of the king's tenants ... to the king's hurt and impoverishing of his said tenants'. Others lacked the 'cunning and discretion' to order and direct the king's business appropriately, 'with many more inconveniences'. Where possible, the document suggested, it would be 'most profitable' for stewards of the lordships to be 'learned men in the law ... for many causes concerning the king's profit and the weal of his tenants'.[44] Yet despite Richard's concern over the depletion and wastage of natural resources on crown land, the practices seem to have continued regardless, with wood sales replacing monetary transactions.[45] Three years later, in 1488, an enquiry into the condition of the New Forest found that 500 deer had been killed during Richard's reign by a group identified only as 'the northern men'.[46]

Emergency measures were taken to help restore the king's finances, with orders issued to Sir James Tyrrell on 20 January to take from the merchants of the Staple wool sacks worth £3,000, 'to sell and utter for our use and profit'.[47] In February, the convocation at Canterbury had voted for another clerical tenth, worth around £10,000. An additional £5,120 may have also been raised by the clergy. By late February, Richard decided to finance the extra cost of military operations and defences by sending out urgent appeals for loans to his nobility and gentry. Royal commissioners were appointed and given a copy of a letter from the king, with which to approach potential lenders. The decision to raise a benevolence was destined to be unpopular – this Richard must have known, having campaigned to end the practice during his brother's reign. The need to do so suggests that Richard was in serious financial difficulty.

Royal servants were assigned counties and were issued with individual letters, containing the amount of money requested, but most left with the names of the recipient blank, to be decided at their discretion. Along with a list of named individuals, potential lenders were to be approached for sums of money ranging from £40 to £200, with the commissioners given template letters in which they were to fill out the blanks, accruing to their 'politique and wise means'. To assist their work, the commissioners were provided with a 'remembrance' of words that they should attempt to use to persuade their pliant victims.

'Sir, the king's grace greeteth you well', the rubric ran:

> and desireth and heartily prayeth you that by way of loan ye will let him have such sum as his Grace hath written to you for; and ye shall truly have it again at such days as he hath showed and promised to you in his letters. And this he desireth to be employed for the defence and surety of his royal person and the weal of this his realm. And for that intent his Grace and all his lords, thinking that every true Englishman will help him in this behalf, of which number his Grace reputeth and taketh you for one; and that is the cause he this writeth to you before other, for the great love, confidence, and substance that his Grace hath and knoweth in you; which trusteth undoubtedly that ye, like a loving subject, will at this time accomplish this his desire.[48]

Richard had, the Crowland chronicler believed, 'resorted to the exactions of King Edward which he himself had condemned in Parliament, only avoiding in every case the word "benevolence".' Yet the practice seemed effectively the same; 'selected men were sent out', he wrote, 'who extorted great sums of money from the coffers of persons of almost every rank in the kingdom, by prayers or threats, by fair means or foul'.[49] The chronicler's view of Richard's financial activities may have been a poor one, but it seems to have been distorted by his belief that Richard had squandered and spent a large treasure left by Edward IV, a view that the surviving records of the financial legacy left to Edward V cannot sustain. In fact, the loans that Richard organised were not strictly in the same category as the benevolences of Edward IV that had been condemned in the previous Parliament. With repayment due by June 1486, Richard was still technically able to request the loans. Yet the Crowland chronicler's reaction may reflect the wider feeling of ill-will that the loans generated. The commissioners chosen by the king were almost all the king's household men, although where possible Richard used men who were native to their local counties, perhaps for local knowledge or to help sway local opinion. If Richard had hoped that this would lead to a rapid generation of income, he was to be disappointed. The commissioners were first provided with a number of unaddressed letters for various amounts, with the name left blank for the commissioners to fill in themselves once they had found a suitable donor. Three weeks after their original instructions they received a much longer and detailed list of men to be asked for specific sums. This suggests that attempts to bargain with local gentry figures to become potential lenders had proved more difficult than first thought. The status of the commissioners chosen must have been partly to blame. Once again they were not local figures, and came from humble backgrounds, such as was the case with Walter Grant, a yeoman of the queen's chamber who was appointed a commissioner for Worcestershire, Warwickshire and Leicestershire.[50]

Nevertheless, the surviving Exchequer records indicate that the loans did have some effect on revitalising Richard's ailing finances. The roll for Michaelmas 1484–5 indicates that royal revenue had more than doubled since Easter 1484, to a total of £18,720 18s, with large increases in the amount of cash raised from the customs, with Southampton bringing in a payment of £2,000 on 17 February. Fifty-four loans raised £4,485 in 1484.[51] By Easter 1485, revenue had increased to £24,496 5s 8½d, with the loans raising around £11,000, the highest total since 1478. Blank bonds amounting to £18,600 were to be placed by the king's agents where it was possible, but there was no guarantee that this money would be raised. In the end, less than a seventh of the hoped-for total for the blank bonds actually made it onto the receipt roll, with a total of £4,420 being raised from seventy-six loans.[52]

Still sedition continued, with a steady drip of conspiracies or rumours of conspiracies to come. One involved two fellows of Peterhouse at Cambridge, possibly connected to John Morton, while another involved a group of Sussex gentry, including Thomas and Roger Fiennes, and other gentlemen at Winchelsea.[53] In April, Edward Gower was ordered to seize the land of the 'king's rebel' John Peke, who previously had been bound over to appear before the royal council in October 1483.[54] On 29 April 1485, Ralph Ashton and Robert Rydon were appointed vice-constables to proceed against and try crimes of lèse-majesty 'summarily and plainly without noise and show of judgement on simple fault'.[55] On 2 May, Sir Robert Clifford, a Lancastrian knight who had been involved with

Buckingham's rebellion and captured at Southampton, was taken out of the Tower of London to be tried at Westminster. Found guilty, Clifford was to be dragged by a cart immediately to Tower Hill to be executed. Yet when Clifford passed by the church of St Martin's le Grand, with the help of a friar who had acted as his confessor 'and one of them that was next about him, his cords were so loosed or cut' that Clifford attempted to flee into sanctuary. 'And likely it had been ye he should haue so done', one chronicler noted, had it not been for the efforts of the sheriffs and the king's men, who forced him onto the ground and bound him tighter, and 'so harried him to the said place of execution, where he was divided in two pieces, and after his body with the head' was taken to Augustine Friars to be buried.[56]

Henry Tudor was never far from Richard's mind. 'At length rumours grew daily that those in rebellion against the king were making haste and speeding up the plans for their invasion of England', the Crowland chronicler wrote; Richard, however, remained uncertain as to where Tudor intended to land, 'for his spies were not able to bring any certain information'. Instead Lord Lovell was sent to near Southampton, 'to deploy his fleet carefully so as to keep a faithful watch on all the ports of those parts and not to miss the chance of engaging the enemy with the united forces of the whole neighbourhood if they tried to land there'. The chronicler remained highly critical of 'this unnecessary policy', which resulted in 'stores and money' being lost. 'The king incurred such great expenses so that he might not be deceived by the ambiguity of the name of the port which was said by many people to be chosen for descent', the chronicler noted, since 'some people, as though gifted with the spirit of prophecy, foretold that these men would land at the port of Milford'. Since there were two ports named Milford – a small bay near Southampton and the other, more familiar, location at Milford Haven in Pembrokeshire, and it was reckoned that 'such prophecies were customarily fulfilled not at the better known but most often at another place of the same name', Richard 'saw fit to set up so many forts, at this time in that southern part of the kingdom'.[57]

Preparations for war continued in earnest. On 18 June, Richard wrote to Edward Benstead, a gentleman usher of the chamber, ordering that he go to the Tower and 'shoot certain our guns we have been making there for their prove and assay' while they were to be 'stoked and cauted'. 'And also that the long scaling bridge that is making there' be finished, 'after the mind of him that devised the same.' Benstead was also to repay all creditors for the charges 'as shall grown from time to time . . . so that there be none exclamation upon our said servant by the said creditors'.[58] Calais too was victualled with an extra two barrels of gunpowder, three hundred-weight of lead and two serpentines.[59]

At Nottingham Castle on 21 June, Richard signed a warrant for a second proclamation against Henry, to be issued two days later. The text of the proclamation was mostly a reissue of the warrant that had been sent before, in December 1484; however, as if to underline Richard's own fury at Henry Tudor's pretensions to rule, new material was included to stress the illegitimate nature of Tudor's claim, not merely through Owen Tudor's relationship with Katherine of Valois, but by debasing the Beaufort line of his mother, Margaret, also. Henry, the 'captain' of the rebels, was merely:

> descended of bastard blood both of father side and of mother side, for the said Owen the grandfather was bastard born, and his mother was daughter unto John, Duke of Somerset, son unto John, Earl of Somerset, son unto Dame Kateryn Swynford, and of her in double avourty [adultery] gotten, whereby it evidently appeareth that no title can nor may be in him, which fully intendeth to enter this Realm, purposing a conquest. And if he should achieve his false intent and purpose, every man his life, livelihood, and goods should be in his hands, liberty and disposition, whereby should ensue the disinheriting and destruction of all the noble and worshipful blood of this Realm forever, and to the resistance and withstanding whereof every true and natural Englishman born must lay to his hands for his own surety and weal.

Revealingly, the revised text of the proclamation now stated how Henry not merely 'encroached' upon the royal title, but had now 'usurped upon him the name and title of royal estate of this Realm of England'.[60] Once again Richard set out the familiar claim from the previous proclamation that Henry, having obtained the 'assistance of the King's said ancient enemy of France', had struck a deal with the French king, Charles. The proclamation added one further detail, that Henry was planning to 'exclude the arms of France out of the arms of England for ever'. Perhaps Richard was gambling under the impression that Tudor was hardly likely to be allowed to sail from France and launch his invasion with French

mercenaries with his royal arms quartered with those of France. The proclamation then launched into what might be placed at risk by a successful
invasion; Richard had done so in the December proclamation, but now
chose to be more specific as to whose titles specifically might be at risk,
claiming that Tudor had already parcelled out rewards to his followers.

After the proclamation had been read, men were to be instantly prepared, with the king commanding 'all his said subjects to be ready in their
most defensible array to do his Highness' service of war, when there be
open proclamation, or otherwise shall be commanded so to do, for the
resistance of the King's said rebels, traitors and enemies'.[61] The following
day, 22 June, the king's proclamation was reinforced by the issuing of a
new commission of array that had also been sent out the previous December. 'Forasmuch as certain information is made unto us', the commission
declared, 'that our Rebels and traitors associated with our ancient enemies
of France and other strangers intend hastily to invade this our Realm
purposing the destruction of us, the subversion of this our Realm and
disinheriting of all our true subjects', all commissioners who had been appointed were now to muster their soldiers 'in all haste possible' according
to a set of instructions included with the orders. After the commissioners
had assembled their men, they were to thank them on the king's behalf,
'exhorting them so to continue'. The assembled forces were to be checked
to ensure they were 'able persons, well horsed and harnessed to do the king
service of war. And if they be not to put other able men into their places.'
The commissioners were to send letters in particular to all 'knights, squires
and gentlemen to prepare and ready themselves in their proper persons to
do the king service' upon an hour's warning, with the menacing threat
'that they fail not so to do upon the peril of lessening of their lives, lands
and goods'. Likewise the commissioners were to announce that 'all men be
ready to do the king service within an hour warning whensoever they be
commanded by proclamation or otherwise'. The same day, Richard sent
another letter to every sheriff, ordering that upon receiving their instructions from the Commissioners of Array, they were to remain within their
shire town or at least ensure that their deputy was present, in order to
assist the commissioners with their tasks, 'not failing hereof in any ways,
as ye will answer unto us at your uttermost peril'.[62]

Richard's orders were quickly acted upon. On 28 June 1485, the city of

London promised the king a loan of £2,000 'for the defence of the king against his rebels'.[63] The mayor, aldermen and commons of the city 'and specially every person as his true and faithful subject and friend' were ordered to 'have and be ready with his harness', though ominously orders were given that no man was 'to send or to loan any harness out of this city to any person, but to hold and keep it with him for the surety and safeguard of the King'.[64]

Preparations for battle were hard to miss. On 28 July, the city authorities in London ordered a new watch over the capital each night and mustered 3,178 citizens, from seventy-three companies. At Leadenhall, under four overseers, they rehearsed their proposed battle formation, with bowmen followed by two aldermen on horseback, followed by 'the brigandines', men in full body armour, then the mayor and two sheriffs on horseback, followed by 'armed men'. The remaining aldermen brought up the rear on horseback, with 'the jakkes', self-armed citizens wearing 'sleaveless tunics', at the very back.[65] Meanwhile back at Nottingham, Richard sent a letter to the Chancellor, John Russell, 'in which it was contained that the said chancellor for certain reasons moving the king' should send the Great Seal to the king by the Keeper of the Rolls, Thomas Barowe.[66] The last time that Richard had requested the Great Seal to be in his personal possession had been after the outbreak of rebellion back in autumn 1483. On Friday, 29 July, Russell handed over the seal to Barowe. Two days later, on 1 August, Barowe arrived at Nottingham Castle, carrying the Great Seal in a white leather bag, sealed with Bishop Russell's signet, bearing the image of an eagle. At seven o'clock in the evening, in the oratory of the chapel of the castle, and in the presence of the archbishop of York, John, earl of Lincoln, Thomas, Lord Scrope, George, Lord Strange, and the king's secretary, John Kendall, Barowe delivered the seal to Richard, 'whereupon the king, for causes and considerations him moving', returned the seal into Barowe's hands, appointing him Keeper of the Great Seal 'then and there'.[67]

With the Great Seal in Richard's hands and preparations for war made, all that was needed was to wait for Henry Tudor's arrival.

20

'INTENDING OUR UTTER DESTRUCTION'

The same day that Richard received the Great Seal at Nottingham, across the Channel at Le Havre port, nestled in the mouth of the Seine, Henry Tudor sensed that, with a favourable breeze blowing westwards, the time had come to set sail. For weeks, together with his band of exiles, he had busied himself preparing a fleet of thirty ships, to be commanded by the French naval captain Philippe de Crèvecoeur. Crèvecoeur, a noted pirate of the seas who had launched a campaign against English ships in the Channel shortly after Edward IV's death, was not the only suspect character whom Tudor had come to rely upon for his final invasion. Henry had long understood that he would be unable to invade England with the small band of Englishmen who had clustered around him, their loyalty forged only through the desperation of their circumstances. His uncle Jasper and the earl of Oxford aside, many of his followers who had joined him in exile had been devout Yorkists who had fought against Henry's Lancastrian relatives in previous battles. To shore up his invasion force, Henry would have to pay men to fight his cause, and recruited 2,000 mercenaries from the remnants of a standing army based at the nearby Pont d'Arche, men described as no less than 'beggarly Bretons', and 'of the worst sort, raised from the refuse of the people', with other reports that some French soldiers had been gathered from Norman gaols.[1]

Henry also knew that his ultimate success would lie not in the strength of his invading party, but in the strength of support that he would be able to gather upon landing. His bitter memories of the abortive landing at Poole Harbour in November 1483, when Richard's armed soldiers had lined the coast, while wild storms had beaten his ships back to Normandy, had caused him to think twice about launching a second invasion on the south coast, where Richard had strengthened his military defences. It seems that Henry had taken the decision to land in Wales in early 1485, after receiving news that the Welshmen John Morgan, Rhys ap Thomas and John Savage would be prepared to defect to his cause. Henry's uncle Jasper, as earl of Pembroke, remained a popular figure in the region, while Welsh bards such as Robin Dhu had already begun to pen their verse, welcoming Henry as their saviour, stating, 'we look forward to the coming of Henry; our nation puts its trust in him'.[2]

Henry made landfall a week after his flotilla had sailed out of the mouth of the Seine, not at Milford on the south coast, as Richard had been told to expect by his informers, but instead at the small hidden cove of Mill Bay, near the village of Dale on the northern shore of the Milford estuary. 'Judge me, O Lord, and determine my cause', Henry is supposed to have cried while kneeling down in the sands. His army quickly advanced northwards, making its way through Haverfordwest and Cardigan to Machynlleth within a week.

On 11 August, Richard was at his hunting lodge at Beskwood, near Nottingham, when he was informed that Henry Tudor had landed. According to the Crowland chronicler, 'on hearing of their arrival, the king rejoiced, or at least seemed to rejoice, writing to his adherents in every quarter that now the long-wished-for day had arrived, for him to triumph with ease over so contemptible a faction, and thenceforth benefit his subjects with the blessings of uninterrupted tranquillity'.[3] Vergil wrote that Richard soon learnt from his spies that Tudor's army 'did not exceed two thousand men', and remained confident that Walter Herbert and Rhys ap Thomas, whom he had tasked with defending Wales and the Marches, 'in whose valour he had great confidence, would easily put an end' to Tudor's march.

Richard did not waste any time in mobilising his forces in all areas of the realm. With the commissions of array having been issued in June, the country had remained on a war footing, with men prepared to mobilise their weapons and march towards the king with a day's notice. Messages were sent to Henry, earl of Northumberland, 'in whom he had great confidence' to muster a force in the north and 'to come with speed to him at

Nottingham', while, 'with many messages and letters', Sir Robert Brackenbury was summoned to the king's presence, and instructed to arrange
transport of the weapons and ordnance in the Tower of London, with
further orders to 'bring with him as fellows in war Thomas Bourchier,
Walter Hungerford and many others, men of the equestrian order, whom
he had suspicion of'. Meanwhile, 'manifold letters' were sent throughout
the realm, containing 'orders of the greatest severity, commanding that no
men . . . should shun taking part in the approaching warfare', with Richard
threatening that 'whoever should be found in any part of the kingdom
after the victory should have been gained, to have omitted appearing in
his presence on the field, was to expect no other fate than the loss of all his
goods and possessions, as well as his life'.⁴

Evidence of Richard's determination to raise men at all costs can be
found in a surviving letter given under Richard's sign manual, 'given
under our signet at our lodge of Beskwood the xi day of August', addressed
to Henry Vernon, a squire of the king's body, and his brother Richard
Vernon. 'Trusty and welbeloved we greet you well', the letter begins:

> And forasmuch as our rebels and traitors accompanied with our ancient
> enemies of France and other strange nations departed out of the water of
> the Seine the first day of this present month making their course westwards
> been landed at Nangle [Angle] besides Milford Haven in Wales on Sunday
> last passed, as we be credibly informed, intending our utter destruction, the
> extreme subversion of this our realm and disinheriting of our true subjects
> of the same, towards whose re-countering, God being our guide, we be
> utterly determined in our own person to remove in all haste goodly that
> we can or may. Wherefore we will and straightly charge you that ye in your
> person with such number as ye have promised unto us sufficiently horsed
> and harnessed be with us in all haste to you possible, to give unto us your
> attendance without failing, all manner [of] excuses set apart, upon pain of
> forfeiture unto us of all that ye may forfeit and lose.⁵

Roger Wake later wrote how he had journeyed to Richard's forces at
Nottingham 'against his will and mind' since the king's letters commanded him 'upon pain of forfeiture of his life, land, and as much as he
might forfeit'.⁶

During his ascent to the throne and Buckingham's rebellion two years previously, Richard's greatest supporters had been the members of the nobility in whom he once again placed his trust. John Howard, the duke of Norfolk, had pledged to deliver a force of over 1,000 men to Richard if it were needed: receiving orders from the king that he was to march 'in all haste' to join the royal army at Nottingham, the duke now desperately attempted to live up to his promise. Writing to his 'welbeloved friend' John Paston on Sunday, 14 August, 'by this bill delivered in haste . . . letting you to understand that the King's enemies be a land', Norfolk explained that a servant of his had brought him news that the king had intended to 'set forth' on Monday, 15 August, 'but only for Our Lady Day; but for certain he goeth forward upon Tuesday'. Norfolk now requested that Paston 'meet with me at Bury, for, be the grace of God, I purpose to lie at Bury upon Tuesday night'. Norfolk ordered Paston to bring with him 'such company of tall men as ye may goodly make at my cost and charge, be said that ye have promised the King; and I pray you ordain them jackets of my livery, and I shall content you at your meeting with me'.

It must have been just before he departed for Norfolk's camp at Bury that Thomas Longe of Ashwelthorpe in Norfolk, a manor with close associations with the Howards, chose to draw up his will by a 'nuncupative' or oral testament. Stating that he was 'whole of his body and of a good mind, willing to die as a child of the church the said day and time going forth unto the king's host at Nottingham to battle', Longe commended his soul to God, requesting only that if he met his death in battle, his body was 'to be buried amongst Christian people in such place as god would dispose for him'. Longe was not alone in drawing up his final testament before the march towards battle from East Anglia: William Allington, the Commissioner of Array for Cambridgeshire, made his final will too, on 15 August.[7]

Richard's confidence that he would be able to defeat Tudor's army seems to have stemmed from the early information he had received that Henry's army was 'utterly unfurnished and feeble in all things', in comparison to his own well-organised plans for raising an army established by the commissions of array. The king still believed that Tudor's small army would be intercepted and destroyed by the forces of Walter Herbert or Rhys ap Thomas. Jean Molinet wrote how Richard had given £700 'to a rich man named Thomas to raise an army' to gather troops to muster with 'Lord Herbert' and others in order to resist Henry's march.[8] 'He flattered himself that Walter Herbert with Richard Thomas and the rest of the nobles of his region', Vergil later wrote, 'in whose valour he had great confidence, would easily put an end to the adversaries, at the first approach of them.'⁹ Richard may even have been counselled that Tudor's invasion posed no concern. According to Molinet, when Richard signalled his desire to join with his nobility to meet Henry's march, he was dissuaded by those who replied, 'Do not move, we shall do well.'¹⁰

As men poured into Nottingham to join the king's army, still Richard waited to hear back from Thomas, Lord Stanley, and Henry, earl of Northumberland. Despite both men having mustered 'great companies', according to the *Great Chronicle*, they 'made slow speed' towards the king.¹¹ Northumberland was probably on his estate at Wressle in East Yorkshire when he received the king's messengers: even if he received the news of Tudor's landing on the same day as Norfolk, 14 August, with many of his retainers spread across the north-east, it would have taken days to assemble his men, and been impossible to accomplish before 19 August. Yet the earl seems to have delayed even informing the city of York of his intentions: the same day that Norfolk was preparing to march from Bury, on Tuesday, 16 August, the council at York assembled to discuss the news that they had received of Tudor's landing. Since they had received no official message of whether to muster their troops, the council recorded how 'It was determined that John Sponer, Sergeant to the Mace, should ride to Nottingham to the King's grace to understand his pleasure as in sending up any of his subjects within this city to his said grace for the subduing of his enemies late arrived in the parts of Wales, or otherwise it be disposed at his most high pleasure.'¹² With the plague raging, the council agreed that any aldermen and members of the council 'sojourning' outside the city should be sent for 'to give their best advices in such things as concerned the weal and safeguard of this said city'. In the meantime, each warden was to search the inhabitants of his ward, making sure 'that they have sufficient weapons, and array for their defence and the weal of this city'. Proclamations were also to be made throughout York, 'that every man . . . within this City be ready in their most defensible array to attend upon the Mayor, for the welfare of this City, within an hour warning, upon pain of imprisonment'.¹³

John Nicholson's arrival at Richard's lodge at Beskwood must have raised Richard's suspicions. It was Northumberland's responsibility to muster the city and send orders to the council: the earl had clearly failed to do so. Richard requested that York send 400 men as soon as possible.[14] Thomas, Lord Stanley's absence from the king's court was even more concerning. Richard had requested that Stanley join him earlier in the summer; Stanley had refused, claiming that he was ill and unable to travel. Instead he sent his son, George, Lord Strange, to join Richard at court. Strange was certainly present in Nottingham by 1 August, where he is recorded as attending the ceremony of the handing over of the Great Seal.[15] Richard hoped that his father would arrive soon from his residence at Lathom; Stanley had departed with his troops on 15 August, and had headed for Newcastle under Lyme. Meanwhile, his brother, Sir William Stanley, had journeyed from his castle at Holt to Nantwich. Keeping their two armies separate, Thomas Stanley took a more easterly route, arriving at Lichfield by 17 August. What Stanley's exact intentions were, Richard could not be certain: perhaps Stanley intended to act as an advance guard, protecting against Tudor's advance. Stanley had a history of doubtful loyalty; over twenty-five years earlier, he had refused to obey orders to bring his troops to the battle of Blore Heath, countering the instructions by refusing to move unless he be given command of the vanguard. There could be no doubt that, in refusing to join the king, Stanley was undermining Richard's authority. The king had long suspected that Thomas, married to Henry Tudor's mother, Margaret Beaufort, would fall under his wife's influence, and that she 'might induce her husband to support her son's party'.[16] Then suddenly news reached him confirming his fears.

Lord Strange had attempted to make an escape from Nottingham, but instead had been 'discovered by a snare and seized'. On his arrest and imprisonment, Strange confessed that there was a conspiracy between himself, his uncle Sir William Stanley and Sir John Savage 'to support the party of the earl of Richmond'. Strange begged for forgiveness, promising that if his life was spared, 'his father would come to the king's aid, as fast as possible, with all his power'.[17] Strange wrote to Lord Stanley making clear his own precarious situation, together with a plea for urgent support.

Strange does not seem to have been the only person arrested in the hunt for clues about the plot. A Welsh poem by Lewis Mon dedicated to William Gruffudd, significantly a nephew by marriage to Lord Stanley, suggests that Gruffudd was also arrested and taken to Nottingham at the same time as Strange, describing how 'manifestly by deceit he was put unwillingly somewhere out of his own country ... the arrest and the taking away of Lord Strange ... was a double misfortune'. Another poem described how Gruffudd was 'under God's care while at the mercy of King Richard, a man who is cruel to a prisoner'.[18]

Lord Strange's confession provided Richard with the news that he had possibly expected, though Strange had been cautious not to name his father in the conspiracy to place Tudor on the throne. For Richard, it meant that Stanley's loyalty could still be bought by the threat to his son's life. Yet he needed to send out a clear message that any treason would not go unpunished: orders were issued for both Sir William Stanley and Sir John Savage to be 'publicly denounced ... as traitors to the king' at Coventry, no doubt to ensure that the message reached Lord Thomas as soon as possible, while at the same time possibly intending to prevent Sir William Stanley's further advance.

It was too late. News reached Richard that Henry Tudor had managed to pass through Shrewsbury. The town's gates had been opened to him, allowing his army to pass over the River Severn and into England. Henry's arrival at Shrewsbury transformed everything. According to Polydore Vergil, Richard became 'sickened with fear' and 'immediately sent scouts ahead, who were to observe which road the enemy took'. When they returned, Richard was informed that Tudor was encamped at Lichfield. Arriving at the city, Henry had been 'received as a king with thanksgiving'.

The speed of Tudor's advance, 'making haste and moving by day and night towards a direct confrontation', had taken Richard entirely by surprise.[19] It was time to move as quickly as possible, to cut Henry off before he reached Watling Street, an easy route straight down into the capital. Already within the city walls of Nottingham, Richard 'had collected a vast number of armed men', although the Crowland chronicler noted that 'it was not yet fully assembled'.[20] Sir Robert Brackenbury, carrying with him crucial ordnance from the Tower and travelling on the road from the capital, was still to arrive, though it was agreed that he would rendezvous with the royal forces at Leicester.

Richard ordered his forces, described by Polydore Vergil as 'a vast number of armed men', to prepare to depart from Nottingham, marching in a defensive formation in case they faced any attack en route. 'Leading the soldiers forth in an orderly manner from safety, he ordered the front line of armed men to march in a square, towards the direction they expected the enemy to come, and all impediments gathered together in the middle.' Richard himself followed, 'surrounded by his men, and with the other horsemen riding up and down on both sides'.[21]

Richard's forces reached Leicester by sunset. The following morning, having journeyed through the night, Northumberland appeared, leading a force that included several northern lords, including Lords Scrope of Bolton, Fitzhugh, Scrope of Masham, Ogle and Greystoke. Other peers who were later recorded as being present in Richard's army included the earls of Kent and Westmorland, Surrey, Lincoln and Shrewsbury, and Lords Dudley, Maltravers, Grey of Codnor, and Welles, along with 'a countless multitude of the common people', according to the Crowland chronicler, who barely concealed his amazement that 'here was found ready to fight for the king a greater number of soldiers than had ever been seen before in England assembled on one side'.[22]

Still, chroniclers noted that many of the king's levies were missing. As soon as Tudor's landing had become widely known, the *Great Chronicle* observed, 'many knights and squires of this land . . . gathered much people in the king's name and straight sped them unto that other party, by means whereof his power hugely increased'.[23] Since his arrival in Wales, Tudor's campaign had gathered pace, as Henry sent letters to Welsh gentlemen on his march, stating his intent 'in all haste possible to descend into our realm of England, not only for the adeption of the crown unto us of right appertaining, but also for the oppression of that odious tyrant Richard late duke of Gloucester, usurper of our said right', and commanding them to 'make defensibly arrayed for the war' without any delay, warning them to 'fail not hereof as ye will avoid our grievous displeasure and answer unto at your peril'.[24] Another letter, written from Machynlleth on 14 August, was addressed 'By the king', requesting that Sir Roger Kynaston, the constable of Harlech Castle, should assemble his men, 'and defensibly arrayed for the war' he was to 'come to us for our aid and assistance in this our enterprise for the recovery of the crown of our realm of England to us of right appertaining'. Intriguingly, Tudor's letter stated how he had been promised by his 'trusty and well beloved cousin' Lord Powis that 'at this our coming in to these parts he had fully concluded and determined to have do us service'.[25] Powis had travelled to Brittany in 1484 to agree a peace treaty with Duke Francis of Brittany, negotiating the delivery of English archers to help with the Breton campaign against France. If Henry's letter is correct, then it seems that Powis had secretly offered his support to Henry, and that Henry had planned in painstaking detail his invasion of Wales, taking a northern route towards the Shropshire Marches, passing near to Powis's castle en route.

Other letters were sent in haste upon Tudor's arrival. An early manuscript version of Polydore Vergil's history indicates that Henry sent Christopher Urswick to Thomas Stanley and his mother, Margaret Beaufort, then residing in Lathom Castle, with additional messages for Sir William Stanley, Gilbert Talbot 'and many others' that he intended to cross into England through Shropshire, with instructions that 'they should tell others, how they could meet him on the way, when, at a suitable place and time, he would communicate to them more of his intentions'.[26] Arriving at Shrewsbury, Henry had initially been refused entry into the town by its bailiff, Thomas Mitton. Yet, overnight, Mitton suddenly changed his mind: it seems that the influence of Sir William Stanley, sending messages to the town to open its gates, had been the deciding factor. Sir William, by now declared a traitor by Richard, had nothing to lose in declaring his support for Henry. Unlike his elder brother, Lord Thomas, still fearful that any open gesture of support for Richard could lead to his imprisoned son's death, William and his armed force marched to Stone, where he met Henry, offering his support, but refused to join with his army for the moment. Sir William then departed for Lichfield, where he seems to have been instrumental in organising the welcome reception for Henry on his arrival the following day. Instead Sir William rejoined his brother Thomas, the Stanley army stationing itself on the Warwickshire border near Atherstone, where it could legitimately claim to be guarding Watling Street from a rebel advance, blocking the road to London, and locating itself at the point where Richard, moving down from Nottingham, would seek to intercept Tudor's army. If Henry had hoped for the Stanleys' support at this stage, their determination to remain resolutely independent must have come as a disappointment. Henry's anxiety was further heightened when he heard that Richard 'was approaching with an innumerable army'.[27] It seems that his nerve almost failed him; one evening, with twenty armed men, he departed from his army as they journeyed to Tamworth, spending the night alone. When Henry returned to his army the following dawn, he claimed that he had got lost by accident; his men must have feared that, having been deserted by their leader before and stranded in Brittany while Henry escaped to France, once more they had been left alone to their fate.

Meanwhile, arriving at Leicester, Richard would have discovered the news that Rhys ap Thomas, one of the Welshmen in whom he placed so much trust, had in fact defected to Henry, bringing with him 1,500 mounted cavalry. Gilbert Talbot, an uncle of the young earl of Shrewsbury, had also joined Tudor's forces, bringing with him 500 men. Sir Robert Brackenbury arrived with further bad news. As his force travelled up from London, after it had passed Stony Stratford the gentlemen he had been given the task of bringing to the battle, including Walter Hungerford and Thomas Bourchier, 'perceiving that Richard had no trust in them because they would not be brought to the enemy against their will', managed to desert his camp during the night. That was the story that Brackenbury at least was prepared to tell the king. The *Great Chronicle* gives a different account, describing how the men had 'held good countenance' with Brackenbury, who had 'for many of them done right kindly'. It seems that Brackenbury was powerless to prevent their departure, or at the least did little to oppose the desertion, for 'many gentlemen' simply 'took their leave of him', though before their departure they gave him 'thanks for his kindness before showed, and exhorted him to go with them, for they feared not to show unto him that they would go unto that other party'. Once they had departed, the chronicler wrote, Brackenbury 'lost much of his people', and was left 'almost alone'.[28] Other men, including John Savage, Brian Sandford and Simon Digby, were also missing, while two days previously Richard's sheriff for Leicestershire and Warwickshire, Richard Boughton, was killed. It seems that he may have been caught in a skirmish with Stanley's forces on their march into the region.

Richard could no longer afford any further delay. He had been informed by his scouts 'where the enemy most probably intended to spend the next night', eight miles away, near Merevale Abbey on the Warwickshire border, close to Watling Street.[29] On Sunday, 21 August, the king led his army out of Leicester. The Crowland chronicler wrote how Richard departed 'amid the greatest pomp, wearing his diadem on his head, and accompanied by John Howard, duke of Norfolk, and Henry Percy, earl of Northumberland, and other great lords, knights and esquires and a countless multitude of commoners'.[30]

Marching west, Richard's army would have passed nearby the unfinished brick country residence at Kirby Muxloe that William, Lord Hastings, had been building before his execution, as they rode in the direction towards Market Bosworth. Two years earlier, in August 1483, Richard had ridden across the same terrain in the opposite direction, on his summer progress from Warwick to Leicester. Richard's memories of the area, however, were more likely to have been scarred by the treason of the lord of the manor, John Harcourt, who had joined the rebellion in October 1483, before fleeing overseas with his son Robert. Richard had instead granted the manor to Sir Marmaduke Constable, who cannot have been anything other than an absentee landlord, yet whose own agents may have been able to provide information about the terrain and best location to pitch camp later that evening. The chosen location to rest was at the base of a tongue of high ground several hundred feet above sea level known as Ambion Hill, named after an Anglo-Saxon settlement long disappeared.

After setting up camp, pitching their tents on the surroundings of Ambion Hill stretching down to the nearby village of Sutton Cheyney, Richard's forces were allowed to refresh themselves from their march, while the king himself took the opportunity and 'revived his men and with many words exhorted them to the coming battle'.[31] As the night sky darkened, they would have been able to discern the flickering lights of campfires in the distance: a sign that Tudor's army, and their final confrontation with the enemy, was not far away. Richard retired to his tent early, taking with him his Book of Hours for comfort and consolation, with its prayers for the king to be delivered from his enemies, calling on Christ to 'defend me from all evil and from my evil enemy . . . and free me from all tribulations, griefs and anguishes which I face', never so relevant as it was now.

Outside, in the king's camp, the mood remained uncertain, as anxiety about the fate of the following day's battle began to grow amid the darkening night sky. Rumours would later circulate of the king's own crown being stolen that evening by a Scottish highlander called MacGregor, and though it was hastily retrieved, later that evening it was reported that the duke of Norfolk found pinned to his tent a verse, warning: 'Jack of Norfolk be not so bold, For Dickon thy master is bought and sold'.[32]

Whether these words, recorded in the sixteenth century history of Edward Hall, were ever written or not, they reflect the dilemma that must have been faced by thousands of men camping in the fields surrounding Ambion Hill that night. In their strength of numbers alone, it seemed that their king would surely defeat the rebel forces of Henry Tudor. Some may have considered it their duty to defend their kingdom against the assault of what must have seemed to many nothing less than a French-backed invasion. Others, like Thomas Longe, considered it their Christian duty to defend their anointed king, even if it meant they might die 'as a child of the church'. Yet many would have felt the same as Roger Wake, faced with no other choice but to fight on the king's side, 'upon pain of forfeiture of his life', or Geoffrey St German, 'so manashed' by Richard's threatening letters that he attended upon the king 'full sore against his will'.[33]

Among the thousands of men settling down to sleep that night, news of defections must have already reached them: anxiously, they awaited the morning uncertain whether the Stanleys and their own powerful army would be ranged on their side, or against them. Not since the last major battles of the civil wars, wounds that many had assumed long healed, did the future of the nation seem so uncertain; yet the passage of fourteen years meant that many men would have been untried and untested in the heat of battle. Then, at the fields of Barnet and Tewkesbury, men had at least been faced with a clear choice: to return to the hapless Lancastrian rule of Henry VI, or retain their faith in the certainty of the dynamic kingship of Edward IV. Now the future was far less certain. Richard III may have been crowned their king, but how many genuinely believed that his right to rule had been ordained by God? He had ruled for just over two years, during which time the kingdom had been beset by rebellion, leaving the realm plagued by instability; the king's only son and heir had died suddenly, while only recently his wife too had succumbed to a mystery illness. It did not appear that divine favour, at least, was on Richard's side. Publicly, their king had been forced to deny rumours that he planned to marry his own niece; still, it could not be denied that with Richard as king, childless and without a wife, the Yorkist dynasty hung by a thread.

If God brought victory to the king the following day, many must have been uncertain about what the future of that victory would mean for them and their country. For Richard's favoured councillors and followers, they at least could count upon their king's continued support. For the rest of the nation, the king's determination to place his trust in his northern supporters at the expense of the traditional local frameworks of government indicated that they would continue to be ruled by a king who could not shake off his sympathies as a northern overlord. Richard had won his kingship through the influence and strength that his northern hegemony and power had given him; yet to have done so had begun to erode his ability to rule on behalf of the whole kingdom. Obliged to reward his own supporters, he was unable to secure the full support of the realm. Richard was duty bound to ensure their own ambitions were fulfilled, yet even this was something he had been unable to achieve. Failed promises to initial supporters of his regime, noblemen such as the earl of Northumberland or Ralph Neville, the earl of Westmorland, who had hoped that Richard's elevation to the kingship would have guaranteed a greater role for themselves in the north, now cast doubt on their loyalties.

For a king whose motto translated as 'loyalty binds me', Richard now found himself in a spiralling descent, bound by the loyalties that he owed his supporters, or at least loyalties that men such as Northumberland believed that they were owed. The more his supporters were rewarded, the less others considered the king's loyalty lay with them. Epitomised by the ballad of the ill-fated William Collingborne was the belief that the king was being ruled by his own councillors, Sir Richard Ratcliffe, 'the Rat', and William Catesby, 'the Cat'. Richard, it seemed, was increasingly making the same mistake as his brother Edward had done.

For the past two years, Richard's own reign had stalled, beset by the threat of rebellion posed by Henry Tudor. Tudor's threat should have been weak: just as both his claim to the throne and the number of men at his command were weak. But it is testament to Richard's own weakness as king that Tudor could even be considered a credible alternative to the throne. Foreign alliances and skilful diplomacy could have seen Tudor alienated as a mere pretender; instead Richard's threats of war on two fronts, against both France and Scotland, propelled Tudor's claim to be taken seriously to the point that it was given legitimacy and financial backing by the French.

Still, the defeat of his enemies the following morning would at least grant Richard the legitimacy that he ultimately craved, demonstrating that God's blessing, at last, was upon him. What the future held for his reign, no one could be clear; all that mattered lay in the present, and in victory.

21

'AN END EITHER OF WARS OR OF HIS LIFE'

During the night, as the hours slowly went by, Richard could barely sleep, suffering from a 'terrible dream'. The Crowland chronicler claimed that Richard himself in the morning 'declared that during the night he had seen dreadful visions, and had imagined himself surrounded by a multitude of demons'.[1] Vergil wrote how the king had 'reported his dream to many in the morning', that 'he thought in his sleep to see about him horrible images appearing as if they were evil demons and they would not let him rest'. For those who were able to catch sight of the king early that morning, he seemed not to be himself; the Crowland chronicler described how Richard 'presented a countenance which, always drawn, was on this occasion more livid and ghastly than usual'. Vergil believed the dream had filled Richard 'with anxious cares. For immediately after, being troubled in spirit, indeed he presaged a sorrowful outcome for the coming battle, not having the spirit or appearance of eagerness with which before he had looked forward to it.'[2]

To add to Richard's woes, the Crowland chronicler reported how 'at day-break ... there were no chaplains present to perform Divine service on behalf of king Richard, nor any breakfast prepared to refresh the flagging spirits of the king'. Ralph Bigod, serving as the king's Master of the Ordnance, recalled years later how 'king Richard called in the morning for to have had mass said before him, but when his chaplain had one thing ready, evermore they wanted another, when they had wine they lacked bread, and ever one thing was missing'.[3] Still there was time for Richard to make one last rallying cry. He addressed his troops, asserting according to the Crowland chronicler that 'the outcome of this day's battle, to whichever side the victory was granted, would be the utter destruction of the kingdom of England', declaring that it was his intention, 'if he proved the victor, to crush all the traitors on the opposing side', while he predicted that Tudor 'would do the same to the supporters of his party, if victory should fall to him'.[4]

The Scottish chronicler Pittscottie described how Richard sent for his crown from his royal tent, and in the presence of several lords and the bishop of Dunkeld had it placed upon his head in some form of ceremony. Richard's possession of the crown seems to have struck writers such as John Rous, who observed how the king had 'with him the crown itself, together with a great mass of treasure'. The spectacle of the king's troops preparing for battle was an impressive sight. Later it would be described how Richard's host had been assembled 'with banners spread, mightily armed and defenced with all manner of arms, as guns, bows, arrows, spears, glaives, axes, and all other manner of articles apt or needful to give and cause mighty battle'. An observer encamped with the Stanleys on a nearby hill wrote how, overlooking the king's army, they could see little else but for 'armed men and trapped steeds' arranged into three battles.[5] One hundred and forty serpentines were chained together, locked into a row, 'and as many bombards, and thousands of morice pikes, hackbushes'.[6]

The king's army was described as 'a line of battle of remarkable length, and closely packed with infantry and cavalry, so that from afar it would strike terror in the beholders because of the great number of armed men'. In front of the line of infantry, Richard placed his archers, 'like a well-fortified rampart', under the command of the duke of Norfolk who led the vanguard, together with Sir Robert Brackenbury. Richard, with the 'chosen cream of the soldiers', followed behind this 'long battle-line', while placed behind the king was his rearguard, to be led by the earl of Northumberland, commanding several thousand men.[7] As his army assembled at the base of Ambion Hill, Richard had taken good advantage of his position to place it on the higher ground. In front of them, a plain land stretched out, punctuated by a solitary windmill. Several rivers ran across the landscape, acting as a defence to any attack from the south, while a large marshy area known locally as 'Redemore' stretched out alongside the road that led to Witherley and Mancetter, where his scouts had informed him that Henry Tudor and his army had camped the previous night. To

Richard's left, the villages of Dadlington and Stoke clung to the upland ridge of land that framed the landscape, with the spire of the church at Stoke, St Margaret of Antioch, in the distance, overlooking the basin of the chosen site for battle. In the growing light of dawn, Richard and his troops waited, knowing Tudor's advance to be imminent.

Henry and his forces had already been camped in the area for several days, causing significant disruption to the surrounding fields that were flattened to make way for the soldiers' camp. Henry's arrival at Atherstone had been marked with welcome news. Not only had Walter Hungerford and Thomas Bourchier managed to join his camp 'and bound themselves to his faith', but Henry had discovered that both the Stanley brothers were encamped near Merevale Abbey. Henry arrived at the abbey to find both William and Thomas, Lord Stanley, ready to welcome him; 'taking each by the hand', Henry was overjoyed to discover that both brothers were now willing to join his forces. The following day, Henry met with the Stanley brothers again, where they 'disputed between them how to attack the enemy whom they had heard was not far away'. After vespers that evening, Sunday, 21 August, the arrival of John Savage, renowned as 'an excellent warrior', Brian Sandford and Simon Digby, 'and many others defecting from Richard', brought Henry further hope for the battle.[8]

With the support of the Stanleys, themselves commanding over 6,000 men, everything seemed to be falling finally into place. Henry and his forces had moved from their previous encampment at Witherley, and had camped close by to Richard's forces. As the sky was 'barely growing light', waking the camp, Henry had given the order for his soldiers to arm. He then sent messengers to Thomas Stanley that 'he should approach with his forces putting them in battle-order'. If Henry had hoped that Stanley would deliver the men he had promised only the previous day, he was to be disappointed. Thomas, Lord Stanley, he was informed, was prepared to 'lead his men into the line of battle when he himself was present with his army drawn up', but not before, and certainly was not prepared at this moment to join his own forces with Tudor's. Once more Henry's anxieties were heightened; maybe Stanley would, as his past history had shown, sit out the battle altogether.

There was no time to argue. Henry needed to organise his army into battle now. With a clear shortage of men, lacking the additional 6,000 that the Stanley forces would have provided, 'making a virtue out of necessity' Henry was forced to make a 'simple line of battle', formed out of a single line with two wings 'as best he could because of shortage of men'.⁹ With his archers placed out in front, under the command of John, earl of Oxford, on the right wing he placed Gilbert Talbot in command, and John Savage in charge of the left wing. The French forces, commanded by Philibert de Chandée, had been arranged separately from the English army, and had assembled alongside the right wing of Henry's forces, stationed 'a quarter of a league away' from Tudor's vanguard. Henry himself followed behind on foot; according to Vergil's original account, he progressed 'with difficulty' and was only 'surrounded by one squadron of cavalry and a few infantry' that comprised his standard-bearer, Sir William Brandon, and other French mercenaries. A French solider later recalled how Tudor 'wanted to be on foot in the midst of us'.¹⁰ In total, Henry's troops did not amount to more than 5,000 men compared to the royal army of 15,000.¹¹ Henry must have realised that the odds were stacked against him.

With the battle lines on either side drawn up, it was not long before both sides had caught sight of each other's standards in the distance. As men rushed to put on their helmets, Richard's men awaited the king's 'signal to advance with ears pricked'. Yet Richard remained uncertain of his enemies' precise movements. As Henry's forces approached the marsh between the two armies, suddenly they snaked leftwards, keeping the marsh to their right. It was an ingenious decision, with the marsh providing a natural defence from sudden attack. Until the army passed the marsh, Richard calculated, it would prove impossible for his own left flank to attack. Waiting, he held back his attack for now. According to Vergil, Henry's chosen path around the marsh had also allowed him to have 'the sun behind them'; if this was the case, then Tudor would also have gained the advantage of having sunlight shining in the eyes of the enemy.¹²

When Richard saw that Henry and his men had 'passed by the marsh' he ordered his army to attack. 'Raising a sudden shout', the archers fired a volley of arrows at Tudor's forces; in return, 'not slowing the fight', the enemies' archers returned fire. The melee of battle was well captured by a supporter of the Stanleys, who later set down his experiences into ballad form. 'The archers let their arrows fly; they shot of guns; many a banner began to show that was on Richard's party; with ground weapons they joined.'[13] Soon the armies had drawn near enough for close combat to begin with drawn swords. As both sides became immersed in bloody strokes and hand to hand conflict, however, there was a sudden change in the formation of Tudor's army.

What exactly occurred at this point in the confusion of battle is difficult to discern. According to the chronicler Jean Molinet, after Richard's cannon and artillery opened fire, the French mercenaries seem to have been able to establish 'by the king's shot the lie of the land and the order of his battle'. Molinet believed that it was this opening salvo that allowed the French to urge the main force to be reassembled, and 'in order to avoid the fire, to mass their troops against the flank rather than the front of the king's battle'.

For a while, no one on Richard's side seemed to know what was happening. 'As if terrified because they suspected a trick', momentarily they ceased fighting. In their amazement, it seemed as if the enemy were withdrawing, as orders were shouted that no soldier was to advance more than ten feet from the standards. The order had come from John, earl of Oxford: the earl, fearing that his own men were becoming swamped in the king's far larger army, understood the dangers of an over-enthusiastic army that sacrificed discipline. At the battle of Barnet, he had commanded the Lancastrian vanguard that, having assumed victory, had later been hacked down and crushed in the thickening mist, as they confused their Yorkist opponents for men on their own side. Oxford was not prepared to make the same mistake. Now, his troops, following their commanders' orders, 'all pressed close together and withdrew a little way from the battle'.[14]

Any hopes that Tudor's forces had fallen back were illusory. Instead, having collected his forces together in a tight formation, the earl of Oxford ordered his forces to attack Norfolk's vanguard 'on the one side', possibly outflanking the royal vanguard from the left, while 'others on the other side made a wedge' which they drove straight through Richard's front line, causing the king's formidable line of troops to become separated. Acting as a co-ordinated pincer movement, 'together they pushed forward and they renewed the battle'.[15]

'There now began a very fierce battle between the two sides', the Crowland chronicler wrote, describing how Tudor's own forces separated into two wings, with the earl of Oxford, 'a very valiant knight, with a large force of French as well as English troops' taking up a renewed position opposite the duke of Norfolk. After 'several feats of arms on both sides', Richard's vanguard was broken and soon dispersed as the French, according to Molinet, 'obtained the mastery of his vanguard'. Norfolk and his son, the earl of Surrey, were now left fatally isolated. For Oxford, who had his own scores to settle with the duke, having lost his confiscated lands to Norfolk, there could be only one outcome. Molinet wrote how the duke was captured, and taken to Tudor, and was then sent to the earl, 'who had him dispatched'.[16] While this cannot be corroborated, another ballad account described how the elderly duke was killed near the windmill, dispatched by John Savage.[17]

As Richard watched with disbelief as his vanguard crumbled under the attack of Oxford and the French forces, something else had caught his eye. In the distance, the king could make out the fluttering of Thomas, Lord Stanley's banner. Finally Stanley had revealed his true intent; he had chosen to bear arms against the king. Richard would have no choice but to order the execution of his hostage, Stanley's son, George, Lord Strange. The Crowland chronicler described how, as 'the leader and troops of the enemy moved steadily up on the king's army', Richard ordered that Strange be beheaded 'on the spot'. 'However, those to whom this task was given, seeing that the matter in hand was at a very critical stage and that it was more important than the elimination of one man, failed to carry out that king's cruel command and, on their own judgement, let the man go and returned to the heart of battle'.[18]

Meanwhile the fighting continued on the front lines, described as 'a battle of the greatest severity'. It was soon apparent that something was wrong. Vergil later wrote how Oxford and his men, 'after a brief fight, also routed the others who were fighting in the first battle line, of whom a great number were killed in the flight itself'. Norfolk's vanguard had been crushed, but Richard's rearguard, led by the earl of Northumberland, should have stepped up to renew the fighting.[19] Yet, according to the Crowland chronicler, 'in the place where the earl of Northumberland was posted, with a large company of reasonably good men, no engagement could be discerned, and no battle blows given or received'. 'Many, especially northerners in whom the king so greatly trusted', the chronicler observed, 'took to flight without engaging, and there was left no part of the opposing army of sufficient significance or substance.'[20] Vergil wrote how 'many more, who had followed Richard against their will, easily abstained from fighting and slipped secretly away, inasmuch as they were not desiring the safety, but rather the destruction, of their king, whom they hated.' The majority of Richard's army, Vergil believed, would have done so 'from the beginning if it had been possible', but had been prevented from doing so by Richard's 'scouts flying about hither and thither'. Northumberland, Jean Molinet observed, should have 'charged the French' but instead 'did nothing except to flee, both he and his company, and to abandon his King Richard'.[21] For the chronicler Robert Fabyan, the battle had been 'sharp', although 'sharper it should have been, if the king's party had been fast to him. But many toward the field refused him, and went unto that other party. And some stood hoving afar off till they saw to which party the victory fell.'[22]

Northumberland's inaction, and the flight of his men, was treason enough, yet other accounts of the battle suggest that the earl may have even taken up arms against the king. A Spanish account of the battle written by Diego de Valera, but based on a first-hand account given by Juan de Salazar, who was present with Richard at Bosworth, described how Lord 'Tamerlant', who had been entrusted with Richard's left wing, 'left his position and passed in front of the king's vanguard', at which point, 'turning his back on Earl Henry, he began to fight fiercely against the king's van, and so did all the others who had plighted their faith to Earl Henry'.[23] Could this possibly have been the case? Valera later wrote how 'Tamerlant' had given his assurance to Henry Tudor, along with 'sundry other leading men' who had given Tudor their oath, that they 'would give him assistance when they came to battle and would fight against King Richard, and so they did'.[24] Jean Molinet also believed that the earl 'had an undertaking with the earl of Richmond, as had some others who deserted him in his need'.[25]

Whether Northumberland and part of Richard's army had actively turned against the king and taken up arms for Tudor, or whether the earl was simply unable to engage in the battle, trapped behind the marsh and unable to support the king's vanguard as it was being decimated by Oxford's attack, it was clear that the battle was already ending before any effective engagement had begun. Polydore Vergil later wrote how Richard's own commanders recognised that defeat seemed on the cards, and how they 'saw the soldiers wielding their arms languidly and slowly and others leaving the battle secretly. They suspected treachery and urged him to flight. And as the battle had now manifestly turned against him, they offered a fast horse.' Richard refused outright. Whether, as Vergil inferred, 'he knew the people to be hostile towards him and threw away all hope for the future that would come after this' or whether at this stage he believed outright in his cause, Richard replied that 'he would make an end either of wars or of his life', a comment that drew even the admiration of the Italian, who noted 'such was that great courage and great strength of spirit in him'.[26]

Vergil's manuscript account of the battle was written over twenty years after the event, yet the moment when Richard refused to flee and instead fought on is mirrored in other, more contemporary accounts. According to de Valera's letter detailing the battle, when Juan de Salazar saw for himself 'the treason of the king's people', he confronted Richard, urging the king to flee the battlefield immediately. 'Sire, take steps to put your person in safety', he was later reported to have said, 'without expecting to have the victory in today's battle, owing to the manifest treason of your following.' 'Salazar', Richard replied, 'God forbid I yield one step. This day I will die as a king or win.'[27]

All accounts of the battle confirm that Richard then placed the crown upon his helmet, ready to enter the fray himself. Valera wrote that Richard then 'placed over his head armour the crown royal which they declare to be worth one hundred and twenty thousand crowns', along with his *côte d'armes* over his armour. The very act of wearing the crown, which the Crowland chronicler described as the 'pretiosissima corona' – the priceless crown – indicates that Richard viewed the battle as nothing less than a moment of divine intervention, one in which he would either emerge as God's favoured and anointed king, or nothing. He had already informed his army of the apocalyptic choice that faced either side that morning, declaring that 'the outcome of this day's battle, to whichever side the victory was granted, would totally destroy the kingdom of England'.[28] For the Yorkist dynasty, it had been battle itself that had won Edward IV the crown; it was at the battle of Mortimer's Cross that God had supposedly revealed his divine favour in the three suns in the sky, an optical illusion of the light that had been taken as a miracle representing the three 'sons' of York. Now Richard hoped for one last miracle; with God on his side, he hoped for nothing less than a second coronation. Polydore Vergil explained that Richard, 'because he knew for certain that that day would either give him his kingdom at peace again, or take it away for ever, he went into the battle wearing the royal crown on his helmet, so that, indeed, if he was victorious wearing his crown, that would be the day which would give him an end of his troubles. But if indeed he was defeated, he would fall more honourably with the insignia of royalty.'[29]

Richard was informed by his scouts that Henry Tudor 'was in the distance with a few armed men gathered round him'.[30] Now looking across the landscape, Richard himself could see Henry drawing nearer, recognising him 'more surely from his standards'. It seemed that Tudor, together with his knights, was riding towards the king himself, the Crowland chronicler wrote, intending to make 'straight for king Richard'.[31] Richard suddenly became 'enraged with anger'. Throwing himself onto a horse, he ordered that his closest cavalry men should join him in his final charge. Spurring his horse until it reached a galloping pace, the king and his cavalry sped towards Tudor and the men around his standard, 'from other side beyond the battle lines', making use of the little territory that had opened up between the battle between the vanguards and the marsh to Richard's left. When Henry perceived that the king had launched his attack and would soon be upon him, he prepared 'eagerly' for battle, 'because all hope of safety was in arms'.[32]

As Richard and his men crashed into the side of Henry's defences, it seemed as though the king had the upper hand. In the first onslaught, several of Tudor's men were killed and even Henry's standard ended up being 'thrown to the ground' together with William Brandon, who was fatally wounded in his attempts to defend his master's honour and keep the tattered pennants from being ground into the mud. Richard then confronted John Cheyne, his brother Edward IV's Master of the Horse, who had helped lead the rebellion against him in autumn 1483. The six-foot-eight Cheyne, undoubtedly renowned for being the tallest soldier of his day, was noted by Vergil as being one of the 'bravest' men, yet even Cheyne was no match for the king riding towards him, 'whom Richard pushed to the ground with great force making a pathway everywhere for himself with his sword.'[33] The battle around the standards was both fierce and bloody: Richard's own standard-bearer, Sir Percival Thirlwall, had his legs cut from underneath him, yet still managed to keep a tight grasp upon the king's standard. It seemed that as Richard and his cavalry renewed their attack, the situation was becoming increasingly desperate. Henry's own men, Vergil later admitted, were 'now wholly distrustful of victory', yet Henry himself, despite his complete lack of military experience, was still managing to withstand the force of the blows from Richard's cavalry.[34] It seemed that victory was now in Richard's grasp: his foe, untrained in the arts of war, stood no chance against the king.

Meanwhile, watching the drama of the battle unfold, Thomas, Lord Stanley, and his brother Sir William Stanley had barely moved from the positions they had taken up at dawn, their forces arranged on the hills to the south, near the villages of Dadlington and Stoke. Richard's possession of Thomas's son, George, and the threat that the king might order his execution if either one of the brothers moved against the royal forces had made it impossible for either Thomas or William to join Henry Tudor's forces, though by this stage Richard most likely viewed their inaction as treason itself. Sir William Stanley, having already been declared a traitor by the king several days previously, had nothing to lose, though he may have wished to follow his elder brother's command. If Thomas, Lord Stanley, and his troops still refused to engage, Sir William realised that Tudor's life was in the balance. If Richard were to defeat

Henry, then William must have known that he too would be a dead man soon.

With Richard and his cavalry pressing down on Henry Tudor and his small detachment of soldiers, Stanley decided to act. Giving the order for his forces to thunder into battle, Stanley's move came too fast for Richard. 'Down at a bank he hyed, and set fiercely on the king', one ballad later recalled, while another observed how Stanley's soldiers appeared as a flash of red and white jackets.[35] Richard's small band of 200 cavalry were no match for Stanley's 3,000-strong army. Nevertheless, according to Valera, Richard 'began to fight with much vigour, putting heart into those that remained loyal, so that by his sole effort he upheld the battle for a long time'. For others, many knew that flight would be their only chance of survival. As Richard's forces began to turn and take flight, the deserters were 'picked off' by Stanley's forces, with Vergil describing how 'a great number . . . were killed in the rout'. Still Richard fought on to the last, until he was simply overwhelmed. 'On his standard then fast they did light', one observer recalled, 'they hewed the crown of gold from his head with dowtfull dents.'[36]

Only the Burgundian chronicler Jean Molinet suggests that Richard, witnessing the desertion of his army, and finding himself 'alone on the field, fled with the others'.[37] It was then that his horse in flight impaled itself and the king was 'soon met by Welshmen, one of whom with a halberd killed him'.[38] While Richard's army may have deserted him, Molinet is alone in believing that Richard attempted to flee; the Crowland chronicler was explicit that Richard died 'not in the act of flight'.[39] There are several, speculative accounts of how Richard met his final end. The Crowland chronicler states that he was 'pierced with numerous deadly wounds'; a later ballad described vividly how the king's helmet was beaten into his skull until his brains poured out, while another Welsh poet believed that it had been a Welshman, possibly Rhys ap Thomas according to later legend, who had 'killed the boar, and shaved his head'.[40] The discovery of Richard's remains allows further speculation as to what exactly were the wounds that Richard may have suffered in his final moments. While we cannot know what injuries Richard sustained to the soft tissue of his body, his skeleton bears witness to several severe wounds, some of which would have proved instantly fatal. It is certain that Richard was not wearing a helmet by the time he was killed: a cut mark to his jawbone suggests that his helmet strap had been severed, and his helmet removed. There is evidence that Richard had been involved in a struggle, for another wound, this time a diamond-shaped puncture to his right cheekbone, indicates that he had been stabbed in the face with what was likely to have been a roundel dagger. Usually employed to deliver a final death blow in battle and able to pierce through plate armour, the weapon seems to have been used in the act of wrestling the king to the ground: the angle of the wound suggests that it had been delivered from behind, as if Richard was being pinned back by his assailant.

These wounds were neither severe nor deep enough to have resulted in Richard's death; yet more would follow. Aside from other, smaller sword and dagger wounds – further evidence of a prolonged struggle – the back of Richard's skull indicates that the king suffered massive trauma through two separate blows that would have killed him instantly. There is no way of knowing in what sequence they occurred, but it is possible that one of them was delivered by a halberd, as referred to by Molinet, crashing down onto Richard's skull as its axe was held aloft on its six-foot-long pole. An entire piece of bone has been sheathed clean off from the skull, the incision so clean that the offending weapon must have been used with incredible velocity and power. By this time, Richard may have been on his knees, at the mercy of his captives. Yet they would show none. Another blow confirms that the king's demise was immediate: a sword thrust – delivered at the base of the occipital bone of the skull, near the first vertebrae of the spine – driven straight through his brain. The wielder of the sword delivered the thrust with such aggression that the weapon did not stop until it reached the opposite side of Richard's skull, the pointed tip leaving a small mark as evidence of the horrific violence that Richard had succumbed to.

It was a brutal and bloody death, yet Richard had been determined to end his life defending his crown and his honour. No one, not even Richard's most determined enemies, would deny that the king's final end came in a display of chivalric bravery. 'As for King Richard', the Crowland chronicler noted, 'like a spirited and most courageous prince, he fell in battle on the field and not in flight.'[41] Even John Rous had to admit that despite Richard having been 'unexpectedly destroyed in the midst of his army by an invading army small by comparison ... let me say the truth to his credit: that he bore himself like a noble soldier and despite his little body and feeble strength, honourably defended himself to his last breath, shouting again and again that he was betrayed, and crying "Treason! Treason! Treason!"'[42] Rous's open admiration of Richard's courage in battle was echoed by Polydore Vergil, who, despite his antagonism towards the enemy of his Tudor patron, could not but admire Richard's 'proud and fierce spirit which did not desert him even in death, which, abandoned by his men, he wished to approach rather than to save his life by shameful flight.'[43]

EPILOGUE

'HIS FAME IS DARKENED'

At the sight of Richard's last stand and death, his forces 'threw down their weapons and willingly surrendered' to Henry. 'Which the majority would have done of their own accord even when Richard was alive', Polydore Vergil later commented, 'assuming it could have been done without danger.' 'Many northerners, in whom, especially, King Richard placed so much trust, fled even before coming to blows with the enemy', the Crowland chronicler wrote, 'and so there remained no worthy or trained troops to make the glorious victor, Henry VII, submit himself again to the trial of battle.'[1] The *Great Chronicle* described how Sir William Stanley 'won the possession of King Richard's helmet with the crown being upon it', but only after doing so 'incontinently, as it was said'. Sir William 'came straight to King Henry and set it upon his head saying, "Sir, here I make you King of England."'[2]

The day after the battle, 23 August, the mayor and aldermen of York met in their council chamber. John Sponer, who once again had been sent to 'the field of Redemore to bring tidings from the same to the city', had managed to flee the site of the battle, bringing with him the awful news that the city most feared: 'that King Richard, late mercifully reigning upon us, was through great treason of . . . many others that turned against him, with many other lords and nobles of this north parts, was piteously slain and murdered'; the clerk writing the minutes of the meeting added, 'to the great heaviness of this city'.[3]

A thousand men had been killed in the battle, including John, duke of Norfolk, Lord Ferrers, Robert Brackenbury and Richard Ratcliffe. Francis, Viscount Lovell, managed to escape the battlefield, finally seeking refuge

in the sanctuary of St John at Colchester. William Catesby was not so fortunate. Arrested on the battlefield, he was taken to Leicester. On 25 August,
Catesby narrated his final will and testament, asking for 'all lands that I
have wrongfully purchased' to be restored to their owners. He hoped that
his wife and children would be safe: 'I doubt not the King will be a good
and gracious Lord to them, for he is called a full gracious prince', adding,
perhaps hopeful of a last-minute reprieve, that he had 'never offended him
by my good and free will; for god I take to my judge I have ever loved him'.
Almost as an afterthought, Catesby added a bitter, final, note: 'My lords
Stanley, Strange and all that blood help and pray for my soul for ye have not
for my body as I trusted in you.'[4] The following day Catesby was executed
in the Market Square at Leicester, his head being cut off 'as a last reward for
his excellent service', the Crowland chronicler wrote mockingly.

Richard's body, the Crowland chronicler wrote, was 'discovered
amongst the dead'. Stripped of all its armour and clothes, the king was
thrown naked over the back of a horse by one of Henry's Welsh troops,
his head and arms hanging down on one side and his legs on the other, his
'hair hanging as one would bear a sheep', while a rope was placed around
his neck.[5] The *Great Chronicle* went further in providing the detail of how
Richard, his 'body despoiled to the skin and nought being left about him
so much as would cover his privy member, was trussed behind a pursuiv-
ant called Norroy, as a hog or other vile beast, and so, all besplattered with
mire and filth, was brought to a church in Leicester for all men to wonder
upon, and there lastly irreverently buried'.[6] 'A wretched sight indeed',
Polydore Vergil mused, 'but very worthy of the man's life.' 'And so he who
had miserably killed numerous people', Jean Molinet reflected, 'ended his
days iniquitously and filthily in the dirt and the mire, and he who had
despoiled churches was displayed to the people naked and without any
clothing.'

Taken to Leicester, Richard's body was placed on public display for two
days, 'with everyone wishing to look at it'. There could be no doubting
that the king was dead. 'The king ascertaineth you', Henry Tudor's first
proclamation as King Henry VII read, 'that Richard duke of Gloucester,
late called King Richard, was slain at a place called Sandeford, within the
shire of Leicester, and brought dead off the field unto the town of Leicester, and there was laid openly, that every man might see and look upon

him.' At some point after his death, it seems Richard was to suffer the final indignity of having a dagger thrust between his buttocks, the blow being delivered with such force it lacerated to the bone; perhaps with this in mind, the Crowland chronicler described how 'many other insults were offered' to the corpse. Richard was given a simple burial in the Greyfriars' Church, wrapped in merely a shroud. It would not be until ten years later that Henry VII would finally pay a meagre £10 1s for an alabaster tomb, 'with his picture cut out, and made thereon' to mark the king's grave.[7]

With the despoliation of Richard's body, so too the king's reputation would need to be destroyed. Within days of the battle, the Welsh bard Dafydd Llwyd ap Llywelyn ap Gruffudd of Mathafarn wrote an ode 'to King Richard who destroyed his two nephews ... Poets are in better heart', Dafydd rejoiced, 'that the world prospers and little R. is killed – a grey, cheerless forked letter which had no respect in England.' Richard, he wrote, 'could neither rule nor govern England. He could not carry the part, he would not fit the breach where Edward stood.' Describing Richard as 'a pale leg, vain overseer', he continued: 'A servile boar wrought penance upon Edward's sons in his prison. If he slew without favour of the bench his two young nephews, I marvelled in a measure of anger at God, that the earth did not swallow him. Shame on the sad-lipped Saracen that he slew Christ's angels ... The little boar lives not, no killing was more charitable', the poem continues, variously describing Richard as 'the little caterpillar of London', 'the old cock', 'a little ape, the magpie's love', adding, 'he is slain, my wish was that God prosper him who killed him. Success to whomsoever killed the dog slain in the ditch.'[8]

Elsewhere in the country, it was a different story, for the moment at least. The city of York remained in a state of denial over Henry Tudor's victory; instead of recording the royal style, its ledger merely read 'the throne being vacant'. When Henry sent Sir Roger Coton to the city the following day, he was met by the mayor and aldermen within the protection of the castle, since Coton 'durst not for fear of death come through the city'. The choice of an inn named the Boar for the meeting must have made Coton feel just as unwelcome. When Coton officially proclaimed the new king, the city council merely wrote that he was 'the king named and proclaimed Henry the VII'; in contrast, several months later, they were still referring to 'the most famous prince of blessed memory, King Richard, late deceased'.

When, in 1486, Henry attempted to replace the city's recorder, one of Richard's chief adherents, Miles Metcalfe, the city refused to accept the king's nominee and instead chose another Ricardian supporter, John Vavasour. Later, in June 1486, the city again rejected Henry's choice of swordbearer for the city, resolving that he 'should never enjoy the office . . . or other office within the said city'.[9]

Gradually, however, the establishment of Tudor rule and the defeat of Richard's final supporters, among them Francis, Viscount Lovell, and John, earl of Lincoln, at the battle of Stoke in June 1487, brought with them an acceptance of the new version of Richard's reign, as seen through Tudor eyes. For the Italian poet Pietro Carmeliano, who had sought patronage at Richard's court, dedicating a *Life of St Catherine* to him in fulsome terms, new masters now needed to be served. In a poem celebrating the birth of a son and heir, Arthur, to Henry Tudor and his new wife, Elizabeth of York, Richard was now portrayed as a 'murderous tyrant' responsible for killing Henry VI, running a sword through his entrails. Carmeliano's slavish efforts paid off: by 1490, he was employed as Henry's Latin secretary.

Around the same time, the Warwickshire monk John Rous wrote a short *History of the Kings of England*, ending with Richard's reign. Conveniently forgetting the praise he had lavished upon Richard during his progress to Warwick in 1483, Rous now wrote that Richard was 'small of stature, with a short face and unequal shoulders, the right higher and the left lower', though the words 'right' and 'left' were added later, possibly by a second hand. 'This King Richard, who was excessively cruel in his days, reigned for three years and a little more', Rous concluded, 'in the way that the Antichrist is to reign. And like the Antichrist to come, he was confounded at his moment of greatest pride . . . Although his days were short', Rous closed, 'they were ended with no lamentation from his groaning subjects.' Taking the work he had composed in 1483, Rous now translated his English text into Latin, conveniently removing all mention of his previous praise of the dead king, describing Richard only as the 'unhappy husband' of Anne Neville.[10]

While both Rous and Carmeliano had a new patron to impress, other near-contemporary chroniclers, recording events somewhat more dispassionately, came to the same conclusions. 'And thus ended this man with dishonour as he that sought it', the author of the *Great Chronicle* wrote at the turn of the century, 'for had he continued still protector and have suffered the children to have prospered according to his allegiance and fidelity, he should have been honourably lauded over all, whereas now his fame is darkened and dishonoured as far as he was known, but God, that is all merciful, forgive him his misdeeds.'[11]

At York, the capital of Richard's own adopted heartland, memories of the dead king lingered. In December 1490, a quarrel broke out in a house between one John Painter and a schoolmaster, William Burton. Burton had arrived at the house, 'busy of language' and 'distempered either with ale or wine', when he took exception to Painter's presence, and ordered him out of the house. Some months later, details of their exchange were leaked to the city authorities. Painter, William Burton claimed, had told him that the earl of Northumberland 'was a traitor and betrayed King Richard, with much other unfitting language concerning the said earl'. Painter denied this, and gave his own version of events, describing how Burton himself had stated that 'King Richard was an hypocrite, a crouchback, and buried in a dike like a dog.' Painter retorted that he lied, 'for the king's good grace hath buried him like a noble gentleman'. Attempting to resolve the situation, the prior of Bolton wrote to inform the city council that 'where it is reported they should be busy with King Richard, they were not, but that the said schoolmaster said, he loved him never, and was buried in a dike'.

Richard's reputation would continue to be shaped by later commentators and historians, men such as the Italian Polydore Vergil, who did not arrive in England until 1502, and of course Thomas More in his famous history of Richard's reign. Both versions of events would contribute significantly to the fashioning of the so-called 'black legend' of Richard III. Their observations, even their words themselves, would be copied directly to form material for other chronicles and histories, which in turn became the historical basis for Shakespeare's own drama.

In the months that followed Richard's death, however, for the Crowland chronicler, dwelling upon Richard's life and short reign, it proved a time for reflection. 'I observe from the chronicles', he noted in an addition to his narrative, 'that no such end for a king of England, being killed that is on a battlefield in his own kingdom, has been heard since the time of King

Harold, who was an intruder and was defeated in battle by William the Conqueror coming from Normandy whence also these men had come.' It was at this point that the chronicler chose to include a poem, written 'taking into account the banners and badges of today's victor and vanquished and at the same time those of King Edward's sons whose cause, above all, was avenged in this battle, and what befell all three kings who after the Conquest of England were called Richard'. Like his namesakes Richard I and Richard II, Richard had 'in common an end without issue of their body, a life of greed and a violent fall'. He was, the poem continued, 'not content until he suppressed his brother's progeny and proscribed their supporters; at last, two years after taking violent possession of the kingdom he met these same people in battle and now has lost his grim life and his crown'. The poem ends: 'In the year 1485 on the 22nd day of August the tusks of the Boar were blunted and the red rose, the avenger of the white, shines upon us.'[12]

'Since it is the custom of writers of history normally to keep silent about the actions of living persons', the Crowland chronicler stated, he had 'decided to put an end to his labours with the death of King Richard.'[13] Completing his work at Crowland Abbey on the last day of April 1486, he turned to a final poem:

> You who read all these changes in the fortunes of great men, why do you not scorn all the mutabilities of the world; why does the glory of vain pomp touch you or your mind? For kings have fallen who would not submit to kings and who, abandoning the front door, entered through the back, confounding at the same time themselves and their own, not to mention mixing up the public with the private, so that neither blood, age, nor valour in battle, after this, could make a king . . .[14]

There are few words better suited to reflect upon the turbulent, transitory nature of Richard's own life. He had reigned as Richard III for 788 days; in battle he died aged 32 years, 10 months and 21 days.

ACKNOWLEDGEMENTS

This book has taken far longer than I anticipated to write, yet its completion would not have been possible without a number of people who have helped, inspired and provided their tireless support along the way. I am extremely grateful to my dedicated editorial team at Weidenfeld & Nicolson, whose patience and enthusiasm for this book has been truly appreciated. Alan Samson commissioned the book, and has been generous with both his time and advice throughout the project. Bea Hemming, the editor of my previous two books, dedicated herself to working on the first draft of the manuscript, helping to shape the final version; Simon Wright expertly helped to finish editing the book, patiently guiding me to completion. Celia Hayley brilliantly helped to weave different drafts of the manuscript together seamlessly, providing the encouragement to finish off the final material needed for the book. Mark Handsley has been an expert copyeditor, and Holly Harley diligently helped to finish the final stages of the book. Throughout the entire process, Georgina Capel has been a wonderful agent, kind and supportive, her commitment to the book and to myself never wavering.

There has been an outstanding amount of scholarship written about Richard III, to which I am indebted. The works of Michael Hicks, Rosemary Horrox, Tony Pollard and Anne Sutton are essential reading; I am grateful to Dr Horrox for sharing her expertise with me. Sean Cunningham and Hannes Kleineke have given generously both with their time and sharing documents and translations with me: I am extremely grateful for their friendship, advice and help. Peter Hammond and Carolyn Hammond have been incredibly generous in providing me with materials and transcripts from the Richard III Society; likewise the Society has been equally supportive and helpful in lending me back issues of *The Ricardian*. I owe a debt of gratitude to those who have helped with this book but have now sadly passed on, including the late Lesley Boatwright, Cliff Davies and David Baldwin. Others who have helped fashion my thinking on

Richard, through conversations and correspondence, include Peter Foss, Bob Woosnam-Savage from the Royal Armouries in Leeds, Michael K. Jones, Geoffrey Wheeler, and Richard Knox. I am grateful also to Margaret Lynch for her assistance in translating Polydore Vergil's Latin manuscript and other documents, and to Erkin Gozutok, Greg Howard, Jessica Lutkin and Callum Warren for their help with research. My mother has, as always, been a valued proofreader. Of course, any mistakes and errors, whether in fact or judgement, that I have made in writing this book are mine alone.

Finally, this book would simply not have been possible without the loving support and dedication of my wife, Lydia. Ever since I began researching Richard III four years ago, she has been both amazingly supportive and patient, allowing me to find the time to write late into the evening, listening to my ideas and providing constructive feedback. During this time, our two children, Clementine and Henry, have joined our family; juggling work, family life and writing a book has been difficult at times, but I could not have done it without her dedicated and loving support constantly in the background. Writing *Richard III*, has taken us both on a journey; I look forward to many more. For the moment, however, I am proud to dedicate this work to her.

SELECT BIBLIOGRAPHY

ABBREVIATIONS

Arrivall   J. Bruce (ed.), *Historie of the Arrivall of Edward IV in England and the Finall Recoverye of his Kingdomes from Henry VI A.D.MCCCC. LXXI*, London, 1838.

BL, Har 433   R. E. Horrox, and P. W. Hammond (eds.), British Library, Harleian Manuscript 433, 4 vols., 1979–83.

CC   *The Crowland Chronicle Continuations, 1459–1486*, ed. N. Pronay and J. Cox, London, 1986. Supplemented with H. T. Riley (ed.), *Ingulph's Chronicle of the Abbey of Croyland*, London, 1854.

CCR   *Calendar of the Close Rolls Preserved in the Public Record Office: 1468–76* (Edward IV), vol. 3, London, 1953; *1476–85* (Edward IV, Edward V, Richard III), vol. 4, London, 1954.

CPR   *Calendar of the Patent Rolls Preserved in the Public Record Office: 1461–7* (Edward IV), London, 1897; *1467–77* (Edward IV, Henry VI), London, 1900; *1476–85* (Edward IV, Edward V, Richard III), London, 1901.

CSP, Milan   Allen B. Hinds (ed.), *Calendar of State Papers and Manuscripts in the Archives and Collections of Milan: 1385–1618* (online at www.british-history.ac.uk)

CSP, Venice   R. Brown (ed.), *Calendar of State Papers and Manuscripts Existing in the Archives and Collections of Venice*, vol. I, *1202–1509*, London, 1864.

GC   *The Great Chronicle of London*, ed. A. H. Thomas and I. D. Thornley, London, 1938.

LPL   Lambeth Palace Library

Mancini   Dominic Mancini, *Usurpation of Richard III*, ed. C. A. J. Armstrong, 2nd edn, Oxford, 1969.

More   Thomas More, *History of King Richard III*, ed. R. S. Sylvester, New Haven, Conn., 1963.

PL   J. Gairdner (ed.), *The Paston Letters 1422–1509*, 6 vols., London, 1904. Latest edition: N. Davis et al. (eds.), *Paston Letters and Papers of the Fifteenth Century*, Oxford, 2004–5.

PROME   C. Given-Wilson et al. (eds.), *The Parliament Rolls of Medieval England*, 16 vols., Woodbridge, 2005.

Rous   'John Rous's account of the reign of Richard III', translated from *Historia Regum Angliae* in A. Hanham, *Richard III and His Early Historians*, Oxford, 1975, pp. 118–24.

RP   J. Strachey et al. (eds.), *Rotuli Parliamentorum*, 6 vols, 1777.

TNA   The National Archives, Kew.

Vergil   H. Ellis, *Three Books of Polydore Vergil's English History*, London, 1844.

Warkworth   John Warkworth, *A Chronicle of the First Thirteen Years of the Reign of Edward IV* (1461–74), ed. J. O. Halliwell, London, 1839.

YCR   A. Raine (ed.), *York Civic Records*, 2 vols., Yorkshire Archaeological Society Record Series, 98 (1939) and 103 (1941).

YHB   L. C. Atreed (ed.), *York House Books, 1461–90*, 2 vols., Stroud, 1991.

MANUSCRIPTS CITED

BRITISH LIBRARY (BL)

Additional MS 7099, 12,060, 12,520, 19,393, 19,398, 48,976
Additional charter 5987, 67,545
Cotton MS Julius B XII
     Vespasian F III
     Vitellus A XVI
Harleian charter 58.F.49
Harleian MS 433, 542, 787, 793, 1546
Sloane MS 3479

THE NATIONAL ARCHIVES (TNA)

C	1	Early Chancery proceedings
	4	Chancery answers
	56	Confirmation rolls
	66	Patent rolls
	67	Pardon rolls
	81	Chancery warrants, series 1
	82	Chancery warrants, series 2
	244	Corpus cum causa

CP	25	Feet of fines
DL	5	Duchy of Lancaster, council minutes
	29	Accounts of auditors, receivers, feodaries and ministers
	37	Chancery rolls
	39	Forest records
	42	Miscellaneous books
E	101	Exchequer, KR, accounts various
	159	Memoranda rolls and enrolment books
	207	Bille
	208	Brevia baronibus
	361	Enrolled wardrobe and household accounts
	401	Exchequer of receipt, receipt rolls
	402	Tellers' bills
	403	Issue rolls and registers
	404	Warrants for issues
	405	Tellers' rolls
KB	9	King's bench, ancient indictments
	29	Controlment rolls
PROB	2	Inventories, pre-1661
	11	Prerogative Court of Canterbury wills
PSO	1	Privy seal warrants, series 1
SC	1	Ancient correspondence, chancery and exchequer

BIBLIOTECA APOSTOLICA VATICANA, ROME

Urbini Latini 498

BODLEIAN LIBRARY, OXFORD

Ashmole MS 1448

CANTERBURY RECORD OFFICE (CRO)

FA 7 City Accounts

COVENTRY CITY ARCHIVES

BA/H/Q/A79/8 Richard III Letter

DEVON RECORD OFFICE, EXETER

ECA Book 51, Hooker's commonplace book
Exeter receivers' accounts

KINGSTON UPON HULL RECORD OFFICE

BRG 1/1 fo. 133v

LONDON METROPOLITAN ARCHIVES (LMA)

Journals of Common Council VII, VIII, IX
Col/cc/01/01/009

NORFOLK RECORD OFFICE

King's Lynn Hall Books, KL/C7/4

WARWICKSHIRE COUNTY RECORD OFFICE

CR 26/4

YORK CITY ARCHIVES (YCA)

House Books, 1, 2/4, 7

PRINTED PRIMARY SOURCES

Attreed, L. C. (ed.), *York House Books 1461–1490*, 2 vols., Stroud, 1991
Barnard, F. P., *Edward IV's French Expedition of 1475: The Leaders and Their Badges*, Gloucester, 1975
Basin, Thomas, *Histoire de Louis XI*, ed. C. Samaran and M.-C. Garand, 3 vols., Paris, 1963–72
Bentley, S., *Excerpta Historica, or, Illustrations of English History*, London, 1833
Bishop Percy's Folio Manuscript, ed. J. W. Hales and F. J. Furnivall, 3 vols., London, 1868
Blair, C. H. Hunter, 'Two Letters Patent from Hutton John near Penrith, Cumberland', *Archaeologia Aeliana*, 4th series, vol. 39 (1961), pp. 367–70
British Library, Harleian MS 433, ed. R. E. Horrox and P. W. Hammond, 4 vols., London, 1979–83
Bruce, J. (ed.), *Historie of the Arrivall of Edward IV in England and the Finall Recoverye of his Kingdomes from Henry VI A.D.MCCCC.LXXI*, London, 1838
Buck, Sir George, *The History of King Richard the Third*, ed. A. N. Kincaid, Gloucester, 1979
Calendar of Close Rolls (CCR), 1461–85, 3 vols., HMSO, 1949–54
Calendar of Patent Rolls (CPR), 1441–1509, 8 vols., HMSO, 1908–16
Campbell, W. (ed.), *Materials for a History of the Reign of Henry VII*, 2 vols., London, 1873–7
Cely Letters 1472–1488, The, ed. A. Hanham, London, 1975
Christ Church Letters, ed. J. B. Sheppard, London, 1877

Chronica Monasterii S. Albani: registra quorundam abbatum monasterii S. Albani, qui saeculo xvmo flouere II Registra Johannis Whethamstede, Willelmi Albon et Willelmi Walingforde, ed. H. T. Riley, Rolls Series, 1873

Collier, J. P. (ed.), *Household Books of John Duke of Norfolk and Thomas Earl of Surrey, 1481–1490*, Roxburghe Club, 1844

Commynes, Philippe de, *Memoirs*, trans. M. Jones, Harmondsworth, 1972

The Crowland Chronicle Continuations, 1459–1486, ed. N. Pronay and J. Cox, London, 1986

Davies, R. (ed.), *Extracts from the Municipal Records of the City of York during the Reigns of Edward IV, Edward V and Richard III*, London, 1843

Dobson, R. B. (ed.), *York City Chamberlains' Account Rolls, 1396–1500*, Gateshead, 1980

Ellis, H. (ed.), *Original Letters Illustrative of English History*, 2nd series, vol. I, 1827

—, *Three Books of Polydore Vergil's English History*, London, 1844

Fabyan, Robert, *The New Chronicles of England and France*, ed. H. Ellis, London, 1811

Foedera, Conventiones, Literae, et cujuscunque generis acta publica, inter Reges Angliae, ed. Thomas Rymer, 20 vols., London, 1704–5

Gairdner, J. (ed.), *The Paston Letters 1422–1509*, 6 vols., London, 1904

Great Chronicle of London, The, ed. A. H. Thomas and I. D. Thornley, London, 1938

Green, R. Firth, 'Historical Notes of a London Citizen, 1483–1488', *English Historical Review*, vol. 96 (1981), pp. 585–90

Halle, Edward, *The Union of the Two Noble and Illustrious Families of Lancaster and York*, London, 1550; reprinted in facsimile, Menston, 1970

Halliwell, J. O. (ed.), *Letters of the Kings of England*, vol. I, London, 1848

Hardyng, John, *The Chronicle of John Hardyng, with the Continuation by Richard Grafton*, ed. H. Ellis, London, 1812

Hicks, M. A., 'The Last Days of Elizabeth Countess of Oxford', *English Historical Review*, vol. 103 (1988), 76–95

Historical Manuscripts Commission (HMC), 12th Report, *Rutland Manuscripts*, vol. I (1888)

—, 78, *Report on the Manuscripts of the late R. R. Hastings*, vol. I (1928)

Holinshed, Raphael, *Chronicles of England, Scotland and Ireland*, 6 vols., London, 1807–8

Horrox, R. E. (ed.), 'Financial Memoranda of the Reign of Edward V: Longleat Miscellaneous Manuscript Book II', London, 1987, pp. 199–244

Horrox, R. E and P. W. Hammond (eds.), British Library, Harleian Manuscript 433, 4 vols., 1979–83

Leathes, S. M. (ed.), *Grace Book A*, Cambridge, 1897

Leland, J., *The Itinerary of John Leland*, ed. L. Toulmin-Smith, 5 vols., 1906–10

Lyell, L. and F. D. Watney (eds.), *Acts of Court of the Mercers' Company, 1453–1527*, Cambridge, 1936

Mackay, A. J. G. (ed.), *The Historie and Chronicles of Scotland ... Written and Collected by Robert Lindesay of Pittscottie*, 3 vols., vol. I, Edinburgh, 1899–1911

Mancini, Dominic, *Usurpation of Richard III*, ed. C. A. J. Armstrong, 2nd edn, Oxford, 1969

More, Thomas, *The History of King Richard III*, ed. R. S. Sylvester, New Haven, Conn., 1963

Molinet, Jean, *Chroniques de Jean Molinet*, ed. J. A. Buchon, 2 vols, Paris, 1828

Nichols, J. G. (ed.), *Grants etc from the Crown during the Reign of Edward the Fifth*, London, 1854

—, (ed.), *Camden Miscellany*, vol. I: *Chronicle of the Rebellion in Lincolnshire, in 1470*, London, 1847

Nicolas, N. H., *Testamenta Vetusta*, London, 1826

The Paston Letters and Papers of the Fifteenth Century, ed. N. Davis, 2 vols., Oxford, 1971–6

Plumpton Correspondence, ed. T. Stapleton, London, 1839

Raine, A., ed., *York Civic Records*, vol. I, Wakefield, 1939

Raine, J., 'The Statutes Ordained by Richard, Duke of Gloucester, for the College of Middleham. Dated 4 July, 18. Edw. IV, (1478)', *Archaeological Journal*, vol. 14 (1857)

Registrum Thome Bourgchier, Cantauriensis Archiepiscopi A.D. 1454–86, ed. F. R. H. du Boulay, Oxford, 1957

Reisebeschreibung Niclas von Popplau, Ritters, bürtig von Breslau, ed. Piotr Radzikowski, Kraków, 1998

Riley, H. T. (ed.), *Ingulph's Chronicle of the Abbey of Croyland*, London, 1854

Rotuli Parliamentorum, ed. J. Strachey et al., 6 vols., London, 1767–77

Rous, John, *Historia Regum Angliae*, Oxford, 1745

Stonor Letters and Papers, 1290–1483, The, ed. C. L. Kingsford, 2 vols., London, 1919

Stowe, John, *The Annales of England*, London, 1592

Sutton, A. F. and P. W. Hammond (eds.), *The Coronation of Richard III: The Extant Documents*, Gloucester, 1983

Sutton A. F. and L. Visser-Fuchs, *The Hours of Richard III*, Stroud, 1990

—, *The Reburial of Richard Duke of York 21–30 July 1476*, London, 1996

Thomas A. H. and I. D. Thornley (eds.), *The Great Chronicle of London*, Gloucester, 1983

Turner, T. H. (ed.), *Manners and Household Expenses of England in the Thirteenth and Fifteenth Centuries*, London, 1841

W.W.E.W., 'Grant from Richard, Duke of Gloucester to Reginald Vaughan – 10 Edw. IV', *Archaeologia Cambrensis*, 3rd series, vol. XXXIII (1863), p. 55

Warkworth, John, *A Chronicle of the First Thirteen Years of the Reign of King Edward IV*, ed. J. O. Halliwell, London, 1839

Waurin, Jehan de, *Recueil des Croniques et Anchiennes Istories de la Grant Bretaigne, a present nomme Engleterre*, ed. W. and E. L. C. P. Hardy, 5 vols., London, 1864–91

SECONDARY WORKS

Antonovics, A. V., 'Henry VII, King of England, "by the grace of Charles VII of France"', in Griffiths and Sherborne (eds.), *Kings and Nobles*, Gloucester, 1986, pp. 169–84

Armstrong, C. A. J., 'The Inauguration Ceremonies of the Yorkist Kings and Their Title to the Throne', *Transactions of the Royal Historical Society*, 4th series, vol. 30 (1948), pp. 51–73

Ashdown-Hill, J., 'Walsingham in 1469: The Pilgrimage of Edward IV and Richard, Duke of Gloucester', *The Ricardian*, vol. 11, no. 136 (March 1997), pp. 2–16

Attreed, L. C., 'The King's Interest: York's Fee Farm and the Central Government, 1482–92', *Northern History*, vol. 17 (1981), pp. 24–43

—, 'An Indenture between Richard Duke of Gloucester and the Scrope Family of Masham and Upsall', *Speculum*, vol. 58, no. 4 (1983), pp. 1018–25

Baldwin, D., 'King Richard's Grave in Leicester', *Transactions of the Leicestershire Archaeological and Historical Society*, vol. 60 (1986), pp. 21–2

—, *Richard III*, Stroud, 2013

Barnfield, M., 'Diriment Impediments, Dispensations and Divorce: Richard III and Matrimony', *The Ricardian*, vol. 17 (2007), pp. 84–98

Bennett, M., *The Battle of Bosworth*, Gloucester, 1985

Breeze, A. A., 'A Welsh Poem of 1485 on Richard III', *The Ricardian*, vol. 18 (2008), pp. 46–53

Britnell, R., 'Richard, Duke of Gloucester and the Death of Thomas Fauconberg', *The Ricardian*, vol. 10, no. 128 (1995)

Carlin, M., 'Sir John Fastolf's Place, Southwark: The Home of the Duke of York's Family 1460', *The Ricardian*, vol. 5, no. 72 (1981), pp. 311–14

Chrimes, S. B., *Henry VII*, London, 1972

Chrimes S. B., C. D. Ross and R. A. Griffiths (eds.), *Fifteenth-Century England 1399–1509: Studies in Politics and Society*, Manchester, 1972

Clarke, P. D., 'English Royal Marriages and the Papal Penitentiary in the Fifteenth Century', *English Historical Review*, vol. 120, no. 488 (2005), pp. 1014–29

Coles, G. M., 'The Lordship of Middleham, Especially in Yorkist and Early Tudor Times', unpublished MA thesis, Liverpool University, 1961

Condon, M., 'The Kaleidoscope of Treason: Fragments from the Bosworth Story', *The Ricardian*, vol. 7, no. 92 (March 1986), pp. 208–12

Conway, A. E., 'The Maidstone Sector of Buckingham's Rebellion', *Archaeologia Cantiana*, vol. 37 (1925), pp. 97–120

Crawford, A., 1985, 'The Mowbray inheritance' in Petre (ed.), *Richard III: Crown and People*, pp. 79–85

—, 'The Private Life of John Howard', in Hammond (ed.), *Richard III: Loyalty, Lordship and Law*, pp. 6–24

Cunningham, S., '"More through fear than love": The Herefordshire Gentry, the

Alien Subsidy of 1483 and Regional Responses to Richard III's Usurpation', *The Ricardian*, vol. 13 (2003), pp. 159–73

Davies, C. S. L., 'Bishop John Morton, the Holy See, and the Accession of Henry VII', *English Historical Review*, vol. 102 (1987), pp. 2–30

Dobson, R. B., 'Richard Bell, Prior of Durham (1464–78) and Bishop of Carlisle (1478–95)', *Transactions of the Cumberland and Westmorland Antiquarian and Archaeological Society*, new series, vol. 65 (1965), pp. 182–221

—, 'Richard III and the Church of York', in Griffiths and Sherborne (eds.), *Kings and Nobles*, pp. 130–54

Dunham, W. H., 'Lord Hastings' Indentured Retainers, 1461–83', *Transactions of the Connecticut Academy of Arts and Sciences*, vol. 39 (1955), reprinted Hamden, Conn., 1970

Edwards, R., *The Itinerary of King Richard III, 1483–1485*, London, 1983

Gairdner, J., *History of the Life and Reign of Richard the Third*, new edn, Cambridge, 1898

Gillingham, J., *The Wars of the Roses: Peace and Conflict in Fifteenth-Century England*, London, 1981

—, (ed.), *Richard III: A Medieval Kingship*, London, 1993

Goodman, A., *The Wars of the Roses: Military Activity and English Society, 1452–97*, London, 1981

Goodman, A. and A. MacKay, 'A Castilian Report on English Affairs, 1486', *English Historical Review*, vol. 88 (1973), pp. 92–9

Griffiths, R. A. and J. Sherborne (eds.), *Kings and Nobles in the Later Middle Ages: A Tribute to Charles Ross*, Gloucester, 1986

Griffiths, R. A. and R. S. Thomas, *The Making of the Tudor Dynasty*, Gloucester, 1985

Guth, D. J., 'Richard III, Henry VII and the City: London Politics and the "dun cowe"', in Griffiths and Sherborne (eds.), *Kings and Nobles*, pp. 185–204

Hairsine, R., 'Oxford University and the Life and Legend of Richard III', in Petre (ed.), *Richard III: Crown and People*, pp. 307–32

Hammond, P. W., 'The Illegitimate Children of Richard III', *The Ricardian*, vol. 5, no. 66 (September 1979), pp. 92–6

—, (ed.), *Richard III: Loyalty, Lordship and Law*, London, 1986

Hammond, P. W. and A. F. Sutton, *Richard III: The Road to Bosworth Field*, London, 1985

Hanham, A., *Richard III and His Early Historians 1483–1535*, Oxford, 1975

Harris, O. D., 'The Transmission of the News of the Tudor Landing', *The Ricardian*, vol. 4, no. 55 (December 1976), pp. 5–12

Helmholz, R. H., 'The Sons of Edward IV: A Canonical Assessment of the Claim That They were Illegitimate', in Hammond (ed.), *Richard III: Loyalty, Lordship and Law*, pp. 91–103

Hicks, M. A., 'Dynastic Change and Northern Society: The Career of the Fourth Earl of Northumberland, 1470–89', *Northern History*, vol. 14 (1978), pp. 78–107

—, 'The Changing Role of the Wydevilles in Yorkist Politics to 1483', in Ross (ed.), *Patronage, Pedigree and Power*, pp. 60–86

—, 'Descent, Partition and Extinction: The Warwick Inheritance', *Bulletin of the Institute of Historical Research*, vol. 52 (1979), pp. 116–28

—, *False, Fleeting, Perjur'd Clarence: George, Duke of Clarence, 1449–78*, Gloucester, 1980

—, 'Richard, Duke of Gloucester and the North', in Horrox, *Richard III and the North*, pp. 11–26

—, *Richard III and Duke of Gloucester: A Study in Character*, York, 1986

—, *Richard III: The Man behind the Myth*, Stroud, 1991

—, 'Unweaving the Web: The Plot of July 1483 against Richard III and Its Wider Significance', *The Ricardian*, vol. 9, no. 114 (September 1991)

—, 'One Prince or Two? The Family of Richard III', ibid., vol. 9, no. 122 (September 1993)

—, 'Richard Lord Latimer, Richard III and the Warwick Inheritance', ibid., vol. 12, no. 154 (September 2001)

—, *Anne Neville: Queen to Richard III*, Stroud, 2006

Horrox, R. E., 'Richard III and Allhallows Barking by the Tower', *The Ricardian*, vol. 6, no. 77 (June 1982), pp. 38–40

—, 'Preparation for Edward IV's Return from Exile', ibid., vol. 6, no. 79 (December 1982), pp. 124–7

—, 'Henry Tudor's Letters to England during Richard III's Reign', ibid., vol. 6, no. 80 (March 1983), pp. 155–8

—, 'Richard III and London', ibid., vol. 6, no. 85 (June 1984), pp. 322–9

—, *Richard III and the North*, Hull, 1986

—, *Richard III: A Study in Service*, Cambridge, 1989

Horrox R. E. and A. F. Sutton, 'Some Expenses of Richard, Duke of Gloucester 1475–7', *The Ricardian*, vol. 6, no. 83 (December 1983), pp. 266–9

Hughes, J., *The Religious Life of Richard III*, Stroud, 1997

Ives, E. W., 'Andrew Dymmock and the Papers of Anthony, Earl Rivers, 1482–3', *Bulletin of the Institute of Historical Research*, vol. 41 (1968), pp. 216–29

Jones, E. W., *Bosworth: A Welsh Retrospect*, Liverpool, 1984

Jones, M. K., 'Richard III and the Stanleys', in Horrox, *Richard III and the North*, pp. 27–50

—, 'Richard III and Lady Margaret Beaufort: A Re-assessment', in Hammond (ed.), *Richard III: Loyalty, Lordship and Law*, pp. 25–37

—, 'Sir William Stanley of Holt: Politics and Family Allegiance in the Late Fifteenth Century', *Welsh History Review*, vol. 14 (1988), pp. 1–22

—, 'Richard, Duke of Gloucester and the Scropes of Masham', *The Ricardian*, vol. 10, no. 134 (September 1996), pp. 454–60

—, *Bosworth 1485: Psychology of a Battle*, Stroud, 2002

Kelly, H. A., 'Canonical Implications of Richard III's Plan to Marry his Niece', *Traditio*, vol. 23 (January 1967), pp. 269–311

Kendall, P. M., *Richard the Third*, London, 1955

Kleineke, H., 'Alice Martyn, Widow of London: An Episode from Richard's Youth', *The Ricardian*, vol. 14 (2004), pp. 32–6

—, 'Richard III and the Court of Requests', ibid., vol. 17 (2007), pp. 22–32

—, *Edward IV*, London, 2008

Lander, J. R., *Crown and Nobility 1450–1509*, London, 1976

Langley, P and M. Jones, *The King's Grave: The Search for Richard III*, London, 2013

Levine, M., 'Richard III – Usurper of Lawful King?', *Speculum*, vol. 34 (1959), pp. 391–401

McFarlane, K. B., *The Nobility of Later Medieval England*, Oxford, 1953

—, 'The Wars of the Roses', *Proceedings of the British Academy*, vol. 1 (1964)

—, *England in the Fifteenth Century*, ed. G. L. Harriss, London, 1981

Metcalfe, W. C., *A Book of Knights Banneret, Knights of the Bath and Knights Bachelor*, London, 1885

Myers, A. R., 'The Character of Richard III', *History Today*, August 1954

Nokes, E. M, and G. Wheeler, 'A Spanish Account of the Battle of Bosworth', *The Ricardian*, vol. 2, no. 36 (1972), p. 2

Orme, N., 1984, 'The education of Edward V', *Bulletin of the Institute for Historical Research*, vol. 57, no. 136 (November 1984), pp. 119–30

Palliser, D. M., 'Richard III and York', in Horrox, *Richard III and the North*, pp. 51–81

Petre, J. (ed.), *Richard III: Crown and People*, London, 1985

Pollard A. J., 'The Tyranny of Richard III', *Journal of Medieval History*, vol. III, no. 2 (1977)

—, 'Richard Clervaux of Croft', *Yorkshire Archaeological Journal*, vol. 50, no. 9 (1978), pp. 151–69

—, 'The Richmondshire Community of Gentry during the Wars of the Roses', in Ross (ed.), *Patronage, Pedigree and Power*, pp. 37–59

—, 'North, South, and Richard III', *The Ricardian*, vol. 5, no. 74 (September 1981), pp. 384–9

—, *The Middleham Connection. Richard III and Richmondshire 1471–1485*, Middleham, 1983

—, (ed.), *Property and Politics: Essays in Later Medieval English History*, Gloucester, 1984

—, 'St Cuthbert and the Hog: Richard III and the County Palatine of Durham, 1471–85', in Griffiths and Sherborne (eds.), *Kings and Nobles*, pp. 109–29

—, *North-Eastern England during the Wars of the Roses: Lay Society, War and Politics 1450–1500*, Oxford, 1990

—, *Richard III and the Princes in the Tower*, Stroud, 1991

Potter, J., *Good King Richard? An Account of Richard III and His Reputation*, London, 1983

Radzikowski, P., 1998, 'Niclas von Popplau – His Work and Travels', *The Ricardian*, vol. XI, no. 140 (March 1998), pp. 239–48

Reeves, A. C., 'King Richard III at York in Late Summer 1483', ibid., vol. 12, no. 159 (December 2002), pp. 542–53

Richmond, C. F., 'Fauconberg's Kentish Rising of May 1471', *English Historical Review*, vol. 85, no. 337 (1970), pp. 673–92

—, 'The Death of Edward V', *Northern History*, vol. 25 (1989), pp. 278–80

—, 'The Nobility and the Coronation of Richard III', *The Ricardian*, vol. 12, no. 148 (March 2000), pp. 653–9

Roskell, J. S., 'The Office and Dignity of the Protector of England, with Special Reference to Its Origins', *English Historical Review*, vol. 68 (1953), pp. 193–233

—, 'William Catesby, Counsellor to Richard III', *Bulletin of the John Rylands Library*, vol. 42 (1959), pp. 145–74

Ross, C., *Edward IV*, New Haven, Conn., 1974

—, 'Some "Servants and Lovers" of Richard in his Youth', *The Ricardian*, vol. 4, no. 55 (December 1976), pp. 2–4

— (ed.), *Patronage, Pedigree and Power in Later Medieval England*, Gloucester, 1979

—, *Richard III*, New Haven, Conn., 1981

Ross, J., 'Richard, Duke of Gloucester and the De Vere Estates', *The Ricardian*, vol. 15 (2005), pp. 20–32

Rowney, I., 'Resources and Retaining in Yorkist England: William Lord Hastings and the Honour of Tutbury', in Pollard (ed.), *Property and Politics*, pp. 139–55

—, 'The Hastings Affinity in Staffordshire and the Honour of Tutbury', *Bulletin of the Institute for Historical Research*, vol. 57 (1984), pp. 35–45

Scofield, C., *The Life and Reign of Edward the Fourth*, 2 vols., London, 1923

Seward, D, *Richard III: England's Black Legend*, London, 1983

Skidmore, C., *Bosworth: The Birth of the Tudors*, London, 2013

Sutton, A. F., 'The Return to England of Richard of Gloucester after His First Exile', *The Ricardian*, vol. 3, no. 50 (September 1975), pp. 21–2

—, 'The Administration of Justice whereunto We be Professed', ibid., vol. 4, no. 53 (June 1976), pp. 4–15

—, 'Richard III's "Tytylle & Right": A New Discovery', ibid., vol. 4, no. 57 (1977), pp. 2–8

—, 'Richard III, the City of London and Southwark', in Petre (ed.), *Richard III: Crown and People*, pp. 289–95

—, '"A curious searcher for our weal public": Richard III, Piety, Chivalry and the Concept of the "Good Prince"', in Hammond (ed.), *Richard III: Loyalty, Lordship and Law*, pp. 58–90

—, '"And to be delivered to the Lord Richard Duke of Gloucester, the other brother . . ."', *The Ricardian*, vol. 8, no. 100 (March 1988), pp. 20–25

Sutton, A. F. and L. Visser-Fuchs, 'Richard III and St Julian: A New Myth', ibid., vol. 8, no. 106 (September 1989), pp. 265–70

—, 'The Prophecy of G', ibid., vol. 8, no. 110 (September 1990), pp. 449–50

—, '"Richard Liveth Yet": An Old Myth', ibid., vol. 9, no. 117 (June 1992), pp. 262–9

— , 'Richard III's Books: Ancestry and "True Nobility"', ibid., vol 9, no. 119 (December 1992), pp. 343–58

—, 'Richard III's Books Observed', ibid., vol. 9, no. 120 (March 1993), pp. 374–88

—, 'Richard of Gloucester and La Grosse Bombarde', ibid., vol. 10, no. 134 (1996), pp. 461–5

—, *Richard III's Books: Ideals and Reality in the Life and Library of a Medieval Prince*, Stroud, 1997

—, 'Richard III, the Universities of Oxford and Cambridge, and Two Turbulent Priests', *The Ricardian*, vol. 19 (2009), pp. 95–109

Thompson, J. A. F., 'Richard III and Lord Hastings – a Problematical Case Reviewed', *Bulletin of the Institute of Historical Research*, vol. 48 (1975), pp. 22–30

—, 'Bishop Lionel Woodville and Richard III', ibid., vol. 49 (1986)

Tudor-Craig, P. (ed.), *Richard III*, London, 1973

Virgoe, R., 'Sir John Risley (1443–1512), Courtier and Councillor', *Norfolk Archaeology*, vol. 38 (1981), pp. 140–48

Visser-Fuchs, L., 'Richard in Holland, 1461', *The Ricardian*, vol. 6, no. 81 (June 1983), pp. 182–9

—, 'Richard in Holland, 1471–2', ibid., vol. 6, no. 82 (September 1983), pp. 220–28

—, 'Edward IV's "Memoir on Paper" to Charles, Duke of Burgundy: The So-called "Short Version of the Arrivall"', *Nottingham Medieval Studies*, vol. 36 (1992), pp. 167–227

—, '"He hardly touched his food": What Niclas von Popplau Really Wrote about Richard III', *The Ricardian*, vol. 11, no. 145 (June 1999), pp. 525–30

—, 'Richard was late', ibid., vol. 11, no. 147 (December 1999), pp. 616–19

Warnicke, R. M., 'Lord Morley's Statements about Richard III', *Albion*, vol. XIV (1983)

—, 'Sir Ralph Bigod: A Loyal Servant to Richard III', *The Ricardian*, vol. 6, no. 84 (March 1984), pp. 299–303

Weiss, M., 'A Power in the North? The Percies in the Fifteenth Century', *The Historical Journal*, vol. 19, no. 2 (June 1976), pp. 501–9

White, W. J., 'The Death and Burial of Henry VI, A Review of the Facts and Theories', *The Ricardian*, vol. 6, nos. 78 (September 1982), pp. 70–80, and 79 (December 1982), pp. 106–17

Wilkinson, J., *Richard, the Young King to Be*, Stroud, 2009

Williams, B., 'The Portuguese Connection and the Significance of "the Holy Princess"', *The Ricardian*, vol. 6, no. 80 (March 1983), pp. 138–45

Wood, C. T., 'The Deposition of Edward V', *Traditio*, vol. 31 (1975), pp. 247–86

—, 'Richard III, Lord Hastings and Friday the Thirteenth', in Griffiths and Sherborne (eds.), *Kings and Nobles*, pp. 155–68

NOTES

PROLOGUE

1 *Reisebeschreibung Niclas von Popplau*, p. 44.
2 Ibid., pp. 51–2.
3 Ibid., p. 53.
4 Ibid., pp. 54–5.
5 Popplau noted: 'For the English use these words towards persons of both high and low rank, whether they come from this land or elsewhere. They also use them at gatherings, invitations to meals, and occasions when one blessed another, saying: I welcome you. In the same way the King's councillors, princes and lords, and gentry addressed me to do me honour.'
6 Ibid. pp. 58–9.
7 The word here is *dick*, which can mean fat, but that seems improbable.
8 Ibid., p. 59.
9 Radzikowski, 'Niclas von Popplau – His Work and Travels', pp. 239–48, at pp. 242–3.
10 Mancini, pp. 22–3; Seward, *Richard III*, p. 253 n.11; *Reisebeschreibung Niclas von Popplau*, p. 59.
11 Quoted in Ross, *Richard III and His Rivals*, p. ix.
12 Hanham, *Richard III and His Early Historians*, pp. 106, 120, 123; BL, Additional MS 48976; C. Ross, *The Rous Roll*, Gloucester, 1980.
13 See G. R. Elton, *England 1200–1640*, London, 1969, p. 22; Ross, *Edward IV*, Appendix I: 'Note on Narrative Sources', pp. 429–35.
14 For some of the debate on the authorship of the *Crowland Chronicle*, see H. A. Kelly, 'The Last Chroniclers of Croyland', *The Ricardian*, vol. VII, no. 91 (1985), pp. 142–77; H. A. Kelly, 'The *Croyland Chronicle* Tragedies', *The Ricardian*, vol. VII, no. 99 (1987), pp. 498–515; A. Hanham, 'Richard Lavender, Continuator?', *The Ricardian*, vol. VII, no. 99 (1987), pp. 516–19; L. Visser-Fuchs, 'A Commentary on the Continuation', *The Ricardian*, vol. VII, no. 99 (1987), pp. 520–22; D. Williams (ed.), 'The *Crowland Chronicle*, 616–1500', in *England and the Fifteenth Century*, (Woodbridge, 1987), pp. 371–90; M. Condon, 'The *Crowland Chronicle Continuations 1459–1486*', *History and Archaeology Review*, vol. 3 (1988), pp. 5–11; A. Hanham, 'Croyland Observations', *The Ricardian*, vol. VIII, no. 108 (1990), pp. 334–41; A. Hanham, 'Author! Author! Crowland Revisited', *The Ricardian*, vol. XI, no. 140 (1998), pp. 226–39; M. A. Hicks, 'The Second Anonymous Continuation of the Crowland Abbey Chronicle 1459–86 Revisited', *English Historical Review*, vol. CXXII (2007), pp. 346–70.
15 *CC*, p. 171.
16 See Kelly, 'Last Chroniclers', pp. 143, 153; Lincolnshire Archives Office, Register of John Russell, fo. 78v.
17 Vatican, MS *Urbs Lat* 498, fo. 235r.

1. SONS OF YORK

1 Warkworth, p. 21; *Arrivall*, p. 38.

2 'Yorkist Notes, 1471', printed in C. L. Kingsford, *English Historical Literature in the Fifteenth Century*, Oxford, 1913, p. 375.

3 *CC*, p. 129.

4 *Arrivall*, p. 38.

5 Ibid.

6 *CC*, p. 129.

7 Warkworth, p. 21.

8 *CSP, Milan* I, p. 157.

9 Warkworth, p. 21.

10 *CCR*, pp. 229–30.

11 Hanham, *Richard III and His Early Historians*, p. 210; More, p. 8: 'The Duchess his mother had so much a do in her travail, that she could not be delivered of him uncut: and that he came into the world with the feet forward, as men be born outward, and (as the fame runneth) also not untoothed.'

12 Hanham, *Richard III and His Early Historians*, p. 210.

13 Lambeth Palace Library, MS 474 fo. 7v: 'hac die natus erat Ricardus Rex Anglie iii apud ffodringay anno domini MCCC[Clii]'.

14 H. K. Bonney, *Historic Notices in Relation to Fotheringhay*, Oundle, 1921, p. 27.

15 Anne Crawford (ed.), *Letters of Medieval Women*, Stroud, 2002, pp. 234–5.

16 *PL*, vol. II pp. 295–6.

17 *PL*, vol. II p. 13.

18 Whetehamstede, J., Registrum, ed. H. T. Riley, 2 vols., Rolls Series, 1872–3, I p. 164; R. Griffiths, *The Reign of Henry VI*, London, 1981, pp. 740–41 n. 144.

19 Whetehamstede, vol. I p. 341.

20 *The Chronicles of the White Rose of York*, ed. J. A. Giles, London, 1843, pp. 5–6.

21 *An English Chronicle of the Reigns of Richard II, Henry IV, Henry V, Henry VI*, London, 1856, p. 83.

22 *RP*, vol. V, pp. 349–50.

23 *The Historical Collections of a Citizen of London in the 15th Century, Containing . . . Gregory's Chronicle*, ed. J. Gairdner, London, 1876, pp. 206–7.

24 Ross, *Edward IV*, Appendix I: 'Note on Narrative Sources', pp. 22–6.

25 William Worcester, *Annales rerum anglicarum*, 1728, p. 775; *Three Fifteenth-Century Chronicles*, ed. J. Gairdner, London, 1880, p. 172. See also *Registrum Abbatiae Johannis Whethamstede*, in *Chronica monasterii S. Albani*, vol. I, p. 382.

26 Riley (ed.), *Ingulph's Chronicle of the Abbey of Croyland*, p. 422; *Registrum Abbatiae Johannis Whethamstede*, p. 390; F. W. D. Brie (ed.), *The Brute of England; or the Chronicles of England*, London, 1906, vol. II, p. 531; *Historical . . . Gregory's Chronicle*, p. 211; Edward Halle, *Chronicle, Containing the History of England . . .*, ed. H. Ellis, London, 1809, p. 251.

27 *PL*, vol. I, p. 198; See also 'The Rose of Rouen', *Archaeologia*, vol. XXIX (1842), p. 344.

28 *PL*, vol. II, pp. 216–17; Carlin, 'Sir John Fastolf's Place, Southwark', pp. 311–14.

29 TNA, PSO1/23/1247B; Kleineke, 'Alice Martyn, Widow of London', pp. 32–6.

30 *GC*, p. 195.

31 See Frederic W. Madden, *Political Poems Written in the Reigns of Henry VI and Edward IV*, London, 1842, p. 345.
32 Visser-Fuchs, 'Richard in Holland, 1461'.
33 *CSP, Milan*, p. 73, no. 90.
34 Visser-Fuchs, 'Richard in Holland', p. 188.
35 HMC, 9th Report, vol. I, Appendix, p. 140; *The Chronicle of John Stone, Monk of Christ Church*, ed. W. G. Searle, Cambridge, 1902, p. 83.
36 Sutton, 'The Return to England of Richard of Gloucester', pp. 21–2.
37 TNA, E404/72/1/4.
38 *Historical Collections of a Citizen of London*, p. 215; Ross, *Edward IV*, p. 32.
39 *CSP, Venice* I, no. 374.

2. THE WHEEL TURNS

1 TNA, E404/72/1/59.
2 TNA, E361/6 m.53d; Hicks, *False, Fleeting, Perjur'd Clarence*, p. 20; Sutton, 'And to be delivered to the Lord Richard Duke', p. 24.
3 TNA, E361/6 rot. 54–54d: 2 EIV.
4 *CPR*, 1461–7, p. 66.
5 TNA, E404/73/1/130, 4 February 1462.
6 Sir John Fortescue, *De laudibus legum Angliae*, ed. S. B. Chrimes, 1942, pp. 111, 137; Sutton and Visser-Fuchs, 'Richard III's Books', pp. 5–6.
7 *A Collection of Ordinances and Regulations for the Government of the Royal Household Made in Divers Reigns*, London, 1790, pp. 27–8; *PL*, vol. I, pp. 56–9.
8 Hardyng, *Chronicle of John Hardyng*, p. i.
9 TNA, E404/72/4/2.
10 TNA, DL 37/31/36.
11 *CPR*, 1467–77, pp. 295–6.
12 Ibid., p. 308; *The Chronicle of John Stone, Monk of Christ Church*, ed. W. G. Searle, Cambridge, 1902, p. 88.
13 *PL*, vol. III, p. 310, 24 September 1461: 'for men seyn there, as I have be [told], that my Lord of Gloucester should have Caister'.
14 *CPR*, 1461–7, pp. 197, 214.
15 *CPR*, 1461–7, pp. 212–13.
16 *CSP, Milan*, p. 100; M. A. Hicks, *Warwick the Kingmaker*, Oxford, 2002, p. 256.
17 TNA, E405/43 m.2.
18 Warwick County Record Office, CR 26/4, p. 69; Hicks, *Warwick the Kingmaker*, p. 26.
19 TNA, E361/6 m.55d.
20 Ibid.: '1 chaffer, 7 brushes of heather, 4 saddles, 3 belts of white cloth, 2 belts of cloth of grey, 3 over-belts of cloth of grey, 10 bits, 5 pairs of pasterns, 4 reins, 14 leading reins, 3 false reins, 2 halters simple, and 3 halters simple with reins.'
21 Rous Roll no. 56.
22 R. Warner, *Antiquitates Culinariae*, London, 1791, pp. 94, 96; Hammond and Sutton, *Richard III*, p. 31.
23 Warner, *Antiquitates Culinariae*, pp. 94, 96; Hammond and Sutton, *Richard III*, p. 31.
24 Waurin, *Recueil des Croniques et Anchiennes Istories*, vol. II, pp. 327–8.
25 Mancini, p. 63.

26　*PL*, vol. III, pp. 203–4.

27　*CSP, Milan*, I, p. 109.

28　Warkworth, p. 3; *GC*, pp. 202–3.

29　Mancini, p. 69.

30　*CSP, Milan*, p. 131.

31　William Worcester, *Annales rerum anglicarum*, 1728, p. 783; Ross, *Edward IV*, p. 93.

32　*CCR*, 1461–8, pp. 456–7; Worcester, *Annales rerum anglicarum*, p. 786.

33　*GC*, p. 207.

34　*CC*, p. 115.

35　*CC*, p. 115.

36　TNA, KB9/320; Ross, *Edward IV*, p. 123.

37　HMC 78, *Report on the Manuscripts of the late R. R. Hastings*, 4 vols., vol. I, pp. 290–91.

38　*A Collection of Ordinances and Regulations*, p. 98.

39　*CSP, Milan*, p. 122.

40　Hicks, *False, Fleeting, Perjur'd Clarence*, p. 44; Bodleian Library MD Dugdale 15, p. 75.

41　BL, Cotton MS Vespasian F III, no. 19; Ellis, *Original Letters*, 2nd series, vol. I, pp. 143–4.

42　*CC*, p. 117.

43　Ibid.

44　*PL*, vol. II, pp. 389–90.

45　BL, Cotton MS Julius B XII, fo. 121v.

46　TNA, E404/74/2, 56.

47　Ross, *Edward IV*, p. 141.

48　Nichols (ed.), *Chronicle of the Rebellion in Lincolnshire*, p. 11.

49　For events in France, see Commynes, *Memoirs*, vol. I, pp. 192–200; Waurin, *Recueil des Croniques et Anchiennes Istories*, vol. III, pp. 28–46; 'The Manner and Guiding of the Earl of Warwick at Angers', in Ellis, *Original Letters*, 2nd series, vol. I, pp. 132–5; background in Ross, *Edward IV*, pp. 146–7; Scofield, *Life and Reign of Edward the Fourth*, vol. I, pp. 518–36.

50　Warkworth, p. 9.

51　*PL*, vol. V, p. 83.

52　*The Chronicles of the White Rose of York*, ed. J. A. Giles, London, 1843, pp. 239–40.

53　'Hearne's Fragment' in *Thomae Sprotti Chronica*, 1715, p. 306; Waurin, *Recueil des Croniques et Anchiennes Istories*, vol. V p. 611; Warkworth, p. 11; Ross, *Edward IV*, pp. 153–4.

54　W. I. Haward, 'Economic aspects of the Wars of the Roses in East Anglia', *English Historical Review*, vol. 41 (1926), p. 179.

55　Norfolk Record Office, King's Lynn Hall Books, KL/C7/4, p. 284, fo. 142. I am grateful to Dr Hannes Kleineke for this reference.

56　Commynes, *Memoirs*, p. 187.

57　Ibid., p. 187.

58　Warkworth, p. 11.

59　*GC*, p. 211; P. W. Hammond, *The Battles of Barnet and Tewkesbury*, Gloucester, 1990, p. 40.

60　TNA, E404/71/6/18; A. R. Myers (ed.), *English Historical Documents IV, 1327–1485*, p. 507.

61 Maaike Lulofs, 'King Edward IV in Exile', *The Ricardian*, vol. 3, no. 44 (March 1974), p. 10.

62 BL Additional MS 48031 fo.146; HMC 12 Rutland MSS I p. 4.

63 Commynes, *Memoirs*, p. 188.

64 Ibid.

65 Scofield, *Life and Reign of Edward the Fourth*, vol. I, p. 546.

66 *CSP, Milan*, I, p. 144.

67 Waurin, *Recueil des Croniques et Anchiennes Istories*, vol. 5, pp. 608–10; Basin, *Histoire de Louis XI*, vol. 2, pp. 68–72.

68 Visser-Fuchs, 'Richard in Holland', p. 224.

69 *Arrivall*, p. 10.

70 Ibid.

71 Ibid., p. 11.

72 Vergil, p. 141.

73 *GC*, pp. 215–16, Hammond, *Battles of Barnet and Tewkesbury*, p. 68.

74 *GC*, p. 215.

75 CLRO Journal 7 fo. 232b, Journal 8 fo. 4; Hammond, *Battles of Barnet and Tewkesbury*, pp. 67–70.

76 *GC*, p. 216.

77 Jean de Haynin, *Memoires*, ed. D. D. Brouwers, 2 vols, Liege, 1905–6, vol. II, pp. 125–9.

78 *Arrivall*, pp. 19–20.

79 Ross, 'Some "Servants and Lovers" of Richard in his Youth', pp. 2–3.

80 Warkworth, p. 38.

81 Ibid., p. 16.

82 *CC*, p. 125.

83 Warkworth, p. 17.

84 Ibid., p. 17.

85 H. Kleineke, 'Gerhard von Wesel's newsletter from England, 17 April 1471', *The Ricardian*, vol. 16 (2016), pp. 66–82, p. 82.

86 *Arrivall*, p. 21.

87 *PL*, vol. V, pp. 99–100.

88 *Arrivall*, p. 29.

89 Ibid.

90 Raphael Holinshed, *Chronicles of England, Scotland and Ireland*, vol. III, p. 319.

91 *Arrivall*, pp. 28–30.

92 Ibid., p. 29.

93 Ibid., p. 30.

94 A. H. Smith, *The Place Names of Gloucestershire*, Cambridge, 1965, p. 267.

95 *Arrivall*, pp. 30–31.

96 Warkworth, p. 18.

97 *CC*, p. 127.

98 *GC*, p. 218.

99 Vergil, p. 152.

100 Edward Halle, *Chronicle, Containing the History of England . . .*, ed. H. Ellis, London, 1809, p. 301; Holinshed, *Chronicles of England, Scotland and Ireland*, vol. III, p. 320; *The Chronicle of Fabyan*, London, 1559, p. 662.

101 HMC, 12th Report, Appendix IV, p. 4.

102 L. Visser-Fuchs, 'Edward IV's "Memoir" on Paper to Charles, Duke of Burgundy: The So-called "Short Version of the Arrivall"', Nottingham Medieval Studies, 36, 1992, pp. 167–227.

103 Arrivall, p. 30.

104 Warkworth, p. 18.

105 Hammond, Battles of Barnet and Tewkesbury, pp. 98–9; C. L. Kingsford, English Historical Literature in the Fifteenth Century, Oxford, 1913, p. 377; Gloucestershire Notes and Queries, 1887, vol. 3, p. 505.

106 Arrivall, p. 31.

107 GC, p. 218.

108 BL, Cotton MS Vitellus A XVI, fo. 133; GC, p. 220.

3. 'NOT ALTOGETHER BROTHERLY EYES'

1 Arrivall, p. 17; Waurin, Recueil des Croniques et Anchiennes Istories, vol. III, p. 211.

2 BL Royal MS 17 D XV fo.327v; T. Wright, Political Poems and Songs Relating to English History, 2 vols., Rolls Series, London 1859–61, vol. II, p.280.

3 CPR, 1467–77, pp. 260, 262.

4 Ibid., p. 262; TNA, C76/155 m.31; TNA, C81/1310/4.

5 Chronicles of London, ed. C. L. Kingsford, Oxford, 1905, p. 185.

6 Vergil, p. 154.

7 CPR, 1467–77, p. 288; PL II, pp. 14, 17.

8 Waurin, Recueil des Chroniques et Anchiennes Istories, vol. V, p. 675: 'mais son fait fut descouvert et sceu par ledit duc de Clocestre, quy luy fist la teste tranchier'.

9 Ibid.

10 Warkworth, p. 20.

11 TNA, SCI/44/61.

12 TNA, E405/54 m.4v; GC, p. 221.

13 RP, VI 193.

14 CC, pp. 132–3; PL I, p. 447.

15 CSP, Milan I, no. 255, p. 177.

16 Clarke, 'English Royal Marriages and the Papal Penitentiary', p. 1028 n. 42.

17 CC, p. 153.

18 Ibid., p. 133.

19 BL, Cotton MS Julius B xii, fos. 314r–v.

20 Hanham, Richard III and His Early Historians, p. 121; 'electio': Rous Roll, no. 56.

21 Ibid.

22 RP, VI 100–101; BL, Cotton MS Julius B XII, fos. 136v–137v.

23 RP, VI 124–5.

24 Hammond and Sutton, Richard III, p. 64, citing A. R. Scoble (ed.).

25 CC, p. 137.

26 CSP, Milan, I, no.313.

27 CC, pp. 143–5.

28 TNA, C81/1512/51–2.

29 CC, p. 145.

30 Third Report of the Deputy Keeper of the Public Records, 214.

31 CC, p. 145.

32 *CC*, p. 147.

33 Jean de Roye, *Journal de Jean de Roye connu sous le nom de Chronique Scandaleuse*, vol. II, Paris, 1896, p. 64.

34 *Christ Church Letters*, ed. J. B. Sheppard, pp. 36–7.

35 More, p. 6.

36 Vergil, p. 168.

37 Ibid.

38 Hicks, 'Changing Role of the Wydevilles in Yorkist Politics', in Ross, *Richard III and His Rivals*, p. 226.

39 More, p. 6.

40 Mancini, pp. 62–3.

41 *CC*, p. 133.

42 *CC*, p. 147.

43 Mancini, pp. 63–5.

44 TNA, DL37/46/15.

45 TNA, C81/863/4658, 4665, 4669–71.

4. A NORTHERN AFFINITY

1 YCA, Book I, fo. 42v; *YHB*, I, p. 78.

2 *YHB*, I, pp. 128–9.

3 YCA, Book I, fo. 76r; *YHB*, I, p. 130.

4 R. H. Skaife (ed.), *The Register of the Guild of Corpus Christi in the City of York*, Durham, 1872, p. 101.

5 *York City Chamberlains' Account Rolls 1396–1500*, ed. Dobson, p. 152; *Historia Dunelmensis*, pp. ccclvii–viii.

6 W. G. Searl, *The History of the Queen's College of St Margaret and St Bernard in the University of Cambridge*, vol. I, Cambridge, 1867, p. 87.

7 W. Dugdale, *Monasticon Anglicanum*, ed. J. Caley, 6 vols., London, 1846, vol. II, p. 65; Ms. Bodl. Top. Glouc. D. 2, fo. 40. Hicks, 'One Prince or Two?', pp. 467–8.

8 TNA, DL29/637/10360A.

9 TNA, C263/2/1/6 no.2; Hicks, 'Last Days of Elizabeth', pp. 308–16.

10 D. Dunlop, 'The "Redresses and Reparacons of Attemptates": Alexander Legh's Instructions from Edward IV, March–April 1475', *Bulletin of the Institute of Historical Research*, vol. 63, 1990, pp. 340–53.

11 Alnwick Castle, MS Y II 28; *Camden Miscellany*, vol. XXXII, pp. 177–8.

12 Ross, *Edward IV*, p. 202.

13 R. Surtees, *The History and Antiquities of the County Palatine of Durham*, London, 1840, vol. IV, pp. 114–15.

14 BL, Additional Ch.67545.

15 A. Raine, *Testamenta Eboracensia*, Durham, vol. III, pp. 238–41.

16 *PL*, vol. III, p. 306.

17 TNA, Durh 3/168/14; Pollard, 'St Cuthbert and the Hog', p. 119.

18 Sutton and Visser-Fuchs, *The Reburial of Richard Duke of York 21–30 July 1476*; M. K. Jones, *Bosworth 1485*, p. 51; M. K. Jones, '1477 – The Expedition that Never Was', *The Ricardian*, vol. 12, no. 153 (June 2001), pp. 275–92. TNA, C81/880/5513; *CPR*, 1476–85, p. 254.

19 TNA, E404/77/1/28; *CPR*, p. 205.
20 TNA, E404/77/2/67; E404/77/3/87.
21 TNA, E404/77/3/90.
22 One medical recipe in a surviving manuscript gives the ingredients for a remedy specially prepared for the duke himself: 'For the Lord Gloucester. Take betony, bugle, sanicle, plaintain, stitchwort, pimpernel, of each 2 pounds, of wax 4 pounds, resin, perosin, of each 2 pounds, turpentine, 1 pound.' The amount of wax suggests that the medicine was some form of ointment; the herbs used were traditionally employed as treatments for wounds, and the recipe is similar to another dating from the fifteenth century in which stitchwort, sanicle, pimpernel and betony were mixed with fats, resins, wine and wax to produce an 'ointment for consowndynge and gendrynge of fleshce'. T. Lang, 'Medical Recipes from the Yorkist Court', *The Ricardian*, vol. 20 (2010), pp. 97–8.
23 TNA, E39/92/38; *Foedera*, ed. Rymer, vol. XII, pp. 156–7.
24 TNA, E405/70.
25 TNA, C81/1520/5268.
26 Metcalfe, *Book of Knights*, pp. 5–7.
27 Vergil, p. 170.
28 Edward Halle, *Chronicle, Containing the History of England . . .*, ed. H. Ellis, London, 1809, p. 334.
29 *CC*, p. 149.
30 M. K. Jones, 'Richard III and the Stanleys', p. 33.
31 *CC*, p. 149.
32 *CSP, Venice 1202–1509*, no. 483.
33 *CC*, p. 149.
34 *YHB* I, p. 273.
35 *CC*, p. 149.
36 *CSP, Venice 1202–1509*, pp. 87–8.
37 *RP*, VI, pp. 204–6.
38 T. B. Pugh, *Glamorgan County History*, vol. 3: *The Marcher Lordships of Glamorgan and Morgannwg and Gower and Kilvey*, Cardiff, 1971, p. 202.
39 TNA, E403/848, m. 2.
40 TNA, CP25/1/281/164.
41 M. A. Hicks, 'Richard III and Romsey', in Ross, *Richard III and His Rivals*, pp. 317–21.
42 TNA, DL42/19, fo. 105v.
43 TNA, CP25(1)/281/164/32; Pollard, *North-Eastern England*, p. 340.
44 TNA, CP25(1)/281/165/23; BL, Cotton MS Julius B XII fos 241v–243v; *CCR, 1476–85*, p. 189.
45 Pollard, *North-Eastern England*, p. 340.
46 Mancini, p. 93.
47 Rous, p. 118.
48 Orme, 'Education of Edward V', p. 127.
49 Ibid., pp. 129–30.
50 Ibid., p. 124.
51 BL, Sloane MS 3479, fos. 54v–55; Orme, 'Education of Edward V', p. 130.
52 Ives, 'Andrew Dymmock', pp. 226–7.
53 *CCR*, 1478–85, no. 612.

54 Ives, 'Andrew Dymmock', p. 229.
55 *RP*, VI, pp. 215–16.
56 *CC*, p. 139.
57 *The Travels of Leo of Rozmital through Germany, Flanders, England, France, Spain, Portugal and Italy, 1465–1467*, ed. M. Letts, Cambridge, 1957, p. 47.
58 *CC*, p. 149.
59 Mancini, pp. 3–4.
60 Ibid., p. 103.
61 *CC*, p. 149.

5. 'THE KING IS DEAD, LONG LIVE THE KING'

1 Mancini, pp. 73, 81–3.
2 *CC*, pp. 150–52.
3 More, p. 5.
4 *CC*, p. 483.
5 Mancini, p. 73.
6 *YHB* I, p. 282.
7 Mancini, p. 69; More, p. 11.
8 More, p. 85.
9 Ibid., *CC*, p. 155.
10 TNA 315/486/6,12,13,14; E. W. Ives, 'Andrew Dymock and the papers of Antony, Earl Rivers, 1482-3', *Bulletin of the Institute of Historical Research*, vol. 41 (1968), pp. 221–4.
11 More also reported that there had been allegations that Hastings had been preparing to betray Calais to the French, 'although this accusation was the merest slander'. More, pp. 10–11.
12 Mancini, p. 85.
13 *CC*, p. 153.
14 St George's Chapel, Dean and Canons of Windsor mss, XI.B.6, endorsement, rot. 2.
15 *CC*, p. 153.
16 Bentley, *Excerpta Historica*, pp. 366–79.
17 Ross, *Edward IV*, p. 418.
18 Lyell and Watney (eds.), *Acts of Court*, pp. 146–7.
19 Ibid.
20 C. Richmond, 'A letter of 19 April 1483 from John Gigur to William Wainfleet', *Historical Research*, vol. 65 (1992), pp. 112–16.
21 *CC*, p. 155.
22 Ibid., p. 153.
23 Ibid., p. 155.
24 Ibid.
25 Mancini, p. 87.
26 Hanham, *Richard III and His Early Historians*, pp. 121–2.
27 Mancini, p. 71.
28 Ibid., p. 73.
29 *CC*, p. 155.
30 Ibid.
31 Mancini, p. 73.

32 Ibid., p. 83; C. E. Moreton, 'A Local Dispute and the Politics of 1483: Roger Townsend, Earl Rivers and the Duke of Gloucester', *The Ricardian*, vol. 8, no. 107 (1989), pp 305–7.

33 Mancini, p. 73.

34 Ibid., pp. 73–5.

35 CLRO Journal IX fo. 18r–v.

36 Lyell and Watney (eds.), *Acts of Court*, p. 147.

37 A. Carson, 'Convocations', *The Ricardian*, vol. XXII (2012), p. 40.

38 *CC*, p. 155.

39 More, p. 90.

40 Mancini, p. 91.

41 C. Rawcliffe, *The Staffords, Earls of Stafford and the Dukes of Buckingham, 1394–1521*, Cambridge, 1978, pp. 28–31.

42 More, p. 15.

43 Mancini, pp. 91–3.

44 The following day, 24 April, the city agreed that John Brackenbury should ride to London to 'attend upon my lord of Gloucester's good grace to labour to have pardon of the king's good grace' regarding the toll of £50 for the fee farm. *YHB* I, p. 282.

45 Rous, p. 118.

46 *CC*, p. 155.

47 Ibid.

48 Ibid., p. 157

49 Ibid.

50 Mancini, pp. 93–5.

51 Ibid., p. 95.

52 Rous, p. 118.

53 *CC*, p. 157.

54 Mancini, p. 97.

55 Ibid., pp. 81–3.

56 Ibid., p. 83.

57 BL Cotton MS Vespasian F XIII fo. 123.

58 BL, Har 433 I, p. 3.

59 Ibid., III, p. 10.

60 TNA, E159/261 Dorse 490 (Anglo-American Legal Tradition).

61 *Chronicles of London*, ed. Kingsford, p. 190.

62 Drapers' Company: Wardens' Accounts 1475–1509, fo. 26; Pewterers' Wardens' Accounts 1451–1530, GL MS 7086.1, fo. 80b; Goldsmiths' Company: Minute Book A, 229–32.

63 Mancini, pp. 101–3.

64 Ibid., p. 83.

65 More, pp. 24–5.

66 Rous, p. 119.

67 Mancini, p. 83.

6. 'PROTECTOR AND DEFENDER OF THIS OUR REALM'

1 Household Accounts II, pp. 390–91.

2 Hanham, *Richard III and His Early Historians*, p. 118.

3 *CC*, p. 159.

4 Ibid., p. 157.

5 Ibid., pp. 157–9.

6 BL, Har 433 III, p. 16.

7 Mancini, p. 85.

8 TNA, E404/78/1/1.

9 BL, Additional Charter 5987. On 20 May, a letter was to be sent to the Abbot of St Mary's, York, requesting that he attend personally the forthcoming Parliament, yet the king had been 'informed by my lord protector of the impotency and age' of the abbot. Sir John Neville was appointed constable of Pontefract Castle on 21 May, together with an appropriate reward, 'by the advice of our dearest uncle the duke of Gloucester'. On 27 May, Walter Felde was appointed the king's almoner, 'by the advice of the king's uncle Richard, duke of Gloucester, protector and defender of the realm during the king's minority'. BL, Har 433 III, pp. 4, 5; *CPR*, 1476–85, p. 349.

10 TNA, E404/78/2/3.

11 *CC*, p. 157.

12 Horrox, 'Financial Memoranda', p. 220.

13 Ibid., p. 216.

14 Mancini, p. 83.

15 Ibid., p. 85.

16 Ibid.

17 Horrox, *Richard III*, p. 102.

18 Nichols, *Grants etc from the Crown*, pp. 2–3.

19 HMC, 9th Report (1883), pt 1, Appendix, p. 145. Richard understandably suspected the loyalty of the local sheriff, Robert Poyntz, who had married Rivers' illegitimate daughter, so replaced him with William Berkeley on 13 May. Richard's choice of replacement seems to have been carefully made so as not to upset local sensibilities and, as far as possible, Poyntz's pride: Berkeley himself was the nephew of Poyntz's stepfather, Sir Edward Berkeley. Horrox, *Richard III*, p. 101.

20 Mancini, p. 87.

21 Nichols, *Grants etc from the Crown*, p. 54.

22 BL, Har 433 III, p. 216.

23 Ibid., pp. 2, 216.

24 TNA, E101/949; Horrox, *Richard III*, p. 99.

25 BL, Har 433 I, p. 36; Horrox, *Richard III*, p. 101.

26 Nichols, *Grants etc from the Crown*, p. 50.

27 Ibid., p. 51.

28 Horrox, *Richard III*, pp. 104–5.

29 TNA, PSO1/56/2840.

30 TNA, PSO1/56/2844.

31 *CPR*, 1476–85, p. 350.

32 Ibid., p. 356.

33 Hanham, *Richard III and His Early Historians*, p. 122.

34 The grant of Monmouth to Buckingham had directly dispossessed its holder, John Mortimer, which was hardly likely to ease men's fears. Horrox, *Richard III*, p. 108.

35 Horrox, 'Financial Memoranda', p. 230.

36 Ibid., pp. 230–31.

37 *Registrum Thome Bourgchier*, pp. 52–3.
38 Ibid., pp. 54–5.
39 Horrox, 'Financial Memoranda', pp. 220–21.
40 Ibid., p. 218.
41 *PL*, vol. II, p. 440.
42 TNA, E404/78/2/37.
43 BL, Har 433 III, pp. 12–13.
44 Horrox, 'Financial Memoranda', pp. 214–15, 225.
45 Ibid., pp. 230–31.
46 *Registrum Thome Bourgchier*, p. 53.
47 BL, Har 433 I, p. 16; A. Carson, 'Convocations', *The Ricardian*, vol. XXII (2012), p. 42.
48 *Foedera*, ed. Rymer, vol. XII, p. 181.
49 BL, Cotton MS Vitellus Ex fos.170–76; printed in Nichols, *Grants etc. from the Crown*, pp. xxxviv–xlix.
50 Nichols, *Grants etc. from the Crown*, pp. xlviii–xlix.
51 Ibid., p. xl.
52 Ibid., p. xli.

7. 'THEIR SUBTLE AND DAMNABLE WAYS'

1 *Registrum Thome Bourgchier*, pp. 52–3.
2 Mancini, pp. 124–5 n. 74.
3 Ibid., p. 89; *CC*, p. 157.
4 BL, Har 433 III, p. 11.
5 *YHB* I, p. 283.
6 Collier, *Household Books* II, p. 399.
7 Ibid., p. 391.
8 TNA, SC1/46/206. The letter continues: 'Also my lord [Richard] commends himself to you and gave me in commandment to write to you and prays you be a good master to Edward Johnson of Thame he was with my lord and sued to be made a denizen for fear of the payment of his subsidy, and my lord sent to Jeves the clerk of the crown and saw the commission and showed to him that he should pay but 6s 8d for himself, and so were he better to do than to be made denizen, which would cost him the third part of his goods. And as for such as have troubled within the lordship of Thame, my lord will be advertised by you at your coming for the reformation, if you take note or you come, for he thinks that they shall be punished in example of others.'
9 Horrox, 'Financial Memoranda', p. 217.
10 Ibid., pp. 216–18.
11 Ibid., p. 224.
12 Ibid., p. 218.
13 TNA, SC1/46/206.
14 *YCR*, vol. I, pp. 73–4.
15 *PL*, vol. III, p. 306.
16 *YHB* I, p. 284.
17 On 13 June, Northumberland had been presented by the council at York with '2 shillings of mayn bread, six gallons of Gascon wine and two pikes', indicating that the earl was in the city by that date at the latest. *YHB* I, pp. 283–4.

18 Hull City Archives, BRG 1/1, fo. 133v.
19 YCA, E 32, fo. 27v; *YHB* II, Appendix III, p. 714.
20 *YHB* I, pp. 284–5.
21 *YHB* I, p. 285.

8. 'GREAT CONFUSION AND GREAT FEAR'

1   *CC*, p. 159.
2   More, p. 46.
3   *CPR*, 1477–85, p. 257; ibid., 1485–94, pp. 232–3.
4   *The English Works of Sir Thomas More*, ed. W. E. Campbell, 1931, p. 53.
5   Hanham, *Richard III and His Early Historians*, p. 122.
6   Vatican, MS *Urbs Lat* 498, fos. 216v–217r; Mancini, p. 111.
7   Dunham, 'Indentured Retainers', p. 131.
8   Vatican, MS *Urbs Lat* 498, fo. 217r.
9   Mancini, p. 91.
10 *CC*, p. 159.
11 Vatican, MS *Urbs Lat* 498, fo. 217r.
12 Mancini, p. 91.
13 Vatican, MS *Urbs Lat* 498, fos. 217v–218r.
14 *GC*, p. 231.
15 Ibid.
16 More, p. 54; Mancini, p. 111.
17 Green, 'Historical Notes of a London Citizen', p. 588.
18 TNA, C1/144/42.
19 Ibid.
20 Sutton and Visser-Fuchs, 'Richard III, the Universities of Oxford and Cambridge', pp. 308–9.
21 Hanham, *Richard III and His Early Historians*, p. 26.
22 *PROME*, vol. XV, p. 219.
23 Hanham, *Richard III and His Early Historians*, p. 27.
24 *PROME*, vol. XV, p. 219.
25 BL, Har Ch. 58 F 49.
26 According to More, who apparently had seen Elizabeth Shore as an old woman, she 'delighted not men so much in her beauty as in her pleasant behaviour'. She had a 'proper wit', and being able to both read and write was 'merry in company, ready and quick of answer, neither mute nor full of babble, sometime taunting without displeasure and not without disport'. More, *Richard III*, pp. 56–7.
27 Ibid., pp. 55–6.
28 Mancini, p. 113.
29 TNA, SC1/46/207.
30 Ibid.
31 *CC*, p. 159.
32 Vatican, MS *Urbs Lat* 498, fo. 218r.
33 TNA, SC1/53/19A.
34 Mancini, p. 92.
35 Ibid., p. 113.

36 Collier, *Household Books*, p. 402.
37 Mancini, p. 109.
38 *Chronicles of London*, ed. C. L. Kingsford, Oxford, 1905, p. 190.
39 Vatican, MS *Urbs Lat* 498, fo. 216v.
40 *GC*, p. 231.
41 Mancini, p. 89.
42 *CC*, p. 159.
43 Mancini, p. 115.
44 More, p. 45.
45 Mancini, p. 95.
46 CLRO Journal 9, fo. 25b; also Green, 'Historical Notes of a London Citizen', 1981, p. 588.
47 HMC, V, 547a.
48 Mancini, p. 117.
49 *Stonor Letters*, vol. II p. 161.
50 Michael Hicks, *Edward IV*, London, 2004, p. 151 n.20; *CPR*, 1476–85, p. 352.
51 PRO E 401/949; C244/133/15.

9. 'UNDOUBTED SON AND HEIR'

1 Mancini, p. 95.
2 *GC*, pp. 232–3.
3 More, p. 68.
4 *Chronicles of London*, ed. Kingsford, p. 190.
5 Vergil, 156 LHS.
6 *Excerpta Historica*, ed. Bentley, pp. 246–8.
7 Hanham, *Richard III and His Early Historians*, pp. 119–20.
8 Ibid.
9 TNA, PSO1/57/2904.
10 Mancini, p. 83.
11 Bodleian Library, MS Ashmole 1448, fo. 287.
12 *Chronicles of London*, ed. Kingsford, pp. 190–91.
13 *GC*, p. 232.
14 See Armstrong, 'Inauguration Ceremonies', p. 130 n. 97.
15 Vatican, MS *Urbs Lat* 498, fo. 219v.
16 Mancini, p. 97.
17 Rous, p. 120; *CC*, p. 161.
18 *RP* VI, pp. 240–2.
19 *RP* VI, p. 240.
20 Commynes, *Memoirs*, pp. 353–4.
21 C. N. L. Brooke, *The Medieval Idea of Marriage* (Oxford, 1989), p. 169; Helmholz, 'Sons of Edward IV', pp. 95–6.
22 John Ashdown-Hill, 'Edward IV's Uncrowned Queen: The Lady Eleanor Talbot, Lady Butler', *The Ricardian*, vol. 11, no. 139 (December 1997), p. 177.
23 Commynes, *Memoirs*, p. 354.
24 Helmholz, 'Sons of Edward IV', p. 94.
25 Mancini, p. 97.

26 TNA, E159/260, Recorda Easter Term, rot. 4
27 BL, Har 433 III, p. 29.
28 Sutton and Hammond (eds.), *Coronation of Richard III*, pp. 25, 154.
29 BL, Har 433 III, p. 29.
30 *Chronicles of London*, ed. Kingsford, p. 191.
31 Richard Grafton, *History of the Reigns of Edward IV, etc.* (ed. H. Ellis), London, 1812,
    p. 133.
32 *GC*, p. 232.
33 *CCR*, 1476–85, p. 346.
34 Sutton and Hammond (eds.), *Coronation of Richard III*, p. 53.

10. 'GOING IN GREAT TRIUMPH'

1 BL, Har 433 III, pp. 31–2.
2 *PL*, vol. I, no. 114; *CSP, Milan* I, p. 39; Frederic W. Madden, *Political Poems Written in
   the Reigns of Henry VI and Edward IV*, London, 1842, p. 345; *CC*, p. 159.
3 Lyell and Watney (eds.), *Acts of Court*, pp. 155–6.
4 Stowe, *Annales of England*, pp. 766–7.
5 Mancini, p. 99.
6 Lyell and Watney (eds.), *Acts of Court*, pp. 155–6.
7 Sutton and Hammond (eds.), *Coronation of Richard III*, p. 159.
8 Ibid., p. 164.
9 Ibid., p. 28.
10 Ibid., p. 291.
11 Ibid, pp. 292–3.
12 Mancini, p. 101.
13 *GC*, p. 234.
14 Sutton and Hammond (eds.), *Coronation of Richard III*, pp. 34–5.
15 The text survives in the archbishop's register:
    Will ye grant and keep to the people of England the laws and customs to them of
    old rightful and devout kings granted and the same ratify and confirm by your oath,
    and specially the laws, customs and liberties granted to the clergy and people by your
    noble predecessor and glorious king saint Edward?
    I grant and promise.
    Ye shall keep after your strength and power to the Church of God to the clergy and
    the people whole peace and godly concord.
    I shall keep.
    Ye shall make to be done after your strength and power equal and rightful justice in
    all your domes and judgements and discretion with mercy and thought.
    I shall do.
    Do ye grant the rightful laws and customs to be holden and promise ye after your
    strength and power such laws as to the worship of God shall be chosen by your people
    by you to be strengthened and defended?
    I grant and promise.
    After the archbishop had requested that Richard be 'perfectly given and granted
    unto us that ye shall keep to us and to all the churches' the privileges of canon law, 'and
    them defend as a devout Christian king ought to do', Richard replied:

With glad will and devout soul I promise and perfectly grant that to you and to every of you and to all the churches to you committed I shall keep the privileges of canon law and of holy church and due law and rightfulness, and I shall in as much as I may be reason and right with God's grace defend you and every of you, every bishop and abbot through my realm and all churched to you and them committed. All these things and every of them I Richard king of England promise and conform to keep and observe, so help me God and by these Holy Evangelists by me bodily touched upon this holy altar.

Registrum Thome Bourgchier, pp. 60–61.

16 The anointing took place concealed from the congregation by a canopy carried by four knights, specially chosen by Richard, including Sir William Parr, Sir Richard Ratcliffe and Sir Edmund Hastings. Oil was placed on Richard's hands, giving them symbolic healing power, his breast, the middle of his back, his shoulders, to symbolise strength, the crook of his elbows, representing wisdom, and finally on the crown of his head in the shape of a cross, symbolising glory. As the choir sang first the anthem *Zadoc the Priest*, then a psalm and a prayer, a coif was brought forward by Buckingham and placed on Richard's head, which would remain fastened for the next eight days, until 13 July.

17 Sutton and Hammond, *Richard III: The Road to Bosworth Field*, pp. 121–2; Sutton and Hammond (eds.), *Coronation of Richard III*, pp. 275–82.

18 Sutton and Hammond (eds.), *Coronation of Richard III*, pp. 285–309.

19 Sutton and Hammond, *Richard III: The Road to Bosworth Field*, p. 123.

20 Sutton and Hammond (eds.), *Coronation of Richard III*, pp. 275–82.

21 Ibid., p. 83.

22 Ibid., p. 124.

23 BL, Har 433, fo. 22.

24 TNA, C53/198 mm.1.

25 Collier, *Household Books*, p. 399.

26 TNA, C81/1529/5.

27 TNA, C81/1529/8.

28 Horrox, *Richard III*, p. 129.

29 *YHB*, I, p. 290; TNA, C66/544 m.20; *CPR*, 1476–85, p. 409.

30 *PL*, vol. III, p. 306.

31 TNA, E404/78/2/3.

32 Horrox, *Richard III*, pp. 198–9.

33 Ibid., pp. 142–3.

34 Ibid., p. 142.

35 BL, Har 433 II, pp. 2–4.

36 BL, Har 433 I, pp. 65, 69, 72; BL, Har 433 II, pp. 2–4.

37 *CPR*, 1476–85, pp. 362–3, 16 July and 25 July.

38 TNA, C81/1529/15.

39 Collier, *Household Books*, vol. II, pp. 411–13. A surviving letter of Buckingham's in the Staffordshire Record Office is dated 20 July from London, responding to someone claiming ownership of his manor of Penshurst. The duke wrote: 'we are not advised to make you any further answer until the king and his council be made privy to the title'.

40 BL, Har 433 II, pp. 4–5.

41 TNA, C81/1392/2.

42 *CPR*, 1476–85, p. 559.

43 Ibid., pp. 559, 577.

44 Magdalen College Register A, fo. 27b; Sutton and Visser-Fuchs, 'Richard III, the Universities of Oxford and Cambridge', pp. 308–9.

45 Hanham, *Richard III and His Early Historians*, p. 122.

46 *The Ricardian*, vol. 19 (2009), pp. 108–9.

47 *CC*, p. 161.

48 N. M. Herbert, Charter of Richard III to Gloucester, in *The 1483 Gloucester Charter in History* (1983), pp. 9–15.

49 BL, Har 433 II, p. 7.

50 Rous Roll, no. 63.

51 Ibid., no. 62.

52 Rous noted how 'there were then with the king at Warwick the bishops of Worcester, Coventry, Lichfield, Durham and St Asaph's; the Duke of Albany, brother of the King of Scotland; Edward, earl of Warwick; Thomas, earl of Surrey, the steward of the king's household; the earl of Huntingdon; John, earl of Lincoln; and the Lords Stanley, Dudley, Morley, and Scrope; Francis, Lord Lovell, the king's chamberlain, and William Hussy, chief justice of England, and many other lords. And ladies of similar rank with the queen.'

53 On land she pledged the use of knights, cavalrymen and infantry, 'strong and armed', at fair wages. The ambassador's oration in Richard's presence was in reality less than diplomatic, for in a remarkable speech he told the king that Isabelle had been 'turned in her heart from England in times past, for the unkindness the which she took against the king last deceased, whom God pardon, for his refusing of her, and taking to his wife a widow of England'. Edward's marriage to Elizabeth Woodville, de Saisola recalled, had caused 'mortal war' between Edward and the earl of Warwick, whose side Isabelle had taken 'to the time of his death'; afterwards, 'she took the French king's part and made leagues and considerations with him'. Now that Edward, 'that showed her this unkindness', was dead, and Louis XI had recently, she considered, broken his treaty with her, she was willing to make a new alliance with England; 'the number of spears and horsemen the which the king shall have of Spain shall be at his pleasure 10,000 spears if he will or more and 30,000 footmen'. BL, Har 433 III, pp. 24–5.

54 De la Forssa was not only to present his letters to the king and queen of Castile, but also to show the 'tender love, trust and affection that the king our brother now deceased' had borne them, 'letting them wit that his highness is and ever intendeth to be of like disposition towards them in all things that he may conveniently do'. Richard hoped that a peace treaty that had been previously signed between Edward and the late king of Castile, Henry, and which Edward himself had looked to renew in the last year of his life, might now be concluded. Ibid., p. 35.

55 Ibid., p. 44.

56 James Gairdner (ed.), *Letters and Papers Illustrative of the Reigns of Richard III and Henry VII*, vol. I, London, 1861, pp. 35–6.

57 BL, Har 433 III, pp. 47–8.

58 Ibid., p. 48.

59 Ibid., pp. 34–5.

60 Gairdner (ed.), *Letters and Papers . . . Richard III and Henry VII*, vol. I, pp. 37–43.

61 Vergil, p. 155.

62 Ibid., p. 158.

63 Ibid. p. 159.

64 WAM 123,20; Sutton and Hammond (eds.), *Coronation of Richard III*, pp. 167, 169, 278–81; M. K. Jones and M. G. Underwood, *The King's Mother: Lady Margaret Beaufort, Countess of Richmond and Derby*, Cambridge, 1992 p. 62.

65 Edward Halle *Chronicle, Containing the History of England . . .*, ed. H. Ellis, London, 1809, pp. 388–9.

66 On 2 February 1483, Henry made an offering of £6 7s 1d at the cathedral, on the holy day of the Purification of Our Lady.

67 BL, Har 433 III, pp. 22–3.

11. 'THE FACT OF AN ENTERPRISE'

1 BL, Har 433, II, pp. 82–3.

2 *YCR*, vol., I, pp. 78–9.

3 Religious imagery of St John the Baptist, in particular the head of the Baptist, was closely associated with representations of the body of Christ, the Corpus Christi, the springtime feast of which was a significant event in the city, and the responsibility of York's renowned Corpus Christi Guild, of which both Richard and Anne had been members since 1477. As Richard's procession took the same route as the Corpus Christi mystery plays, the symbolism of the procession would have been noted by onlookers.

4 *YCR*, vol. I, p. 79.

5 *CC*, p. 161.

6 BL, Har 433 II, p. 42. Curtys was ordered to deliver not only doublets of purple satin, tawny satin, two short gowns of crimson cloth of gold and other cloths of velvet and silk, and yards of black velvet, silk and buckram, but also a 'banner of sarcenet of our lady, one banner of the Trinity, one banner of Saint George, one banner of Saint Edward, one of Saint Cuthbert, one of our own arms all sarcenet, iii coats of arms beaten with fine gold for our own person'.

7 *CC*, p. 161.

8 York Minster Library, Bedern College Statute Book, p. 48; Sutton and Hammond (eds.), *Coronation of Richard III*, pp. 140–41.

9 BL, Har 433 I, p. 2.

10 19 August 1483: BL, Har 433 II, pp. 9, 27.

11 Hanham, *Richard III and His Early Historians*, p. 50.

12 Ibid., p. 121.

13 BL, Har 433 II, p. 8.

14 Vatican, MS *Urbs Lat* 498, fo. 221v.

15 *GC*, p. 234.

16 Mancini, p. 93.

17 Ibid., p. 105.

18 Those reimbursed included Edward John, John Melyonek, Sir Oliver Underwood, Master Robert Cam, one 'Master Smythe', Sir William Sulby, Sir William Preston, Sir William Lucy, Richard Holme, John Martyn, Edward Wakefield, Henry Muschamp, John London, John Bunting, Thomas Bladesmith, Robert Ham and Thomas Coke. BL, Har 433 II, p. 2.

19 Nestfield did a thorough job of apprehending anyone who seemed suspicious. Several entries in the legal records of King's Bench include the arrest of the yeoman John Proctor, 'by John Nestfield', and the apprehension of Simon Wagstar, a labourer from Westminster by Nestfield's servants. TNA, KB9/366/16; TNA, KB9/950/24.

20 TNA, C81/1392/1.

21 TNA, C81/1529/20; *CPR*, 1476–85, p. 362.

22 *CC*, p. 163.

23 Stowe, *Annales of England*, p. 767.

24 TNA, E101/107/15, fo. 18; TNA, E404/77/3/49; *CPR*, 1476–85, p. 272; E 404/78/1/3.

25 BL, Har 433 II, pp. 8–9.

26 Ibid., p. 7.

27 Ibid., pp. 8–9.

28 TNA, C66/556 m.7 dorse; *CPR*, 1476–85, pp. 465–6.

12. 'CONFUSION AND MOURNING'

1 BL, Har 433 II, p. 28.

2 Ibid.

3 Ibid., p. 29.

4 Ibid., p. 28; TNA, SC1/46/102.

5 PL VI, p. 73.

6 *Cely Letters*, ed. Hanham, *Richard III and His Early Historians*, pp. 287–8.

7 BL, Har 433 II, p. 19; for further information of Southampton's involvement in unrest see Horrox, *Richard III*, pp. 187–8.

8 Ibid.

9 J. A. F. Thompson, 'Bishop Lionel Woodville and Richard III', *Bulletin of the Institute of Historical Research*, vol. 39 (1986), pp. 130–5, pp. 132–3.

10 *Cely Letters*, ed. Hanham, p. 122.

11 R. A. Griffiths, 'The Crown and the Royal Family in Later Medieval England', in Griffiths and Sherborne, *Kings and Nobles*, pp. 19–20.

12 More, p. 92.

13 TNA, SC1/44/75.

14 *CPR*, 1476–85, p. 465.

15 TNA, E159/260; Anglo-American Legal Tradition website: Fronts IMG 130.

16 Christopher Collyns hired 200 soldiers and mariners to take to the sea in a ship called the *Carrigan* and another 100 men in the ship *Michael of Queensbrugh* for six weeks, between 29 September and 11 November. TNA E404/78/3/49. On 1 October, William Milfield was given control of Portsmouth and Portchester, 'by our special commandment . . . continually abiding in the said castle upon the safeguard and defence thereof and of the country thereabouts' with a porter, groom, artilleryman and watchman, paid 6d and 3d a day respectively. TNA E159/261 Dorse IMG 509–10. Several days later, on 10 October, the same day as his arrival in Lincolnshire, Richard ordered for receivers of 'the west parts' of the kingdom to pay Sir Richard Ratcliffe 500 marks, 'to be employed in such ways as we have commanded him by mouth'. BL, Har 433 II, p. 29.

17 Vatican, MS *Urbs Lat* 498, fo. 224r.

18 TNA C81/1392/6.

19 TNA C81/1531/61.

20 BL, Cotton MS Vitellius A XVI, p. 191.
21 *CC*, p. 163.
22 *Chronicles of London*, ed. Kingsford, pp. 191–2.
23 *GC*, p. 234.
24 R. Ricart, *The Maire of Bristowe is Kalendar*, ed. L. Toulmin-Smith, London, 1872, p. 46.
25 J. Ashdown-Hill, "The Death of Edward V: New Evidence from Colchester", *Essex Archaeology and History*, 3rd series, no. 35 (2004), pp. 226–30.
26 C. S. L. Davies, 'A Requiem for King Edward', *The Ricardian*, vol. 9, no. 114 (September 1991), pp. 102–5.
27 Commynes, *Memoirs*, vol. II, p. 305: 'mais le roy ne volulut responder a ses lettres ne oyr le messaige et estima tres cruel et mauvais ... ledict duc de Clocestre ... Et incontinent commis ce cas'.
28 Helmholz, 'The Sons of Edward IV', p. 109.
29 *Cely Letters*, ed. Hanham, p. 108.
30 Green, 'Historical Notes of a London Citizen', p. 588.
31 Commynes, *Memoirs*, p. 397.
32 Maaike Lulofs, 'King Edward IV in Exile', *The Ricardian*, vol. 3, no. 44 (March 1974), p. 13; Pollard, *Richard III and the Princes in the Tower*, p. 123.
33 Vatican, MS *Urbs Lat* 498, fo. 221r.
34 *CC*, p. 163.
35 Mancini, p. 115.
36 *GC*, pp. 234, 236–7.
37 *CC*, p. 163.
38 *GC*, pp. 236–7.
39 *CC*, p. 163.
40 Vatican, MS *Urbs Lat* 498, fo. 222v.
41 BL, Royal MS 12 G I, fos. 1–2v: 'Per exspoliationem regis Ricardi, ego existens incarcerates in turre Londonarum'; P. Kibre, 'Lewis of Caerleon: Doctor of Medicine, Astronomer and Mathematician', *Isis*, vol. 43 (1952), pp. 100–108.
42 Vatican, MS *Urbs Lat* 498, fo. 224r.
43 *CC*, pp. 163–5.
44 *YCR*, vol. I, pp. 83–4.
45 HMC, 11th Report, Appendix III, p. 103.
46 *Stonor Letters and Papers*, ed. Kingsford, vol. II, no. 333.
47 *PL*, no. 383.
48 See A. Hanham, 'A Rebel Manifesto of 1483', *The Ricardian*, vol. 20 (2010), pp. 66–9.
49 TNA E207/21/16/12.
50 Southampton Record Office SC5/1/19 fos. 28–28v, 31–31v.
51 *Stonor Letters and Papers*, ed. Kingsford, vol. II, pp. 70, 122–4.
52 *CPR*, 1476–85, pp. 362, 461.
53 Ibid., p. 375.
54 Ibid., p. 371; *Foedera*, ed. Rymer, vol. XII, p. 204.
55 *Foedera*, ed. Rymer, vol. XII, p. 204.
56 TNA E404/78/2/20.
57 John Bell, the bailiff of Cambridge, was rewarded 'forasmuch as he came to our highness with four men defensibly arrayed to Leicester and so continued still in our service awaiting upon us all our journey in repressing our rebels and traitors unto the time we came

to our City of London to his great cost and charge without any reward or recompense'. TNA E404/78/2/24. During October, Thomas Grayson, one of the king's customers in the ports of Exeter and Dartmouth, 'armed, manned and vitialled a ship' carrying eighty men, at his own personal cost of 100 marks. The following month, Grayson also spent £40 in rewards to 'a hundred men of war being upon the sea in divers ships . . . to take and resist the Earl of Richmond and other our rebels and traitors in his company then being upon the sea'. In total, Grayson spent £156 13s 4d, for which he was repaid the following November. TNA E404/78/3/25. William Gaske of Saltash would later be repaid £85 19s 8d 'which he hath at divers times employed of his own money in sundry wise to our full good pleasure and to the resistance of our rebels and traitors'. TNA PSO1/57/2903.

58 *Plumpton Correspondence*, ed. Stapleton, pp. 60–61.

59 Thomas Nandyke survived the rebellion: he died in 1491, leaving a will that included an inventory of his possessions. Among his goods were two astrolabes, equipment for conducting alchemy, 'books of physic' and thirty-seven pounds of lead. TNA, PROB 2/48.

60 BL, Additional MS 19398, no. 16.

61 Vatican, MS *Urbs Lat* 498, fos. 226r–226v.

62 Robert Picart, *The Maire of Bristowe is Kalendar*, ed. L. Toumin Smith, Camden Society, new series, vol. 5 (1872), p. 46.

63 TNA, PSO1/59/3013.

64 *Adam's Chronicle of Bristol*, Bristol, 1910, p. 74.

65 According to Dr Steve Bell of the HM Nautical Almanac Office: 'There was a total eclipse of the moon on 15th/16th October 1483 (Julian calendar) when the moon was full. The penumbral eclipse starts at 21:43 UT and becomes partial at 22:45 UT. The total phase is at 23:47 UT and mid-eclipse is at 00:32 UT on the 16th. The total phase ends at 1:17 UT and the partial phase ends at 2:19 UT on the 16th. The penumbral phase ends at 3:20 UT on the 16th. The moon was at a declination of +12.1 degrees at mid-eclipse and a distance of 373,159 km – neither of these would suggest particular high tides in their own right. If the Moon was on the celestial equator (0 degrees) and closer to Earth (around 360,000 km) then it would have had a more significant effect on the tides. The presence of a low pressure system and strong winds from the appropriate direction would have a more significant effect than the moon in this case.' I would like to thank Dr Evan Jones for his help in providing this reference.

66 *CC*, p. 165; BL, Har 433 II, pp. 58–9.

67 *CC*, p. 165.

13. 'TRUE AND FAITHFUL LIEGEMEN'

1 The same day as the duke's execution, on 2 November, Thomas Fowler, a gentleman usher of the chamber, was ordered to seize all the property within Buckingham and Bedford that had belonged to the duke of Buckingham, the marquess of Dorset, Sir William Norreys, Sir William Stonor, Sir Thomas Saintleger, Sir Richard Enderby, Sir John Done, Sir Thomas Delamare, Sir Roger Tocotes, Sir Richard Beauchamp, Walter Hungerford and John Cheyney. BL, Har 433 II, pp. 32–3.

2 Ibid., p. 30.

3 Lancashire Record Office DD K 1/20.

4 BL, Har 433 II, pp. 58–9.

5 *CPR*, 1476–85, pp. 368, 367.

6 Leland, *The Itinerary of John Leland*, ed. Toulmin-Smith, p. 255.

7 Exeter City Archives Book 51, fo. 321v.

8 According to an account of the king's visit, Richard 'took the view of the whole city', which he 'did very well like and commend', paying a visit to the castle, which 'he was in a marvellous great liking thereof both for the strength of the place' and 'the godly and pleasant aspects' of its surroundings. When Richard was told that it was called Richmond, according to the account 'he was suddenly fallen into a great displeasure . . . at length he said "I see my days be not long."' Ibid., fo. 322r.

9 TNA, C82/55/6.

10 *CC*, p. 165.

11 BL, Har 433 II, pp. 45–6.

12 Ibid., p. 47.

13 Ibid., pp. 48–9.

14 *Chronicles of London*, ed. Kingsford, p. 192.

15 *CCR*, no. 1171.

16 Letters were sent to the Abbot of Beaulieu, ordering 'in our straightest wise' to deliver to the council within six days all 'muniments and writings by the which ye claim to have a sanctuary', 15 December 1483: BL, Har 433 II, p. 59. Master John Chester, the prior of Beaulieu, was accused of having 'harboured and succoured certain our rebels and traitors'; his brother was bound by recognisance for the prior to answer the charges in person; however, Chester was 'so greviously vexed with bodily infirmity' that he was unable to make the journey. The king granted the prior 'respite' until the following autumn, where in front of the council he was able to prove his innocence 'in such effectual ways'. TNA, C81/1392/18.

17 Horrox, *Richard III*, pp. 160–61.

18 BL, Har 433 II, p. 36.

19 Green, 'Historical Notes of a London Citizen', p. 588.

20 BL, Har 433 I, pp. 87, 88.

21 Ibid., pp. xxiii–xxiv.

22 The eleven rebels were Thomas Arundel, William Berkeley, William Uvedale, John Cheyne, Thomas Fiennes, Nicholas Gaynesford, Walter Hungerford, Thomas Audley, John Norreys, Robert Poyntz and John Wingfield.

23 Thomas St Leger, William Stonor, William Norreys, George Brown, Giles Daubeney, Thomas Bourchier.

24 *CC*, p. 169.

25 Campbell (ed.), *Materials for a History*, vol. I, p. 214.

26 *GC*, pp. 235–6.

27 BL, Har 433 II, pp. 66–7.

28 TNA, E404/78/2/28, 22 January 1484.

29 TNA, E404/78/2/18.

30 *CPR* 1476–85, p. 374.

31 BL, Har 433 II, p. 43.

32 CLRO, Journal of Common Council, 9 fo. 43.

33 The city's gates were repaired with flint and stone from Maidstone that year, suggesting damage: HMC, 9th Report, vol. I, p. 145.

34 BL, Har 433 I, p. 3.

35 In spite of being a knight of the body in Richard's household, and in receipt of an annuity of £40, local man Philip Courtenay had to stand by as a fellow knight of the body, the Yorkshireman Thomas Everingham, was given lands worth £200, centred on Barnstaple, just sixteen miles from Courtenay's home at Molland. Philip's brother John was an esquire of the body, yet received nothing, while his fellow esquire, Halneth Malyverer, another northerner, received lands in his home county worth £66 as well as being granted the office of constable of Launceston. Horrox, 'Financial Memoranda', pp. 288–9.

36 See William Hampton's review of Ross, *Richard III*, in *The Ricardian*, vol. 6, no. 77 (June 1982), pp. 46–7.

37 BL, Har 433 II, p. 37.

38 *CC*, p. 171.

39 Vatican, MS *Urbs Lat* 498, fo. 226v.

40 Vergil, p. 203.

14. *TITULUS REGIUS*

1 Sutton and Hammond (eds.), *Coronation of Richard III*, p. 53.

2 *PROME* vol. XV, p. 8.

3 *RP*, VI, p. 241.

4 *PROME* vol. XV, p. 58.

5 Ibid., pp. 60–61.

6 Pewterers' Wardens' Accounts 1451–1530, GL MS 7086.1, I, p. 57.

7 *CPR*, 1476–85, p. 494.

8 *CC*, p. 171.

9 *RP*, VI, p. 240.

10 Ibid.

11 *CC*, p. 169.

12 *RP*, VI, pp. 244–51.

13 *CC*, p. 171.

14 On 12 January, Richard Fogge had been granted permission 'to go at his liberty in all places ... at our pleasure'. On 10 February, John Norreys, the brother of William Norreys, was ordered to appear at the king's presence 'in all goodly haste possible'. Three days later, Lionel Woodville was requested to be taken by Richard's chaplains Edmund Chaterton and John Doket 'unto our presence in all goodly haste'. BL, Har 433 II, pp. 74, 91, 92.

15 TNA, C81/1531/48: 'Please it your noble grace in consideration of the princely pity which ye have showed to your most sorrowful and repentant subjects whose names be marked with your own gracious hand in the book of exception delivered to Master Chaterton to grant to all them whose names ensue your gracious letters of pardon in form following. Forasmuch as the said book can be no sufficient warrant to make out their pardons available for their lives according to your blessed intent. And that this is the same form no more nor less that passed your grace at Nottingham to them that ye gave your pardon to, being then at Beaulieu and that there is none of these names but such as your grace appointed in the said book that should have your pardon'. See also BL, Har 433 I, p. 181 for a draft pardon list.

16 P. M. Barnes, 'The Chancery Corpus Cum Causa File 10–11 Edward IV', in R. F.

Hunnisett and J. B. Post (eds.), *Medieval Legal Records*, London, 1978, p. 440; *CCR*, pp. 365, 369.

17 *CCR*, 1476–85, no. 1242; TNA, C244/134/31.

18 *RP*, VI, p. 298.

19 BL, Har 433 II, p. 207.

20 BL, Har 433 I, pp. 259–60.

21 *PROME* vol. XV, p. 36.

22 *RP*, VI, p. 250.

23 *CPR*, 1476–85, pp. 389, 423–8, 501; BL, Har 433 I, pp. 173, 186.

24 Vergil, p. 204.

25 BL, Additional MS 12060, fo. 22v.

26 Vergil, p. 204.

27 *PROME* vol. XV, p. 79.

28 BL, Har 433 III, p. 190.

29 *CC*, p. 171.

30 BL, Har 433 I, pp. 81–2.

15. 'THEIR SUDDEN GRIEF'

1 *CPR*, 1476–85, p. 422.

2 Ibid., p. 377.

3 Ibid., p. 385.

4 BL, Har 433 II, p. 88. Three days later, Richard issued a similar licence to John Legh from Nottingham after it was 'unto us showed how that two of his barns full of corn and other goods were of late during his being in our service at Dunbar in Scotland by infortune and negligence suddenly burnt to his utter desolation and undoing', with Richard urging those who read the licence to give alms, 'wherein ye shall not only as we verily trust do a right meritory deed to go and to us a singular pleasure'. Ibid., p. 92. On 20 February Richard gave £46 13s 4d to the monastery of Creyke, 'we moved with pity herein' that a large part of the monastery, having been burnt down, 'is like to fall to extreme desolation and divine service to be withdrawn and diminished without charitable remedy'. Ibid., p. 96.

5 *CPR*, 1476–85, p. 444.

6 Ibid., p. 450.

7 Ibid., p. 452.

8 Christie's Sale 5334/Lot 23.

9 BL, Har 433 III, p. 109.

10 Sir John Fortescue, *De natura legis naturae*, II, viii, quoted in Chrimes, *Henry VII*, p. 14.

11 BL, Har 433 III, p. 133; BL, Har 433 II, p. 49.

12 TNA, C1/67/36; BL, Har 433 II, p. 146.

13 C. Wedgwood, *History of Parliament: Biographies of the Members of the Commons House 1439–1509*, HMSO 1936, p. 690.

14 TNA, KB9/953/45–46.

15 BL, Har 433 I, p. 66; C. H. Cooper, *Annals of Cambridge*, Cambridge, 1842, vol. I, p. 230.

16 BL, Har 433 II, pp. 207, 192.

17 BL, Har 433 III, p. 139.

18 Ibid., p. 123.

19 BL, Har 433 II, pp. 104–5.

20 Ross, *Richard III and His Rivals*, pp. 133–4.

21 A. F. Sutton and L. Visser-Fuchs, "'As dear to him as the Trojans were to Hector'": Richard III and the University of Cambridge', in L. Visser-Fuchs (ed.), *Richard and East Anglia* (2010), pp. 130–34; Ross, *Richard III and His Rivals*, p. 134.

22 Ross, *Richard III and His Rivals*, pp. 134–5; Sutton and Visser-Fuchs, "'As dear to him as the Trojans were to Hector'", in Visser-Fuchs (ed.), *Richard and East Anglia*, pp. 122–3.

23 BL, Har 433 II, p. 63. Two days later, orders were sent to the mayors and bailiffs of every port, instructing them that a fleet had been sent to encounter a Breton fleet lying off Flanders, 'wherefore we will desire and nonetheless command you to have good watch and espial if be fortune it happen them to meet together and fight upon your coast, that then ye in all the diligence ye can possible, man out your small vessels and boats with such people as ye can make defensibly arrayed'. Ibid., p. 65.

24 *Cely Letters*, ed. Hanham, p. 201.

25 B. A. Pocquet du Haut-Jusse, *Francois II, Duc de Bretagne, et l'Angleberre (1458–88)*, Paris, 1929 pp. 254–5.

26 On 6 November, James III had proposed a temporary truce to last until 15 March, requesting safe conduct for an embassy to visit the royal court. Responding on 2 December, Richard formally agreed to the safe conduct, issuing letters authorising it under the Great Seal; however, Richard remained cautious about agreeing to any truce, arguing that it would take too long to notify the wardens of the marches and across the entire border on land and at sea, and wished to delay any agreement until the arrival of the Scottish embassy. BL, Har 433 III, pp. 50–51.

27 Halliwell, *Letters of the Kings of England*, pp. 156–7.

28 Norman Macdougall, *James III*, Edinburgh, 2009, pp. 209–10; BL, Har 433 II, pp. 101–2; A. Grant, 'Richard III and Scotland', in A. J. Pollard (ed.), *The North of England in the Age of Richard III*, Sutton, 1996, p. 131.

29 BL, Har 433 II, p. 123.

30 In a letter to the Vatican, dated 31 March, he detailed how the bishop of Durham was forced to consume 'a vast quanity of money' defending the border, 'that even at the height of peace he is compelled to keep at his own expense a hundred armed soldiers in a single castle. What then of the multitude of other places of this kind in the whole Durham estates, especially at this time when we are waging a determined war with the very cruel and obstinate Scottish people? . . . For almost all the towns and castles which we have mentioned above have fallen into decay, partly by the fault and negligence of former times, and partly by being ravaged and shattered by the calamity of wars, so that the income of many years is not sufficient to restore them'. BL, Har 433 III, p. 70.

31 Ibid., p. 62.

32 Ibid., p. 65.

33 On 3 March, William, earl of Huntingdon, was given an annuity of 400 marks. On 8 March, Thomas FitzAlan, Lord Maltravers, was granted an annuity of 300 marks from the customs of the ports in London and Southampton. On 21 March, Lord Dacre was granted an annuity of 100 marks. On 25 March, Lord Neville was given lands worth £200 and an annuity of £80, while, on 30 March, John, Lord Dudley, was given

lands worth over £100 a year and an annuity of £100. On 13 April, for his 'good service against the rebels', John, earl of Lincoln, was granted lands with a yearly value of over £350. The same day Lincoln was also granted an annuity of £176 13s 4d. On 18 May, Henry, Lord Grey of Codnor, was granted lands worth over £250 a year, on which he only had to pay a rent to the king of £20 for knight-service. On 20 May, Lord Cobham was granted an annuity of £160, while Lord Welles was given an annuity of 100 marks on 22 May. *CPR*, 1476–85, pp. 431, 388, 423, 428, 452, 388–9, 448, 430, 453.

34 Pollard, *North-Eastern England*, p. 354. It was not just Richard's ducal estates which would be raided to pay for the support Richard was attempting to buy. The four duchy of Lancaster lordships in Yorkshire had thirty-three new grants of annuities charged to them, costing £118 in Knaresborough, £106 in Pickering, £318 in Pontefract and £286 from Tickhill.

35 Coventry City Archives, BA/H/Q/A79/8. I am grateful to Keith Stenner for the reference. See also the *Ricardian Bulletin*, Autumn 2005, pp. 25–6.

36 *CC*, pp. 171–3.

37 On 5 March, Richard gave an order for 'carpenters called "whelers" and "cartwrightes" and other workmen, cannons and necessaries for the king's ordinance, and bows, arrows, crossbows and winches for the same for defence against divers revels and enemies of the king who intend to invade the realm'. *CPR*, 1476–85, p. 385. On 10 March, the gunner William Nele was granted an annuity of 6d a day 'for his good service in making cannons within the Tower of London and elsewhere' since 7 July, 'from which day he has attended to the making of the cannons'. Ibid., p. 448. The following day, Patrick de la Mote was appointed to the 'office of chief cannoner or master founder and surveyor and maker of all the king's cannon in the Tower of London and elsewhere', with a salary of 18d a day with wages for two men, Theobald Ferrount, 'gunner', and Gland Pyroo, at 6d a day. Ibid., p. 405. On 23 March, having reached Nottingham, Ralph Bigod, a knight of the king's body and master of the ordinance, was appointed 'to take carpenters and all other workmen and cannons and other necessaries for the ordnance and carriage' while Thomas Beere, the yeoman purveyor of the carriage of the ordnance, was 'to take cars and waggons and horses called "hakeneys"'. Ibid., p. 387. 2,228 lb of saltpetre was also purchased from London, for £64 19s 1d. TNA, E404/78/3/9.

38 Richard explained how 'we have committed to him certain matters to be explained to your holiness and we humbly ask and beg that with your customary goodwill to us and our kingdom you will listen with ready and willing ears to all the things that the same venerable father will open to you in this matter and graciously deign to show him favour in the business he is to do there', adding, 'this will be more pleasing to us than anything else could be'.

39 *CPR*, 1476–85, no. 1152.

40 BL, Har MS 433 II, pp. 24–5.

41 *CC*, pp. 496–7.

42 TNA, DL42/20, fo. 64r, 14 September 1484.

43 *Cely Letters*, ed. Hanham, p. 123.

44 BL, Har 433 II, p. 126.

45 Ibid.; BL, Har III, p. 71; *Foedera*, ed. Rymer, vol. XII, pp. 226–7.

46 J. T. Fowler (ed.), *Rites of Durham*, Durham, 1903, p. 106; M. O'Regan, 'Richard III and the Monks of Durham', in Petre (ed.), *Richard III: Crown and People*, pp. 339–42.

47 TNA, C81/897/557–9; Edwards, *Itinerary of King Richard III*, p. 19.

48 BL, Har 433 II, p. 138.

49 Edwards, *Itinerary of King Richard III*, pp. 20–22.

50 *CPR*, 1476–85, pp. 415, 455, 484, 509; Sir Robert Somerville, *History of the Duchy of Lancaster*, London, 1953, vol. I, p. 149n; A. Rowntree (ed.), *The History of Scarborough*, London, 1931, p. 134; Hicks, 'Dynastic Change', p. 376.

51 *CPR*, 1476–85 p. 455.

52 TNA, E404/78/3/42: 31 January 1485.

53 BL, Har 433 III, pp. 107–8.

54 Ibid., p. 114.

16. 'DEFEND ME FROM ALL EVIL'

1 BL, Har 433 II, p. 122.

2 Ibid., p. 163.

3 Vergil, p. 208.

4 Ibid., p. 142.

5 *CPR*, 1476–85, p. 439; BL, Har 433 II, p. 71.

6 BL, Har 433 II, p. 51.

7 A. Hanham, *The Celys and Their World: An English Merchant Family of the Fifteenth Century*, Cambridge, 1985, pp. 311, 413.

8 BL, Har 433 II, pp. 212–13; LMA, Col/cc/01/01/009 fo. 114v. I am grateful to Sam Harper for this reference.

9 BL, Har 433 II, pp. 115–16.

10 TNA, E404/78/3/9.

11 TNA, E404/78/3/33.

12 BL, Har 433 III, pp. 109–11.

13 Ibid.

14 Ibid., p. 259.

15 BL, Har 433 II, p. 82.

16 BL, Har 433 III, p. 259.

17 BL, Har 433 I, p. 3.

18 *CPR*, 1476–85, p. 441.

19 BL, Har 433 I, p. 3.

20 LPL, MS 474 fos.139v–140v.

21 LPL, MS 474 fos. 184–184v.

22 J. Raine, 'The Statutes Ordained by Richard, Duke of Gloucester, for the College of Middleham, Dated 4 July, 18 Edward IV 1478', *Archaeological Journal*, vol. IV (1847), pp. 161–70.

23 Ibid.

24 W. G. Searl, *The History of the Queen's College of St Margaret ad St Bernard in the University of Cambridge*, vol. I, Cambridge, 1867, pp. 89–92.

25 Sutton, '"A Curious Searcher"', p. 65.

26 P. W. Hammond, 'Richard III's Books: III. English New Testament', *The Ricardian*, vol. 7, no. 98 (1987), pp. 479–85.

27 TNA, DL29/648/10485; J. K. Allison, *Victoria County History: East Riding*, vol. I: *Hull*, Oxford, 1969, p. 398; Sutton, '"A Curious Searcher"', p. 67.

28 LPL, MS 474, fo. 179v.

29 BL, Additional MS 38,603, fos. 57v–58.

30 LPL, MS 474, fo. 183v; Raine, *Archaeological Journal*, vol. IV (1847), pp. 169–70.

31 J. Hughes, '"True Ornamens to Know a Holy Man": Northern Religious Life and the Piety of Richard III', in A. J. Pollard (ed.), *The North of England in the Age of Richard III*, Sutton, 1996, pp. 178–9.

17. 'COMMOTION AND WAR'

1 On 16 June, orders were sent to the constable of the Tower of London to deliver two serpentines, two guns, twelve hackbushes, ten steel crossbows, sixty longbows, a hundred sheaves of arrows and two barrels of gunpowder. BL, Har 433 II, p. 142. Two weeks later, a letter was sent to all sheriffs and constables, announcing that the king had appointed his councillor and clerk Alexander Lye 'to take up in our name all victuals, soldiers, mariners, artificers, labourers, all carts, boats and all other stuff and horses waynes, all timber stones as he shall think necessary requisite to our use'. BL, Har 433 II, p. 145. John Papedy was to raise mariners and soldiers 'in our name at our price and wages . . . to do us service in certain our ships'. Ibid.

2 CC, p. 173.

3 BL, Har 433 II, pp. 134, 145, 149–50.

4 Since arriving in England, Albany had proved more a hindrance than a help to Richard. Richard must have already had doubts over Albany's competence after his abandonment of the Scottish campaign in 1482, but was hardly pleased when one of Albany's ships seized two Burgundian wine ships bound for London on 12 March 1484, robbing them of goods worth £375. Richard was later forced to make restitution to the unfortunate wine merchant involved, who himself was imprisoned by Albany for six weeks, TNA, E404/78/3/26. A sign that Richard no longer regarded the pair as influential guests came in his decision to cut the annual pension granted Douglas by Edward IV from £500 to £200. Cal Docs Scot IV, nos. 1494, 1496, 1497; Norman Mac-Dougall, 'Richard III and James III', in Hammond (ed.), *Richard III: Loyalty, Lordship and Law*, p. 167.

5 CC, p. 173.

6 L. Visser-Fuchs, 'Richard III, Tydeus of Calydon and their Boars in the Latin Oration of Archibald Whitelaw, Archdeacon of St Andrews, at Nottingham on 12 September 1484', *The Ricardian*, vol. 17 (2007), pp. 1–22.

7 Ibid. This is hardly surprising; having had over ten years' experience of border warfare, Richard was perhaps the most qualified person to do so. Richard understood well that his subjects near the border longed for peace: in 1483, he had given private authorisation for Lord Dacre and Sir Thomas Percy to make local truces along the borders. Clause 16 of the truce provided for the provision of justice for the border area, linked to the Council of the North in England and the Scottish king's council, a move in which Richard's own hand has been detected.

8 TNA, C81/1531/62.

9 TNA, C81/1392/14.

10 TNA, C81/1392/16; KB9/369/19, 22; CPR, 1476–85, p. 393.

11 TNA, KB9/952/9.

12 GC, p. 236.

13 Durham, Dean and Chapter Muniments, Reg Parv III, fo. 188v, printed in Pollard, *Richard III and the Princes in the Tower*, p. 238.

14 *Calendar of Ancient Deeds* iv A10182, A7654, iii A4303; *Registrum Thome Bourgchier*, p. 65.

15 BL, Har 433, fos. 45v, 286v.

16 *CPR*, 1476–85, p. 479.

17 Hanham, *Richard III and His Early Historians*, pp. 122–3; White, 'The Death and Burial of Henry VI: Part 2', *The Ricardian*, vol. 6, no. 79 (1982) pp. 100–18.

18 W. H. St John Hope, 'The Discovery of the Remains of King Henry VI in St George's Chapel, Windsor Castle', *Archaeologica*, vol. 62, part 2, pp. 533–42; J. Ashdown-Hill, *The Last Days of Richard III and the Fate of His DNA*, Stroud, 2013, p. 52.

19 Edwards, *Itinerary of King Richard III*, p. 23.

20 Ibid., pp. 25–7.

21 *Foedera*, ed. Rymer, vol. XII, pp. 226–7.

22 Duke Francis even had to grant compensation of £200 *tournois* to the widowed Georget le Cuff, whose husband was killed by one of the exiles. The chronicler Commynes noted how the exiled community was becoming a financial burden upon Francis: in June 1484, he gave £3,100 *tournois* to the Englishmen for their lodging; in addition, he paid a pension of £400 a month to the marquess of Dorset and his men, £200 to John Halewell, and £100 each to Sir Edward Woodville and the Willoughbys.

23 Vatican, *MS Urbs Lat* 498, fo. 227r; Vergil, p. 205.

24 *CPR*, 1476–85, pp. 493–4.

25 TNA, C81/1531/3.

26 C. S. L. Davies, 'Richard III, Brittany, and Henry Tudor 1483–1485', *Nottingham Medieval Studies*, vol. 37 (1993), p. 116.

27 J. Allanic, *Le Prisonnier de la tour d'Elven; ou le jeunesse*, Vannes, 1909, p. 38.

28 Ibid., p. 49.

29 Vatican, *MS Urbs Lat* 498, fo. 227r–v; Vergil, p. 206.

30 Vatican, *MS Urbs Lat* 498, fo. 227v; Vergil, p. 207.

31 Archives de la Loire-Atlantique, E212/93, fos. 15r, 17v.

32 A. Spont, 'La marine française sous le règne de Charles VIII, 1483–1493', *Revue des questions historiques*, new series II (1894), p. 393; Antonovics, 'Henry VII, King of England', p. 173.

33 *Proces-verbaux des séances du Conseil de Régence du Roi Charles VIII*, ed. A. Bernier, Paris, 1836, pp. 128, 164.

18. REBELS AND TRAITORS

1 TNA, E404/78/3/49. Colyns seems to have been some kind of professional bounty hunter; in January 1482, under orders from Edward IV, he put to sea with sixty armed mariners, 'defensibly armed and arrayed', 'to take and oppress divers rovers and ill disposed persons'. Colyns soon arrested John Myles and others, for which he was rewarded with £97 and £3 for the wages for his men. TNA, E404/78/2/44.

2 TNA, C81/1392/17.

3 HMC, 2nd Report, p. 91.

4 TNA, C81/1392/17.

5 TNA, C81/1392/20, 21.

6 T. H. Lloyd, *The English Wool Trade in the Middle Ages*, Cambridge, 1977, pp. 281–2.

7 A. Hanham, *The Celys and Their World: An English Merchant Family of the Fifteenth Century*, Cambridge, 1985, p. 299.

8 Lyell and Watney (eds.), *Acts of Court*, pp. 157–8.

9 Ibid., pp. 159–60.

10 TNA, KB9/952/3, 9; *GC*, pp. 235–6.

11 Fabyan, *New Chronicles*, pp. 671–2.

12 TNA, C81/1392/19.

13 TNA, C67/53 m.6; CRO, FA 7, fo. 26; Horrox, *Richard III: A Study in Service*, p. 279.

14 Vatican, MS *Urbs Lat* 498 fo. 228r; Vergil, p. 208.

15 Vatican, MS *Urbs Lat* 498, fo. 228v.

16 Edwards, *Itinerary of King Richard III*, p. 27.

17 TNA, KB9/953/2,15,17–18.

18 TNA, C82/329/25.

19 TNA, C244/129/144A; 244/136/92; *CPR* 1476–85, p. 533.

20 Horrox, *Richard III: A Study in Service*, p. 279.

21 Virgoe, 'Sir John Risley', pp. 142–3; Horrox, *Richard III: A Study in Service*, p. 282. Risley was also an old associate of John Fortescue, who seems to have encouraged the rising at the same time as assisting in the earl of Oxford's escape from Hammes. Fortescue's home was at Ponsbourne in Hertfordshire, close to the property of other rebels, though Risley also had close ties with Oxford as the steward of the de Vere lordship of Lavenham. The initial idea for the rebellion could not have come from the imprisoned earl; instead it seems a more likely accomplice was John Morton, the wily bishop of Ely, who had links with both the Brandons and Fortescue.

22 Edwards, *Itinerary of King Richard III*, p. 27.

23 At Canterbury that same month, 12d was spent on 'leavened bread allowed for the Lord Bastard riding to Calais' as well as 3s 4d 'paid for a pike given to Master Brackenbury Constable of the Tower who at that time returned from Calais from the Lord Bastard'. City of Canterbury, Chamberlains' Accounts, Michaelmas 1484–Michaelmas 1485, fo. 26.

24 BL, Har 433 I, p. 230.

25 *CPR*, 1476–85, p. 535.

26 TNA, KB 9/369/5.

27 TNA, C255/8/7.

28 TNA, KB9/369/5, 24–5.

29 BL, Har 433 II, p. 183.

30 *YHB*, I, pp. 347–8.

31 BL, Additional MS 12,520, fo. 2r; BL, Har MS 787, fo. 2v.

32 BL, Harleian MS 787 fo. 3; BL, Additional MS 12,520, fo. 3r–3v.

33 BL, Additional MS 19,398, fo. 33.

34 A. Spont, 'La marine française sous le règne de Charles VIII, 1483–1493' *Revue des questions historiques*, new series 11 (1894), p. 393; Antonovics, 'Henry VII, King of England', p. 173.

35 BL, Har 433 III, p. 125. The Commission for the County of Gloucester survives: 'For the safety and defence of our kingdom of England against the malice of rebels and our foreign enemies who intend to attack various parts of our said kingdom near the coast, we have appointed you jointly and separately to array and inspect all and singular

men-at-arms and all other defensible men, both light horsemen and archers, dwelling within the said county, and when they have been arrayed and inspected in such array, to cause them to be set and put in thousands, hundreds and scores or otherwise as may be convenient and necessary, and lead them or cause them to be led to our presence with all possible speed to attack and expel the aforesaid rebels and enemies from time to time as the need arises from imminent peril. Also to hold and superintend diligently the muster or review of the same men-at-arms, light horsemen and archers from time to time as need shall arise. And we enjoin and command you and each one of you as strictly as we may that on the sight of these presents you will at once cause to be armed and arrayed and to come before you all and singular the defensible and able-bodied men of the said county and array and arm them according to their grades and ranks and when they have been thus arrayed and armed, to keep them in such array. Ibid., pp. 127–8.

36 Ibid., pp. 124–8. 'Forasmuch as the king our sovereign lord hath certain knowledge that Peter Bishop of Exeter, Thomas Grey late Marquess of Dorset, Jasper late Earl of Pembroke, John late Earl of Oxford and Sir Edward Woodville with other divers his rebels and traitors disabled and attainted by authority of the high court of Parliament, of whom many be known for open murderers, avoutrers and extortioners contrary to truth, honour and nature, have forsaken their natural country taking them first to be under the obeisance of the Duke of Brittany and to him promised certain things which by him and his council were thought things too greatly and unnatural and abominable for them to grant, observe, keep and perform. And therefore the same utterly refused. They seeing that the said duke and his council would not aid and succour them nor follow their ways, privily departed out of his country into France, there taking them to be under the obeisance of the king's ancient enemy Charles calling himself king of France.'

37 Ibid., pp. 124–5.

38 Ibid., p. 124.

39 No date had been set for any troops to muster, only for the men to be prepared to 'do the king's grace service ... when they shall be thereunto warned and commanded without any excuse'. On 18 December, however, further instructions were sent to commissioners of array in Surrey, Middlesex and Hertfordshire, to explain how 'forasmuch as we have late sent unto you certain instructions for the direction of our said county and subjects of the same against the malice of our rebels and traitors if the case require', the commissioners were now to call all knights and squires together, and to explain that they were to be prepared to journey 'unto us upon half a day warning if any sudden arrival fortune of our said rebels and traitors'. The commissioners were to confirm in writing 'showing every man's deposition and of what number of persons of every of them we shall be assured, and that this be done with all diligence as ye will answer unto us at your perils'. BL, Har 433 II, p. 182.

40 Vatican, MS *Urbs Lat* 498, fo. 229v.

41 *CC*, pp. 174–5.

42 TNA, C244/136/130, 132; *CPR*, 1476–85, pp. 511, 543.

43 BL, Har 433 I, p. 268; *CPR*, 1476–85, pp. 504, 507, 534.

44 *CPR*, 1476–85, p. 528.

45 Vatican, MS *Urbs Lat* 498, fo. 229v; Vergil, pp. 210–11.

46 Vatican, MS *Urbs Lat* 498, fo. 229v.

47 TNA, C81/1530/27; TNA, C244/134/31; CCR, 1476–85, no. 1393; Horrox, *Richard III: A Study in Service*, p. 274.
48 BL, Har I, p. 287; Horrox, *Richard III: A Study in Service*, pp. 282–3.
49 Campbell, *Materials for a History*, vol. I, p. 274.
50 *CC*, p. 173.
51 Ibid.
52 Ibid.

19. 'GRIEF AND DISPLEASURE'

1 *CC*, p. 175.
2 Vatican, MS *Urbs Lat* 498, fo. 228v.
3 Ibid.
4 Ibid.
5 *CC*, p. 175.
6 Ibid.
7 L. Visser-Fuchs, 'Where Did Elizabeth of York Find Consolation?', *The Ricardian*, vol. 9, no. 122 (September 1993), pp. 469–74.
8 Buck, *History of King Richard the Third*, ed. Kincaid, pp. 190–91.
9 A. Hanham, 'Sir George Buck and Princess Elizabeth's Letter: A Problem in Detection', *The Ricardian*, vol. 7, no. 97 (June 1987), p. 399.
10 *CC*, p. 175.
11 BL, Har 433 II, p. 216.
12 Ibid.
13 TNA, DL 42/20 fo. 67Ar.
14 TNA, E404/78/3/45.
15 *CC*, pp. 174–5; *GC*, p. 234.
16 TNA, E404/78/3/47.
17 Williams, 'The Portuguese Connection', pp. 138–45, 235–6; Barnfield, 'Diriment Impediments, Dispensations and Divorce', pp. 95–8.
18 J. Ashdown-Hill, *The Last Days of Richard III and the Fate of His DNA*, Stroud, 2013, p. 26.
19 A. S. Marques, 'Alvaro Lopes de Cheves: A Portuguese Source', *The Ricardian Bulletin*, Autumn 2008, pp. 25–7; J. Ashdown-Hill, *The Last Days of Richard III*, pp. 28–30.
20 Lyell and Watney (eds.), *Acts of Court*, pp. 173–4.
21 *GC*, p. 234.
22 *CC*, pp. 175–7.
23 Ibid., p. 177.
24 *YHB*, I, pp. 359–60.
25 Vatican, MS *Urbs Lat* 498, fo. 229v.
26 Vatican, MS *Urbs Lat* 498, fo. 230r.
27 Richard wrote to the bishop of London on 22 January 1485 about how the cleric Richard Fox had been granted the advowson of the parish church of St Dunstan in Stepney, in spite of the fact that Fox was 'now and that time being with our great rebel Henry ap Tudder, called Earl of Richmond'. Richard now took the side of the priest Degory Watur, who claimed the living for himself, and 'has mournfully complained to us and our Council, beseeching us to provide a fitting remedy in this matter'. When the

bishop refused to grant the office to Watur, sending a message to the king that it had
not been proved that Fox was with Tudor, Richard wrote to confirm how 'we certainly
know' that Fox was 'with our said rebel to counsel, assist and help as much as he is
able, against us and our kingdom, in disturbance of us and our peace and all our
faithful subjects'. BL, Har 433 I, pp. 200–201.

28 Vatican, MS *Urbs Lat* 498, fo. 230r.

29 P. Pelicier, *Essai sur le gouvernement de la Dame de Beaujeu*, Chartres, 1882, pp. 252–3;
Antonovics, 'Henry VII, King of England', p. 175

30 Michael J. Jones, 'The Myth of 1485: Did France Really Put Henry Tudor on the
Throne', in *The English Experience in France, c.1450–1558: War, Diplomacy and Cultural Exchange*, ed. D. Grummitt, Aldershot, 2002, p. 103.

31 Commynes, *Memoirs*, p. 397.

32 BL, Har 433 II, p. 189.

33 TNA, E404/78/3/32. A ship, the *Nicholas of London*, was purchased for 100 marks from
a London merchant, Thomas Graston, while another, the *Margaret of Scotland*, was
purchased from Exeter for £40. TNA, E404/78/3/41, dated 31 January 1485; BL, Har 433
II, p. 196, 2 February 1485. Two London merchants were reimbursed £100 when the
king, 'by the advise of our council', appointed Lord Scrope to requisition their ship,
the *Grace Dieu*, which they had planned since the previous summer to sail from Dartmouth to Italy. The ship was now to be taken for the king's use, 'for the safekeeping
of the sea and the defence of this our realm against the malicious disposition of our
rebels and traitors being beyond the sea'. Another ship, the *George*, was also purchased
from the merchants for £500, though the king at that moment in time could only raise
£300 in part payment. TNA, E404/78/3/40, dated 31 January 1485.

34 Vatican, MS *Urbs Lat* 498, fo. 229r.

35 BL, Har 433 I, p. 133; BL, Har 433 II, pp. 102–3; BL, Har 433 III, p. 145.

36 TNA, C81/1531/2; BL, Har 433 III, pp. 144–5.

37 BL, Har 433 II, p. 197.

38 BL, Har 433 I, p. 282.

39 BL Har 433 iii p. 29; *Letters and Papers of Richard III and Henry VI*, vol I. pp. 11–16.

40 TNA, C 76/169/m.26; *Foedera*, ed. Rymer, vol. XII, pp. 265–6; BL, Har 433 I, p. 271.

41 TNA, E404/78/3/45. In addition, on 15 March, Robert Brackenbury was paid £215 7s
5d for his services, including 'in his journeys riding to Sandwich, Dover and Maidstone', as well as 'keeping and finding of our prisoners within our said Tower of
London as for the provision and reparation of our ordnances and artilleries'. TNA,
E404/78/3/46. On 29 March, the master of the ordnance was ordered to deliver fifty
bows, a hundred sheaves of arrows, a barrel of gunpowder, fifty armed spears and
three carts of ordnance 'for the defence of Harwich'. BL, Har 433 II, p. 223. On 10
April, Christopher Colyns, by now constable of Queenborough Castle, was given
authority to command masons and tilers, and procure stones and carriages for works
there. On 29 April, for 'the hasty speed of the king's works in the Tower of London
and Westminster' a commission was issued to seize as many carpenters and wood
sawers, and to fell as much oak, elms and timber as needed. BL, Har 433 II, p. 223, 29
April 1485.

42 *CC*, p. 173.

43 BL, Har 433 III, pp. 116–20.

44 Ibid., pp. 118–20.

45 In February 1485, William Catesby was granted a warrant to fell wood in Rockingham forest and sell 'by his wisdom shall be thought expedient' for the reparation of the castle there. In February, two squires of the king's body, Richard Crofts and Thomas Fowler, were ordered to pay for the cost of a mutton, worth £6 5s, 'to the use of our household', with a promise that the sum would be repaid by a 'woodsale ... to be made in our county of Buckingham'. In March, Queenborough Castle in Kent had nearby woods raided so that its drawbridge at four gates could be rebuilt, and porters' lodgings repaired. Sir Richard Huddlestone, having been appointed constable of Beaumaris Castle, was given a warrant 'to have as much wood for fuel to be taken of our gift' to serve his household for the next two years. BL, Har 433 II, pp. 202, 203, 104.

46 Horrox, *Richard III: A Study in Service*, p. 283.

47 BL, Har 433 II, p. 191.

48 BL, Har 433 III, pp. 128–30.

49 *CC*, pp. 173–5.

50 Horrox, *Richard III: A Study in Service*, p. 307.

51 TNA, E401/952; Steel 1954, p. 320; Horrox, *Richard III: A Study in Service*, pp. 306–7.

52 A. Steel, *The Receipt of the Exchequer 1377–1485*, Cambridge, 1954, pp. 320–21.

53 Davies, 'Bishop John Morton', pp. 9–10; PRO, C244/136/27, 28, 20; *CCR*, 1476–85, no. 1456.

54 BL, Har 433 II, p. 215; TNA, C244/134/119.

55 *Foedera*, ed. Rymer, vol. XII, p. 255–71.

56 *Chronicles of London*, ed. Kingsford, pp. 192–3.

57 *CC*, p. 177.

58 TNA, PSO1/60/3116.

59 BL, Har 433 II, p. 222. 12 May 1485.

60 BL, Har MS 787, fo. 2r.

61 *PL*, vol. VI, pp. 81–4.

62 BL, Har MS 433 II, pp. 228–9.

63 CLRO, Journal IX, fo. 78v.

64 Lyell and Watney (eds.), *Acts of Court*, p. 180.

65 CLRO, Journal IX, fos. 81v–82r.

66 *Foedera*, ed. Rymer, vol. XII, pp. 271–2.

67 *CCR*, 1476–1485, nos. 1454, 1457, 1458.

20. 'INTENDING OUR UTTER DESTRUCTION'

1 Bennett, *Battle of Bosworth*, p. 83.

2 'Y mae hiraeth am Harri /Y mae gobaith I'n hiaith ni': H. T. Evans, *Wales and the Wars of the Roses*, Stroud, 1995, pp. 218–23.

3 *CC*, p. 177; Bennett, *Battle of Bosworth*, p. 157. Richard was informed that a messenger sent by Richard Williams, the constable of Pembroke Castle, had arrived at his court. He had ridden uninterrupted throughout the day and night, using post horses stationed along the way to make his 150-mile journey from Pembroke to Nottingham. The messenger brought news from his master that Richard had been expecting. Henry Tudor had landed, he informed the king, at Angle, on the eastern side of Milford Haven. Williams's information was evidently wrong, though it can be explained by the fact that Angle was the first in a network of beacons established to signal the alarm

of Tudor's arrival that, once lit, triggered off a chain of further beacons being lit along the Haven, until the news had reached Pembroke Castle itself. Williams was not to know that Tudor had in fact landed on the western side of the Haven; nor was the official who had been given the task of lighting the beacon at St Anne's Head, near Dale, for Tudor's forces had chosen the site of their landing at Mill Bay well, it being obscured from view and from any guards on duty. Perhaps the flotilla of ships floating into the harbour had been spotted first, triggering the beacon at Angle to be lit first; nevertheless it would prove a crucial piece of misinformation, leading Richard to believe that Tudor was cut off in the southern region of the Haven. This might explain the accounts of Richard's initial reaction to Tudor's landing. O. D. Harris, 'The Transmission of the News of the Tudor Landing', *The Ricardian*, vol. 4, no. 55 (1976).

4   *CC*, pp. 177–9.

5   HMC, 12th Report, Rutland MSS I (1888), p. 7.

6   TNA, C82/5.

7   *PL*, vol. III, p. 320.; TNA, PROB11/8, fos. 17d–18; CIPM, Henry VII, I, pp. 13–14.

8   Molinet, *Chroniques*, p. 407: 'il avoit donne sept cents livres sterlins a un riche nomme Thomas pour lever gens d'armes; et se debvoit trouver avecs le seigneur de Herbat et aultres, pour resister a la descente; mais ils firent le contraire'.

9   Vatican, MS *Urbs Lat* 498, fo. 232r.

10 Molinet, *Chroniques*, p. 407: 'Le roy Richard se vouloit joindre avecq les seigneurs d'Angleterre, pour ester a la descente, mais ils lui manderent: "Ne vous bougez, nous ferons bien."'

11 *GC*, p. 237.

12 *YCR*, I, pp. 117–18; YCA House Books 2/4 fos. 169–169v.

13 *YCR*, pp. 117–18.

14 When John Nicholson returned to report back on 19 August, it was resolved that the city would send just eighty men 'defensibly arrayed' with John Hastings, gentleman to the Mace, acting as captain, and 'should in all haste possible depart towards the King's grace for the subduing of his enemies foresaid'. Each soldier was to be paid twelve pence a day in wages for only ten days, totalling ten shillings each. The council resolved that they should meet at two o'clock that same afternoon at the Guildhall to appoint persons to 'take wages'. Finally, the next day, men from York set out on the 120-mile journey to the king's court at Nottingham. Few could doubt their loyalty: on 20 August 1485, the Yorkshire squire Robert Morton of Bawtry made his will, in which he stated proudly he was 'going to maintain our most excellent king Richard III against the rebellion raised against him in this land'. Unfortunately, Morton and his Yorkshire contingent had left their departure far too late to reach Richard's forces in time.

15 *CCR*, 1476–1485, nos. 1454, 1457, 1458.

16 *CC*, p. 179.

17 Ibid.

18 Ibid.; Jones, *Bosworth 1485*, pp. 57–8.

19 *CC*, p. 179.

20 Ibid.

21 Vatican, MS *Urbs Lat* 498, fo. 232r.

22 *CC*, p. 179; Bennett, *Battle of Bosworth*, pp. 157–8.

23 *GC*, pp. 237–8.

24 *The History of the Gwydir Family, Written by Sir John Wynn*, ed. J. Ballinger, Cardiff, 1927, p. 28.

25 G. Grazebrook, 'An Unpublished Letter by Henry Earl of Richmond', *Miscellanea Genealogica et Heraldica*, 4th Series, vol. V (1914), pp. 30–39; Horrox, 'Henry Tudor's Letters', 1983 pp. 155–8.

26 Vatican, MS *Urbs Lat* 498, fo. 231r.

27 Vatican, MS *Urbs Lat* 498, fo. 232v.

28 *Great Chronicle*, ed. Thomas and Thornley, pp. 237–8; see also Vatican, *MS Urbs Lat* 498, fo. 232r.

29 *CC*, pp. 179–81.

30 Ibid., p. 179.

31 Vatican, MS *Urbs Lat* 498, fo. 232v.

32 Halle, *Union of the Two Noble and Illustrious Families*, fos. 29d–35; Bennett, *Battle of Bosworth*, p. 169.

33 *RP*, vol. I, p. 328.

21. 'AN END EITHER OF WARS OR OF HIS LIFE'

1   *CC*, p. 181; Bennett, *Battle of Bosworth*, p. 157.

2   Vatican, MS *Urbs Lat* 498, fo. 233r.

3   BL, Additional MS 12,060, fo. 19v–20r.

4   *CC*, p. 181. Bennett, *Battle of Bosworth*, pp. 157–8.

5   W. Hutton, *The Battle of Bosworth Field*, London, 1813, p. 128.

6   Ibid., pp. 128–9.

7   Vatican, MS *Urbs Lat* 498, fo. 234r.

8   Ibid., fo. 232v.

9   Ibid., fo. 233v.

10 'il voult ester a pye au milieu de nous'. A. Spont, 'La malice des francs-archers (1448–1500)', *Revue des questions historiques*, vol. 59 (1897), p. 474.

11 Vatican, MS *Urbs Lat* 498, fo. 234r.

12 Ibid.

13 Hutton, *Battle of Bosworth Field*, p. 129.

14 G. Doutrepont and O. Jodogne (eds.), Chroniques de Jean Molinet, Brussels, 1935–7, vol. I, pp. 434–6; Vatican, MS *Urbs Lat* 498, fo. 234r.

15 Ibid., fo. 234v.

16 Bennett, *Battle of Bosworth*, p. 161; translation of G. Doutrepont and O. Jodogne (eds.), *Chroniques de Jean Molinet*, Brussels, 1935–7, vol. I, pp. 434–6.

17 BL, Har MS 367, fos. 89–100, printed in *Bishop Percy's Folio Manuscript*, vol. III, pp. 319–63.

18 *CC*, p. 181.

19 Vatican, MS *Urbs Lat* 498, fos. 234r–234v.

20 *CC*, p. 183; Bennett, *Battle of Bosworth*, p. 158.

21 Bennett, *Battle of Bosworth*, p. 161.

22 *The Chronicle of Fabyan*, London, 1559, pp. 519–20; Bennett, *Battle of Bosworth*, p. 163.

23 Bennett, *Battle of Bosworth*, p. 160. See text in E. Nokes and G. Wheeler, 'A Spanish Account of the Battle of Bosworth', *The Ricardian*, vol. 2, no. 36 (1972), pp. 1–5. A later

Scottish chronicle, written by Robert Lindsay of Pittscottie, but drawing heavily on the oral tradition of Scottish warriors present at the battle, similarly described how Richard's forces 'that should have opposed' the march of Tudor's army 'gave them place and let them go by', while 'themselves turned around and faced King Richard as if they had been his enemies'. Mackay (ed.), *Historie and Chronicles of Scotland . . .*, pp. 190–99; Bennett, *Battle of Bosworth*, p. 162.

24 Bennett, *Battle of Bosworth*, p. 160.

25 Tudor had previously sought Northumberland's support when he had sent Christopher Urswick on a mission to England earlier in the year; while Urswick was supposedly unable to make contact with Northumberland; nevertheless the earl and Tudor had been childhood acquaintances, growing up at Raglan Castle together at the court of William Herbert, earl of Pembroke. Vatican, MS *Urbs Lat* 498, fo. 230r.

26 Ibid., fo. 235r.

27 Salazar's pleas for Richard to flee that battle can be compared to the prose account of 'Richard the Third, his Deathe, which records how an unnamed knight requests that Richard depart the battlefield before it is too late, to which Richard replies: 'Bring me my battle axe in my hand, and set the crown of gold on my head so high; for by him that shape both sea and sand, King of England this day will I die.' BL, Har MS 542, fo. 34.

28 *CC*, p. 181.

29 Vatican, MS *Urbs Lat* 498, fo. 235r.

30 Ibid., fo. 234v.

31 Riley (ed.), *Ingulph's Chronicle of the Abbey of Croyland*, p. 504.

32 Vatican, MS *Urbs Lat* 498, fo. 234v.

33 Ibid.

34 Ibid.

35 Hutton, *Battle of Bosworth Field*, p. 129.

36 Ibid., p. 129.

37 Molinet, *Chroniques*, p. 409: 'mais quand il vit ceste desconfiture et se trouva seul sur le camp, il cuida courre après les autres'.

38 Ibid., p. 409: 'son cheval saulta en un palud duquel ne se povoit ravoir; et lors fut approche d'un de ceulx de Galles'.

39 *CC*, p. 183.

40 'Lladd y baedd, eilliodd ei ben'; R. Griffith, *Sir Rhys ap Thomas and His Family: A Study in the Wars of the Roses and Early Tudor Politics*, Cardiff, 1993, p. 43.

41 *CC*, p. 183.

42 Hanham, *Richard III and His Early Historians*, p. 123.

43 Vatican, MS *Urbs Lat* 498, fos. 234v–235r.

EPILOGUE: 'HIS FAME IS DARKENED'

1 *CC*, p. 183.

2 *Great Chronicle*, ed. Thomas and Thornley, pp. 237–8.

3 York City Archives, House Book B2-4, fo. 169v.

4 D. T. Williams, *The Battle of Bosworth, 22 August 1485*, 1975, p. 49.

5 Vergil; Vatican, *MS Urbs Lat*, fo. 235r: 'Iterim corpus Ricardi omnibus indumentis nudatum ac dorso equi resupinum impositum una ex parte equi capite cum brachiis

et ex altera tibiis pendentibus Leycestram deportatur'. For Molinet, see Bennett, *Battle of Bosworth*, p. 161. *CC*, p. 183.

6 *GC*, pp. 237–8.

7 BL, Additional MS 7099, fo. 129; TNA, C1/206/69; W. Burton, *The Description of Leicester Shire* (1622), p. 163; D. Baldwin, 'King Richard's Grave in Leicester', *Transactions of the Leicestershire Archaeological and Historical Society*, lx (1986), pp. 21–4.

8 Tudor-Craig, *Richard III*, p. 95.

9 YCA, B6, fo. 23r; *YCR*, vol. I, p. 160.

10 Hanham, *Richard III and His Early Historians*, pp. 118–24; BL, Additional MS 48,976; C. Ross, *The Rous Roll*, Gloucester, 1980.

11 *GC*, p. 238.

12 *CC*, p. 185.

13 Ibid., p. 189.

14 Ibid., p. 191.

INDEX